Next-Gen Supply Chains

Next-Gen Supply Chains

AI, Automation, and Sustainability in a Disrupted World

Edited by

Pankaj Bhambri
Pushan Kumar Dutta
Mudassir Khan
Marta Starostka-Patyk

ISTE

WILEY

First published 2026 in Great Britain and the United States by ISTE Ltd and John Wiley & Sons, Inc.

ISTE Ltd
27-37 St George's Road
London SW19 4EU
UK

www.iste.co.uk

John Wiley & Sons, Inc.
111 River Street
Hoboken, NJ 07030
USA

www.wiley.com

Library of Congress Control Number: 2026932019

British Library Cataloguing-in-Publication Data
A CIP record for this book is available from the British Library
ISBN 978-1-83669-074-0

The manufacturer's authorized representative according to the EU General Product Safety Regulation is Wiley-VCH GmbH, Boschstr. 12, 69469 Weinheim, Germany, e-mail: Product_Safety@wiley.com.

Contents

Preface

The global supply chain is no longer a linear, predictable backbone of commerce but rather a dynamic, interconnected and often fragile ecosystem. The convergence of pandemic disruptions, geopolitical tensions, climate change and escalating consumer demands has exposed the limitations of traditional models. In this new paradigm, resilience, agility and sustainability are not merely strategic advantages but fundamental requirements for survival and growth. This book, *Next-Gen Supply Chains: AI, Automation, and Sustainability in a Disrupted World*, was conceived to provide a comprehensive roadmap for navigating this complex transformation.

Our mission is to bridge the critical gap between the theoretical potential of emerging technologies and their practical implementation. We move beyond siloed discussions to present an integrated view of how generative AI, blockchain, the Internet of Things and autonomous systems are converging to create truly intelligent and self-orchestrating supply networks. The book is structured to guide readers from understanding the transformed risk landscape, through the technological foundations, to the strategic imperatives and organizational change required for success. A unique emphasis is placed on the symbiotic relationship between technological innovation and the human element, ensuring that workforce transformation and ethical governance are central to the discourse.

This volume is the product of a truly global collaboration, bringing together the insights of leading academics and practitioners from diverse geographical and industrial contexts. We are deeply grateful to our international panel

---

Preface written by Pankaj BHAMBRI, Pushan KUMAR DUTTA, Mudassir KHAN and Marta STAROSTKA-PATYK.

of contributors for sharing their expertise, and to our reviewers for their rigorous feedback. Our hope is that this book will serve as an indispensable resource for supply chain professionals, executives, students and policymakers alike, empowering them to build the robust, efficient and sustainable supply chains of the future.

January 2026

1

AI and Automation: Building Resilient and Sustainable Supply Chains in Uncertain Times

This chapter discusses how the Covid-19 crisis laid systemic weaknesses in global supply chains and drove action from efficiency-based to resilience-based models. It gives a holistic approach to building resilient and sustainable supply chains, built on flexibility, agility and redundancy while underpinned by the latest technologies including AI/automation/blockchain. The chapter compares old-style with new approaches to risk management, drawing on what we believe are major lessons from the pandemic, and emphasizes the growing need for transparency, sustainability and strategic diversification. Practical recommendations are provided to help organizations prepare for future disruptions and build adaptive, future-ready supply chains. In addition to technological advancements, the chapter describes how sustainability principles such as circular economy models, ethical sourcing and carbon footprint reduction must be incorporated into supply chain strategies. With cases and examples from around the world, it offers a model that shows how digital innovation combined with sustainability systems can help organizations respond faster to change, more effectively manage risks and develop innovative approaches long-term competitive advantage in- or out-of-industry.

1.1. Introduction

In a post-pandemic world, resilience is no longer just the capacity to bounce back from shock (Leach et al. 2021). It is also the ability to foresee, absorb, adjust to and recover from a broad range of threats that are often unexpected, whether from pandemics or geopolitical tension or natural and cyber disaster (Nandi et al. 2021; Thakur-Weigold and Miroudot 2024). The pandemic hastened a shift in the paradigm, forcing companies to rebalance their priorities away from just-in-time

Chapter written by Sanam SOOMRO, Mingyue FAN, Ranjeeta SADHWANI and Safia SOOMRO.

efficiency and towards just-in-case preparedness. At the heart of this transformation lies the integration of disruptive technologies, such as artificial intelligence (AI), automation and blockchain (Drissi Elbouzidi et al. 2023).

This chapter provides a thorough overview of resilience in the supply chain from the perspectives of technology and sustainability. It starts by clarifying the term resilience for supply chain scenarios, and then describes the three dimensions of resilience (flexibility, agility and redundancy) and its measurable indicators. It then discusses risk management frameworks, comparing traditional ones to AI-enabled predictive analytics. Based on lessons from the pandemic and other global crises, the chapter focuses on structural vulnerabilities and uses case studies to show what were important failures and important strategies. Finally, it offers practical ways to develop future-ready supply chains that are resilient, sustainable and tech-enabled to survive the vagaries of a fast-evolving world.

1.2. Understanding supply chain resilience

The resilience of a supply chain is no longer viewed as a reactive response, but rather as a systemic characteristic, a dynamic feature incorporated into the design, the governance and the technological infrastructure of supply chain networks. In an era of black swan events, geopolitical instability, climate shocks and cyber threats, supply chains must both run efficiently in regular principal terms and act robustly under stresses and adapt themselves during recovery. Resilience, then, is not the act of avoiding disruption, but having the capability to withstand, adjust and grow through it (Rana and Bhambri 2024b).

Fundamentally, supply chain resilience is a combination of three interconnected elements: flexibility, agility and redundancy (Kamalahmadi et al. 2022). These three things together create a core triad that lets organizations respond to disruption as a condition to be designed for not an existential threat which brings a problem we can solve for you (Garavelli 2003).

1.3. Risk management frameworks

In a supply chain, risk management is to identify, assess and prioritize the expected risk and disruptions that may have an effect on the continuity of supply chain operations (Olufunke Olawale et al. 2024).

The risk management can be improved with the help of AI by analyzing the potential impact of various risks related to financial, operational, environmental or political risk.

1.4. Impact of the pandemic on supply chain vulnerabilities

1.4.1. *Disruptions caused by global crises*

The Covid-19 crisis acted as an earthquake to the world supply chain in highlighting the fragility of the conventional supply chain practices and significantly hindering the movement of goods. Factories, transport networks and international borders were locked down, abruptly and globally. Factory shutdowns, especially in China, led to shortages in core raw materials and parts that left impacts throughout the electronics and auto sectors (Liu et al. 2022). At the same time, transportation slowdowns particularly in air and ocean freight left backlogs and starved product inventories, causing significant product delays. Labor shortages from sickness, quarantines and lockdowns worsened the situation. Companies had to operate with limited staff, leading to reduced output and slowdowns at various stages of the supply chain (Ganesan et al. 2021).

1.4.2. *The cascading effects on global supply networks*

1.4.2.1. *Domino effect of disruptions*

The aftershocks of the Covid-19 pandemic reverberated through global supply chains, as one trouble spot in the supply chain frequently led to subsequent delays and shortages further downstream. For example, shortages of semiconductors, as a result of plants shutting in Asia, hit the automotive sector particularly hard. The factories, which produced the chips, closed.

1.4.2.2. *Vulnerabilities in just-in-time (JIT) inventory systems*

The Covid-19 pandemic has exposed stark weaknesses in JIT (Just-In-Time) inventory systems that value cost efficiency over supply chain resilience. Such systems are optimized to reduce stock and holding costs and do not have buffer stock that can be used in the event of a shock. With firms experiencing sudden surges or breaks in the demand for products, many realized the folly of relying on JIT strategies for critical products. Witness the automobile industry as an example, relying on JIT inventory systems. Shortages, particularly of critical components such as semiconductors, led to long delays in production, underscoring the challenges that lean inventory models can run into in times of crisis (Mohammad et al. 2022).

1.4.2.3. *Supply chain complexity*

During the Covid-19 pandemic, however, the real nature of the challenges implicit in global supply chains became far more readily apparent. At that time, businesses had a long and stretched tie with the suppliers who could not quickly adapt to disruptions. This complexity not only made it difficult to troubleshoot issues quickly, but was also slow to change. No one was immune, even businesses with supposedly mighty technological engines such as Walmart and Amazon saw big disruptions (Rose et al. 2023).

1.4.3. *Case studies of major supply chain disruptions during the pandemic*

1.4.3.1. *Case study: Amazon and inventory shortages during the pandemic*

The global supply chain was thrown into disarray by the Covid-19 pandemic, especially e-commerce giants such as Amazon. With the pandemic leading to factory closures and delays in transportation across the globe, Amazon had great difficulty in keeping stock of its essential goods (Rana and Bhambri 2024a). With factories shut down and significant disruptions in shipping routes resulting from factories and ports closing and labor shortages, the company experienced widespread out-of-stocks (Jyani 2024).

In early 2020, Amazon faced shortages of items such as sanitizers, cleaning products and nonperishable foods. After demand for these items skyrocketed, the company quickly realized it could not meet demand, and that demand had been accelerated by the health crisis and the migration of people shopping online. To solve the problem, Amazon deprioritized nonessential goods, adjusted its logistics to ship critical items first and hired 175,000 new workers (Strauss-Wieder 2023).

1.4.3.2. *Case study: 3M and the N95 mask shortage*

The healthcare and pharmaceutical supply chains were put under huge stress by the Covid-19 pandemic, which came with an unprecedented surge in demand for life-saving medical equipment, including PPE, ventilators and test kits (Mathew and Mathew 2020). This was exacerbated by production slowdowns and plant closures led by lockdowns, as well as dislocations in global logistics networks. One prime example is 3M, but they are far from alone; the N95 mask manufacturer simply could not keep pace with the explosive demand for personal protective equipment (PPE) when the pandemic began. As hospitals worldwide experienced dire shortages of these critical supplies, 3M had difficulty meeting demand if it boosted production to meet global, rather than simply domestic, needs. The company was in a bind. Its own manufacturing capacity was limited, and global supply chains were in disarray. This resulted in a lag of distribution of N95s to the front-line health care workers as well as health catastrophe. At the same time, drug makers such as Pfizer were pushed to ramp up the production of Covid-19 vaccines with their own challenges of meeting supply chain bottlenecks (Yu et al. 2022).

1.4.3.3. *Case study: Tyson Foods and meat supply disruptions*

The food sector was among the hardest hit during the Covid-19 pandemic, with labor shortages, plant shutdowns and massive disruptions to supply chains. They included hard-hitting plant closures in meat processing that were enacted after Covid-19 outbreaks among workers. This forced the largest shutdown in meat supply in history resulting in shortages and price spikes across the board (Anderson et al. 2021). Tyson Foods, a major American meat processor, faced significant challenges during the pandemic. Tyson had to shut down multiple plants as Covid-19 outbreaks rampaged through some of its facilities, hammering its production volume. That led to shortages of beef, chicken and pork in the nation's grocery stores, as the supply of processed meats became tight. The disturbance left shelves bare, and also drove up food prices as demand for meat overwhelmed supply (Aday and Aday 2020).

1.5. Building resilience post-pandemic

The Covid-19 pandemic has undeniably exposed the fragility of modern supply chains while simultaneously highlighting its strategic role. It has served as a wake-up call for organizations, encouraging them to develop robust contingency plans for addressing future uncertainties and enhancing supply chain resilience in the post-pandemic world. Despite the significant disruptions, one positive outcome is the realization that traditional approaches to supply chain resilience are insufficient for managing such large-scale shocks (Ivanov and Dolgui 2020).

1.5.1. *The role of technology in strengthening resilience: AI, automation and blockchain*

Strengthening the resilience and sustainability of supply chains and manufacturing processes requires the integration of more advanced technologies associated with the fifth industrial revolution (Industry 5.0) (Bhambri et al. 2024). Core AI-driven components of Industry 5.0 such as cyber-physical systems, automation, IoT and blockchain work in synergy with human intelligence to open new frontiers in innovation and preparedness. These technologies have played a crucial role in addressing the unprecedented disruptions brought on by the Covid-19 pandemic and in shaping more agile, adaptive and future-ready operations. As discussed by Ahmed et al. (2023), Industry 5.0 (I5.0), in conjunction with AI, presents a transformative opportunity to create a digitally inclusive future by enhancing supply chain resilience and sustainability. They documented that real-time supply chain monitoring enabled by IoT emerged as the most critical factor in enhancing the resilience and survivability of manufacturing supply chains.

1.5.2. *Strategic sourcing and diversification of suppliers*

The literature has discussed different sourcing strategies to increase the resilience and performance of the supply chain. The single sourcing strategy involves only one supplier; this translates to more modest production costs, lower inventory levels, better supplier relations and lastly secure information. However, this is at the cost of an increased risk of failure (Namdar et al. 2018). On the other hand, multiple sourcing involves many suppliers. This strategy can mitigate risks during periods of disruption and foster competitiveness among suppliers (Shan et al. 2023). Yet, managing multiple suppliers leads to greater operational complexity and increased costs (Burke et al. 2007).

The prolonged disruptions caused by the Covid-19 pandemic have provoked new discussions regarding existing sourcing and resilience strategies to ensure supply chain viability (Ivanov and Dolgui 2020).

Echefaj et al. (2024) presented a framework combining elements of the circular economy with more resilient sourcing strategies. The latter highlights the requirement to effectively coordinate resource loops, supply chain interdependencies and common uncertainties across a connected network.

1.5.3. *Collaboration and transparency within supply chains for better risk management*

A company is considered to be transparent when it publicly shares detailed information about its suppliers, sustainability standards and purchasing practices (Egels-Zandén et al. 2015). Supply chain transparency refers to the extent to which firms possess essential information about upstream and downstream activities in their supply networks. It also involves the willingness of an organization to publicly share this information (Chen et al. 2019; Gualandris et al. 2021). It is also highlighted that supply chain transparency can reduce supply chain risk and improve resilience (i.e. Sodhi and Tang 2019; Dubey et al. 2021).

In order to get benefit from stakeholders and to meet government requirements, companies are now disclosing information proactively (Villena and Dhanorkar 2020).

Historically, global supply chains have struggled with transparency and traceability, issues that require the coordination of many parties and new technological processes. Recent developments, however, indicate a shift toward using innovation to solve these problems. Among these solutions, blockchain technology is becoming increasingly popular for improving supply chain visibility and accountability (Yang 2019).

1.6. The future of supply chain resilience

1.6.1. *Lessons learned and long-term strategies*

The importance of resilient supply chains became a wake-up call for businesses around the world during the Covid-19 pandemic. Looking ahead, businesses must not only recover from the pandemic's effects but also prepare for future disruptions, such as economic, environmental or technological challenges.

1.6.1.1. *Adaptability over efficiency*

The supply chains of the future will have to be agile enough to switch gears rapidly if and when disruptions arise. Businesses will have to find the right trade-off between efficiency and resilience by building more flexibility into their sourcing, manufacturing and distribution (Berendes et al. 2025).

1.6.1.2. *Diversification of suppliers*

The pandemic demonstrated the dangers of relying too much on single-source suppliers or regions (Bhambri and Paweloszek 2024). Firm should aim to develop globalized supply networks and make them immune to disruption due to natural disasters or pandemics (Li et al. 2022).

Tactics such as regional sourcing, the use of alternative suppliers to source critical products and partnerships in local markets can help companies to insulate themselves from future shocks.

1.6.1.3. *Digital transformation*

A critical long-term strategy for enhancing supply chain resilience is the adoption of digital technology. Disruptions like the pandemic demonstrated that agility and the ability to pivot quickly depend on real-time information flows and digital tools. Technologies such as AI, IoT, cloud computing and blockchain provide the capabilities needed for advanced analysis, allowing organizations to anticipate future challenges. As noted by Chauhan et al. (2023), better predictions ultimately lead to better decisions.

1.6.1.4. *Building stronger relationships with suppliers*

Businesses will also need to diversify and be less opaque with regards to their supplier. That is, the sharing not just of data but also sustainability objectives, including committed ethical labor practices and co-risk-management operations. Under the best conditions, this practice would facilitate faster communication and earlier detection of threats in times of crisis (Baah et al. 2021).

1.6.2. *How organizations can prepare for future disruptions*

To get ready for the next disruption, organizations need to take a proactive approach at seeing what the possible risks could be. This involves putting in place systems and frameworks that increase transparency, improve inventory alignment and support better risk assessment.

1.6.2.1. *Predictive analytics and risk modeling*

Predictive risk modeling using AI and machine learning will play a critical role in predicting potential disruptions (Bhambri and Khang 2025). Companies can employ these technologies to crunch huge volumes of data and forecast disruptions before they occur.

For instance, using AI algorithms, companies can forecast any delay in the shipment on the basis of historical data, weather and geopolitical events months ahead and regulate their supply chain operations in advance (Aljohani 2023).

1.6.2.2. *Real-time monitoring and agile responses*

The business ability to follow goods and assets everywhere in the supply chain will be enabled by IoT-based devices and real-time monitoring systems. This greater visibility will allow organizations to better react when inevitable surprises occur causing a disruption at a port, a supplier going offline, demand changes in the market. Real-time data makes businesses agile and able to make smart decisions (Rane and Narvel 2022).

1.6.2.3. *Inventory optimization*

Firms will also have to reevaluate their inventory strategies to strike a balance between lean and resilient operations (Bhambri and Khang 2024).

The just-in-time model confers many advantages, but the pandemic made it clear that maintaining buffer stock for crucial products was essential, particularly during uncertain times (Choi et al. 2023). The supply chains of the future will have to include more flexible inventory systems that are able to react to demand bends and possible disruptions.

1.6.2.4. *Scenario planning and business continuity*

Enterprises should also regularly conduct scenario planning exercises in which disruptions are simulated to see how supply chains would respond. It can draw attention to vulnerabilities that the supply chain needs to fix.

1.6.3. *The integration of sustainable practices into resilient supply chains*

Long-term supply chain resilience is no longer optional. Sustainability is now a key part of building strong, lasting supply chains. As the world addresses environmental and social problems, businesses need to bring sustainability to the supply chain, not only to minimize long-term risks, but more importantly to prove their competitive edge (Bhambri and Kumar 2024).

1.6.3.1. *Circular economy models*

More and more companies are using circular economy principles, which means that products are designed for longevity, repair and ultimately recycling. Less reliance on limited resources and less waste allows companies to develop more sustainable and robust supply chains (Kazancoglu et al. 2023). For example, IKEA is striving to use environmentally friendly resources and promote products that are recyclable or reusable after their life time.

1.6.3.2. *Sustainable sourcing and ethical supply chains*

Organizations need to be concerned not just with where raw materials are sourced, but with the environmental and ethical practices of the suppliers to whom they outsource. Working with suppliers who support sustainable and ethical labor standards, organizations can help to combat the long-term environmental and social risks (Kandil et al. 2022). It is also beneficial for a company's branding, because consumers and investors are leaning more and more towards businesses that have a strong sustainable image.

1.6.3.3. *Energy efficiency and carbon footprint reduction*

Companies can also build supply chain resiliency by increasing their energy efficiency and lowering their carbon footprint. Moving towards energy from renewables, optimizing transport routes to waste as little fossil fuel as possible or implementing green logistics are all key in the move towards creating supply chains that are more sustainable (Bhambri and Bajdor 2024). Furthermore, reducing the environmental impact can help businesses to meet changing regulatory requirements, such as carbon tax policies or sustainability reporting obligations (Xu et al. 2023).

1.6.3.4. *Supply chain transparency*

Both sustainability and resilience depend on transparency. Visibly tracking the sustainability impact of each step in the supply chain allows companies to guarantee that they are meeting their sustainability goals and not taking on risks such as greenwashing. A technology such as blockchain can provide transparency by allowing stakeholders to track products from origin to end-consumer to guarantee that ethical and sustainable practices are adhered to at every stage in the supply chain.

1.6.4. *Preparing for an unpredictable future*

The future of supply chain resilience is the capability to cope with an increasingly volatile, uncertain, complex and ambiguous (VUCA) world. The acceleration of technological progress, geopolitical change, and economic and societal transformation is the new reality, and businesses will need to be brave, agile, creative and resilient to deal with this.

1.6.4.1. *Continuous learning and improvement*

Developing resilience means having the willingness to learn from such occurrences. Businesses must look to the past, whether the Covid-19 pandemic or other forms of disruption, and refine their supply chain strategies on an ongoing basis. This includes regular examination of risk management systems, technology investment and supplier relations.

1.6.4.2. *Collaboration across industries*

Resilience should not be sole duty of an individual organization, but necessitates cooperation among industries. Trading best practices, creating partnerships and working together on common risk factors can help develop a predictable and more resilient supply chain ecosystem for businesses. This is particularly critical in companies such as the pharmaceutical industry, where collaboration during the pandemic helped speed up vaccine distribution and response.

1.7. Conclusion

The Covid-19 global pandemic has changed the way companies have looked at supply chains. Where it used to be all about efficiency and effectiveness, it is now shifting towards resiliency and agility. This chapter touches on the notion that at its heart, resilience is more of an expansive ability than a reactive posture, built upon flexibility, agility and over-provisioning. The utilization of futuristic technologies such as AI, automation, blockchain, predictive analytics is enabling organizations to brace for upcoming disruptions and change gears with a forward-looking focus. In addition to this, it makes sure that the environmental factor gets due importance as well. Supply chains for the future must operate on the principles of circular economy, ethical sourcing and environmental responsibility/social accountability to meet stakeholder expectations as well as be prepared for any risks looming ahead. The Quad nations can strengthen their collective security by working together to make supply chains more transparent and resilient. This is not a one-time project, but a continuous effort requiring digital infrastructure, cross-industry cooperation, and shared risk. Success also depends on shifting priorities from simply minimizing costs to preserving value amid uncertainty, backed by new investment. Organizations that embrace this approach will not only survive future crises but thrive in a complex world.

1.8. References

Aday, S. and Aday, M.S. (2020). Impact of COVID-19 on the food supply chain. *Food Quality and Safety*, 4(4), 167–180. doi: 10.1093/fqsafe/fyaa024.

Ahmed, T., Karmaker, C.L., Nasir, S.B., Moktadir, Md.A., Paul, S.K. (2023). Modeling the artificial intelligence-based imperatives of industry 5.0 towards resilient supply chains: A post-COVID-19 pandemic perspective. *Computers & Industrial Engineering*, 177, 109055. doi: 10.1016/j.cie.2023.109055.

Aljohani, A. (2023). Predictive analytics and machine learning for real-time supply chain risk mitigation and agility. *Sustainability*, 15(20). doi: 10.3390/su152015088.

Anderson, J.D., Mitchell, J.L., Maples, J.G. (2021). Invited review: Lessons from the COVID-19 pandemic for food supply chains. *Applied Animal Science*, 37(6), 738–747. doi: 10.15232/aas.2021-02223.

Baah, C., Acquah, I.S.K., Ofori, D. (2021). Exploring the influence of supply chain collaboration on supply chain visibility, stakeholder trust, environmental and financial performances: A partial least square approach. *Benchmarking: An International Journal*, 29(1), 172–193. doi: 10.1108/BIJ-10-2020-0519.

Berendes, K., Arabmaldar, A., Hammerschmidt, M., Loske, D., Klumpp, M. (2025) Measuring the resilience-efficiency trade-off: An empirical application for retail logistics. *Logistics Research*, 18(1–2), 110–134. doi: 10.1108/LORE-12-2024-0016.

Beta, K., Nagaraj, S.S., Weerasinghe, T.D.B. (2025). The role of artificial intelligence on supply chain resilience. *Journal of Enterprise Information Management*, 38(3), 950–973. doi: 10.1108/jeim-12-2023-0674.

Bhambri, P. and Bajdor, P. (eds) (2024). *Handbook of Technological Sustainability: Innovation and Environmental Awareness*. CRC Press, Boca Raton.

Bhambri, P. and Khang, A. (2024). Machine learning advancements in E-health: Transforming digital healthcare. In *Medical Robotics and AI-Assisted Diagnostics for a High-Tech Healthcare Industry*, Khang, A. (ed.). IGI Global, New York, London, Beijing. doi: 10.4018/979-8-3693-2105-8.ch012.

Bhambri, P. and Khang, A. (2025). Edge computing for enhancing efficiency and sustainability in green transportation systems. In *Driving Green Transportation System through Artificial Intelligence and Automation*, Khang, A. (ed.). Springer, Cham. doi: 10.1007/978-3-031-72617-0_3.

Bhambri, P. and Kumar, S. (2024). Protecting sustainable supply chains from cyber threats. In *Digital Sustainability: Navigating Entrepreneurship in the Information Age*, Bhambri, P. and Paweloszek, I. (eds). CRC Press, Boca Raton. doi: 10.1201/9781003484226-9.

Bhambri, P. and Paweloszek, I. (2024). Introduction to digital sustainability and entrepreneurship. In *Digital Sustainability: Navigating Entrepreneurship in the Information Age*, Bhambri, P. and Paweloszek, I. (eds). CRC Press, Boca Raton. doi: 10.1201/9781003484226-2.

Bhambri, P., Rani, S., Khang, A. (2024). AI-driven digital twin and resource optimization in Industry 4.0 ecosystem. In *Intelligent Techniques for Predictive Data Analytics*, Singh, N., Birla, S., Ansari, M.D., Shukla, N.K. (eds). Wiley-IEEE Press, Hoboken. doi: 10.1002/9781394227990.ch3.

Burke, G.J., Carrillo, J.E., Vakharia, A.J. (2007). Single versus multiple supplier sourcing strategies. *European Journal of Operational Research*, 182(1), 95–112. doi: 10.1016/j.ejor.2006.07.007.

Chauhan, S., Singh, R., Gehlot, A., Akram, S.V., Twala, B., Priyadarshi, N. (2023). Digitalization of supply chain management with Industry 4.0 enabling technologies: A sustainable perspective. *Processes*, 11(1), doi: 10.3390/pr11010096.

Chen, S., Zhang, Q., Zhou, Y. (2019). Impact of supply chain transparency on sustainability under NGO Scrutiny. *Production and Operations Management*, 28(12), 3002–3022. doi: 10.1111/poms.12973.

Choi, T.Y., Netland, T.H., Sanders, N., Sodhi, M.S., Wagner, S.M. (2023). Just-in-time for supply chains in turbulent times. *Production and Operations Management*, 32(7), 2331–2340. doi: 10.1111/poms.13979.

Drissi Elbouzidi, A., Ait El Cadi, A., Pellerin, R., Lamouri, S., Tobon Valencia, E., Bélanger, M.-J. (2023). The role of AI in warehouse digital twins: Literature review. *Applied Sciences*, 13(11), doi: 10.3390/app13116746.

Dubey, R., Gunasekaran, A., Childe, S.J., Fosso Wamba, S., Roubaud, D., Foropon, C. (2021). Empirical investigation of data analytics capability and organizational flexibility as complements to supply chain resilience. *International Journal of Production Research*, 59(1), 110–128. doi: 10.1080/00207543.2019.1582820.

Echefaj, K., Charkaoui, A., Cherrafi, A., Ivanov, D. (2024). Design of resilient and viable sourcing strategies in intertwined circular supply networks. *Annals of Operations Research*, 337(1), 459–498. doi: 10.1007/s10479-024-05873-1.

Egels-Zandén, N., Hulthén, K., Wulff, G. (2015). Trade-offs in supply chain transparency: The case of Nudie Jeans Co. *Journal of Cleaner Production*, 107, 95–104. doi: 10.1016/j.jclepro.2014.04.074.

Ganesan, B., Al-Jumaily, A., Fong, K.N.K., Prasad, P., Meena, S.K., Tong, R.K.-Y. (2021). Impact of coronavirus disease 2019 (COVID-19) outbreak quarantine, isolation, and lockdown policies on mental health and suicide. *Frontiers in Psychiatry*, 12. doi: 10.3389/fpsyt.2021.565190.

Garavelli, A.C. (2003). Flexibility configurations for the supply chain management. *International Journal of Production Economics*, 85(2), 141–153. doi: 10.1016/S0925-5273(03)00106-3.

Gualandris, J., Longoni, A., Luzzini, D., Pagell, M. (2021). The association between supply chain structure and transparency: A large-scale empirical study. *Journal of Operations Management*, 67(7), 803–827. doi: 10.1002/joom.1150.

Ivanov, D. and Dolgui, A. (2020). Viability of intertwined supply networks: Extending the supply chain resilience angles towards survivability. A position paper motivated by COVID-19 outbreak. *International Journal of Production Research*, 58(10), 2904–2915. doi: 10.1080/00207543.2020.1750727.

Jyani, N. (2024). Cruising through the crisis: How Amazon became the biggest gainer in the pandemic. *Journal of Information Technology Teaching Cases*, 20438869241246809. doi: 10.1177/20438869241246809.

Kamalahmadi, M., Shekarian, M., Mellat Parast, M. (2022). The impact of flexibility and redundancy on improving supply chain resilience to disruptions. *International Journal of Production Research*, 60(6), 1992–2020. doi: 10.1080/00207543.2021.1883759.

Kandil, N., Hammami, R., Battaïa, O. (2022). Insourcing versus outsourcing decision under environmental considerations and different contract arrangements. *International Journal of Production Economics*, 253, 108589. doi: 10.1016/j.ijpe.2022.108589.

Kazancoglu, Y., Ozkan-Ozen, Y.D., Sagnak, M., Kazancoglu, I., Dora, M. (2023). Framework for a sustainable supply chain to overcome risks in transition to a circular economy through Industry 4.0. *Production Planning & Control* 34(10), 902–917. doi: 10.1080/09537287.2021.1980910.

Leach, M., MacGregor, H., Scoones, I., Wilkinson, A. (2021). Post-pandemic transformations: How and why COVID-19 requires us to rethink development. *World Development*, 138, 105233. doi: 10.1016/j.worlddev.2020.105233.

Li, G., Liu, M., Zheng, H. (2022). Subsidization or diversification? Mitigating supply disruption with manufacturer information sharing. *Omega*, 112, 102670. doi: 10.1016/j.omega.2022.102670.

Liu, B., Zhang, Q., Liu, J., Hao, Y., Tang, Y., Li, Y. (2022). The impacts of critical metal shortage on China's electric vehicle industry development and countermeasure policies. *Energy*, 248, 123646. doi: 10.1016/j.energy.2022.123646.

Mathew, J.L. and Mathew, T.L. (2020). Invention, innovation, and imitation in India – Necessity arising from the COVID-19 pandemic. *Annals of the National Academy of Medical Sciences (India)*, 56, 77–86. doi: 10.1055/s-0040-1713719.

Mohammad, W., Elomri, A., Kerbache, L. (2022). The global semiconductor chip shortage: Causes, implications, and potential remedies. *IFAC-PapersOnLine*, 55(10), 476–483. doi: 10.1016/j.ifacol.2022.09.439.

Namdar, J., Li, X., Sawhney, R., Pradhan, N. (2018). Supply chain resilience for single and multiple sourcing in the presence of disruption risks. *International Journal of Production Research*, 56(6), 2339–2360. doi: 10.1080/00207543.2017.1370149.

Nandi, S., Sarkis, J., Hervani, A.A., Helms, M.M. (2021). Redesigning supply chains using blockchain-enabled circular economy and COVID-19 experiences. *Sustainable Production and Consumption*, 27, 10–22. doi: 10.1016/j.spc.2020.10.019.

Olawale, O., Ajayi, F.A., Udeh, C.A., Odejide, O.A. (2024). Risk management and HR practices in supply chains: Preparing for the future. *Magna Scientia Advanced Research and Reviews*, 10(2), 238–255. doi: 10.30574/msarr.2024.10.2.0065.

Rana, R. and Bhambri, P. (2024a). AI-driven MCDM tools for optimizing industrial wastewater treatment. In *Modern SuperHyperSoft Computing Trends in Science and Technology*, Smarandache, F. and Majumder, P. (eds). IGI Global, New York, London, Beijing. doi: 10.4018/979-8-3693-6875-6.ch003.

Rana, R. and Bhambri, P. (2024b). Environmental challenges and technological solutions. In *Handbook of Technological Sustainability: Innovation and Environmental Awareness*, Bhambri, P. and Bajdor, P. (eds). CRC Press, Boca Raton. doi: 10.1201/9781003475989-17.

Rane, S.B. and Narvel, Y.A.M. (2022). Data-driven decision making with Blockchain-IoT integrated architecture: A project resource management agility perspective of industry 4.0. *International Journal of System Assurance Engineering and Management*, 13(2), 1005–1023. doi: 10.1007/s13198-021-01377-4.

Rose, N., Rowe, F., Dolega, L. (2023). How consumer behaviours changed in response to COVID-19 lockdown stringency measures: A case study of Walmart. *Applied Geography*, 154, 102948. doi: 10.1016/j.apgeog.2023.102948.

Shan, X., Xiong, S., Zhang, C. (2023). Mitigating supply disruption risks by diversifying competing suppliers and using sales effort. *International Journal of Production Economics*, 255, 108637. doi: 10.1016/j.ijpe.2022.108637.

Sodhi, M.S. and Tang, C.S. (2019). Research opportunities in supply chain transparency. *Production and Operations Management*, 28(12), 2946–2959. doi: 10.1111/poms.13115.

Strauss-Wieder, A. (2023). Evolving with rapidly shifting supply chains and freight systems: The past, the present, and the emerging future. *Transportation Research Record*, 2677(2), 1–14. doi: 10.1177/03611981221109583.

Thakur-Weigold, B. and Miroudot, S. (2024). Supply chain myths in the resilience and deglobalization narrative: Consequences for policy. *Journal of International Business Policy*, 7(1), 99–111. doi: 10.1057/s42214-023-00170-3.

Villena, V.H. and Dhanorkar, S. (2020). How institutional pressures and managerial incentives elicit carbon transparency in global supply chains. *Journal of Operations Management*, 66(6), 697–734. doi: 10.1002/joom.1088.

Xu, H., Pan, X., Li, J., Feng, S., Guo, S. (2023). Comparing the impacts of carbon tax and carbon emission trading, which regulation is more effective? *Journal of Environmental Management*, 330, 117156. doi: 10.1016/j.jenvman.2022.117156.

Yang, C.-S. (2019). Maritime shipping digitalization: Blockchain-based technology applications, future improvements, and intention to use. *Transportation Research Part E: Logistics and Transportation Review*, 131, 108–117. doi: 10.1016/j.tre.2019.09.020.

Yu, Z., Razzaq, A., Rehman, A., Shah, A., Jameel, K., Mor, R.S. (2022). Disruption in global supply chain and socio-economic shocks: A lesson from COVID-19 for sustainable production and consumption. *Operations Management Research*, 15(1), 233–248. doi: 10.1007/s12063-021-00179-y.

2

Generative AI's Impact on Supply Chain Decision-Making

This chapter discusses recent progress in applying generative artificial intelligence (Gen-AI) to supply chain decision-making. Studies from manufacturing, retail, pharmaceuticals, e-commerce and green supply chains point to the increasing role of technologies such as large language models (LLMs), generative adversarial networks (GANs), retrieval-augmented generation (RAG), reinforcement learning (RL) and digital twins. Literature uniformly indicates that there are improvements in forecasting accuracy, cost savings and operating efficiency with significant benefits such as better demand forecasting, lower costs of inventory, decreased processing time and higher supply chain resilience. In addition to efficiency, Gen-AI facilitates risk management, scenario planning and sustainability programs through which organizations are able to respond more dynamically to disruptions. Still, there are hurdles to overcome, especially regarding data quality, ethical and privacy threats, algorithmic prejudice, integration with legacy systems and the requirement for skilled professionals. Research also indicates that technological advantage is optimized through bundling with human capital, managerial support and coordinated adoption plans. Overall, Gen-AI illustrates transformative capability within predictive analytics, logistics optimization and strategic decision-making, and future development will rely on explainability, domain-specific frameworks and responsible implementation practices.

2.1. Introduction

Generative artificial intelligence, or Gen-AI, is a group of sophisticated machine learning methods that can create new, contextually applicable data, solutions and insights. Unlike conventional predictive models, generative models such as large language models (LLMs), generative adversarial networks (GANs), retrieval-augmented generation (RAG), and digital twins not only examine patterns in data but also create

Chapter written by Pankaj BHAMBRI and Himani SHARMA.

novel outputs, facilitating applications that go beyond mere forecasting. In tandem, supply chain decision-making has grown more sophisticated with globalization, fluctuating demand, geopolitical uncertainty, and sustainability issues. Organizations need to make swift yet precise decisions on procurement, inventory management, logistics, risk, and long-term strategy. Traditional approaches frequently find it challenging to deal with the dynamic, uncertain, and data-driven nature of contemporary supply chains. Gen-AI convergence with supply chain management holds great promise in mitigating these challenges.

Through facilitating improved demand forecasting, disruption management, resource optimization, and real-time scenario simulation, Gen-AI offers decision-makers more adaptive and robust strategies (Bhambri and Kumar 2024). For instance, generative models can model "what-if" scenarios for demand spikes, optimize transport in disruption, or create low-carbon supply networks. In retail, Gen-AI can propel personalized recommendations and adaptive inventory planning, while in pharmaceuticals, it can speed up logistics for drug distribution. Understanding this convergence is imperative as organizations look to strike a balance between efficiency, resilience and sustainability in extremely dynamic environments.

Recent studies identify both benefits – enhanced forecasting precision, lower costs and greater agility – and pitfalls, such as data privacy threats, legacy system integration and the requirement for ethical stewardship. This review adds value by integrating current evidence to establish a systematic framework regarding how Gen-AI can revolutionize supply chain decision-making. It examines the dominant technologies, claimed advantages, real-world applications and existing limiting factors, as well as emerging gaps in research and future guidance for ethical and effective uptake.

2.2. Literature review

Workforce perception influences and challenge: Kumar and Jauhar (n.d.) demonstrate that Gen-AI increases productivity and automation within SCM but acceptance is dependent on skills, job satisfaction and management support; the pragmatic benefit is quicker decisions with improved role definitions; constraints are resistance, training overhead and ethics/privacy threats.

Generative AI and management innovation include Zhang and Zhang (2025) contending that Gen-AI enhances managerial sense-making, mitigates information asymmetry, and facilitates wiser algorithms between functions. The benefit is improved strategic decisions and knowledge combination; constraints are bias, privacy and the necessity for governance.

Gen-AI impact on SCM operational excellence

– Quantitative proof of enhanced lead time, on-time delivery and inventory turnover; benefit is measurable performance improvement; limitation is ambiguity of causality and sector generalizability. AI and Gen-AI control towers in retail SCM include Bathina reporting significant gains in visibility, disruption detection and decision latency; benefit is end-to-end situational awareness; limitation is integration complexity and socio-technical alignment (Singh et al. 2025).

Gen-AI

– Widespread industry-wide benefits – predictive maintenance, virtual prototyping, creative design; benefit is multi-domain leverage; constraints are data fragmentation, high expense and interoperability (Sai et al. 2024).

AI/Gen-AI in E-Commerce and SCM (review)

– Veluru (2024) identified enhancement in forecasting, personalization, fraud detection and logistics optimization; benefit is customer-centric efficiency; constraints are privacy, cost and skills deficiencies. Generative and adaptive AI for sustainable SC design (Necula and Rieder 2025) VAE+NSGA-II+DQN produces low-carbon, low-cost trade-offs; strength is explicit cost–emission balancing; weakness is synthetic data reliance and computational overhead. The Collaboration Paradox (Dhar 2025) includes multi-agent LLM configurations that can exacerbate bullwhip without sturdy execution (e.g. VMI); strength is strategic policy generation; weakness is instability from naïve agent cooperation.

Gen-AI and strategic entrepreneurship decisions (SLR)

– Improved accuracy/effectiveness and innovativeness in SMEs; strength lies in decision-making support in uncertainty; weaknesses are data bias and poor longitudinal validation (López-Solís et al. 2025).

Multi-case study of Gen-AI in work/decisions

– Actual organizational proof of quicker tasks, creativity and departmental productivity where AI culture is present; strength lies in augmentation across functions; weaknesses are single-firm focus and qualitative bias (Sandelin 2024).

Gen-AI + RAG agents in SCM

– Gaddala (2023) places RAG for forecasting, supplier management and real-time decision-making; benefit is foundation on grounded answers with retrieval; constraints are dependence on data and limited industrial experiments. (Seiti et al. 2024).

Human-centric Gen-AI in SC risk (EDAS + R. Graph)

– This sets GPT-class models first for food-chain risk with causal MCDM; benefit is criteria clarity and interdependency model development; constraints are preprint nature and modeling assumptions.

Gen-AI-enabled SCM

– Coordination and dynamism includes intensified usage which enhances performance through buyer/supplier coordination, enhanced in dynamic markets; benefit is proof of mediation mechanisms; constraint is single-country survey and correlational design (Li et al. 2024). Gen-AI and DNNs in Pharma SC enables demand prediction, risk forecasting and discovery-logistics connection; benefit is domain-specific automation; constraint is regulatory/privacy issues and proprietary data (Chava and Saradhi 2024).

Gen-AI for improved Ops and SCM

– Systematic review indicates advantages in forecasting, risk and supplier assessment; strength is holistic opportunity map; constraints are legacy integration, compute expense and ethics (Khlie et al. 2024).

Gen-AI resilience of SC (Fuzzy AHP)

– Prioritizes agility > flexibility > visibility > info-sharing > collaboration; strength is actionable prioritization; constraints are limited expert sample and subjectivity (Maghroor et al. 2024).

Gen-AI for new SC strategies – trends/innovation

– Emphasizes self-learning systems, digital twins and collaborative ecosystems; benefit is strategic horizon scanning; constraints are cost, security and regulatory hurdles (Francis Onotole et al. 2022).

Gen-AI in SCM (conceptual)

– Integrates use in risk, inventory, procurement, logistics with XAI need; benefit is widespread applicability; constraints are skills gaps and data quality (Shekhar et al. 2023).

Gen-AI-revolutionizing SCM

– Cites case reductions in cost (~15%) and inventory (~35%) along with improved service; benefit is measurable business effect; downside is change-management and scalability challenges (Yandrapalli 2023).

Gen-AI

– Opportunities and research directions for SC resilience: eight areas of resilience, focus on digital twins and proactive adaptation; benefit is research/roadmap perspective; drawback is hallucination/security threats and human-in-the-loop requirements (Boone et al. 2025).

Are Gen-AI/ChatGPT game-changers for OSCM?

– Survey (UK/USA) indicates greater efficiency, responsiveness, agility among adopters; benefit is macro-market signal; constraints are cross-sectional design and region bias (Wamba et al. 2023).

Gen-AI in SC/operations

– Capability-based framework aligns seven AI capabilities (learning, perception, prediction, interaction, adaptation, reasoning, creativity) to 13 decisions; benefit is theory-grounded scaffolding (RBV/DC); constraints are empirical verification required (Jackson et al. 2024).

LLMs and SLMs for decision-making and sustainability in SCM

– Strategic/ESG LLMs; SME, domain-specific SLMs; benefit is maturity-matched five-step adoption framework; constraints are compute/bias and data fragmentation (Besis 2025).

ChatGPT and Gen-AI in OSCM (exploratory survey)

– Advantage in customer satisfaction, cost, efficiency, risk; industry varies in maturity; benefit is snapshot of adoption; constraints are issues of data quality and conflation with non-generative AI (Fosso Wamba et al. 2024).

Maximizing employee functions in the Gen-AI age (AHP)

– Key criteria include innovativeness, productivity, CX; strategies include adaptive orgs, AI teams, ethics governance; benefit is HR playbook for co-creation; constraints are limited expert pool and economic effects not simulated (Agarwal 2025).

Gen-AI unleashing adaptive workflow design (RPA)

– GPT+RPA reduces processing time ~35% and increases satisfaction; benefit is self-tuning workflows; constraints are complexity of setup, data dependency and security (Bashir et al. 2024; Pingili et al. 2025).

Ethical role of Gen-AI in HR (SLR)

– Suggests hybrid human–AI paradigm for HR choices; benefit is efficiency with ethical guidance; constraints are bias, privacy and explainability gaps.

Generative probabilistic planning for SC networks

– An approach using offline reinforcement learning, graph neural networks, and a generative policy reportedly returns robust, globally optimized plans compared to heuristics. The benefit is end-to-end robustness under uncertainty; constraints are computational cost and transferability.

LLMs + knowledge graphs for SC visibility

– A conceptual approach uses zero-shot NER/RE to construct multi-tier knowledge graphs from public data, revealing underlying supply chain links. The primary benefit is achieving visibility beyond Tier-1 without requiring data sharing; key constraints are handling domain-specific jargon and generating only static snapshots.

Gen-AI for relationship prediction in SC KGs (case study)

– LLM embeddings plus ML enhance link prediction and contextual risk inference; benefit is improved network understanding for decisions; constraints are hallucinations and dataset/embedding reliance (Zheng and Brintrup 2024).

2.3. Comparison table

Table 2.1 collates the major findings, approaches, strengths and weaknesses of current studies focusing on the integration of Generative AI into supply chain decision-making (Bhambri and Starostka-Patyk 2025). It consolidates various studies from manufacturing, retailing, pharmaceuticals, e-commerce, sustainability and workforce planning.

Through systematic comparison of research purposes, settings, methods, technologies used and outcomes reported, the table not only points out the quantifiable advantages, for example, enhanced forecasting accuracy, cost savings and responsiveness but also the ongoing concerns, such as data quality, ethical hazards and implementation difficulty.

Title of paper	Research objective/aim	Domain/context	Methodology/ approach	Technology/ models used	Key findings/ contributions	Challenges/ limitations
Influences and challenges of workforce perceptions...	Study workforce perceptions and ethics in Gen-AI adoption	Supply chain management	Survey (132 professionals) plus modeling	Gen-AI adoption variables	Boosts productivity but skill gaps remain	Resistance, training needs, ethics
The impact of generative AI on management innovation	Explore GAI impact on management innovation	Management/ Org Innovation	Lit review plus conceptual analysis	LLMs, NLP, GANs, knowledge graphs	Improves decision accuracy, reduces info gaps	Privacy, bias, ethical/legal concerns
Impact of generative AI on operational excellence…	Measure Gen-AI effects on SCM performance	SCM (Manufacturing firms)	Quantitative pre/post study (100 firms)	Gen-AI for forecasting, scheduling	Improved lead times, on-time delivery	Biases, causality limits, cultural influence
AI and generative-AI control towers in retail SCM	Analyze GenAI-enabled control towers	Retail SCM	Case evidence plus synthesis	Control towers, NLP, analytics	↑ visibility (88%), ↓ cost (25%)	Integration complexity, ethics, readiness
Generative AI for Industry 5.0	Study Gen-AI in Industry 5.0	Industry 5.0 (multi-sector)	Lit review plus product analysis	ChatGPT, DALL-E, GANs, RL	Optimizes production, prototyping	High costs, privacy, interoperability issues
AI and Gen-AI in E-Commerce SCM	Review AI/GenAI in e-commerce SCM	E-commerce and SCM	Comprehensive lit review	ML, GANs, recommender systems	Enhances forecasting, personalization	Privacy, cost, skills shortage

Title of paper	Research objective/aim	Domain/context	Methodology/ approach	Technology/ models used	Key findings/ contributions	Challenges/ limitations
Gen and Adaptive AI for Sustainable SC Design	Hybrid GenAI, RL for low-cost/low-emission SCM	Sustainable SCM	VAE, NSGA-II, RL agent	VAE, NSGA-II, DQN	50% emission cut, 15% cost rise	Synthetic data, comp. heavy
The Collaboration Paradox	Study collaborative GenAI agents in SCM	Supply chain simulation	Multi-agent simulations	LLMs, RAG, VMI, MAS	Collaboration paradox: hoarding	Simplified sim, no industry validation
Gen-AI and strategic decisions in entrepreneurship	Impact of GenAI on SME strategy decisions	Entrepreneurship/ strategy	Systematic lit review	LLMs, GANs, analytics	Better accuracy, efficiency	Bias, integration, limited SME validation
Multi-case study on GenAI in work	Show real org use of GenAI in departments	Org decision-making (retail)	Multi-case, 31 participants	ChatGPT, multimodal AI	Faster tasks, creativity ↑	One org, qualitative only
GenAI and RAG in SCM	Explore role of GenAI and RAG agents	Supply chain management	Lit review, framework	GANs, GPT, RAG	Better forecasting, supplier mgmt.	Data dependence, interpretability
Human-centric GenAI in SC risk	Risk mgmt. via causal MCDM and GenAI	SC risk management (food chain)	Enhanced EDAS, R. Graph	GPT, BERT, RoBERTa, T5	GPT effective in risk management	Preprint, synthetic assumptions

Title of paper	Research objective/aim	Domain/context	Methodology/ approach	Technology/ models used	Key findings/ contributions	Challenges/ limitations
GenAI in SCM: Coordination and Dynamism	Assess GenAI usage depth on SCM performance	SCM (Chinese firms)	Survey (236 firms), mediation	LLMs, NLP, DL models	Coordination mediates benefits	Chinese context, correlation only
GenAI and DNNs in Pharma SC	GenAI, DNNs in pharma SCM	Pharma supply chains	Lit review, case studies	GANs, VAEs, DNNs	Better forecasting, optimization	Privacy/regulation, bias
GenAI in Ops and SCM	Opportunities/ challenges in SCM	Ops and SCM	Lit review, framework	LLMs, GANs, CV, ML	Improves forecasting, risk management	Legacy integration, ethics
GenAI in SC Resilience (Fuzzy AHP)	Assess GenAI impact on SC resilience drivers	SC resilience	Lit review, expert survey, Fuzzy AHP	GenAI, Fuzzy AHP	Agility most critical driver	Small expert sample
GenAI for SC Strategies and Future Trends	Review GenAI trends in SCM strategies	SC strategy and innovation	Lit review	GANs, transformers, IoT, Blockchain	Supports forecasting, risk, collab	Privacy, costs, regulation
GenAI in SCM Ops	Impact on SCM (risk, inventory, logistics)	Supply chain management	Lit review, examples	GANs, NLP, XAI	Better forecasting, procurement	Skills, data, ethics
Revolutionizing SCM with GenAI	Transform SCM functions with GenAI	SCM	Lit review, industry cases	GANs, ChatGPT, analytics	Reduced costs (15%), lower inventory (35%)	Integration, skill gaps, ethics

Title of paper	Research objective/aim	Domain/context	Methodology/ approach	Technology/ models used	Key findings/ contributions	Challenges/ limitations
GenAI and SC Resilience Research Directions	Explore GenAI for resilience across domains	SC Resilience	Lit review, framework	LLMs, RAG, Digital Twins	8 resilience domains identified	Hallucinations, cyber risk
GenAI/ChatGPT as SCM Game Changers	Survey SCM adopters vs. non-adopters (UK, USA)	Ops and SCM	Survey (315), OL theory	ChatGPT, LLMs	↑ efficiency, agility; risks in data	Early adoption, cross-sectional
GenAI Framework in SCM and Ops	Framework mapping AI/GenAI to SCM functions	SCM and Ops	Conceptual framework (RBV+DC)	GANs, GPT, DALL-E, IoT	7 core AI capabilities mapped	Needs empirical validation
GenAI and LLMs in SCM Sustainability	Impact of LLMs/SLMs on SCM decisions	Sustainable SCM	SLR (88 papers), Framework	LLMs (GPT), SLMs (Phi)	LLMs excel at strategic tasks	SME gaps, high compute cost
ChatGPT and GenAI in OSCM	Explore adoption, benefits, challenges in OSCM	Ops and SCM (US/UK firms)	Survey (300 responses)	ChatGPT, LLMs, NLP	↑ satisfaction, efficiency	Data quality, resistance
Optimizing roles in GenAI Era	Redefine roles for human–AI co-creation	HR/Workforce	SLR, MCDM (AHP), experts	GenAI (LLMs, CV, ML)	Top criteria: Innovativeness, Productivity	Small expert sample

Title of paper	Research objective/aim	Domain/context	Methodology/ approach	Technology/ models used	Key findings/ contributions	Challenges/ limitations
GenAI + RPA Workflow Design	Adaptive workflow automation with GenAI, RPA	Enterprise Workflow (E-commerce)	Framework, Case study	GPT, RPA, Analytics	35% faster processing, ↑ accuracy	High setup cost, security risks
Ethical role of GenAI in HR	Hybrid framework for HR decisions	HR Management.	SLR (50 studies), Bibliometrics	ChatGPT, Bard, LLMs	AI aids HR but humans ensure ethics	Bias, privacy, over-reliance
Gen probabilistic planning in SCNs	Use GenAI, RL for supply chain planning	SC Network Planning	Offline RL, GNN simulation	GNNs, RL, GenAI policies	Resilient plans, better than heuristics	High compute, transfer limits
LLMs + KGs for SC Visibility	Use LLMs, KGs to improve SC visibility	SC Visibility/ Risk	Zero-shot, KG building	LLMs, KGs, NER/RE tools	Extracts hidden SC dependencies	Domain term limits, static data
GenAI for relationship prediction in SC KGs	Improve link prediction in SC knowledge graphs	SC visibility and risk	Embeddings, ML, Case study	LLMs, ML, KGs	Outperforms baselines in SC links	Hallucination, dataset reliance

Table 2.1. *Literature review comparison table*

2.4. Challenges

2.4.1. *Data quality, fragmentation and integration*

The most persistent issue in the studies reviewed is that supply chain data is fragmented and inconsistent. It is spread out among suppliers, manufacturers, third-party logistics providers and retailers, and is more likely than not stored in old ERP or siloed databases (Rana and Bhambri 2024a). Generative AI models based on large, high-quality datasets fall apart when provided with incomplete or inconsistent inputs. For instance, articles on control towers and resilience (Shekhar et al. 2023; Yandrapalli 2023; Khlie et al. 2024; Veluru 2024) highlight that suboptimal data integration translates into errors in forecasting and disruption management. In the absence of strong data pipelines and standardization, even the most sophisticated models stand to amplify existing inefficiencies rather than address them.

2.4.2. *Computational cost and resource intensity*

Large language models, GANs or reinforcement learning agents are computationally costly to deploy and train. They need high-performance computing, GPU clusters and large storage infrastructure. This costs multinational companies but is much less viable for small- and medium-sized businesses. Industry 5.0 and sustainable design studies (Chava and Saradhi 2024; Sai et al. 2024; Besis 2025; Necula and Rieder 2025) observe that although AI may minimize emissions or maximize cost trade-offs, the initial investment is exorbitant. Consequently, scalability is still an issue, and a lot of organizations cannot scale beyond pilots (Rana and Bhambri 2024b).

2.4.3. *Ethical, privacy and security risks*

One of the biggest limitations is the ethical and legal aspects of data utilization. Supply chains deal with sensitive information such as supplier agreements, buyer orders and even financial or identification data (Rana and Bhambri 2024c). Their use in generative models poses risks of privacy violations, intellectual property exposure and regional data protection compliance. A number of papers (Bashir et al. 2024; Khlie et al. 2024; Boone et al. 2025; Zhang and Zhang 2025) caution that data bias can transmit unfair results, including disparate supplier grading or biased personnel decisions. Further, the absence of apparent accountability for AI outputs makes regulation tricky, which makes companies hesitant toward blanket deployment.

2.4.4. *Model limitations: hallucination, bias and explainability*

Generative models, as effective as they are, tend to hallucinate – results that sound plausible but are not necessarily correct. In supply chain situations, one inaccuracy in a forecast or an optimization can cause significant operational disruptions. Several reviews (Shekhar et al. 2023; Yandrapalli 2023; Fosso Wamba et al. 2024; Boone et al. 2025) emphasize the importance of explanation AI (XAI) schemes by which managers can comprehend and validate model results. Bias is another problem: when models are trained on biased or incomplete data, they perpetuate existing inequalities, such as over-prioritizing some suppliers or distorting demand trends. These problems lower organizational trust in AI-driven recommendations.

2.4.5. *Organizational and workforce barriers*

Aside from technical challenges, organizational maturity and employee attitude have a critical impact on adoption. Research in the human-focused and HR environments (Kumar and Jauhar n.d.; Sandelin 2024; Agarwal 2025) indicates that workers tend to view AI as jeopardizing job security, with resistance and reluctance to work alongside AI-powered systems.

Despite management backing for adoption, inadequate training and change management delay integration. The "collaboration paradox" (Dhar 2025) points out that in the absence of proper coordination, AI agents can further exacerbate supply chain uncertainty. This emphasizes that Gen-AI is not a plug-and-play technology; its potential comes to fruition only when supported by managerial intervention, training of employees and co-creation culture (Rana and Bhambri 2025).

2.5. Technologies

Generative AI technologies for supply chain decision-making exhibit uneven maturity and readiness: LLMs without retrieval are still pilot-grade (≈TRL 5–6) – good enough for summaries and drafting but unsafe for high-stake actions because they hallucinate and suffer from knowledge drift; LLMs with RAG are production-ready in document-rich contexts (≈TRL 7–8) when you have versioned corpora, strict access controls and retrieval telemetry; knowledge graphs with LLM extraction fall mid-maturity (≈TRL 5–6), producing multi-tier visibility only if you pay for ontology design, entity resolution and continuous curation; GANs/VAEs offer useful rare-event coverage (≈TRL 6–7) but need independent realism/transfer tests passed before they can inform policy; digital twins are getting close to production where telemetry and master data are on-point (≈TRL 6–8), but rapidly degrade under data gaps and model rot; RL+GNN planners are still deployment-sparse (≈TRL 4–6) due to compute cost, reward/constraint design and the sim-to-real gap – keep on shadow mode with safety shields and rollback; and multi-agent LLMs are research-grade (≈TRL 3–4) because instability risks (e.g. bullwhip, collusion) keep them out of production. Practically, implement LLM+RAG and digital twins initially where data contracts and governance are in place; add KGs when curation is sponsored; utilize GANs/VAEs to stress-test and not substitute ground truth; maintain RL as offline decision support until safety/generalization are established; and limit multi-agent LLMs to sandboxes – with XAI, retrieval/fidelity audits and cost/energy accounting as non-negotiable controls in all.

2.6. Future scope

To turn this future vision into an actionable research agenda in narrative form, we will first cement LLM+RAG for contract review and supplier rating by rigorously comparing retrievers, chunking and re-ranking on corporate documents while keeping retrieval traces logged – tuning factuality, source coverage, freshness and escalation rates to elevate TRL from pilot to production. Concurrently, we will enable decision support explainability through experimental evaluation of counterfactuals, source-attributed rationales and feature attributions within live planning processes, with the aims to achieve reduced overrides, increased SLA conformance and accelerated decisions. We will ensure multi-tier visibility through ongoing knowledge graphs that combine streaming NER/RE with human-in-the-loop curation, auditing precision/recall and time-to-risk-flag to manage staleness. To safely utilize synthetic data, we will cross-validate GAN/VAE scenarios with train-on-synthetic/test-on-real evaluations, causal/temporal diagnostics and out-of-domain tests, subsidizing only those scenarios that enhance policy performance in the real world. Digital twins will be run with clear fidelity goals (MAPE, latency, coverage) and ROI stage gates, such as twin-to-ground variance monitors, kill-switches and data-gap alerts. RL+GNN planners will stay in shadow-mode until safety is established, using constrained/shielded/offline-conservative techniques, off-policy evaluation and rollback triggers to ensure SLA adherence under disturbances. We will design hybrid OR × Gen-AI planners that allow LLMs to propose hypotheses or decompositions while MILP/CP guarantees feasibility/optimality, benchmarking cost-to-serve, solve time, robustness and human rework to warrant handoffs. At scale, we will have cost- and energy-aware goals throughout RAG, twins and RL such that every percent of service enhancement is planned against dollars and kWh/CO_2, and governance and procurement dashboards. Data contracts, access based on roles, retention/lineage, bias tests and red-team exercises will form the governance core which avoids leakage, drift and unfairness while maintaining utility. Lastly, multi-agent LLM negotiation will be limited to sandbox market simulators in order to implement stability protocols (caps, penalties, shared beliefs) that dampen bullwhip and collusion prior to live integration. Throughout all strands, open benchmarks, telemetry schemas, audit trails and reproducibility packages will transform pilots into stable, compliant and cost-efficient deployments.

2.7. References

Agarwal, A. (2025). Optimizing employee roles in the era of generative AI: A multi-criteria decision-making analysis of co-creation dynamics. *Cogent Social Sciences*, 11, 2476737.

Ahn, H.-il, Olivar, S., Mehta, H., Song, Y.C. (2024). Generative probabilistic planning for optimizing supply chain networks. *ArXiv* [Online]. Available at: https://arxiv.org/abs/2404.07511.

AlMahri, S., Xu, L., Brintrup, A. (2024). Enhancing supply chain visibility with knowledge graphs and large language models. *ArXiv* [Online]. Available at: https://arxiv.org/abs/2408.07705.

Bashir, N., Donti, P., Cuff, J., Sroka, S., Ilic, M., Sze, V., Delimitrou, C., Olivetti, E. (2024). The climate and sustainability implications of generative AI. *An MIT Exploration of Generative AI*, 3.

Bathina, S. (2025). AI and generative-AI control towers: Reinventing retail supply chain management. *International Journal of Environmental Sciences*, 11, 2469–2480. doi: 10.64252/ghh8hc73.

Besis, S. (2025). Assessing the role of generative AI and small and large language models in enhancing decision making and sustainability in supply chain management. Master's Thesis, KTH Royal Institute of Technology, DIVA [Online]. Available at: https://kth.diva-portal.org/smash/get/diva2:1984938/FULLTEXT01.pdf.

Bhambri, P. and Kumar, S. (2024). Protecting sustainable supply chains from cyber threats. In *Digital Sustainability: Navigating Entrepreneurship in the Information Age*, Bhambri, P. and Paweloszek, I. (eds). CRC Press, Boca Raton, 125–141. doi: 10.1201/9781003484226-9.

Bhambri, P. and Starostka-Patyk, M. (2025). Integrating AI with blockchain for decentralized security and threat prevention. In *Handbook of AI-driven Threat Detection and Prevention: A Holistic Approach to Security*, Bhambri, P. and Anand, A.J. (eds). CRC Press, Boca Raton, 353–370. doi: 10.1201/9781003521020-21.

Boone, T., Fahimnia, B., Ganeshan, R., Herold, D.M., Sanders, N.R. (2025). Generative AI: Opportunities, challenges, and research directions for supply chain resilience. *Transportation Research Part E: Logistics and Transportation Review*, 199, 104135.

Chava, K. and Saradhi, K.S. (2024). Emerging applications of generative AI and deep neural networks in modern pharmaceutical supply chains: A focus on automated insights and decision-making. *South Eastern European Journal of Public Health*, 20–45. doi: 10.70135/seejph.vi.4441.

Dhar, S. (2025). The collaboration paradox: Why generative ai requires both strategic intelligence and operational stability in supply chain management. *ArXiv*. [Online]. Available at: https://arxiv.org/abs/2508.13942.

Fosso Wamba, S., Guthrie, C., Queiroz, M.M., Minner, S. (2024). ChatGPT and generative artificial intelligence: An exploratory study of key benefits and challenges in operations and supply chain management. *International Journal of Production Research*, 62, 5676–5696.

Francis Onotole, E., Ogunyankinnu, T., Adeoye, Y., Osunkanmibi, A.A., Aipoh, G., Egbemhenghe, J. (2022). The role of generative AI in developing new supply chain strategies-future trends and innovations. *International Journal of Supply Chain Management*, 11, 325–338.

Gaddala, V.S. (2023). Unleashing the power of generative AI and RAG agents in supply chain management: A futuristic perspective. *IRE Journals*, 6, 1411–1417.

Jackson, I., Ivanov, D., Dolgui, A., Namdar, J. (2024). Generative artificial intelligence in supply chain and operations management: A capability-based framework for analysis and implementation. *International Journal of Production Research*, 62, 6120–6145.

Khlie, K., Benmamoun, Z., Jebbor, I., Serrou, D. (2024). Generative AI for enhanced operations and supply chain management. *Journal of Infrastructure, Policy and Development*, 8, 6637.

Kumar, C. and Jauhar, S.K. (n.d.). Influences and challenges of workforce perceptions and decision-making on ethically integrating generative AI in supply chain management. Preprint. doi: 10.2139/ssrn.5071269.

Li, L., Liu, Y., Jin, Y., Cheng, T.E., Zhang, Q. (2024). Generative AI-enabled supply chain management: The critical role of coordination and dynamism. *International Journal of Production Economics*, 277, 109388.

López-Solís, O., Luzuriaga-Jaramillo, A., Bedoya-Jara, M., Naranjo-Santamaría, J., Bonilla-Jurado, D., Acosta-Vargas, P. (2025). Effect of generative artificial intelligence on strategic decision-making in entrepreneurial business initiatives: A systematic literature review. *Administrative Sciences*, 15, 66.

Maghroor, H.R., Madanchi, F., O'Neal, T. (2024). The role of generative AI in supply chain resilience: A fuzzy AHP approach. In *9th North American Conference on Industrial Engineering and Operations Management*, Washington, D.C., 4–6.

Necula, S.-C. and Rieder, E. (2025). Generative and adaptive AI for sustainable supply chain design. *Journal of Theoretical and Applied Electronic Commerce Research*, 20, 240.

Pingili, R. (2025). Generative AI unlocking adaptive workflow design. *Journal of Next-Generation Research 5.0*, 1(2). doi: 10.70792/jngr5.0.v1i2.72.

Porkodi, S. and Cedro, T.L. (2025). The ethical role of generative artificial intelligence in modern HR decision-making: A systematic literature review. *European Journal of Business and Management Research*, 10, 44–55.

Rana, R. and Bhambri, P. (2024a). AI-driven MCDM tools for optimizing industrial wastewater treatment. In *Modern SuperHyperSoft Computing Trends in Science and Technology*, Smarandache, F. and Majumder, P. (eds). IGI Global, Hershey, 61–106. doi: 10.4018/979-8-3693-6875-6.ch003.

Rana, R. and Bhambri, P. (2024b). Generative AI-driven security frameworks for web engineering: Innovations and challenges. In *Generative AI for Web Engineering Models*, Shah, I.A. and Jhanjhi, N.Z. (eds). IGI Global, Hershey, 285–296. doi: 10.4018/979-8-3693-3703-5.ch014.

Rana, R. and Bhambri, P. (2024c). Hybrid MCDM (multi-criteria decision-making) approaches for sustainable energy management. In *Modern SuperHyperSoft Computing Trends in Science and Technology*, Smarandache, F. and Majumder, P. (eds). IGI Global, Hershey, 149–184. doi: 10.4018/979-8-3693-6875-6.ch006.

Rana, R. and Bhambri, P. (2025). Harnessing block chain digital twins for sustainable business operations. In *Practical Frameworks for New-Age Digitalization Business Strategy*, Tee, P., Song, B., Ho, R. (eds). IGI Global, Hershey, 413–446. doi: 10.4018/979-8-3373-2018-2.ch013.

Sai, S., Sai, R., Chamola, V. (2024). Generative AI for Industry 5.0: Analyzing the impact of ChatGPT, DALLE, and other models. *IEEE Open Journal of the Communications Society*, 6, 3056–3066.

Sandelin, F. (2024). A multi-case study on generative AI use in work and decision-making: Exploring applications and potential departmental effects. Master's Thesis, Hanken School of Economics, Helsinki.

Seiti, H., Javadi, R., Ghanbari, H., Kazemiyan, S.K., Hameed, I.A. (2024). Unleashing the potential of human-centric generative AI in supply chain risk management: A casual MCDM approach. *SSRN*. doi: 10.2139/ssrn.5037708.

Shekhar, A., Prabhat, P., Yandrapalli, V., Umar, S., Abdul, F., Wakjira, W.D. (2023). Generative AI in supply chain management. *International Journal on Recent and Innovation Trends in Computing and Communication*, 11, 4179–4185.

Singh, R., Sankhi, A., Sikh, G.H., Nanavati, K. (2025). Impact of generative AI on operational excellence in supply chain management: A quantitative analysis. *International Journal of Research and Analytical Reviews (IJRAR)*, 12(2), 656–668.

Veluru, C.S. (2024). Investigating the impact of artificial intelligence and generative AI in E-commerce and supply chain: A comprehensive literature review. *European Journal of Advances in Engineering and Technology*, 11, 131–143.

Wamba, S.F., Queiroz, M.M., Jabbour, C.J., Shi, C.V. (2023). Are both generative AI and ChatGPT game changers for 21st-century operations and supply chain excellence? *International Journal of Production Economics*, 265, 109015.

Yandrapalli, V. (2023). Revolutionizing supply chains using power of generative AI. *International Journal of Research Publication and Reviews*, 4, 1556–1562.

Zhang, C. and Zhang, H. (2025). The impact of generative AI on management innovation. *Journal of Industrial Information Integration*, 44, 100767.

Zheng, G. and Brintrup, A. (2024). Enhancing supply chain visibility with generative AI: An exploratory case study on relationship prediction in knowledge graphs. *ArXiv* [Online]. Available at: https://arxiv.org/abs/2412.03390.

3

Circular Supply Chain Economics

Circular supply-chain economics investigates the impacts of the transition of the prevailing linear supply-chain of take–make–waste to a circular business model and supply-chain forms on the creation of value, cost, risk, business competitiveness, resource security and environmental performance. This chapter is a field survey of theory, empirical findings, economics models, measures, and policy interventions applicable to the circular supply chain. It integrates multidisciplinary literature – industrial ecology and operations research, macroeconomics and international trade – and gives practitioners and policy makers practical frameworks to appraise, design and scale circular supply chains. Such areas as closed-loop logistics, product-as-service and sharing platforms, remanufacturing and reuse economics, value retention in materials, life-cycle and input–output accounting tools, market and regulatory drivers, case studies of firm-level transitions, barriers and enablers, and research gaps are among the main matters to be considered. This chapter concludes by highlighting policy recommendations, roadmaps of implementation, and future research priorities.

3.1. Introduction

Global economy is constructed on the basis of supplying raw materials, processing and manufacturing goods, distributing goods and mostly discarding them at the end of their life. This neo-liberal paradigm has propelled unprecedented expansion of the economy at an increasing ecological and social cost: resource depletion, accumulation of waste, greenhouse gas emissions and supply–security vulnerabilities. The circular economy (CE) redefines it and attempts to ensure the highest possible value of products, components and materials through their reuse as long as possible, recycle natural systems, and decouple economic activity and virgin resources (Centobelli et al. 2021). The operational support of this transition is based on supply chains. This chapter identifies the subject of circular supply-chain economics as the understanding of the economic processes, motivations and the

Chapter written by Vijay Kumar SINHA and Balajee MARAM.

results that govern circular processes of goods and materials through production, distribution, consumption and recovery (Mayantia and Helob 2024).

The question is: In what ways and at what point does circularity create net economic value (firm profits, consumer surplus, national welfare), what tradeoffs are created and what policies or business model innovations are required to scale circular supply chains? This is naturally interdisciplinary and a mixture of microeconomic (pricing, contracts, inventory), operations research (reverse logistics, production planning), industrial ecology (material flow accounting), and macroeconomic and trade (Stahel 2016). The ensuing discussion is based on top-tier practitioner reports and peer-reviewed literature to offer conceptual and practical advice.

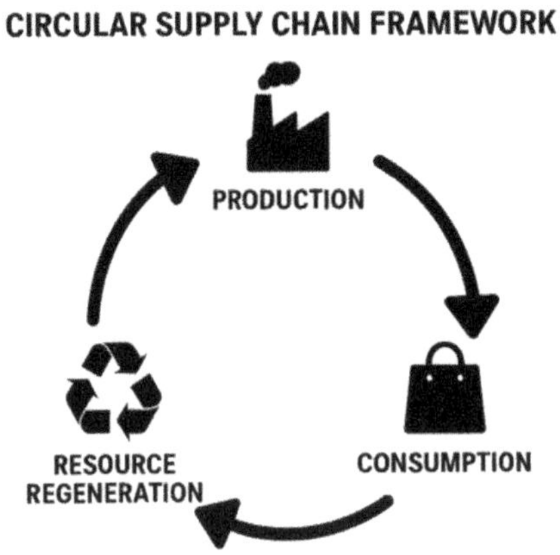

Figure 3.1. *Circular supply-chain framework (Farooque et al. 2019)*

3.2. Conceptual foundations

3.2.1. *Supply chains and principles of the circular economy*

The Ellen MacArthur Foundation (EMF) describes the circular economy through three design principles: the elimination of waste and pollution, the circulating of products and materials at the maximum value, and regeneration of natural systems. In the case of supply chains, they will be converted into lasting and repairable design, modular design to be disassembled, business models that retain ownership (product-as-service), reverse logistics to gather used goods and industrial symbiosis to use inputs (byproducts) in other processes (Dora et al. 2021). Circular supply chains necessitate a rethink on the physical flow as well as the information/financial flow that manage retrieval, refurbishment and redistribution.

Concepts distinction include closed loop, circular loops, and slow/fast loops. Similar terms that are found in the literature include closed-loop supply chains (CLSC), reverse logistics and circular supply chains. Cyclical supply chains integrate CLSC into larger systemic goals (material value retention, ecosystem regeneration): under profit motives, CLSC primarily prioritizes operational optimization of returns, remanufacturing and recycling; and the development of new governance, policy and intersector collaboration is often needed (Kudrenko et al. 2025). Other forms of circular strategies involve the use of so-called slowing loops (durability, repair) and closing loops (recycling, remanufacturing) (Mets et al. 2022).

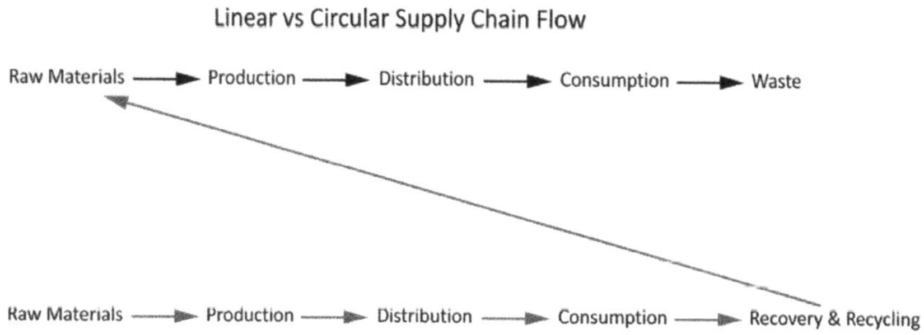

Figure 3.2. *Linear versus circular supply-chain flow. For a color version of this figure, see www.iste.co.uk/bhambri/nextgensupply.zip*

3.3. Circular supply-chain economic mechanisms

Circularity transforms fundamental economic relations. The key mechanisms are described below, and their implications are presented.

3.3.1. *Unit economics and cost structures*

The change of fixed and variable cost composition depending on the circular model:

– Increased initial design and product development (design durability, modular; material R&D) costs. Less material variable costs in case recovered inputs replace virgin feedstock-recovery will include collection, sorting, transportation and quality control expenses (Rana and Bhambri 2024b).

– *New operating expenses:* reverse logistics, refurbishment centers, testing, warranty management and traceability platforms (Lahane et al. 2020). Various depreciation and asset accounting: under product-as-service, the company can keep the ownership and can thus treat the products as long-lived assets which need to be maintained but can also allow the recurring revenue. The net impact is determined by the rates of recovery, the recovered manufacturing rate and the price difference between virgin and recovered materials. Circular cost advantages are even more understandable in firms which are heavily material-intensive and whose product design is stable. The empirical studies of multilateral bodies and case studies show that circular solutions can help lower material prices and risks to commodity price spikes – especially in turbulent markets (Jackson 1996).

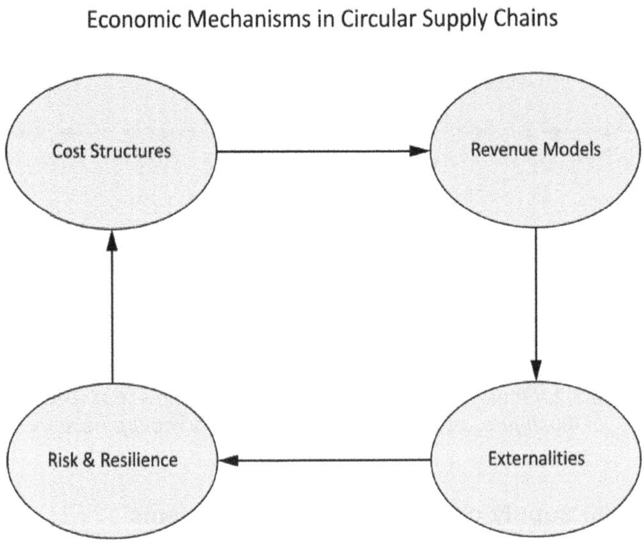

Figure 3.3. *Economic mechanisms in circular supply chains*

3.4. Demand and revenue models

Circular supply chains have frequently been linked to alternative revenue models:

– PaaS (Product-as-Service): firms do not own products but charge per usage (leasing, subscription).

This harmonizes incentives – producers are given a reward on durability and maintainability. Platforms that deal with refurbished goods have markets that can grow and value based on the used products can be harvested (Zardo et al. 2024).

3.4.1. *Performance contracting*

Outcome-linked payment (e.g. uptime, energy efficiency) encourages long product life and effective maintenance. The perceptions (quality, status), price difference and provision of after sales services affect consumer willingness to pay refurbished or leased products (Rana and Bhambri 2024a). In the case of B2B markets, PaaS is more appealing due to the existence of longer relationships and predictable service demands.

World Economic Forum 3.3 Risk and resilience effects

Circular supply chains are capable of enhancing resilience through decreasing dependency on imported virgin materials (strategic stock of recovered materials), using more varied sources of inputs (local recovery networks) and decreasing logistical distance. Nevertheless, transition brings new operational risk, including complicated reverse logistics, variability in the quality of the recovered inputs and regulatory uncertainty. Macroanalyses indicate that reshoring or extreme localization is known to be destructive of GDP, but circular policies that encourage diversification and resource efficiency can enhance resilience without having intense economic impacts.

3.4.2. *Externalities and market failures*

The environmental positive impacts of circularity are also externalities (less pollution, reduced emissions), which are not priced by markets and, as a result, circular solutions are not sufficiently invested. Policy solutions such as standards, incentives or mandates are necessary to internalize externalities in coordination failures across fragmented supply chains to address first-mover disadvantages. Valuation is complicated by measurement issues (embodied emissions, material quality).

3.4.3. *Circular supply-chain economics modeling*

This section outlines major modeling techniques that are applied to measure economic and environmental performance of circular supply chains. Life-Cycle Assessment (LCA) evaluates the environmental effects throughout the life of a product, which includes the extraction of raw materials, the manufacturing phase, distribution, use and end-of-life. The LCA is required to estimate the reduction of the amount of greenhouse gas (GHG) and reduction of resource utilization in the circular cases (e.g. remanufacturing vs. virgin manufacture) (Genovese et al. 2017). Nevertheless, LCA is based on system limits and assumptions (functional unit, division of recycling burdens), which need to be revealed in economic evaluations.

3.4.4. *PMC models for input–output (IO) and material flow analysis (MFA)*

MFA follows how materials move through an economy or industry. A hybrid input–output LCA uses both monetary IO tables and physical data to figure out how circular policies affect the whole economy. OECD and other organizations have created inventories of circular-economy indicators and IO-based analyses to figure out how the macroeconomy is affected (e.g. how material efficiency affects GDP and jobs). These models are useful for looking at systemic effects, rebound effects and effects across sectors.

3.5. Operations research models: closed-loop inventory, pricing and remanufacturing

Operations research gives businesses microeconomic tools to help them make decisions, like the best ways to buy and store items when they return into the supply chain, how to set prices and make products in closed-loop networks, and how to write contracts for third-party returns processors (Bhambri and Kumar 2024).

Classic closed-loop supply-chain models figure out when it makes sense to collect, refurbish or recycle based on return rates, remanufacturing yields and how much people want refurbished goods. These models show threshold effects, which means that circular operations stop being profitable when return rates or quality levels fall below a certain point (Circular Business Models 2020).

3.5.1. *Models based on agents and system dynamics*

Researchers use agent-based and system dynamics models to elucidate behavioral dynamics (such as consumer return behavior and the adoption of PaaS) and feedback loops (including material availability and market prices). These help us to understand path dependence and tipping points, or how adopting circular practices early on can lead to economies of scale that lower costs and encourage more people to do the same.

3.5.2. *Metrics and indicators for circular supply chains*

A strong set of metrics is necessary for judging circular supply chains in terms of cost and environmental impact.

3.6. Metrics for businesses and products

These are material circularity indicator (MCI) or similar metrics that measure the percentage of reused or recycled materials and the extension of product life.

Lifecycle cost (LCC) encompasses acquisition, operation, maintenance and end-of-life expenses across various ownership models.

– Return rate and recovery yield: the percentage of sold units that are returned and the percentage that can be used again or recycled.

– The remanufacturing margin and the index of prices on the secondary market for used goods.

Total cost of ownership (TCO) for customers is an important factor to think about when comparing PaaS to buying (Murray et al. 2017).

3.6.1. *Indicators for the system and the macro*

– Material intensity of GDP (Mi/GDP): how many kilograms of materials are used for every unit of GDP.

– The proportion of sccondary raw materials in the overall material inputs.

– Effects on jobs: how many and what kinds of jobs are created in refurbishment and reverse logistics.

– Metrics for GHG emissions per value added and resource productivity.

The OECD has put together a lot of lists of circular economy indicators for cities and regions to help them make and keep track of policies.

Standardized metrics help prevent bad results, like using more energy when transporting goods in reverse logistics, by showing how different areas affect each other (Ellen MacArthur Foundation 2019).

3.6.2. *Plans for businesses and business models*

Different business models show how circular supply-chain economics works. Below, we talk about the main types of archetypes and how they work.

3.6.3. *Product-as-service (PaaS)*

– Mechanics: the company keeps ownership and charges for use or results (leasing, subscriptions).

– Economics: changes how revenue is recognized from one-time sales to recurring revenue streams and changes product costs into long-term assets that need maintenance investments (Bhambri and Bajdor 2024).

PaaS encourages durability and repair, aligns producers' incentives for material efficiency and can help with demand fluctuations. Success depends on how often assets are used, how much it costs to maintain them, how much they are worth after they are sold and how well customers accept them.

PaaS can help you make more money over the long term and build stronger relationships with your clients for products that cost a lot of money (such as industrial equipment and medical devices) (Hazen et al. 2021).

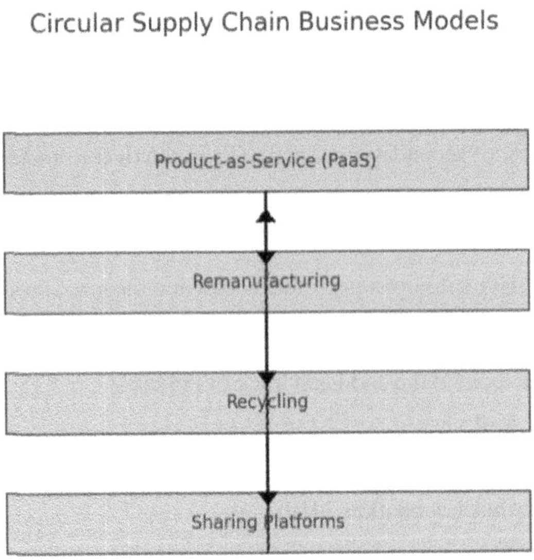

Figure 3.4. *Circular supply-chain business models*

3.6.4. *Rebuilding and refurbishing*

– Mechanics: collect products that are no longer useful, fix them up to like-new condition and sell them again.

– Economics: remanufacturing usually costs less in materials and energy than making new things, but it needs collection networks and skilled workers.

The amount of returns, the modularity of the products and the market price for remanufactured goods all affect how profitable a business is (Bhambri et al. 2022). Remanufacturing can give you good margins and protect you from commodity cycles for many durable goods, such as car parts, industrial parts and electronics.

3.6.5. *Recycling and getting materials back*

– Mechanics: get raw materials back from products that are no longer useful and use them again in manufacturing.

– Economics: recycling turns waste into secondary feedstock. Its economics depend on the value of the materials, the costs of processing them, the levels of contamination and the prices of new materials.

Mechanical recycling may be expensive and not very productive for low-value, mixed waste streams (Rana and Bhambri 2024c). However, metals, which are higher-value materials, usually have good economics. Advanced technologies for sorting and recycling chemicals can help increase yields, but they have problems with scale and energy use.

Reports say that recycling alone cannot fill the gaps in material demand; to raise overall material circularity, it is important to design things so they can be reused and recycled (Abid et al. 2024).

3.6.6. *Platforms for sharing and pooling*

– Mechanics: platforms that let many people share things they do not use much (such as cars and tools).

– Economics: sharing makes things more useful and lowers capital costs for each user, but it needs trust, scheduling and often platform governance.

Scale and network effects are very important. Platforms can centralize reverse logistics and maintenance, which can save money (Vegter et al. 2020).

3.6.7. *Tools for policy and market design*

Market failures and coordination issues make it necessary for public policy to speed up the adoption of circular supply chains. Good tools are:

– Extended producer responsibility (EPR): this makes producers responsible for managing the end of a product's life. It also encourages them to design products that can be recycled and to pay for the costs of recovery.

– Deposit-refund systems: make people want to return things, such as drink containers.

– Tax breaks or credits: for investments in remanufacturing, using secondary materials, or PaaS pilots.

– Tariffs and trade facilitation: carefully planned to make it easier for reverse logistics to happen across borders without any extra barriers. OECD studies show how trade policy makes it possible for goods to move in circles across borders.

3.7. Rules and standards set by the government

– Design standards for how easy it is to fix things and how easy it is to recycle them (e.g. spare parts must be available).

– Minimum recycled content requirements are needed to make people want to use secondary materials.

– Regulations that give people the right to repair things to cut down on planned obsolescence and make it easier for third parties to fix things.

3.7.1. *Support for public procurement and innovation*

Governments can use procurement to make markets for circular products and pay for pilot projects that lower the risk of investments (such as innovation grants and demonstration projects).

3.7.1.1. *Standards and infrastructure for information*

Digital product passports and traceability platforms (material composition, ownership history) make it easier for people to share information and lower the cost of doing business in circular supply chains (Kirchherr et al. 2017).

Standards for the quality of recovered materials are the same everywhere, so that they can be used in manufacturing.

When making policies, you need to find a balance between ambition and trade-offs. For example, aggressive reshoring or poorly calibrated localization measures can hurt welfare, while openness, diversification and circularity can make the economy more resilient without costing a lot of GDP. The OECD warns against simple reshoring plans and stresses the need for consistent policies (Wang et al. 2025).

3.8. Changes in jobs and structures

Circular activities such as repair, remanufacturing, and logistics usually require more people than automated primary manufacturing. This could create jobs in the area, but the skills and pay for these jobs may be different. Research indicates that net employment effects are contingent upon the presence of productivity gains accompanying labor shifts and the ability of declining sectors (e.g. primary extraction) to retrain workers for circular roles.

3.8.1. *Trade flows and logistics in the opposite direction*

To be circular, used goods and secondary materials often have to cross borders. To make it easier for reverse supply chains, trade rules and customs procedures need to change so that recovered goods are not treated as waste. To help reverse flows while protecting environmental standards, the OECD has put out guidelines on how to align trade and circular economy policies (Bhambri et al. 2024).

3.8.1.1. *Geopolitical effects and resource security*

Circular supply chains can minimize the risk of resource geopolitics by decreasing the reliance on virgin material and increasing the supply of secondary material. In the case of resource intensive sectors, such as batteries, rare earths and critical metals, circular strategies (urban mining, battery takeback) are part of national industrial policy.

3.9. Case studies and empirical evidence

This section summarizes empirical evidence, as well as examples of firms/country cases.

According to reports by the World Economic Forum and Ellen MacArthur Foundation, the amount of economic value unlocked by circular interventions and the level of emissions reduction vary by sector. As an illustration, there exists a high potential of recovering and remanufacturing of materials in electronics and automotive industries; textiles have potential opportunities of reuse and resale with challenges of sorting and fiber recycling. Similar to macro-reports, the key issue is that recycling is insufficient to satisfy material demand and the combination of slowing up, narrowing and closing loops is essential (Rana and Bhambri 2024d).

3.9.1. *Firm examples*

– Philips (lighting): experiments with PaaS in the early stages and takeback.

– Programs in the context of lighting as a service generated consistent revenues and possibilities to upgrade products and reuse them (such as service model aligns incentive to create durability).

– Automotive remanufacturing: remanufacturing of engines, transmissions and electronics is also run by many OEMs – recovering high-value parts and saving materials and energy compared to new manufacture.

– Textiles and fashion: non-ownership models are demanded by recommerce and rental models (some fast-fashion companies and niche luxury brands) but the scalability is limited by the logistic costs and cleaning prices.

– Those instances imply that the circular economics is highly predetermined by sectoral features (duration of product, modularity, material worth) (OECD 2021).

3.10. Barriers and enablers

3.10.1. *Technological and operational barriers*

– Low rates of returns: customers are not guaranteed to return with products; incentives and convenience are important.

– Quality variability: recovered materials and components are not of good quality, which makes processing even more expensive.

– Design constraints: circular options are limited by products that are not designed to be disassembled.

– Data gaps: lack of traceability and material data will hinder reuse.

3.10.2. *Economical and market obstacles*

– Price competition of low virgin inputs: recycling and remanufacturing experience the pressure of price when the prices of virgin material are low.

– Capital intensity and scale: refurbishment and reverse logistics systems need to be initially invested.

– Poor incentive alignment: sellers are more likely to choose one-run sales as opposed to service forms; investors may underestimate circular returns in the long run (Viscardi et al. 2022).

3.10.3. *Policies and institutional barriers*

– Regulatory uncertainty: personalized processing of returns and incisive national rules impede cross-border circular flows.

– Absence of standards: there are no quality standards of the secondary materials.

3.10.4. *Enablers*

– Digitalization: IoT, product passes and blockchain have the potential to facilitate automated reverse logistics and decrease information friction.

– Standards and mandates EPR, recycled content mandates and right-to-repair laws can change incentives.

– Finance innovation: the de-risking of circular investments can be done through green bonds, blended finance and performance payments (Noman et al. 2022).

– Consortia: the scale economies and common infrastructure can be attained through industry consortia and urban mining programs.

By lowering the need for new materials and raising the supply of used materials, circular supply chains can make resource geopolitics less of a threat.

For industries that use a lot of resources, such as batteries, rare earths and critical metals, circular strategies such as urban mining and battery takeback are important parts of national industrial policy.

3.11. Evidence from the real-world and case studies

This section puts together real-world data and examples from businesses and countries.

3.11.1. *Results for the whole world and for each sector*

The World Economic Forum and the Ellen MacArthur Foundation say that circular interventions could create a lot of economic value and cut down on emissions, but the results are different in each sector (Patra et al. 2024). For instance, the electronics and automotive industries have a lot of room for material recovery and remanufacturing. Textiles, on the other hand, have opportunities for reuse and resale but problems with sorting and fiber recycling. Macro-reports show that recycling alone cannot meet the demand for materials. Instead, a mix of slowing, narrowing and closing loops is needed (Sehnem et al. 2021).

3.11.2. *Examples of firms*

– Philips (lighting): early PaaS experiments and takeback programs for lighting as a service led to steady sales and chances to upgrade and reuse products (an example of a service model that aligns incentives for durability) (Nohra et al. 2022).

– Automotive remanufacturing: many original equipment manufacturers (OEMs) run programs to remanufacture engines, transmissions and electronics. This saves materials and energy compared to making new ones.

– Textiles and fashion: recommerce platforms and rental models (some fast-fashion companies and niche luxury brands) show that people want models that do not require ownership, but logistics and cleaning costs make it hard for these models to grow (Saari et al. 2024).

These cases show that the characteristics of a sector (product durability, modularity and the value of materials) have a big impact on circular economics.

3.12. Things that get in the way and things that help

3.12.1. *Problems with technology and operations*

– Low return rates: customers might not return items; incentives and ease of use are important.

– Changes in quality: the quality of recovered materials and parts varies, which raises processing costs.

– Design constraints: circular options are limited by products that cannot be taken apart.

– Data gaps: not enough traceability and material data make it hard to reuse.

3.12.2. *Barriers to the economy and the market*

– Price competition with cheap virgin inputs: when the price of virgin materials is low, recycling and remanufacturing have to deal with price pressure.

– Capital intensity and scale: you have to put money into reverse logistics and refurbishment systems up front.

– Misaligned incentives: sellers might like one-time sales better than service models, and investors might not see the value of long-term circular returns.

3.12.2.1. *Barriers in policy and institutions*

– Unclear rules: customs' treatment of returns and different rules in different countries make it hard for circular flows to happen across borders.

– No standards: there are not any clear quality standards for secondary materials.

3.12.3. *Things that help*

– Digitalization: IoT, product passports and blockchain can make it easier to share information and make automated reverse logistics possible.

– Standards and rules: EPR, recycled content mandates and right-to-repair laws can change the way people act (Farooque et al. 2019).

– Finance innovation: green bonds, blended finance and performance payments can make circular investments less risky.

– Collaborative platforms: industry groups and urban mining projects can share infrastructure and get economies of scale (Batista et al. 2018).

3.12.4. *Checking the economic viability*

This checklist can help companies think about circular supply-chain investments:

1. Value of materials and parts: Are the materials that are recovered valuable and can they be used instead of new ones?

2. Return potential: What rate of return and level of quality are realistic based on how customers act and what they are offered?

3. Design flexibility: Is it possible to redesign products so that they can be taken apart and put back together again without incurring too much cost?

4. Logistics and geography: Are collection networks and refurbishment centers possible at a reasonable cost, given the distances and volumes?

5. Regulatory environment: Are there policies that help (such as EPR and tax breaks) or trade barriers that make it hard for reverse flows to happen?

6. Market demand: Are there enough people who are willing to pay for refurbished or service models?

7. Digital readiness: Is it possible to use traceability and quality assurance to lower the cost of transactions?

8. Financing: Are there ways to get money to cover the initial costs and longer payback periods?

Companies should do sensitivity analyses on return rates, remanufacturing yield and price differences for secondary materials to find the break-even points for circular options. Operations research closed-loop inventory and pricing models can provide formal decision rules (Korhonen et al. 2018).

3.12.4.1. *Suggestions for policy*

To grow circular supply chains at the national and regional levels, the following policy priorities are suggested:

– Make or improve EPR frameworks that give producers responsibility for their products after they die, while making sure that costs are clear and that recovery service providers can compete with each other (Kapil Khanna et al. 2025).

– To make reverse logistics easier, customs and trade rules for used goods and secondary materials should be the same. This should be done with environmental protections in place. The OECD's advice on trade and the circular economy shows the way (OECD 2022).

– Require product information and digital passports to make it possible to trace and ensure quality across circular flows that cross borders.

– Support policies that protect the right to repair and design standards to make repairs easier and spare parts more available.

– Use public–private partnerships and green finance tools to pay for circular infrastructure such as collection networks and refurbishment hubs.

– Put money into training and job programs to give workers new skills in repair, remanufacturing and reverse logistics.

– Use procurement policies that favor circular and service-based offers to keep demand steady (Ellen MacArthur Foundation 2020).

– To keep track of progress and avoid greenwashing, keep an eye on and report standardized circularity indicators that are in line with OECD inventories (Prieto-Sandoval et al. 2018).

3.13. A plan for companies to follow to put it into action

The following is a useful phased plan:

– Strategic assessment (0–6 months): find out which product lines have the biggest effect, do a materiality analysis and map the value chain.

– Pilot projects (6–24 months): start pilot programs for PaaS on niche products, remanufacturing lines for certain parts or takeback programs with partner retailers (Singh et al. 2024).

– Scale operations (2–5 years): set up special centers for refurbishing, add digital product passports and grow secondary markets.

– System integration (5+ years): reverse logistics that are networked, platforms for multiple firms to share infrastructure and circular procurement across all operations (Rizos et al. 2017).

Important factors for success include strong leadership, cross-functional teams (R&D, supply chain, legal, finance), partnerships with experts in logistics and refurbishment, and clear KPIs that are linked to both profitability and circular performance (Selvarajan et al. 2024).

3.14. Research priorities and gaps

Even though things are getting better, there are still important research questions to answer:

– Behavioral obstacles to returns: Which interventions most efficiently enhance consumer return rates across various sectors?

– Quality assurance for secondary materials: strong ways to check and standardize the quality of secondary raw materials on a large scale (Duan et al. 2024).

– Macro-modeling of circular transitions: integrated assessment models that connect micro-firm decisions, trade and national accounts to show how they affect the whole economy (Chen et al. 2025).

– How do we price future residual assets and set up contracts for PaaS to get investors interested in finance and valuation?

– Distributional impacts and labor transitions: an examination of the effects of circular transitions on wages, inequality and regional employment, along with the role of policy in facilitating equitable transitions.

Academics ought to integrate empirical firm cases with systemic models to extract contextually relevant policy insights (Hussain and Malik 2020).

3.15. Conclusion

Circular supply-chain economics is a promising way to separate economic activity from the use of virgin resources while also making businesses more resilient and opening up new opportunities. However, to make this promise come true, we need to rethink how we design products, make contracts, handle logistics, measure success and make public policy. Digital traceability, multistakeholder coordination and new ways to handle money are all important enablers. Policymakers should put harmonized rules for reverse logistics, targeted incentives and data infrastructure at the top of their list. Companies should test and grow circular models where the economics are good for material intensity and product design. As research and practice develop together, strong indicators and careful empirical studies will help make sure that the circular transition is good for the economy and the environment.

Dimension	Linear supply-chain economics	Circular supply-chain economics
Core principle	Take → make → dispose	Reduce → reuse → recycle → regenerate
Resource use	Extractive, one-way resource flow	Regenerative, resource loops (materials, energy, water)
Economic model	Focus on volume sales, one-time transactions	Emphasis on value retention, services and multiple life cycles
Cost structures	High raw material cost, low waste management cost	Lower raw material dependence, higher upfront reverse logistics and redesign cost
Revenue models	Product ownership transfers to customer	Product-as-a-service (PaaS), leasing, remanufacturing, recycling credits
Profit drivers	Economies of scale, cheap inputs, faster production cycles	Resource efficiency, extended product value, resilience, premium for sustainability
Externalities	High negative externalities (pollution, waste, carbon footprint)	Reduced externalities via circular flows, improved ESG performance
Innovation focus	Process efficiency, cost-cutting	Eco-design, closed-loop systems, green technologies

Business models	Mass production, linear retail	Sharing platforms, reverse logistics, industrial symbiosis
Risk and resilience	Vulnerable to resource scarcity, geopolitical shocks	More resilient through resource diversification, local loops and recycling
Policy dependency	Dependent on subsidies, deregulation for growth	Strongly linked with government incentives, extended producer responsibility (EPR)
Stakeholder roles	Firms dominate; consumers passive buyers	Multi-stakeholder: firms, governments, consumers, NGOs, Academia
Environmental outcomes	High GHG emissions, landfill growth, biodiversity loss	Lower emissions, waste diversion, improved biodiversity through regeneration
Social outcomes	Short-term job creation, but resource depletion harms future	Green jobs, inclusive models, consumer participation in sustainability
Technology integration	Limited (mostly production automation)	Advanced (IoT for tracking, AI for optimization, blockchain for traceability)
Consumer involvement	Low – consume and dispose	High – return systems, shared use, co-creation
Challenges	Resource depletion, waste crises, policy pressure	High upfront investment, consumer behavior shift, technology cost
Long-term sustainability	Unsustainable, declining returns due to resource scarcity	Sustainable, regenerative, aligned with SDGs and climate goals

Table 3.1. *Circular versus linear supply-chain economics*

3.16. References

Abid, I., Fuad, M.J.M., Chowdhury, M.J.M., Ferdous, S.S. (2024). A structured literature review regarding the application of blockchain technology in the transition to a circular economy. *ArXiv* [Online]. Available at: https://arxiv.org/abs/2408.11664.

Batista, L., Bourlakis, M., Smart, P., Maull, R. (2018). In pursuit of a circular supply chain archetype – A literature review grounded in content analysis. *Prod. Plann. Control.*, 29(6), 438–451. doi: 10.1080/09537287.2017.1343502.

Bhambri, P. and Bajdor, P. (2024). Technological sustainability unveiled: A comprehensive examination of economic, social, and environmental dimensions. In *Handbook of Technological Sustainability: Innovation and Environmental Awareness*, Bhambri, P. and Bajdor, P. (eds). CRC Press, Boca Raton, FL, 80–98. doi: 10.1201/9781003475989-8.

Bhambri, P. and Kumar, S. (2024). Protecting sustainable supply chains from cyber threats. In *Digital Sustainability: Navigating Entrepreneurship in the Information Age*, Bhambri, P., Paweloszek, I. (eds). CRC Press, Boca Raton, FL, 125–141. doi: 10.1201/9781003484226-9.

Bhambri, P., Aggarwal, M., Singh, H., Singh, A.P., Rani, S. (2022). Uprising of EVs: Charging the future with demystified analytics and sustainable development. In *Decision Analytics for Sustainable Development in Smart Society 5.0*, Bali, V., Bhatnagar, V., Lu, J., Banerjee, K. (eds). Springer, Singapore, 37–54. doi: 10.1007/978-981-19-1689-2_3.

Bhambri, P., Rani, S., Khang, A. (2024). AI-driven digital twin and resource optimization in Industry 4.0 ecosystem. In *Intelligent Techniques for Predictive Data Analytics*, Singh, N., Birla, S., Ansari, M.D., Shukla, N.K. (eds). Wiley and Sons, Hoboken, NJ, 47–69. doi: 10.1002/9781394227990.ch3.

Centobelli, P., Cerchione, R., Esposito, E., Passaro, R., Shashi. (2021). Determinants of the transition towards circular economy in SMEs: A sustainable supply chain management perspective. *International Journal of Production Economics*, 242, 108297. doi: 10.1016/j.ijpe.2021.108297.

Chen, M., Wang, T., Zhao, Q., Hu, Y. (2025). Research on the development of a circular supply chain involving multiple entities: Identification and analysis of principal driving factors informed by the technology cycle. *Systems*, 13(5), 365. doi: 10.3390/systems13050365.

Circular Business Models (2020). Supply chains in circular business models: Processes and performance goals. *Resour. Conserv. Recycl.*, 162, 105046.

Dora, M., Bhatia, M.S., Gallear, D. (2021). A multidimensional research agenda for supply chain in a circular economy. Working Paper, Brunel Business School, Brunel.

Duan, W., Liu, M., Xu, D., Han, L. (2024). Remanufacturing closed-loop supply chain contract coordination with quality control in mind. *Systems*, 12(9), 350.

Ellen MacArthur Foundation (2019). *Putting the Pieces Together: How the Circular Economy Fights Climate Change*. Ellen MacArthur Foundation, Cowes, Isle of Wight.

Ellen MacArthur Foundation (2020). Moving toward a circular economy: Speeding up the growth of global supply chains. White Paper, Cowes, Isle of Wight.

Farooque, M., Zhang, A., Thürer, M., Qu, T., Huisingh, D. (2019). A definition and structured literature review of circular supply chain management. *J. Clean. Prod.*, 228, 882–900. doi: 10.1016/j.jclepro.2019.04.303.

Genovese, A., Acquaye, A., Figueroa, A., Koh, S.L. (2017). Sustainable supply chain management and the shift to a circular economy: Evidence and some uses. *Omega*, 66, 344–357. doi: 10.1016/j.omega.2015.05.015.

Hazen, B.T., Russo, I., Confente, I., Pellathy, D. (2021). Supply chain management for a circular economy: A framework for research and ideas. *Int. J. Logist. Manag.*, 32(2), 510–537. doi: 10.1108/IJLM-12-2019-0332.

Hussain, M. and Malik, M. (2020). Facilitators for circular economy within the framework of sustainable supply chain management. *J. Clean. Prod.*, 256, 120375. doi: 10.1016/j.jclepro.2020.120375.

Jackson, T. (1996). *Concerns About Materials: Pollution, Profit, and Quality of Life.* Routledge, Abingdon.

Kapil Khanna, S., Kuik, S., Ban, J. (2025). Circular supply chain management: Connecting business innovation and sustainability through best practices. *J. Circ. Econ.*, 3(1). doi: 10.55845/VLHS2148.

Kirchherr, J., Reike, D., Hekkert, M. (2017). Understanding the circular economy: A study of 114 definitions. *Resour. Conserv. Recycl.*, 127, 221–232.

Korhonen, J., Honkasalo, A., Seppälä, J. (2018). The idea of a circular economy and its limits. *Ecol. Econ.*, 143, 37–46. doi: 10.1016/j.ecolecon.2017.06.041.

Kudrenko, I., Mukhametov, A., Aslanov, E.S. (2025). Structural changes to supply chains are needed for a circular economy. *J. Entrep. Innov.*, 14(51). doi: 10.1186/s13731-025-00515-7.

Lahane, S., Kant, R., Shankar, R. (2020). A cutting-edge review of circular supply chain management and what it could mean for the future. *J. Clean. Prod.*, 258, 120859.

Mayantia, B. and Helob, P. (2024). Circular economy in supply chain management: A framework for developing database tools to improve sustainability. *Int. J. Environ. Stud.*, 81(4), 1962–1979. doi: 10.1080/00207233.2024.2350757.

Mets, L., Chertow, M.R., Althaf, S. (2022). Industrial symbiosis: New supply networks for the circular economy. In *Circular Economy Supply Chains: From Chains to Systems*, Bals, L., Ellram, L.M., Tate, W.L. (eds). Emerald Publications, Leeds.

Murray, A., Skene, K., Haynes, K. (2017). The circular economy: A cross-disciplinary examination of the concept and its implementation on a global scale. *J. Bus. Ethics*, 140(3), 369–380. doi: 10.1007/s10551-015-2693-2.

Nohra, P., Rejeb, H.B., Venkateswaran, S. (2022). The effect of automation on innovative remanufacturing processes within the circular economy: A contemporary analysis. *ArXiv* [Online]. Available at: https://arxiv.org/abs/2209.04040.

Noman, A., Akter, U.H., Pranto, T.H., Haque, A.B. (2022). A bibliometric analysis and systematic literature review of machine learning and artificial intelligence in the circular economy. *ArXiv* [Online]. Available at: https://arxiv.org/abs/2205.01042.

OECD (2021). Policy alignment for international trade and the circular economy. Report, OECD Publications.

OECD (2022). Securing reverse supply chains for an economy that uses resources wisely and goes around in circles. Report, OECD Publications.

Patra, S.P., Wankhede, V.A., Agrawal, R. (2024). A cutting-edge review of circular economy practices in supply chain finance. *Benchmarking: Int. J.*, 31(7), 2197–2216.

Prieto-Sandoval, V., Jaca, C., Ormazabal, M. (2018). Toward a consensus on the circular economy: A systematic review of definitions, practices, and frameworks. *J. Clean. Prod.*, 179, 605–615. doi: 10.1016/j.jclepro.2017.12.224.

Rana, R. and Bhambri, P. (2024a). Hybrid MCDM (multi-criteria decision-making) approaches for sustainable energy management. In *Modern SuperHyperSoft Computing Trends in Science and Technology*, Smarandache, F. and Majumder, P. (eds). IGI Global, Hershey, PA, 149–184. doi: 10.4018/979-8-3693-6875-6.ch006.

Rana, R. and Bhambri, P. (2024b). Environmental challenges and technological solutions. In *Handbook of Technological Sustainability: Innovation and Environmental Awareness*, Bhambri, P. and Bajdor, P. (eds). CRC Press, Boca Raton, FL, 187–200. doi: 10.1201/9781003475989-17.

Rana, R. and Bhambri, P. (2024c). Artificial intelligence and Internet of Things (IoT) facilitated digital twin for Industry 4.0 application domains. In *AI-Driven Digital Twin and Industry 4.0*, Rani, S., Bhambri, P., Kumar, S., Pareek, P.K., Elngar, A.A. (eds). CRC Press, Boca Raton, FL, 168–181. doi: 10.1201/9781003395416-11.

Rana, R. and Bhambri, P. (2024d). Digital twin for sustainable industrial development. In *AI-Driven Digital Twin and Industry 4.0*, Rani, S., Bhambri, P., Kumar, S., Pareek, P.K., Elngar, A.A. (eds). CRC Press, Boca Raton, FL, 241–253. doi: 10.1201/9781003395416-15.

Reike, D., Vermeulen, W.J., Witjes, S. (2018). The circular economy: CE 3.0 as new or refurbished? *Resour. Conserv. Recycl.*, 135, 246–264. doi: 10.1016/j.resconrec.2017.08.027.

Rizos, V., Tuokko, K., Behrens, A. (2017). The circular economy: An overview of definitions, procedures, and effects. Research Report, CEPS, Brussels.

Saari, L., Valkokari, K., Martins, J.T., Acerbi, F. (2024). Circular economy matrix guiding manufacturing industry companies towards circularity – A multiple case study perspective. *Circular Economy and Sustainability*, 4, 2505–2530. doi: 10.1007/s43615-024-00385-3.

Sehnem, S., Kuzma, E., Julkovsky, D.J., Frare, M.B., Vazquez-Brust, D. (2021). Megatrends in the circular economy: Opportunities for meaningful progress in businesses. *Circ. Econ. Sustain.*, 1, 1–24. doi: 10.1007/s43615-021-00036-x.

Selvarajan, S., Manoharan, H., Khadidos, A.O., Shankar, A., Khadidos, A.O., Viriyasitavat, W., Xu, L.D. (2024). SSCM: A secured approach to supply chain management with control management using blowfish optimization. *Enterprise Information Systems*, 18(6), 727–750. doi: 10.1080/17517575.2024.2351871.

Singh, N., Ashish, D.K., Dixit, A. (2024). Construction supply chain: A systematic literature review with bibliometric analysis. *Journal of Global Operations and Strategic Sourcing* 18(3), 471–497. doi: 10.1108/JGOSS-04-2023-0032.

Stahel, W.R. (2016). The economy that goes in circles. *Nature*, 531(7595), 435–438. doi: 10.1038/531435a.

Vegter, D., van Hillegersberg, J., Olthaar, M. (2020). Supply chains in circular business models: Processes and performance objectives. *Resources, Conservation and Recycling*, 162, 105046. doi: 10.1016/j.resconrec.2020.105046.

Viscardi, S., Colicchia, C., Creazza, A. (2022). A literature review on the circular economy and food waste in supply chains. *Int. J. Logist. Res. Appl.*, 26(5), 589–614. doi: 10.1080/13675567.2022.2128095.

Wang, C., Chen, C., Chen, C., Hsieh, H. (2025). Decarbonization of remanufacturing processes in circular supply chains: Case study on rubber recycling industry. *Industrial Management & Data Systems*, 125(10), 2753–2776. doi: 10.1108/IMDS-04-2024-0397.

Zardo, D.J., Granela, A.P., Sehnem, S. (2024). A look at circular supply chains and circular practices from the points of view of sustainability and Industry 4.0. *Corp. Soc. Responsib. Environ. Manag.*, 32(2), 1831–1846. doi: 10.1002/csr.3022.

4

IoT Architecture for End-to-End Visibility

The growing complexity of global supply chains requires new approaches to achieving transparency, efficiency and resilience. This chapter explores the role of the Internet of Things (IoT) as a foundation for end-to-end (E2E) visibility in logistics and supply chain management. IoT enables real-time data collection, transmission and analysis through interconnected devices and sensors, supporting improved monitoring, predictive analytics and decision-making. This chapter presents the layered architecture of IoT – comprising perception, communication, processing and application layers – highlighting its capacity to integrate diverse data sources and provide comprehensive visibility across the entire value chain. Various IoT models, including cloud-centric, distributed, hybrid and agent-based architectures, are discussed in relation to their applicability in different supply chain contexts. Benefits of IoT adoption include enhanced tracking and transparency, optimized inventory management, predictive maintenance, operational efficiency, adaptability to disruptions and contributions to sustainability goals.

At the same time, this chapter identifies challenges such as system integration, data quality, cybersecurity risks, high implementation costs and organizational resistance. Looking ahead, IoT development in supply chains will increasingly integrate with artificial intelligence (AI), big data and blockchain to enable autonomous, predictive and self-optimizing systems. The analysis concludes that IoT is not merely a supportive technology but a strategic enabler of next-generation supply chains, where E2E visibility is essential for competitiveness in dynamic and uncertain markets.

4.1. Introduction

The emergence of the Internet of Things (IoT) has also created an opportunity for creative solutions to supply chain management challenges. IoT technology has the potential to transform the visibility, tracking, management and delivery of goods by integrating intelligent devices, sensors and enhanced networks throughout the supply chain (Rahman and Asyhari 2019).

Chapter written by Marta STAROSTKA-PATYK.

This chapter will explore the revolutionary potential of IoT and its capabilities in improving end-to-end visibility in supply chains. Through real-time data collection and analysis, IoT equips supply chain partners with the means necessary to achieve end-to-end visibility, which in turn leads to meeting ever-increasing customer demands. Real-time supply chain visibility provides a complete, end-to-end view of logistics processes in real time (Somapa et al. 2018; Sunmola and Apeji 2024). Typical supply chains include functions such as product design, ordering raw materials and parts, forecasting demand, organizing deliveries for selected sales channels, and providing customer service and visibility throughout the order process. All of these interdependent processes and elements must be managed synchronously; otherwise, the very concept of supply chains would be meaningless (Bartlett et al. 2007).

4.2. Visibility of supply chains

Supply chain visibility means partner companies' ability to continuously monitor and oversee the flow of raw materials, components and finished products from procurement, through production and warehousing, to delivery to the end customer. This also includes the ability to track inventory levels, production schedules and transportation in real time (Apeji and Sunmola 2022; Razak et al. 2023). Detailed knowledge of inventory levels at various stages of the flow allows for immediate response to irregularities and the avoidance of both overstocks and shortages, which in turn translates into lower storage costs and operational liquidity (Tarigan et al. 2021). If a seller or supplier can constantly indicate the location of a product and when it will be delivered, this information significantly builds mutual trust and customer loyalty, positively impacting customer satisfaction and the purchasing experience. Improved visibility in supply chains also helps identify potential points of failure, responds to delays and shortages, and meets legal and organizational requirements (Ahmed et al. 2021; Hunaid et al. 2022). Monitoring only processes within our own supply chain is not sufficient. Gaining visibility also requires knowledge of what is happening with partners and participants in their supply chains, as well as current market, regulatory and even weather conditions. This knowledge allows for predicting disruptions, risks and volatile supply chain operations (Messina et al. 2023). Collaboration problems arise when partners use different procedures, standards and tools, preventing effective integration and coordination within supply chain visibility (Freichel et al. 2022). Companies can achieve a high level of visibility only when they combine modern technology with the integration of internal and external data, build collaborative and transparent relationships with partners and strive to ensure that processes and the information they generate are consistent and properly managed. This is a difficult and demanding task, primarily due to the costs, organizational and integration requirements (Udeh et al. 2024).

4.3. Internet of Things (IoT) in logistics and supply chains

The communication occurs in real time and involves a vast amount of data regarding processes, flows, objects and the environment. In logistics, IoT is used extensively due to its usefulness and capabilities in automated and continuous tracking of component processes of transport, warehousing, supply, production and distribution, which translates into efficient and effective management of logistics processes (Sallam et al. 2023). The ever-increasing complexity of supply networks, changes in demand requiring faster and more flexible responses than before, and the increased pressure to achieve sustainable development goals and protect the environment, all contribute to the significant and crucial importance of this technology in modern logistics (Anurag and Johnpaul 2025).

4.3.1. *Architecture of IoT*

In the context of modern supply chains, IoT architecture is based on a layered structure. IoT architecture is built on a four-layer, scalable and efficient model that ensures fault tolerance and data security. This structure enables comprehensive tracking, monitoring and supervision, as well as the automation and optimization of logistics processes. In this structure, each layer fulfills a distinct yet complementary role and supports the full cycle of data acquisition, transmission, processing and analysis in real time (Khan et al. 2022; Pal 2023).

4.3.2. *Models of IoT for supply chains*

Logistics today relies on dynamic and multi-layered processes, a consequence of the turbulent market and economic environment. Therefore, it requires flexible and scalable IoT architecture models. These models differ in the degree of decentralization, data processing location, integration with IT systems and level of autonomy. Depending on the operational needs of the enterprise in the supply chain and its digital maturity, there are five basic architectural models for IoT (Zaman et al. 2025).

The first, most classic layered architecture model, divides the IoT system into logically ordered functional layers: sensory, communication, processing and application. It has the following features:

– clear separation of responsibilities within each layer;

– high modularity, facilitating the modernization of individual components;

– scalability and compatibility with existing ERP/WMS/TMS systems (Khan et al. 2022).

This model is most often used in warehouses with a high level of automation, distribution centers and container ports. The second model is the distributed model (distributed/fog-based architecture), where data processing occurs close to the point of generation. This approach minimizes latency and reduces network load. Key features of this model include:

– supporting scenarios requiring a rapid response (e.g. warning of cargo overheating);

– supporting local device autonomy (e.g. warehouse robots);

– operates in conditions of limited cloud connectivity (Khan et al. 2022).

The distributed model is used in refrigerated logistics processes, for real-time transport monitoring and for remote location detection with limited network coverage.

The next model is the cloud-centric model (cloud-centric architecture), in which most functions related to data processing, storage and analysis are performed in the cloud. Here, IoT devices play a primary role in data acquisition. The cloud model is characterized by:

– easy integration with predictive analytics and AI;

– the ability to aggregate data from multiple locations;

– availability of SaaS and PaaS services for companies of all sizes (Khan et al. 2022).

This model finds its application in international supply chains, marketplace platforms and 3PL operators.

The hybrid model (hybrid architecture) is a model that combines elements of the cloud and distributed models. It enables dynamic task redirection, depending on needs. It is characterized by:

– high resistance to communication disruptions;

– flexibility in adapting resources to current requirements;

– ability to intelligently balance workloads (Khan et al. 2022).

It is used in complex logistics networks where multiple locations with varying degrees of technological advancement must be integrated as such.

The final model is the agent-based architecture, which is based on autonomous agents – devices or processes – that communicate and collaborate in a decentralized manner. This model:

– supports adaptive logistics management in real time;

– facilitates flexible response to changes in demand, road conditions or unexpected events;

– can use AI for local decision-making (Khan et al. 2022).

It finds application in dynamic last-mile delivery systems, mobile robotics in warehouses and urban logistics. Choosing the right IoT architecture for a given supply chain primarily depends on the operational specifics of the chain, preferred time constraints, the availability of the necessary network infrastructure and the level of digital integration with other chain partners. Hybrid models are increasingly being used in business practice because they combine the advantages of local and cloud computing, ensuring both speed and strategic data analysis across the entire supply chain (Zaman et al. 2025).

4.3.3. *Benefits of IoT in supply chains*

Implementing IoT solutions in supply chains is yielding positive results in many operational, economic and strategic areas. Integrating IoT devices with existing ICT systems in the supply chain enables the creation of a new value in the form of fully digital, intelligent and flexible systems for managing the flow of both goods and information (Hanaysha and Alzoubi 2022). The benefits of implementing IoT in the supply chain can be seen in the form of (De Vass et al. 2021):

1. Increased visibility, transparency, monitoring, supervision and real-time tracking. All of this is possible thanks to the use of sensors, and sensors that continuously provide information on the location, status and conditions of goods in transit. These benefits are most significant for transportation processes, as they enable the tracking of shipments with exceptionally high accuracy, reduce the number of lost, damaged or stolen goods and facilitate compliance with legal regulations.

2. Improved inventory and warehouse management. In this area, IoT enables automatic monitoring of inventory levels and the rapid detection of shortages or surpluses, which in turn translates into optimized storage space. IoT implementation reduces safety stock without the risk of shortages, enables just-in-time operation through automatic inventory replenishment and shortens order picking and shipping times.

3. Improving operational efficiency, made possible by process automation and predictive analytics. As a result, all processes across the supply chain are streamlined, primarily by detecting and eliminating bottlenecks in real time, optimizing delivery routes and transportation, production and distribution schedules, and reducing human error and unexpected downtime.

4. Predicting and preventing breakdowns. IoT enables supply chains to check and monitor the technical condition of vehicles, machines and equipment in real time. This enables predictive maintenance, which prevents breakdowns by detecting signs of wear before they reach a complete state. This significantly reduces the costs of downtime and repairs to machinery and equipment, and extends the lifecycle of assets.

5. Greater flexibility and adaptability of the supply chain, meaning dynamic response to changes in demand, crisis situations and supply disruptions. The value here lies in the ability to instantly redesign logistics routes and channels, automatically allocate resources based on current needs, and model various scenarios based on preset parameters derived from IoT devices.

6. Data-driven decision-making (data-driven supply chain) by integrating IoT with analytical, ERP and AI systems and leveraging current, accurate data captured in real time. This enables better planning of demand, production and logistics processes, shortens the decision-making cycle and significantly increases the accuracy of forecasts and simulations.

7. Sustainable development and reduced environmental costs, as IoT helps partner companies reduce the consumption of natural resources and reduce carbon dioxide emissions by optimizing logistics processes. This is achieved by reducing mileage and fuel consumption of transportation vehicles, optimizing temperature and energy consumption in cold stores and warehouses, and monitoring carbon footprints in real time and influencing their reduction.

Traditional supply chains are currently being transformed, thanks to the use of IoT, into intelligent, integrated systems capable of rapid response, self-learning and continuous improvement (Hanaysha and Alzoubi 2022). This is a significant step forward, and this development trend should be maintained, as it allows for building a strong competitive position in a volatile, uncertain and complex economic and market environment.

4.4. IoT for end-to-end visibility in supply chains

End-to-end (E2E) visibility in supply chains means the ability to fully and continuously monitor the flow of raw materials, products and information along the entire supply chain and throughout all of its processes, up to the delivery of the finished product to the end customer. This E2E visibility is one of the key goals of digital transformation in logistics. This is because visibility provides better control over all logistics processes and enables quick and informed decision-making at multiple operational levels (Ahmed et al. 2021). In this logistics context, Internet of Things (IoT) technology plays a crucial, even fundamental, role. This is because IoT automatically and continuously acquires data and integrates it in real time.

The main mechanisms enabling E2E visibility include monitoring the location and condition of shipped goods using technologies such as GPS, RFID, environmental sensors and BLE beacons. These solutions enable the tracking of cargo with very high accuracy, regardless of its geographical location. The data obtained in this way also includes detailed information about the transport conditions of the cargo, including not only its current location but also factors such as temperature, humidity, vibration levels and even container openings. With all of this information at hand, companies can immediately respond to any deviations from the norm, improving the safety and quality of logistics services (Moleme et al. 2024).

The currently used IoT architecture enables the integration of data from various sources related to a given supply chain system. Information is collected from warehouses, transportation vehicles, production units and retail outlets, and despite this large number, it can be aggregated on a single platform to provide a unified and consistent view of the entire logistics process. This integration allows partner companies to gain a comprehensive business context, thus avoiding "blind spots" that would be invisible or difficult to detect in a traditional supply chain (Al Mahmud et al. 2025).

E2E visibility in supply chains is also useful for dynamic, real-time management of logistics processes. For example, if delays, congestion or vehicle breakdowns occur during transport, the IoT system can automatically initiate corrective actions, such as rerouting, rerouting cargo to another point, or rescheduling delivery for repairs. Such capabilities significantly increase the supply chain's resilience to all types of disruptions and unforeseen events. Furthermore, data acquired by IoT devices is used as input for predictive algorithms. These algorithms can detect specific risks early and develop solutions to avoid the consequences (Al-Khatib 2023a).

Another aspect of ensuring full E2E supply chain visibility is the ability to share data among all supply chain participants. IoT platforms enable all necessary information to be automatically shared with suppliers, manufacturers, logistics operators, retailers and end customers. This creates a high level of transparency while fostering mutual trust, streamlining communication and facilitating collaboration between all supply chain partners. Furthermore, IoT and the resulting E2E supply chain visibility is combined with other modern technological advancements such as blockchain, ensuring data integrity and full product traceability (this is particularly important in regulated industries such as pharmaceuticals and food) (Al-Khatib 2023a).

The positive effect of achieving E2E visibility through IoT is measurable business benefits for the entire supply chain. Partner companies can significantly reduce their business costs by reducing safety stock, improving resource utilization, and eliminating unnecessary processes and activities. End customers also benefit, as they receive a higher level of customer service through accurate order tracking and predictable delivery dates. Equally important is the fact that IoT systems are exceptionally effective in risk management and respond much more quickly to disruptions. This significantly increases the resilience of the entire supply chain and significantly supports building a competitive advantage in the market (Al Mahmud et al. 2025).

Considering all of the benefits of using IoT to achieve end-to-end visibility, it is worth sustaining these efforts and transforming traditional supply chains into more modern ones, adapted to the requirements of the ongoing digital transformation, which will keep them at the current level of technical and technological development.

4.5. IoT challenges and barriers to end-to-end visibility in supply chains

Despite the numerous benefits of implementing IoT technology for achieving full end-to-end visibility in supply chains, discussed earlier, it is important to note that such implementations also pose a number of challenges and barriers. These must be overcome, and appropriate technical resources will be crucial, including the highest possible digital maturity for a given company, openness to collaboration with supply chain partners, and the need for and willingness to adapt to changes in the company's organizational culture.

One of the greatest challenges in the era of digital technology is the integration of heterogeneous systems and communication standards. As modern supply chains are typically geographically and technologically dispersed, and because their participants use various ERP, WMS, TMS and IoT solutions, it often turns out that all of these systems, and therefore the chains themselves, are incompatible. This lack of uniform data protocols, coupled with difficulties in exchanging information between supply chain partners, leads to the creation of data silos, which significantly limit the effectiveness of IoT solutions and thus hinder the achievement of supply chain visibility. Data security and privacy issues also pose a barrier. The IoT generates vast amounts of information, often sensitive in nature (Al-Khatib 2023b). Therefore, storing, transmitting and processing it in real time significantly increases the risk of security breaches, cyberattacks or unauthorized access.

Preventing such situations requires the implementation of advanced encryption, authentication and access management mechanisms. Another good solution is to use international regulations such as the GDPR and industry standards for data protection in logistics (Moleme et al. 2024).

Another barrier is the high cost of implementing and maintaining IoT infrastructure, especially for small- and medium-sized enterprises, which typically have more limited financial resources than large companies. Purchasing sensors, edge devices and analytical systems, and integrating them with the company's existing IT infrastructure, poses a significant budgetary burden. Added to this is the need for constant hardware upgrades and the maintaining of connectivity and power for all distributed devices, which naturally generates additional costs that can discourage companies from investing in IoT systems (Al-Khatib 2023b).

The lack of technological and analytical skills among employees is also a significant barrier. Successful IoT implementation requires not only the installation of devices but also the ability to configure them and then manage the acquired data, analyze the results and make decisions based on them. Therefore, many companies, typically in the early stages of their digital transformation, encounter difficulties in recruiting or training specialists in IoT, cybersecurity, data analytics and systems integration. These skill gaps constitute a significant barrier to fully realizing the potential of IoT for E2E supply chain visibility. Organizational resistance and a lack of trust between supply chain partners also pose challenges.

Since E2E visibility relies on the principles of transparency and data sharing between multiple participants, this barrier often arises because these companies do not always accept these principles due to their own business beliefs. This can be due to concerns about losing competitive advantage, disclosing confidential commercial information or misusing data by other partners, which can effectively limit full collaboration within the IoT system (Al-Khatib 2023a).

Finally, it is important to point out the barriers resulting from infrastructure deficiencies. If there is a lack of access to stable and fast communication networks, limited data throughput or problems powering IoT devices in harsh environmental conditions, the IoT architecture does not function properly, and the entire system loses supply chain visibility. Although technologies such as 5G, LPWAN and edge computing are designed to gradually alleviate these limitations, they remain a significant risk factor and barrier, especially in international and cross-border logistics processes (Al Mahmud et al. 2025).

The analysis shows that implementing IoT as a tool for end-to-end visibility in supply chains is associated not only with enormous potential for positive benefits but also with numerous challenges and barriers. To overcome these challenges, a systems approach is crucial, investing in employee digital skills and building systems based on trust and collaboration across all processes. All of these actions will enable the full utilization of the opportunities arising from IoT functionality in next-generation logistics.

4.6. The future of IoT in supply chains and their visibility E2E

The current development trend for IoT in logistics continues to accelerate, even entering a new phase where the role of data is no longer limited to passive event tracking. This indicates that future supply chains will be shaped by systems in a new format – systems that not only collect information in real time but also interpret it and make decisions autonomously and with faster response times than humans (Moshood et al. 2021). In this context, visibility itself is losing its importance as a standalone feature and is becoming the foundation for building flexible, predictive and self-optimizing supply chains.

The development of modern digital technologies for supply chains will undoubtedly move toward deeper integration of IoT data with machine learning and AI algorithms. In the future, these systems, instead of simple alerts about delays or deviations from the norm, will predict such events in advance and automatically recommend or implement remedial actions, thus eliminating the need for human intervention in many routine situations. At this point, E2E visibility in supply chains will acquire a new format for the decision-making layer, thus becoming more flexible, dynamic and intelligent. At the same time, all decentralized data processing models, such as edge and fog computing, will develop, as edge information processing will gain a key role in situations where response time is crucial. Modernized systems, instead of transmitting data to the cloud, will analyze it locally, shortening response times and reducing the risk of downtime in critical situations. These capabilities will also be reflected in the increasing resilience of supply chains to disruptions, which is crucial in the current turbulent economic and political environment (Sodhi and Tang 2021).

In addition to the above, there is the issue of trust and information sharing between chain participants, as the future of E2E visibility in supply chains will depend precisely on the extent to which companies are willing to share data, not only with trading partners but also with external systems and consumers. This is where blockchain technology comes into play, enabling data integrity and transparency without the need for centralization. It also enables the development of distributed and open logistics systems in which trust stems from the technology, not just the relationships between partner companies. Currently, a new generation of IoT devices is increasingly appearing on the market. These are smaller, cheaper, more energy-efficient and capable of operating longer without charging. Using these devices will enable the expansion of supply chain visibility into previously overlooked areas, such as the last mile, reverse logistics and product monitoring after leaving the store. Combined with the increasing availability of 5G networks and the development of LPWAN, future supply chains will function like living organisms – constantly monitoring their functions, learning and adapting to changes in the environment (Moshood et al. 2021).

The future direction of IoT technology development in logistics is already clearly outlined, although there are still many challenges and barriers to overcome. Supply chain environments must learn to function in the new digital reality and adapt their operations to current trends. IoT is no longer just a supporting technology but is becoming a central element of supply chain management strategies.

4.7. Conclusions

In the complex and intricate structure of global supply chains, Internet of Things (IoT) technology is significantly transforming the management of physical goods and information flows along the entire chain. In this context, end-to-end visibility is not only a technological goal but also a prerequisite for gaining a competitive advantage in an uncertain and volatile market. IoT, with its ability to collect, process and transmit data in real time, is a foundation for intelligent and flexible supply chains (Rana et al. 2023; Bhambri and Khang 2024; Bhambri and Kumar 2024; Bhambri et al. 2024; Sridhar et al. 2024).

The entire IoT architecture is built in layers, creating a coherent and scalable model enabling comprehensive monitoring and effective management of flows throughout the entire value chain. Additional solutions such as edge computing, ERP systems, predictive platforms and 5G communications contribute to building transparent, resilient and sustainable next-generation supply chains.

Despite existing challenges and barriers hindering the implementation of IoT in the supply chain, it is worth focusing more on the benefits of this implementation, as visibility, transparency, improved customer service quality, cost reduction and many other benefits are worth considering.

Future development of IoT in logistics and supply chain management will move toward greater autonomy, predictability and resilience. Other supporting technologies will be more closely integrated with IoT, building supply chains capable of autonomous learning, predicting events and making real-time decisions. End-to-end supply chain visibility will then no longer be a feature but a prerequisite for the effective operation of any modern enterprise.

4.8. References

Ahmed, S., Kalsoom, T., Ramzan, N., Pervez, Z., Azmat, M., Zeb, B., Ur Rehman, M. (2021). Towards supply chain visibility using Internet of Things: A dyadic analysis review. *Sensors*, 21(12), 4158.

Al-Khatib, A.W. (2023a). Internet of things, big data analytics and operational performance: The mediating effect of supply chain visibility. *Journal of Manufacturing Technology Management*, 34(1), 1–24.

Al-Khatib, A.W. (2023b). The impact of industrial Internet of things on sustainable performance: The indirect effect of supply chain visibility. *Business Process Management Journal*, 29(5), 1607–1629.

Al Mahmud, M.A., Hossan, M.Z., Tiwari, A., Khatoon, R., Sharmin, S., Hosain, M.S., Ferdousmou, J. (2025). Reviewing the integration of RFID and IoT in supply chain management: Enhancing efficiency and visibility. *Journal of Posthumanism*, 5(3), 409–437.

Anurag, A.S. and Johnpaul, M. (2025). The seminal role of Internet of Things in the digital transformation of supply chain management. In *Revolutionizing Supply Chains Through Digital Transformation*, Andaloussi, M.B. (ed.). IGI Global, Hershey, 43–76. doi: 10.4018/979-8-3693-4427-9.ch003.

Apeji, U.D. and Sunmola, F.T. (2022). Principles and factors influencing visibility in sustainable supply chains. *Procedia Computer Science*, 200, 1516–1527.

Bartlett, P.A., Julien, D.M., Baines, T.S. (2007). Improving supply chain performance through improved visibility. *The International Journal of Logistics Management*, 18(2), 294–313.

Bhambri, P. and Khang, A. (2024). Managing and monitoring patient's healthcare using AI and IoT technologies. In *Driving Smart Medical Diagnosis through AI-Powered Technologies and Applications*, Khang, A. (ed.). IGI Global, Hershey, 1–23. doi: 10.4018/979-8-3693-3679-3.ch001.

Bhambri, P. and Kumar, S. (2024). Cloud and IoT integration for smart healthcare. In *Smart Healthcare Systems: AI and IoT Perspectives*, Bhambri, P. Soni, R., Tran, T.A. (eds). CRC Press, Boca Raton, 69–84. doi: 10.1201/9781032698519-6.

Bhambri, P., Rani, S., Khang, A., Soni, R. (2024). AI-driven digital twin and resource optimization in Industry 4.0 ecosystem. In *AI-driven Digital Twin and Industry 4.0: A Conceptual Framework with Applications*, Rani, S., Bhambri, P., Kumar, S., Pareek, P.K., Elngar, A.A. (eds). CRC Press, Boca Raton, 182–201. doi: 10.1201/9781003395416-12.

De Vass, T., Shee, H., Miah, S. (2021). IoT in supply chain management: Opportunities and challenges for businesses in early industry 4.0 context. *Operations and Supply Chain Management: An International Journal*, 14(2), 148–161.

Freichel, S.L., Rütten, P., Wörtge, J.K. (2022). Challenges of supply chain visibility in distribution logistics – A literature review. *Ekonomski vjesnik: Review of Contemporary Entrepreneurship, Business, and Economic Issues*, 35(2), 453–466.

Hanaysha, J.R. and Alzoubi, H.M. (2022). Investigating the impact of benefits and challenges of IOT adoption on supply chain performance and organizational performance: An empirical study in Malaysia. *Uncertain Supply Chain Management*, 10(2), 537–550.

Hunaid, M., Bhurgri, A.A., Shaikh, A. (2022). Supply chain visibility in leading organizations of the shipping industry: Supply chain in shipping industry. *South Asian Journal of Social Review*, 1(1), 8–20.

Khan, Y., Su'ud, M.B.M., Alam, M.M., Ahmad, S.F., Ahmad, A.Y.B., Khan, N. (2022). Application of Internet of Things (IoT) in sustainable supply chain management. *Sustainability*, 15(1), 694.

Messina, D., Soares, A.L., Barros, A.C., Zimmermann, R. (2023). How visible is your supply chain? A model for supply chain visibility assessment. *Supply Chain Forum: An International Journal*, 24(4), 462–474.

Moleme, L.O., Omoruyi, O., Quayson, M. (2024). Supply chain visibility and integration in the age of the Internet of Things: A retail perspective. *Modern Supply Chain Research and Applications*, 6(3), 330–350.

Moshood, T.D., Nawanir, G., Sorooshian, S., Okfalisa, O. (2021). Digital twins driven supply chain visibility within logistics: A new paradigm for future logistics. *Applied System Innovation*, 4(2), 29.

Pal, K. (2023). Internet of Things impact on supply chain management. *Procedia Computer Science*, 220, 478–485.

Rahman, M.A. and Asyhari, A.T. (2019). The emergence of Internet of Things (IoT): Connecting anything, anywhere. *Computers*, 8(2), 40.

Rana, R., Bhambri, P., Chhabra, Y. (2023). Evolution and the future of industrial engineering with the IoT and AI. In *Integration of AI-based Manufacturing and Industrial Engineering Systems with the Internet of Things*, Bhambri, P., Rani, S., Balas, V.E., Elngar, A.A. (eds). CRC Press, Boca Raton, 19–37. doi: 10.1201/9781003383505.

Razak, G.M., Hendry, L.C., Stevenson, M. (2023). Supply chain traceability: A review of the benefits and its relationship with supply chain resilience. *Production Planning & Control*, 34(11), 1114–1134.

Sallam, K., Mohamed, M., Mohamed, A.W. (2023). Internet of Things (IoT) in supply chain management: Challenges, opportunities, and best practices. *SMIJ*, 2(2), 32.

Sodhi, M.S. and Tang, C.S. (2021). Supply chain management for extreme conditions: Research opportunities. *Journal of Supply Chain Management*, 57(1), 7–16.

Somapa, S., Cools, M., Dullaert, W. (2018). Characterizing supply chain visibility – A literature review. *The International Journal of Logistics Management*, 29(1), 308–339.

Sridhar, V., Rani, S., Pareek, P.K., Bhambri, P. (2024). Evolution of IoT in various application domains. In *Blockchain for IoT Systems: Concept, Framework and Applications*, Sridhar, V., Rani, S., Pareek, P.K., Bhambri, P., Elngar, A.A. (eds). CRC Press, Boca Raton, 13–22. doi: 10.1201/9781003460367-2.

Sunmola, F.T. and Apeji, U.D. (2024). Modelling supply chain visibility: A framework with considerations for manufacturing and business. *Journal of Manufacturing Technology Management*, 35(7), 1354–1374.

Tarigan, Z.J.H., Siagian, H., Jie, F. (2021). Impact of internal integration, supply chain partnership, supply chain agility, and supply chain resilience on sustainable advantage. *Sustainability*, 13(10), 5460.

Udeh, E.O., Amajuoyi, P., Adeusi, K.B., Scott, A.O. (2024). The role of IoT in boosting supply chain transparency and efficiency. *Magna Scientia Advanced Research and Reviews*, 11(01), 178–197.

Zaman, J., Shoomal, A., Jahanbakht, M., Ozay, D. (2025). Driving supply chain transformation with IoT and AI integration: A dual approach using bibliometric analysis and topic modeling. *IoT*, 6(2), 21.

5

Building Blocks of a Transparent IoT Ecosystem

The continuous evolution of digital technologies has established the Internet of Things (IoT) as a critical enabler of innovation across both public and private sectors. Domains such as agriculture, healthcare, transportation and smart homes are increasingly leveraging IoT to enhance operational visibility, automation and personalized services. These ecosystems typically consist of interconnected devices, cloud platforms and internet-based services – bringing forth a heightened need for robust data protection mechanisms.

As the IoT attack surface expands, ensuring system-wide security is essential to prevent unauthorized access, data breaches and potential financial losses. This chapter presents a comprehensive exploration of IoT architecture, focusing on its role in enabling end-to-end visibility. It discusses the layered structure of IoT systems – from data generation at the device level to real-time processing and cloud-based analytics. This chapter also introduces key application areas and highlights the transition towards the Everything-as-a-Service (XaaS) model.

Furthermore, it addresses critical architectural design principles that support scalability, interoperability and security. Special emphasis is given to the integration of IoT with cloud computing, outlining how cloud platforms facilitate seamless device connectivity, data storage and on-demand service delivery. This chapter concludes by highlighting the security challenges associated with cloud integration and recommending strategies to build resilient and secure IoT ecosystems.

Chapter written by Bhagwat KAULWAR, Milind GODASE, Chandrani SINGH and Pankaj BHAMBRI.

5.1. Introduction

The term Internet of Things (IoT) was first introduced in 1999 by Kevin Ashton at the MIT Auto-ID Center, in the context of radio-frequency identification (RFID)-based supply chain tracking (Kramp et al. 2013). Since then, advances in information technology and electronics have fueled the proliferation of internet-enabled devices, making it possible for almost any physical object to become an IoT device.

Researchers such as Gubbi et al. (2012) define IoT as the convergence of embedded systems, sensors, actuators and cloud computing to create a ubiquitous network of "things" capable of sensing, communicating and acting without human intervention (Gubbi et al. 2012). The "things" in IoT can include any internet-connected object, such as televisions, smartphones, sensors or wearable devices. The seamless integration of the physical and digital world through IoT results in increased efficiency, accuracy and convenience – benefiting both service providers and end-users.

The IoT is a combination of a technological push and a human pull for more and ever-increasing connectivity with anything happening in the immediate and wider environment – a logical extension of computing power in a single machine to the environment: the environment as an interface. This push–pull combination makes it very strong, unstoppable, fast and extremely disruptive (Kramp et al. 2013).

Efficient storage management helps businesses lower costs and enhances utilization of material and human resources. For example, IoT-based storage management integrates sensors with programmable logic controllers (PLCs). Sensors send analog signals to the PLC, which converts them into digital instructions and transmits them as data strings. On the software side, applications can display relevant information on dashboards – such as the type of product in a tray, product counts and item details (Godase et al. 2023). The integration of AI models with a cloud-based IoT system can enhance the performance, for example crops can be protected from animals by enabling an AI model to detect animals to protect against crop damage from animal intrusions (Milind 2025).

IoT is widely applied across diverse sectors. For instance, logistics companies use IoT sensors to track consignments in real time, enabling timely delivery and proactive issue management. In urban infrastructure, traffic authorities use IoT data to manage congestion. In healthcare, wearable devices monitor patient vitals such as oxygen levels and heart rate, triggering alerts for immediate intervention when necessary. IoT sectors shown in Figure 5.1 illustrate the wide range of domains adopting IoT applications.

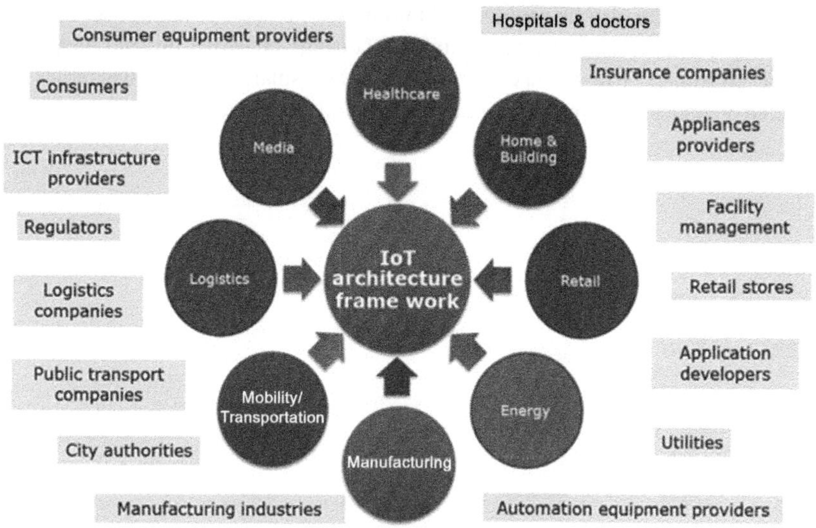

Figure 5.1. *IoT sectors. For a color version of this figure, see www.iste.co.uk/bhambri/nextgensupply.zip*

The concept of Industry 4.0 relies heavily on IoT devices, as almost every modern industry is integrated with internet technologies and information systems. These systems focus on secure data flow and operational optimization. The relationship between Industry 4.0 and the IoT shown in Figure 5.2 highlights this connection (ITU 2017).

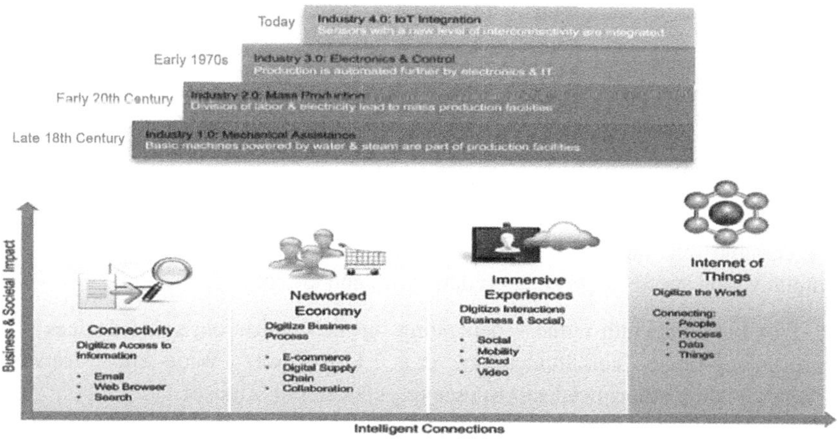

Figure 5.2. *Relationship between Industry 4.0 and IoT (ITU 2017)*

IoT adoption can also be categorized into industrial and consumer use. Industrial IoT covers domains such as retail, manufacturing, construction and healthcare, whereas consumer IoT focuses on electronics, smart homes, wearables and connected vehicles. Figure 5.3 summarizes this classification (GSMA Intelligence 2018).

Category	Sub-category	
Consumer IoT	Consumer electronics	Smart TVs, home entertainment (games consoles, speakers), personal entertainment (MP3 players, portable gaming devices), set-top boxes
	Smart home	Home appliances (fridges, washing machines), home infrastructure (routers), home security (alarms), energy monitoring (thermostats)
	Wearables	Fitness trackers (including personal health trackers), smart watches
	Smart vehicles	Connected cars, connected bikes, insurance telematics
	Consumer - others	Trackers for children, the elderly and pets, as well as drones and robots
Industrial IoT	Smart city	Public transport, surveillance, electric vehicle charging, street lighting, parking, waste management
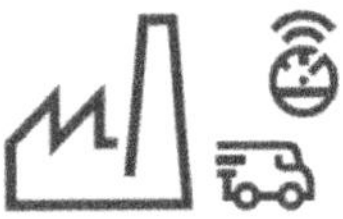	Smart utilities	Energy, water and gas smart metering, smart grid
	Smart retail	PoS, digital signage, vending machines, ATMs
	Smart manufacturing	Inventory tracking, monitoring and diagnostics, warehouse management
	Smart buildings	Heating and air con, security, lighting, hot desks, office equipment
	Health	Remote monitoring of medical devices, emergency vehicle infrastructure
	Enterprise - others	Fleet management, applications in agriculture, oil, mining, construction

Figure 5.3. *Category-wise usage of IoT devices (GSMA Intelligence 2018)*

5.2. Characteristics of IoT

An IoT system is expected to exhibit several key characteristics:

– Low cost – devices should be inexpensive to ensure large-scale deployment.

– Low power consumption – IoT nodes must operate with minimal energy requirements.

– Long battery life – devices often function in remote locations and require extended battery duration.

– High connectivity – IoT systems must support multiple simultaneous connections for data transfer and command exchange with the cloud.

– Variable bit rate requirements – different applications demand varying communication speeds depending on data types and urgency.

– Flexible bandwidth range – depending on the application, some devices may require long-range communication (e.g. Low-Power Wide-Area Network (LPWAN)) while others need short-range (e.g. Bluetooth, Zigbee).

– Limited processing power – most IoT devices operate with low computational capabilities due to hardware constraints.

– Low storage capacity – since storing data locally increases the risk of theft, IoT devices rely on cloud storage.

– Compact design – devices should be small, lightweight and portable for deployment in diverse environments.

– Simple network protocols – IoT architectures typically employ lightweight communication protocols that can be easily adopted by non-expert users.

5.3. IoT architecture

As mentioned earlier, IoT enables analog or digital products to connect to the internet and exchange data or follow instructions. The IoT architecture has four stages, namely sensors/actuators, internet gateways with a data acquisition system, Edge IT and a data center or cloud. Figure 5.4 shows the 4-stage IoT architecture.

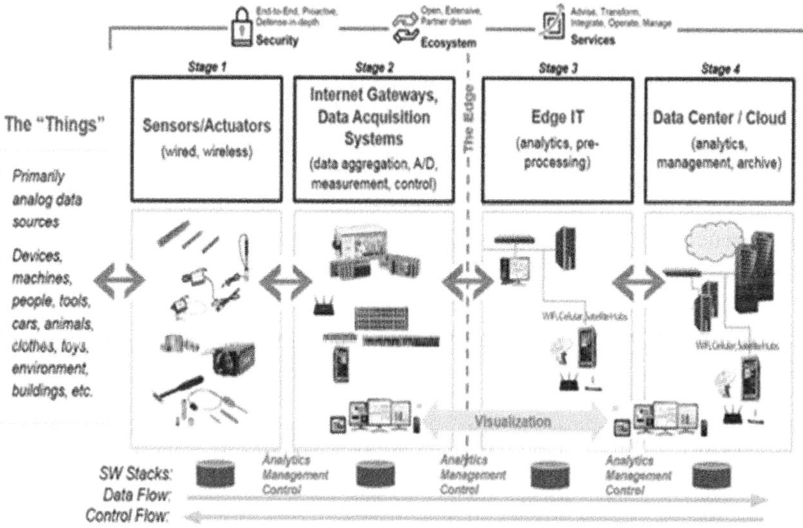

Figure 5.4. *Four-stage IoT architecture*

5.3.1. *Sensors/actuators*

This is the first stage and is responsible for capturing physical data from the environment. Devices used in this layer include analog and digital sensors, RFID tags, cameras, wearables and actuators.

These components are deployed at the physical edge and communicate using wired or wireless protocols. Their primary role is to gather data such as temperature, motion and pressure, and transmit it for further processing. For example, a temperature sensor embedded in an air conditioner adjusts cooling based on real-time room temperature (Greengard 2015).

5.3.2. *Internet gateways with data acquisition system*

The second stage of internet gateways is used to connect sensor networks to Internet Protocol (IP)-based networks. This stage handles protocol translation, signal conditioning and buffering. If needed, tasks like conversion of analog signals to digital signals, aggregating data and applying initial filtering are performed. Gateways serve as the bridge between low-level sensor networks and higher-level computing resources. The devices such as gateways, PLCs, remote terminal unit (RTU), edge routers are used in this stage (Buyya and Dastjerdi 2016). PLCs are industrial digital computers used for the automation of electromechanical processes (e.g. assembly lines, machinery), whereas RTUs are microprocessor-controlled devices that interface with sensors and actuators in the field and communicate data to central control systems, often used in supervisory control and data acquisition (SCADA) systems. For example, a PLC aggregates data from multiple sensors and sends it to the local gateway.

Heterogeneity in device communication protocols is a major challenge in IoT systems (Castellanos et al. 2021). The protocol translation refers to the process of converting communication signals and data formats from one protocol to another to ensure smooth data transmission between heterogeneous devices in an IoT ecosystem.

In IoT, different devices (sensors, actuators, controllers) often speak different communication protocols depending on their manufacturer, purpose or environment. Since these devices need to communicate with each other and with the internet, protocol translation becomes essential. If IoT devices are using non-IP protocols, gateways must convert these into IP-based protocols to ensure smooth cloud connectivity. This also ensures interoperability among different devices from multiple vendors. Thus, protocol translation enables scalable and secure communication across the layers.

The Industrial Internet of Things (IIoT) gateways of the edge layer implement the functions of signal conditioning, data acquisition and signal preprocessing (Li et al. 2022). The sensor-generated signals may be distorted or contain noise. The signal conditioning is the process in which gateways refine these incoming row sensor signals/data by removing noise and normalizing levels.

For example, in a smart manufacturing company, vibration sensors on rotating machines can send analog signals to a nearby PLC. The PLC then amplifies these signals, filters electrical noise from motors, digitizes it using a high-precision ADC and sends it over Ethernet to SCADA or cloud platforms

5.3.3. *Edge IT*

The third stage focuses on near-sensor analytics and data filtering. Its primary objective is to reduce latency, optimize bandwidth and minimize the volume of raw data sent to the cloud.

Key functions of Edge IT includes:

– Local analytics – identifying anomalies in real time.

– Noise reduction – filtering irrelevant or redundant data.

– Event-driven alerts – triggering immediate actions without waiting for cloud processing.

Devices in this stage include Edge servers and local computing nodes. For example, an edge node monitoring a motor can detect abnormal vibrations and trigger immediate local alerts, preventing equipment damage. By processing such data locally, Edge IT reduces reliance on centralized cloud systems and ensures faster decision-making (Shi et al. 2016).

5.3.4. *Data center/cloud*

The fourth stage provides full-scale processing, long-term storage and advanced analytics. The cloud acts as the backbone of IoT integration by offering:

– Scalable storage – handling massive volumes of sensor data.

– Centralized management – integrating inputs from distributed IoT devices.

– Machine learning and AI analytics – enabling predictive maintenance, anomaly detection and optimization.

– Visualization dashboards – presenting insights to end-users in real time.

– APIs for integration – allowing seamless connectivity with business applications.

Cloud services often leverage enterprise servers, big data platforms and IoT hubs. For instance, predictive maintenance solutions use IoT data from thousands of machines across multiple factories, which is aggregated and analyzed on platforms such as AWS IoT Core, Microsoft Azure IoT Hub or Google Cloud IoT (Bahga and Madisetti 2014).

5.4. IoT as XaaS

When IoT capabilities or services are offered to customers on demand, this service is called XaaS. This service is offered through the cloud, where the customer is not burdened to buy or maintain the required full infrastructure. In other words, users can subscribe to XaaS instead of buying and setting up their own IoT hardware, software and analytical platform. The technical and economical glitches in managing and handling of such services are done by service providers, and the user can focus on the use of the service. This saves time and costs for the user who subscribes to it.

In XaaS, the IoT devices are installed at the customer's location, which generates the data. The data transmission from the IoT devices to the cloud platform happens through the service provider's IoT network, such as LPWAN, 5G or Wi-Fi. Once the data is transferred through such a network, the data processing and analytics can be done on the cloud, to which the user has subscribed. The analytical results and other visualization can be shown to the user on their dashboard accessible via web or mobile. Also, the user has the flexibility to pay for services per use such as pay per device, per month or per data volume. Figure 5.5 demonstrates the IoT as XaaS.

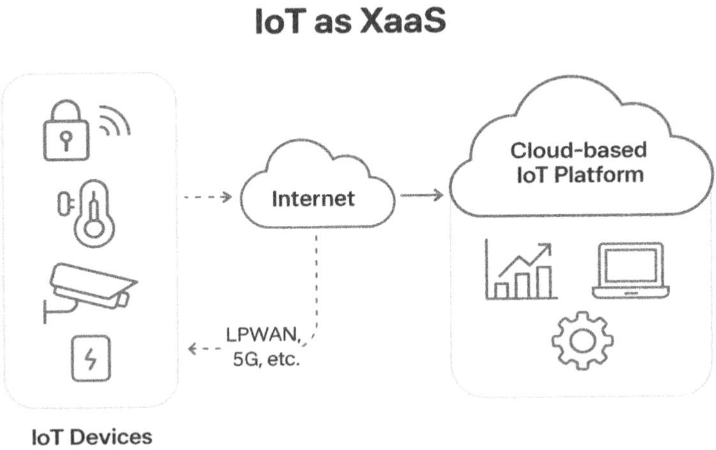

Figure 5.5. *IoT as XaaS*

5.4.1. *Benefits of XaaS*

XaaS provides the following benefits:

– Lower upfront costs as no big capital investment in IoT setup is required.

– Faster deployment as ready-made platform and devices are available.

– Increased scalability as devices can be added or removed devices easily.

– Increased security as automatic updates for firmware, analytics and security patches will be available.

– Better operations as services are managed by experts from the service provider.

For example, farmers can subscribe to IoT soil sensors and weather analytics instead of buying them. Logistics companies can pay monthly for GPS tracking and fuel monitoring. Civic authorities can have street lighting and waste management through IoT as a service. Factories can subscribe to vibration and temperature sensor networks for predictive maintenance. Service providers such as AWS IoT, Bosch IoT Suite, PTC ThingWorx and Siemens MindSphere are providing XaaS services.

5.4.2. *Security challenges*

When IoT and cloud computing are integrated, they create a powerful ecosystem for data collection, storage and processing and also introduce several security challenges at different layers. These challenges can be categorized as device-level challenges, network-level challenges, cloud-level challenges, data security and privacy, and integration and management challenges.

5.4.2.1. *Device-level challenges*

The challenges at the device level can be weak authentication, firmware vulnerability and physical tampering or limited device protection. Coston et al. (2025) conducted a comprehensive study and concluded that IoT devices suffer from weak or hardcoded credentials. Hackers can crack weak credentials or default credentials like admin/admin. This can be dealt with however by using stronger credentials and regularly updating passwords. Device-level challenges can be due to buffer overflows, insecure firmware updates and susceptibility to reverse engineering and physical extraction (Coston et al. 2025). Bakhshi et al. (2024) found that IoT device firmware is frequently targeted via memory corruption (e.g. buffer overflows), misconfiguration and insufficient access controls. Almutairi and Sheldon (2025) conducted a survey and concluded that device-level challenges include limited processing, memory and battery, which hinder the implementation of standard encryption or robust authentication mechanisms. This also points to weak authentication, insecure firmware updates and poor physical security as common vulnerabilities (Almutairi and Sheldon 2025).

5.4.2.2. *Network-level challenges*

The communication of IoT devices with the cloud environment plays an important role in the secure and timely processing of real-time data. Without secure communication (TLS/SSL), attackers can intercept and alter data between IoT and the cloud. Some of the communication protocols may be vulnerable to the secure communication. The compromised IoT devices can be used as a botnet to attack the cloud infrastructure. If data is not encrypted during transmission, sensitive sensor data can be exposed to an open network, and attacks can be made on either of the environments. Using restricted communications, intentional connections, disabling ports and rate limiting can help to tackle network layers (ENISA 2017).

Apart from this, an organization can determine how the device is going to be used. The device might be restricted for some capabilities and disabled for some that are not used. This can prevent the misuse of the capabilities of the IoT device (Boeckl et al. 2019).

5.4.2.3. *Cloud-level challenges*

Although the cloud provides scalability, its use increases the chance of data leakage. A misconfigured cloud storage can expose IoT data. Misconfigurations, inappropriate access control and complexity in managing multi-tenant services are common causes of data exposure and breaches, as cloud security is split between provider and customer[1]. Also, cloud staff or compromised accounts can misuse privileged access. The intricate interaction between these systems and traditional IoT devices demands comprehensive strategies to protect data integrity and user privacy (Singh et al. 2024).

5.4.2.4. *Data security and privacy*

IoT-to-cloud pipelines often carry sensitive personal, location or industrial telemetry. Weak crypto choices, poor key handling and cross-domain data sharing can expose raw data or metadata. Recent work has shown that end-to-end protections can reduce risk to some level with the use of technologies such as blockchain, machine learning, fog and edge computing (Pathak et al. 2024). Post-quantum cryptography options are suitable for edge/IoT so that cloud-stored telemetry remains confidential against future adversaries (Karakaya and Ulu 2024).

1 See: https://en.wikipedia.org/wiki/Cloud_computing_issues?utm_source=chatgpt.com.

5.4.2.5. *Integration and management challenges*

The integration of IoT with cloud services can generate operational challenges such as heterogeneity of devices and protocols, key management complexity, and patch and update management. As integration requires using the services of multiple vendors, the heterogeneity of devices and protocol challenges arise due to different vendors using different standards, complicating interoperability (Farahzadia et al. 2017). Key management complexity arises due to the complexity of the security keys used for encryption during the data transmission stage (Rana et al. 2023a). As such keys are configured with complexity, securely distributing, rotating and managing encryption keys at scale becomes difficult. If these keys are changed frequently for security reasons, updating these keys at all IoT stations and cloud servers can become tedious and lead to human error. As software updates are always an ongoing process, security-related patches need to be downloaded and installed regularly. The patch and update management ensures updated security. But consistent firmware and software updates across thousands of distributed devices can remain a major challenge (Mugarza et al. 2020).

5.5. Conclusion

IoT has emerged as a transformative technology, enabling seamless interaction between physical and digital environments. Through its layered architecture spanning sensors, gateways, edge computing and cloud platforms, IoT delivers end-to-end visibility across diverse domains such as healthcare, logistics, industry and smart cities. The integration of IoT with cloud computing further enhances scalability, real-time analytics and service delivery, particularly under the XaaS model, which reduces operational costs and accelerates adoption (Rana et al. 2023b; Bhambri and Khang 2024; Bhambri et al. 2024; Rana and Bhambri 2024; Sridhar et al. 2024).

However, this integration also introduces substantial security and management challenges. At the device level, IoT systems face threats from weak authentication, firmware vulnerabilities and physical tampering. At the network level, insecure protocols, data interception and denial-of-service attacks threaten communication reliability. At the cloud level, issues such as misconfiguration, multi-tenancy and insider misuse elevate risks of data breaches.

Furthermore, data security and privacy remain critical concerns, as IoT–cloud pipelines often carry sensitive personal and industrial information vulnerable to leakage, tampering or long-term cryptographic threats. Finally, integration and management challenges, including device heterogeneity, complex key management and large-scale patching, add further difficulty in maintaining resilience.

Addressing these concerns requires a multi-layered security approach. End-to-end encryption, lightweight cryptographic schemes, secure firmware management, protocol standardization and zero-trust architectures are essential safeguards. Emerging solutions such as blockchain, federated learning, fog/edge computing and post-quantum cryptography hold promise for enhancing trust, privacy and long-term resilience.

In conclusion, while IoT–cloud ecosystems present unprecedented opportunities for innovation and efficiency, their success depends on robust architectural design principles that balance scalability, interoperability and security. By embedding security and privacy considerations into every layer of the architecture, organizations can build trustworthy IoT ecosystems capable of supporting the next wave of digital transformation.

5.6. References

Almutairi, M. and Sheldon, F.T. (2025). IoT–cloud integration security: A survey of challenges, solutions, and directions. *Electronics*, 14, 1394. doi: 10.3390/ electronics14071394.

Bahga, A. and Madisetti, V. (2014). *Internet of Things: A Hands-on Approach*. Universities Press, Kolkata.

Bakhshi, T., Ghita, B., Kuzminykh, I. (2024). A review of IoT firmware vulnerabilities and auditing techniques. *Sensors*, 24, 708. doi: 10.3390/ s2402070.

Bhambri, P. and Khang, A. (2024). Managing and monitoring patient's healthcare using AI and IoT technologies. In *Driving Smart Medical Diagnosis through AI-Powered Technologies and Applications*, Khang, A. (ed.). IGI Global, New York, London, Beijing. doi: 10.4018/979-8-3693-3679-3.ch001.

Bhambri, P., Rani, S., Khang, A. (2024). AI-driven digital twin and resource optimization in Industry 4.0 ecosystem. In *Intelligent Techniques for Predictive Data Analytics*, Singh, N., Birla, S., Ansari, M.D., Shukla, N.K. (eds). Wiley-IEEE Press, Hoboken, NJ. doi: 10.1002/ 9781394227990.ch3.

Boeckl, K., Fagan, M., Fisher, W., Lefkovitz, N., Megas, K.N., Nadeau, E., O'Rourke, D.G., Piccarreta, B., Scarfone, K. (2019). Considerations for managing Internet of Things (IoT) cybersecurity and privacy risks. National Institute of Standards and Technology, U.S. Department of Commerce. doi: 10.6028/NIST.IR.8228.

Buyya, R. and Dastjerdi, A.V. (2016). *Internet of Things: Principles and Paradigms*. Elsevier, Amsterdam. doi: 10.1016/C2015-0-04135-1.

Castellanos, W., Macias, J., Pinilla, H., Alvarado, J.D. (2021). Internet of Things: A multiprotocol gateway as solution of the interoperability problem. In *Mechatronics, Electronics and Telecommunications Advances Towards Industry 4.0.*, Arcos Legarda, J., Coral-Enriquez, H., Gutierrez, F. (eds). Editorial Bonaventuriana, Bogotá. doi: 10.48550/arXiv.2108.00098.

Coston, I., Plotnizky, E., Nojoumian, M. (2025). Comprehensive study of IoT vulnerabilities and countermeasures. *Applied Sciences*, 15, 3036. doi: 10.3390/ app15063036.

ENISA (2017). *Baseline Security Recommendations for IoT in the Context of Critical Information Infrastructures*. European Union Agency for Network and Information Security (ENISA), Heraklion. doi: 10.2824/03228.

Farahzadia, A., Shams, P., Rezazadeh, J., Farahbakhsh, R. (2017). Middleware technologies for cloud of things – a survey. *arXiv*. doi: 10.48550/arXiv.1705.00387.

Godase, M., Singh, C., Tanpure, A. (2023). IoT-based storage management system. In *Internet of Things (IoT): Key Digital Trends Shaping the Future. ICIoTCT 2022*. Misra, R., Rajarajan, M., Veeravalli, B., Kesswani, N., Patel, A. (eds). Springer, Singapore. doi: 10.1007/978-981-19-9719-8_8.

Greengard, S. (2015). *The Internet of Things*. MIT Press, Cambridge, MA.

GSMA Intelligence (2018). IoT: The next wave of connectivity and services. *GSMA* [Online]. Available at: https://data.gsmaintelligence.com/research/research/research-2018/iot-the-next-wave-of-connectivity-and-services.

Gubbi, J., Buyya, R., Marusic, S., and Palaniswami, M. (2012). Internet of Things (IoT): A vision, architectural elements, and future directions. *arXiv* [Online]. Available at: http://arxiv.org/abs/1207.0203.

International Telecommunication Union (ITU). (2017). Broadband mobile and Internet of Things network planning: ITU Centre of Excellence training [Training programme]. ITU Academy, Bangkok [Online]. Available at: https://academy.itu.int/training-courses/full-catalogue/broadband-mobile-and-internet-things-network-planning.

Karakaya, A. and Ulu, A. (2024). A survey on post-quantum based approaches for edge computing security. *WIREs Computational Statistics*, 16(1), e1644. doi: 10.1002/wics.1644.

Kramp, T., van Kranenburg, R., and Lange, S. (2013). Introduction to the Internet of Things. In *Enabling Things to Talk*, Bassi, A. (ed.). Springer, New York. doi: 10.1007/978-3-642-40403-0_1.

Li, Z., Fei, F., Zhang, G. (2022). Edge-to-cloud IIoT for condition monitoring in manufacturing systems with ubiquitous smart sensors. *Sensors*, 901. doi: 10.3390/s22155901.

Milind, G. (2025). Crop protection system using IoT and AI to prevent animal intrusion. *SSRN Electronic Journal* [Online]. Available at: https://ssrn.com/abstract=5230340. doi: 10.2139/ssrn.5230340.

Mugarza, I., Flores, J.L., Montero, J.L. (2020). Security issues and software updates management in the industrial Internet of Things (IIoT) era. *Sensors*, 20(24), 7160. doi: 10.3390/s20247160.

Pathak, M., Mishra, K.N., Singh, S.P. (2024). Securing data and preserving privacy in cloud IoT-based technologies an analysis of assessing threats and developing effective safeguard. *Artificial Intelligence Review*, 57, 269. doi: 10.1007/s10462-024-10908-x.

Rana, R. and Bhambri, P. (2024). Blockchain for transparent, privacy protected and secure health data management. In *Smart Healthcare Systems: AI and IoT Perspectives*, Bhambri, P., Soni, R., Tran, T.A. (eds). CRC Press, Boca Raton, FL. doi: 10.1201/9781032698519-3.

Rana, M., Mamun, Q., Islam, R. (2023a). Enhancing IoT security: An innovative key management system for lightweight block ciphers. *Sensors*, 23(18), 7678. doi: 10.3390/s23187678.

Rana, R., Bhambri, P., Chhabra, Y. (2023b). Evolution and the future of industrial engineering with the IoT and AI. In *Integration of AI-based Manufacturing and Industrial Engineering Systems with the Internet of Things*, Bhambri, P., Rani, S., Balas, V.E., Elngar, A.A. (eds). CRC Press, Boca Raton, FL. doi: 10.1201/9781003383505.

Shi, W., Cao, J., Zhang, Q., Li, Y., Xu, L. (2016). Edge computing: Vision and challenges. *IEEE Internet of Things Journal*, 3(5), 637–646. doi: 10.1109/JIOT.2016.2579198.

Singh, N., Buyya, R., Kim, H. (2024). Securing cloud-based Internet of Things: Challenges and mitigations. *Sensors*, 1.

Sridhar, V., Rani, S., Pareek, P.K., Bhambri, P. (2024). Evolution of IoT in various application domains. In *Blockchain for IoT Systems: Concept, Framework and Applications*, Sridhar, V., Rani, S., Pareek, P.K., Bhambri, P., Elngar, A.A. (eds). CRC Press, Boca Raton, FL. doi: 10.1201/9781003460367-2.

6

Blockchain Implementation for Supply Chain Transparency Modeling

Blockchain technology, initially popularized through cryptocurrencies, is increasingly recognized as a transformative tool in supply chain management. Its core attributes – transparency, immutability and security – offer solutions to key challenges such as counterfeiting, fragmented information flows and limited traceability. This chapter examines blockchain's potential to enhance supply chain transparency and efficiency, presenting both theoretical insights and empirical findings. A survey was conducted among 219 medium and large non-financial enterprises operating internationally, complemented by case studies from sectors including retail, food logistics, automotive and international trade. The research identifies performance indicators most relevant to blockchain implementation, spanning financial results, customer satisfaction, operational efficiency and employee development. Case studies of Carrefour, Walmart, Renault and Egypt's customs authority demonstrate blockchain's capacity to reduce traceability time, improve compliance and streamline document flows. However, the study also highlights significant barriers to adoption, such as high energy costs, scalability limitations, insufficient legal frameworks and organizational challenges.

Results indicate that while blockchain delivers measurable benefits in cost reduction, quality improvement and customer trust, its widespread adoption requires overcoming technological and regulatory constraints. This chapter concludes that blockchain can revolutionize logistics by reinforcing transparency and stakeholder credibility, although its future impact will depend on aligning technical capabilities with performance measurement systems and addressing external barriers.

6.1. Introduction

In today's economic climate, blockchain technology has gained significant popularity, particularly thanks to cryptocurrencies such as Bitcoin. The literature emphasizes that blockchain is much more than just a foundation for digital

Chapter written by Helena KOŚCIELNIAK.

currencies. Moreover, its unique properties have the potential to revolutionize various areas of business, including supply chain management (Swan 2015; Saberi et al. 2019). Conceptually, in the past, it was neo-Taylorism. Currently, it is lean management and lean production, and in the future, it is Smart Factory, virtual organizations and digital supply chains. In the area of solutions, mechanization and automation (past period) dominated.

Currently, solutions are based on automation and computerization; the future in this area is virtualization and system integration, robotics, artificial intelligence (AI) and cyber-physical systems (CPS) (Pluralsight 2024).

A blockchain is a decentralized database in which information is stored in chronologically linked and cryptographically secure blocks. Each block contains transaction data, a unique block identifier (hash) and a hash of the previous block, ensuring the continuity and immutability of the ledger. Blocks are added to the chain through a process called "mining", which requires solving complex mathematical puzzles, securing the blockchain against manipulation (Nakomoto 2008; World Economic Forum 2016).

There are different types of blockchains, which can be divided into two main categories: public and private. Public blockchains, such as Bitcoin and Ethereum, are open, decentralized networks that anyone can participate in. Private blockchains, such as Hyperledger Fabric and Corda, are closed networks managed by a single organization, accessible only to authorized users (UniCredit 2016).

The innovative potential resulting from the unique features of blockchain technology is being recognized by many businesses. The main features of blockchain are:

– data availability;

– security;

– transparency.

Data availability means that:

– multiple business partners can work on the same document in real time without data loss;

– each user can track all previous information and changes;

– all data is stored digitally, eliminating the need for paper documentation;

– no central institution responsible for data verification and sharing.

Security stems from the fact that:

– blockchain is a decentralized technology and its data is shared via the cloud, meaning records are published online; access to encrypted information is not automatic, as the business partner must verify and consent to access specific data;

– information in blocks cannot be manipulated or falsified because each new record represents information in a new block;

– the distributed and encrypted nature of blockchains makes them difficult to crack, which offers the potential for greater security for the Internet of Things;

– a specific chain can only be viewed by those authorized to open it and view the data contained within it (Swan 2015; Kshetri 2017).

Ensuring security has become one of the greatest challenges facing global supply chains in recent years. Implementing blockchain technology has become one of the greatest challenges facing global supply chains in recent years. Furthermore, blockchain technology can help increase the security of supply chain data flows, as well as IoT data generated throughout the supply chain (IBM 2024).

Blockchain eliminates the possibility of data falsification because every transaction is cryptographically secure and immutable. This means that once recorded, information cannot be changed or deleted without the consent of all network participants. This makes frauds such as document forgery or product substitution virtually impossible (Marciniak 2014).

There are different types of blockchains. They can be divided into two main categories: public and private. Public blockchains, such as Bitcoin and Ethereum, are open, decentralized networks in which anyone can participate. Private blockchains, such as Hyperledger Fabric and Corda, are closed networks managed by a single organization, accessible only to authorized users (Mell and Grance 2023).

6.2. Experimental methods and materials

The study population included companies operating in the global market. Quantitative research was conducted using the CATI (Computer-Assisted Telephone Interviewing) technique. The study population included medium-sized and large enterprises in the non-financial enterprise sector. Respondents were managers of companies implementing blockchain technology. The number of surveys sent was 234, with a return rate of 219. The group of surveyed companies included companies from various industries that had been using blockchain solutions for at least one year. Companies with a short history of blockchain technology implementation predominated in the group of surveyed companies, accounting for 60% of the respondents. Companies with a blockchain usage period of three years accounted for

30%, the remaining 10% were companies with a blockchain usage period of two years.

6.3. Results and discussion: case studies

6.3.1. *Blockchain technology implementation case studies: practical implementation*

By observing the current behavior of enterprises and the ways of using modern technologies in their practical implementation, it is possible to present examples of how to effectively implement the blockchain process in enterprises.

– XCEED (eXtended Compliance End-to-End Distributed). This new blockchain-based solution aims to monitor the compliance of thousands of parts installed in a car in near real time. This new blockchain technology solution was developed and manufactured by Farecia, Groupe Renault, Knauf Industries, simoldes and Coskunz in collaboration with IBM for the European automotive industry. It allows for the certification of compliance of all vehicle components, from design to production. This project has been implemented at partner factories in Bursa (Turkey), Douai (France) and Palencia (Switzerland). The XCEED project is now open to other manufacturers and hundreds of global supply chain suppliers, regardless of size. It is a tool that meets growing transparency requirements.

– Unlike traditional hierarchical management, network governance assumes cooperation between independent stakeholders and develops common rules, processes and management structures that help the whole organization operate effectively and efficiently.

Based on the data in Table 6.1, companies' goals for using blockchain technology revolve around a data exchange system, particularly data updates and authenticity, as well as uninterrupted document flow, where stakeholders – trading partners, government institutions and logistics companies involved in production, transportation, sales and financial processes – can use the same data source. Furthermore, they expect digitally authenticated information and documents. They see potential in the digitization of all stages of transportation, full transparency of production processes and greater quality control.

Real-time access to product information improves control, allows for timely responses to all events and optimizes the flow of transactions and processes. Therefore, this technology combines supply chain control with transparent documentation.

Company	Goal of implementing blockchain technology	Actions/effects	Barriers
Carrefour (Poland + Europe)	Consumers want to know where their food comes from (farm, feed, transport, refrigeration), but traditional systems are difficult to synchronize and prone to errors.	Carrefour implemented blockchain (IBM Food Trust) to track product batches. Each stage of the chain adds a record with the batch number, farm, harvest date, growing conditions, transport (vehicle ID, temperature sensors) and certificates. Customers scan a QR code to view the product's history. Potato passporting was launched in Poland in 2021; participating entities include farmers, processing plants and stores; the chain receives, among other things, quality certificates, transport data and test results.	Supplier integration, implementation costs and format unification (GS1/EPCIS).
Walmart + IBM Food Trust	In food safety incidents, identifying the source of contamination took days. Documents were scattered.	Hyperledger Fabric was implemented. Each participant (farm, packing house, shipper, DC, store) adds a block with batch information. Smart contracts validate the completeness of the steps; the traceability time for a mango was reduced from 7 days to 2.2 seconds.	Label standardization, ERP/WMS system integration and data quality (garbage-in/ garbage-out).
Egipt (government) + CargoX/NAFEZA	Paper bills of lading** caused delays, the risk of forgery and courier costs. A bill of lading (Bill of Landing) is a sea waybill confirming the carrier's receipt of	Egypt has introduced the NAFEZA system, integrated with CargoX (Blockchain Document Transfer). The exporter creates an ACI envelope containing documents (eBLs, invoices,	SME onboarding, eBL legal compliance with conventions and API integration.

	the cargo, constituting proof of the contract of carriage. It documents ownership of the goods. It is a key document in international trade because its holder at the destination port can take delivery of the shipment. It can also be traded, enabling the sale of goods during transport.	certificates). Metadata and hashes are recorded in the blockchain. Customs authorities have real-time access to over 10 million documents, with over 150,000 companies using the system. There is faster and more cost-effective customs clearance.	
Renault – XCEED* (automotive compliance)	Tracking automotive parts compliance required working with thousands of documents and hundreds of suppliers. The process of audits and potential recalls was slow.	Renault and its partners have launched XCEED (Hyperledger Fabric). Suppliers and assemblers maintain records of parts' proof of compliance while maintaining authorization capabilities. XCEED ensures greater responsiveness and efficiency in an era of increasingly stringent regulatory requirements. New market surveillance regulations came into force in September 2020. Increased inspections have been introduced for vehicles already on the market. The entire production chain must adapt its organization to comply with established regulations in a shorter timeframe.	Data privacy between competing vendors, integration with ERP/PLM and Network Governance**, which defines how relationships between various organizations/enterprises operating within a broader network are managed and coordinated to achieve specific goals, managing interdependencies, resources and information in a decentralized manner. Unlike traditional hierarchical governance, network governance involves collaboration between independent actors, developing common rules, processes and governance structures that support the effective and efficient operation of the entire network.

Table 6.1. *Implementation of blockchain solutions in enterprises – selected issues*

Real-time access to product information improves control, allows for timely responses to all events and optimizes the flow of transactions and processes.

Therefore, this technology combines supply chain control with transparent documentation.

However, it is not without its drawbacks, limitations and threats. These include:

– lack of sufficient legal regulations, which limits its practical use;

– dependence on Internet infrastructure, particularly on the policies of Internet service providers;

– reliance on Internet infrastructure, particularly on the policies of Internet service providers;

– scalability, or the ability to maintain acceptable performance in the face of increasing load, means that as the number of website visitors or the amount of data processed increases, performance will decrease;

– very high energy costs of each transaction (electricity consumption per transaction corresponds to the daily energy demand of a typical American household) (Marciniak 2014).

The literature on the subject attempts to organize the barriers to the use of blockchain technology in supply chains. There are four basic groups of barriers in this field:

– organizational;

– technological;

– supply chain-related;

– external.

Organizational barriers include lack of specialized knowledge of the technology, lack of tools for implementing the technology and lack of comparative data for implementing the technology.

Technological barriers stem from the immaturity of the technology, limited IT infrastructure and security concerns.

Supply chain barriers include:

– lack of customer awareness of blockchain technology;

– lack of collaboration among supply chain partners;

– lack of coordination among supply chain partners.

External barriers include:

– market uncertainty related to the use of blockchain technology;

– lack of industry commitment to implementing blockchain technology;

– lack of community involvement in adopting blockchain technology (IBM).

The key issues facing this technology are its complexity and the limited number of IT specialists with the skills to create business solutions using it.

According to the International Data Corporation (IDC), logistics and transportation are among the industries that will benefit most from blockchain solutions in the near future. Global spending on blockchain applications in 2023 reached \$3.1 billion, more than double the figure for 2021 (IBM 2013; Mell and Grance 2023).

6.3.2. *Indicator analysis*

Implementing blockchain technology in supply chains requires measuring performance in this area. Performance management is the foundation for controlling enterprise operations (Haffer 2008). The literature presents performance in four dimensions of performance. The first stage involves defining expected performance. In this stage, the manager describes the expected results of actions that must be performed by the employee. This requires communication between managers and the employee. The second stage involves clarifying expectations for employees. The manager defines what constitutes good performance and provides guidance on how to resolve existing problems. If the employee's actions meet requirements, their performance level is expected and therefore standard. If they allow a problem to arise, their performance level is low and requires managerial intervention. If the performance level is below standard but not yet problematic, the manager must inform the employee what new skills they need to acquire to bring their performance up to standard. This provides room for performance improvement. The final stage is when performance exceeds the standard. This situation allows for the identification of a leading behavioral pattern. Managers can then encourage greater achievements through incentive systems. The presented analysis shows that performance can be quantified. They are the result of actions taken by employees, but from the manager's perspective, performance depends largely on communication (Kaganski et al. 2014; Swan 2015).

The aim of the research is to identify the success factors of companies in this field. To determine these factors, we used the results of surveys on how non-financial companies operating in the international market measure performance. The study group included companies using blockchain technology. Respondents were primarily owners, managers and board members. First, the financial and non-financial indicators used to measure company goals were verified. In the next stage, the types of indicators used in each of these groups were determined. Furthermore, participants were asked to assign weights and importance to each indicator.

The obtained results allowed us to generate core and leading indicators, which, according to respondents, received the most responses and those that are most important in assessing the effects of implemented blockchain technology. Respondents' opinions allowed us to identify four groups of indicators verifying the objectives of the surveyed companies. These include financial indicators, customer indicators, operational indicators including innovation and service and employee indicators (learning and development). The generated and measured responses are presented in Table 6.2.

Variables	% indicators	Indicator wage in scale 1–5
I. Financial	100	
Net profit	81.3	4.55
Sales revenue	82.5C	4.87
Sales profitability	92.3	4.99
II. Customers	77.2	
Customer satisfaction	84.1	4.77
Customer acquisition	83.1	4.59
Customer loyalty	70.1	4.44
Market share	58.4	4.38
Customer profitability	53.7	4.38
III. Operational activities including innovation and service	78.9	
Product and process costs	77.4	4.78
Complaints filed and accepted	77.1	4.50
Number of new products	66.1	4.74
Inventory turnover	77.3	4.78
Machinery and equipment efficiency	56.8	4.69
Project implementation time	40.3	4.37
R&D expenditures	61.7	4.79

IV. Employees, learning and development	77.2	
Employee qualifications	93.1	4.57
Training indicators	81.2	4.38
Employee productivity	80.5	4.75
Average salary	80.4	4.47
Employee satisfaction	90.8	4.66

Table 6.2. *Performance indicators of companies using blockchain technologies – their importance*

The survey results present respondents' opinions on the indicators used to assess the performance of companies using blockchain technology. Financial indicators received 100% of the responses. In this performance evaluation group, the priority is given to return on sales, which depends on net profit and sales revenue. Other financial indicators not included in Table 6.2 include gross profit, revenue growth, receivables turnover, asset turnover and the Internal Rate of Return (IRR).

In the customer dimension, customer satisfaction and acquisition were most frequently mentioned. Market share and customer profitability received equal ratings. The frequency of indicator use matches the assigned weights. Customer profitability received the fewest responses. The frequency of indicator use generally matches the assigned weights.

In the internal processes dimension, the most frequently mentioned indicators were product costs, inventory turnover and complaints submitted and approved. When considering the weighting assigned to individual indicators as the basis for assessment, product and process costs, inventory turnover and the number of new products are important. Table 6.2 shows that the greatest weight is assigned to employees, learning and development, employee qualifications, employee satisfaction, training indicators, labor productivity and average wages. High levels of training qualification indicators correspond to the era of the knowledge economy. In terms of indicator weight, labor productivity is the most significant, followed by employee satisfaction.

Generalizing the research results, it can be concluded that companies implementing blockchain solutions measure their traditional performance using net profit and sales revenue, which are the basis for calculating sales profitability. Positive financial results stem primarily from customer satisfaction and new customer acquisition. Customer satisfaction and customer growth are influenced by business improvement processes, primarily through cost advantages in processes and products, quality improvements and innovation. The research shows that research and development expenditures are crucial for large enterprises, while the number of new products is more important for medium-sized companies. The ability to change and improve efficiency lies primarily in qualifications, their continuous improvement and employee satisfaction.

In conclusion, it should be noted that the surveyed companies implementing blockchain technologies are operating under new conditions and adapting their operations accordingly. They quantify their goals using traditional financial indicators, such as net profit, sales revenue and sales profitability. They place the greatest emphasis on the customer experience. They strive to reach new customer groups with their offerings. They compete in the market by adopting a cost-advantage strategy.

It should be emphasized that they prioritize quality and recognize the need to implement new products. They place significant emphasis on research and development expenditures, which are linked to a policy of reducing the costs of internal processes. Employee qualifications, productivity and satisfaction are highly valued. Regardless of their position, they expect creativity. Suggestions for cost reduction, quality improvement and directions for increasing work efficiency are valued. Managers recognize the relationship between employee engagement and satisfaction.

The approach to measuring performance in the implementation of blockchain solutions encompasses the entire company's operations, all areas, and maintains the measurement of performance according to the indicators analyzed above. The conducted research and the system of performance evaluation indicators describe the owners' goals and the paths to achieving them. They also demonstrate how to align the goals of the company with those of its stakeholders.

Blockchain technology can be expensive, inefficient and technologically challenging for businesses to implement. Furthermore, while blockchain offers transparency by allowing public review of transactions, the lack of a central oversight body can be a double-edged sword. The lack of user identification can attract criminal activity to blockchain transactions. This is one reason why some cybercriminals use cryptocurrencies for illegal transactions.

Furthermore, using blockchain for secure backups comes with its own pitfalls. For example, if someone finds a way to provide more than half of the network's active computing power, they could create a false fork and seize control, as blockchain technology is designed to allow majority control. However, this scenario is unlikely in a mature blockchain.

6.4. Conclusion

Implementing blockchain technology presents certain challenges. The main ones are scalability, regulations and standards, and implementation costs.

Current blockchain technologies have limited scalability, which can be problematic for large supply chains with massive transaction volumes. Implementing global blockchain standards and regulations can be difficult due to legal and regulatory differences across countries. Empirical studies show that blockchain can deliver significant savings over the long term; initial implementation costs can be high, which can be prohibitive for smaller companies.

Despite these challenges, the future of blockchain in supply chain management appears promising. This technology has the potential to revolutionize many sectors, bringing benefits in the form of increased transparency, security and efficiency, while maintaining performance measurement for market success. In the context of future research, it would be interesting to examine, measure and publish the level of indicators after the introduction of blockchains, as this technology will influence the selection of future trading partners. The increasing understanding of blockchain's innovative potential means that the practical applications of the tool will increase. However, this requires significant changes in the functioning of individual entities operating within the network, given the limitations of implementing blockchain technology. The added value of using this tool in supply chain management lies primarily in significantly increasing the transparency of their operations. Recording transactions within a distributed and change-resistant database strengthens the credibility of information flowing between individual links in the chain and throughout the entire chain. Blockchain also has significant potential for storing and recording supply chain data records (Durach et al. 2021). The technology can record every stage of a product's lifecycle, from factory production, through shipping and delivery to the store, all the way to the moment of purchase by the consumer.

Further research should focus on positioning companies according to the indicators used to assess how they cope with future technological challenges and emerging opportunities in the pursuit of maximizing success. The research results can serve as an inspiring source of information to support decisions regarding the effects of applied technologies and blockchain (Bhambri and Kumar 2024; Bhambri and Starostka-Patyk 2024, 2025). The implementation of this technology is a response to growing market needs, greater customer demands and increased competitiveness in the logistics industry. Its application in logistics raises expectations related to improved competitiveness and efficiency, reduced costs, transaction and product security, improved data quality, increased customer satisfaction and increased brand trust. However, comprehensive utilization of blockchain's capabilities and potential will depend on the ability to eliminate existing barriers, such as economic calculations based on appropriate quantitative and qualitative indicators, technological limitations and legal regulations.

6.5. References

Bhambri, P. and Kumar, S. (2024). Protecting sustainable supply chains from cyber threats. In *Digital Sustainability: Navigating Entrepreneurship in the Information Age*, Bhambri, P. and Paweloszek, I. (eds). CRC Press, Boca Raton, 125–141. doi: 10.1201/9781003484226-9.

Bhambri, P. and Starostka-Patyk, M. (2024). Decentralized finance (DeFi) and environmental impact. In *Digital Sustainability: Navigating Entrepreneurship in the Information Age*, Bhambri, P. and Paweloszek, I. (eds). CRC Press, Boca Raton, 142–151. doi: 10.1201/9781003484226-10.

Bhambri, P. and Starostka-Patyk, M. (2025). Integrating AI with blockchain for decentralized security and threat prevention. In *Handbook of AI-driven Threat Detection and Prevention: A Holistic Approach to Security*, Bhambri, P. and Anand, A.J. (eds). CRC Press, Boca Raton, 353–370. doi: 10.1201/9781003521020-21.

Durach, C.F., Blesik, T., von During, M., Bick, M. (2021). Special topic forum: Blockchain: Applications and strategies for supply chain research and practice blockchain applications in supply chain transactions. *Journal of Business Logistics*, 42(1), 7–14.

Haffer, D. (2008). *Performance Management, Leistungserfassung und Leistungsteuerung in Unternehmen und óffentlichen Verwaltungen*. Gabler Editions Wissenschaft, Wiesbaden.

IBM (2013). IBM blockchain platform [Online]. Available at: https://www3.weforum.org/docs/WEF_SCT_EnablingTrade_Report_2013.pdf [Accessed 21 June 2025].

Kaganski, S., Paavel, M., Lavin, J. (2014). Selecting key perfprmance indicators with support of enterprise analyze model. In *Proceedings of the International Conference of DAAAM Baltic, "Industrial Engineering"*, Tallinn, 97–110.

Kshetri, N. (2017). Can blockchain strengthen the Internet of Things? *IT Professional*, 19(4), 68–72.

Marciniak, M. (2014). Significant limitations of blockchain in commercial applications [Online]. Available at: https://itwiz.pl/istotne-ograniczeniablockchain [Accessed 20 April 2024].

Mell, P. and Grance, T. (2011). The NIST definition of cloud computing. Recommendations of the National Institute of Standards and Technology. Report, National Institute of Standards and Technology, Gaithersburg [Online]. Available at: https://nvlpubs.nist.gov/nistpubs/Legacy/SP/nistspecialpublication800-145.pdf [Accessed 7 December 2017].

Mell, P. and Grance, T. (2023). The NIST definition of cloud computing. Recommendations of the National Institute of Standards and Technology. Report, National Institute of Standards and Technology, Gaithersburg [Online]. Available at: https://nvlpubs.nist.gov/nistpubs/Legacy/SP/nistspecialpublication800-145.pdf [Accessed 7 November 2024]

Nakomoto, S. (2008). Bitcoin: A peer-to-peer electronic cash system [Online]. Available at: https://bitcoin.org/bitcoin.pdf.

Pluralsight (2024). Technology in 2025: Prepare for the fourh industrial revolution. Blog [Online]. Available at: https://www.pluralsight.com/blog/career/tech-in-2025.

Saberi, S., Kouhizadeh, M., Sarkis, J. (2019). Blockchains and the supply chain: Findings from a broad study of practitioners. *IEEE Engineering Management Review*, 47(3), 95–103. doi: 10.1109/EMR.2019.2928264.

Swan, W. (2015). *Blockchain: Blueprint for a New Economy*. O'Reilly Media, Santa Rosa.

UniCredit (2016). Blockchain technology and applications from a financial perspective. Technical Report, Version 1.0, Data & Analytics, 6.

World Economic Forum (2016). Top 10 Emerging Technologies 2016. Report.

7

Autonomous Systems in Supply Chain Operations

The purpose of this chapter is to analyze autonomous systems in supply chain operations with a focus on their applications, challenges and future prospects. A systematic literature review (SLR) was conducted covering the period 2015–2025, using databases such as Scopus, Web of Science, ScienceDirect and Google Scholar. The analysis reveals that autonomous system deployments encompass transportation, warehousing and distribution, while their integration with digital technologies – such as artificial intelligence (AI), the Internet of Things and blockchain – constitutes the foundation of future logistics. Findings indicate that these systems enable a reduction of operational costs by 20–40%, an increase in warehouse space efficiency by 30–50% and improved process safety. At the same time, significant implementation barriers are identified, including high investment costs, lack of harmonized legal frameworks and social challenges related to technology acceptance. This chapter also highlights regional differences in implementation: North America focuses on scalability, Europe on sustainable development and Asia on large-scale deployments. The conclusions emphasize the need for integrating sustainability and risk management with autonomous technologies, as well as the importance of phased implementation.

7.1. Introduction

Companies now operate within the paradigm of Industry 4.0, facing increasing pressure to reduce costs, shorten delivery times and enhance process flexibility, all of which accelerate the adoption of technological innovations (Snyder 2019; Ivanov 2020). In logistics, autonomy is understood as the ability of transport, warehousing and distribution systems to make operational decisions based on sensor data, machine learning algorithms and predefined rules (Bogue 2018; Stolaroff et al. 2018).

Chapter written by Agnieszka PACUD.

The International Organization for Standardization (ISO) and the Society of Automotive Engineers (SAE) have developed models of autonomy levels. The most widely cited is the six-level SAE scale (levels 0–5), which has become a key reference point in research and implementation. Although originally created for road transport, it is increasingly being adapted for warehouse logistics and distribution (Kyriakidis et al. 2015; Manyika et al. 2017).

In logistics research, the concept of the *autonomous supply chain* (ASC) has been gaining attention. It refers to a system capable of self-organization and independent decision-making in planning, transportation, procurement and distribution (Geissbauer et al. 2016; Ivanov and Dolgui 2020). Some authors also highlighted the need to distinguish between automation and autonomy. While automation refers to repetitive tasks carried out by machines based on programmed instructions, autonomy assumes the ability to perceive the environment, interpret data and make decisions under uncertainty (Müller and Voigt 2018). Cobots provide operational support to human workers in warehouses and distribution centers, improving ergonomics and safety. They take over heavy, repetitive tasks while offering greater flexibility than traditional industrial robots, as they can be easily reprogrammed and repositioned. In this way, they serve as an intermediary stage between manual labor and full automation, combining the precision of machines with the intuition and adaptability of humans (Bhambri et al. 2024).

One of the most groundbreaking solutions that has recently been applied in logistics practice is the use of autonomous systems. These include autonomous vehicles (AVs), autonomous mobile robots (AMRs), drones and advanced warehouse systems. Their development has been driven by advancements in areas such as machine learning, image recognition, signal processing and next-generation wireless communication technologies (5G, edge computing) (Bogue 2018; Klumpp 2018).

Autonomous logistics systems are part of the broader Industry 4.0 trend, in which automation, digitalization and interconnectivity between intelligent machines, sensors and analytical platforms play a central role (Goodall 2016). The deployment of autonomous solutions has become particularly important in the face of global supply chain disruptions, as revealed during the Covid-19 pandemic (Geissbauer et al. 2016).

Nevertheless, the rapid advancement of autonomous technologies raises a number of questions and challenges related to their implementation. Key issues include integration with existing logistics infrastructure, process standardization, cybersecurity and social acceptance (Snyder 2019). Moreover, the adoption of autonomous solutions requires adequate organizational and investment preparation to fully leverage their potential.

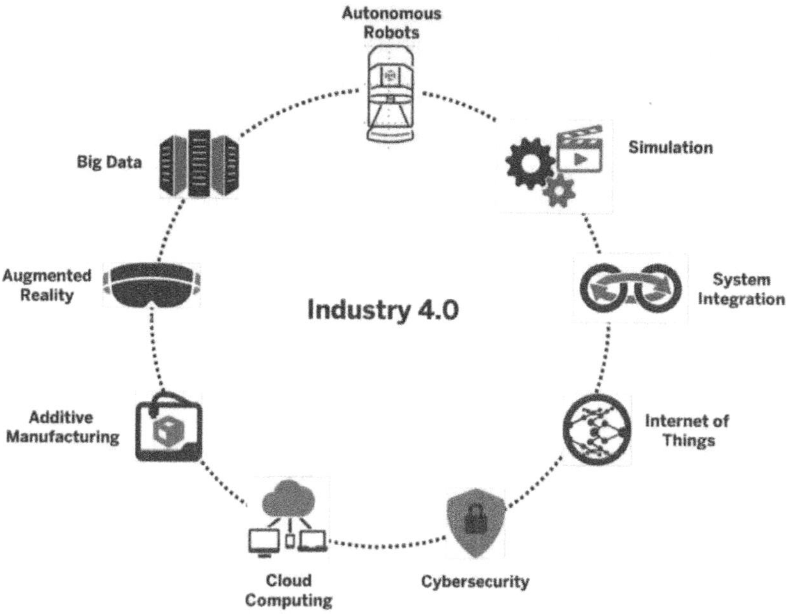

Figure 7.1. *Schematic representation of the role of autonomous systems within the Industry 4.0 concept (Source: author's elaboration based on Winkelhaus and Grosse (2020))*

Feature	AMR (Autonomous Mobile Robot)	AGV (Automated Guided Vehicle)
Navigation	Free navigation (real-time mapping)	Fixed routes, guided by markers
Flexibility	Very high	Limited
Installation costs	Lower (no dedicated route infrastructure required)	Higher (tracks/ guides required)
Applications	Warehouses, distribution centers	Mass production, assembly lines

Table 7.1. *Comparison of key features of AMRs and AGVs (Source: author's elaboration based on Winkelhaus and Grosse (2020))*

As highlighted by numerous scholars (Snyder 2019), these systems are part of a broader trend toward building resilient supply chains, in which flexibility and adaptability to disruptions play a central role.

Autonomous systems in logistics can be defined as automated technical units capable of independently making operational decisions based on sensor data and machine learning algorithms. Their defining feature is the ability to react autonomously to changing environmental conditions without constant human intervention (Denyer and Tranfield 2009).

7.2. Objective and scope of the chapter

The objective of this chapter is to present the current state of knowledge and practical applications of autonomous systems in supply chains, based on scientific literature published over the last decade (2015–2025).

The analysis focuses on three main areas of implementation: transportation, warehousing and distribution, as well as the integration of these systems with other digital technologies such as artificial intelligence (AI), Internet of Things (IoT) and digital twins.

This chapter follows a classical structure: after section 7.1 "Introduction", it presents section 7.2 "Objective and scope of the article", section 7.3 "Research procedure", section 7.4 "Analysis and discussion of results" and section 7.5 "Conclusions". The final summary highlights key recommendations for both practitioners and researchers.

7.3. Research procedure

This chapter uses the *Systematic Literature Review (SLR)* methodology. Literature searches were conducted in the following databases: *Scopus, Web of Science, Science Direct and Google Scholar*, covering the period 2015–2025.

Inclusion criteria include publications in English and peer-reviewed articles addressing logistics, transport, autonomous systems and their applications in supply chains.

Exclusion criteria include publications earlier than 2015, works not related to logistics and non-peer-reviewed texts. A total of 57 studies meeting these criteria were included in the analysis (Braun and Clarke 2006; Bibri 2018; Rana and Bhambri 2025a).

Database	Initial results	After selection
Scopus	312	22
Web of Science	280	18
Science Direct	154	10
Google Scholar	950	7

Table 7.2. *Examples of databases and number of publications included in the analysis (Source: author's elaboration).*

Database	Initial results	After removing duplicates	After abstract screening	Included in the final set
Scopus	312	290	75	22
Web of Science	280	260	65	18
Science Direct	154	150	45	10
Google Scholar	950	870	40	7
Total	**1,696**	**1,570**	**225**	**57**

Table 7.3. *Number of publications included at each stage of selection (Source: author's elaboration based on Denyer and Tranfield (2009). Producing a systematic review. In* The Sage Handbook of Organizational Research Methods *(671–689); Snyder, H. (2019). Literature review as a research methodology: An overview and guidelines.* Journal of Business Research, *104, 333–339)*

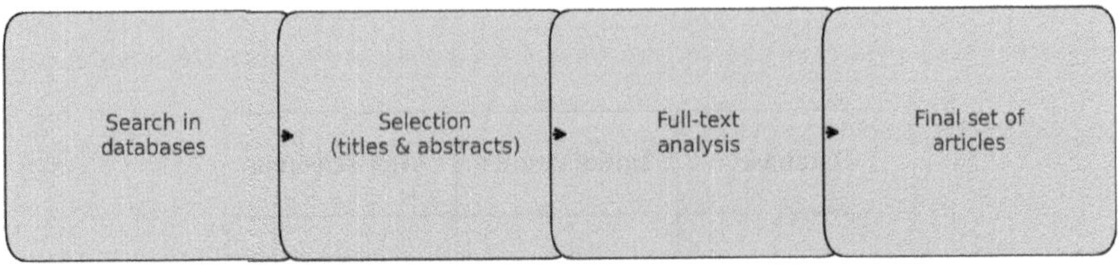

Figure 7.2. *Schematic representation of the SLR procedure (Source: author's elaboration based on Denyer and Tranfield (2009) and Snyder (2019))*

7.4. Analysis of results and discussion

Most publications focus on the integration of autonomous systems with IoT and AI, which is reflected in numerous articles on digital twins, dynamic route planning and automated fleet task scheduling (Rana and Bhambri 2025b).

Empirical studies cover both pilot projects (for example, the use of drones for medicine delivery in Sub-Saharan Africa) and full-scale implementations in distribution centers. Many works report a significant reduction in operational costs, on average by 20–40%, and an increase in warehouse space utilization by 30–50%, depending on the implementation type.

At the same time, the literature reveals clear limitations, such as the lack of coherent legal regulations, difficulties in integrating with existing infrastructure and high initial costs.

Reports suggest (Kiel et al. 2017) that up to 30% of positions involving simple warehouse tasks may be automated by 2030. On the one hand, this raises concerns about large-scale job reductions in logistics; on the other hand, it creates opportunities for new competencies such as robot fleet management, data analysis and autonomous system maintenance.

Studies indicate that the introduction of AMRs and AGVs transforms employment structures – decreasing the demand for manual labor while increasing the demand for technical specialists (Tao et al. 2018).

The first developments in AVs for logistics date back to the 1950s, when early Automated Guided Vehicles (AGVs) were introduced in factories to streamline component transport along assembly lines. Their limited flexibility restricted operations to strictly defined production environments (Snyder 2019). Only the development of Simultaneous Localization and Mapping (SLAM) technology and AI in the early 21st century opened the way for AMRs, capable of navigating dynamic environments and adapting their routes in real time (Bhambri and Kumar 2024).

In the last decade, a breakthrough has arrived with the implementation of Kiva Systems robots in Amazon distribution centers. Their success demonstrated that autonomous systems not only streamline intralogistics but also revolutionize entire business models. Today, similar solutions are used by other global players such as Alibaba, Ocado and Zalando (Braun and Clarke 2006).

AGVs are vehicles moving along strictly predefined paths, typically guided by magnetic tapes, inductive wires or optical markers embedded in warehouse floors. Developed since the 1960s, this technology is characterized by high repeatability and predictability, making it reliable in stable production and logistics environments (Snyder 2019).

In contrast, AMRs represent a newer approach to intralogistics automation. Unlike AGVs, they do not require physical guiding infrastructure but instead rely on perception and navigation algorithms based on SLAM technology, 3D cameras, radars and ultrasonic sensors (Bagloee et al. 2016; Snyder 2019). This enables AMRs to dynamically adapt routes to current warehouse conditions, avoid obstacles and optimize travel paths. They can operate in environments shared with humans and other machines, increasing their suitability for flexible and smart warehouse concepts. The literature emphasizes that AMRs support the idea of adaptive logistics, responding to variable demand and unpredictable disruptions (Thrun 2010).

Companies such as Tesla, Waymo and Einride have been developing vehicles capable of safe road operations with minimal driver intervention (Bagloee et al. 2016). Estimates suggest that full automation of long-distance transport could reduce operational costs by up to 30%. However, safety, liability and public acceptance remain major challenges (Joerss et al. 2016). Comparative studies indicate that AMRs demonstrate 30–40% higher operational flexibility compared to AGVs, although this comes with higher initial costs and more complex integration. Conversely, AGVs are more cost-effective in highly stable, repetitive environments (Tao et al. 2018).

Successful implementation of autonomous systems requires redesigning warehouse processes to fully leverage their potential (Bhambri and Kumar 2024). Autonomous delivery robots moving along sidewalks are being developed for local urban deliveries (Goodall 2016). These solutions help reduce last-mile delivery costs, which traditionally account for up to 53% of total logistics costs. Nevertheless, regulatory and technical challenges remain, particularly regarding drone flight safety and integration with air traffic management (Rana and Bhambri 2024b).

Type of system	Main function	Example implementation	Business effect
AMR	Goods transport	Amazon (Kiva robots)	40% increase in efficiency
AGV	Production line transport	BMW	20% error reduction
Drones	Warehouse inventory	Walmart	70% reduction in inventory time

Table 7.4. *Examples of autonomous system applications in warehousing (Source: author's elaboration based on Bogue (2018))*

Autonomous systems in supply chains operate in synergy with other Industry 4.0 technologies. AI provides learning and real-time decision-making capabilities, while the IoT ensures continuous data inflow from the environment. Blockchain enhances transparency and data security in supply chain transactions (Stolaroff et al. 2018).

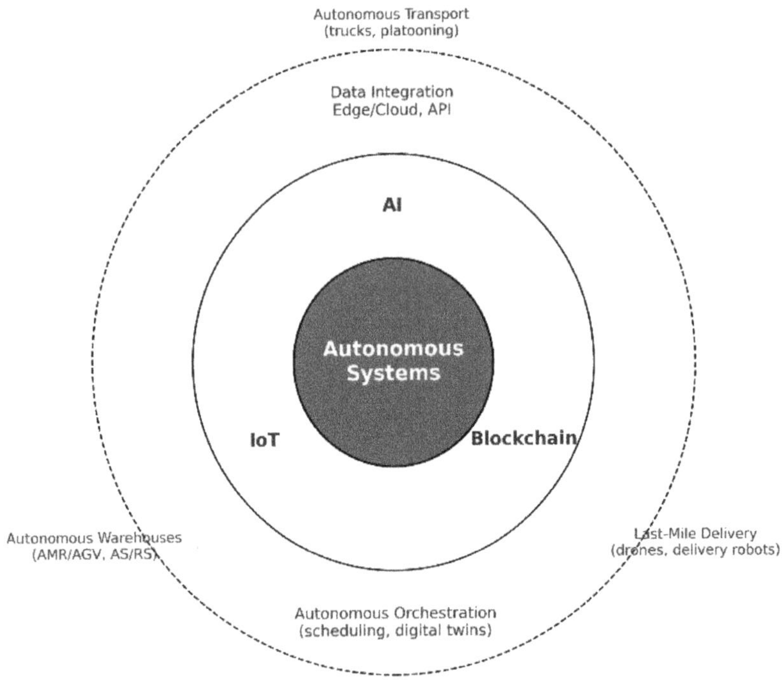

Figure 7.3. *Model of autonomous systems integration with AI, IoT and blockchain in logistics (Source: author's elaboration based on Treiblmaier (2018) and Wang et al (2019))*

In practice, integration enables the creation of ecosystems where autonomous transport and warehouse systems cooperate with IoT sensors and analytics platforms, generating real-time data to optimize processes.

Area	Benefits	Example implementations
Efficiency	Shorter order fulfillment times, fewer errors	Amazon Robotics, Ocado
Costs	Lower labor and operational costs, optimized warehouse space	DHL Supply Chain
Safety	Reduced accidents in transport and warehousing	Waymo Freight, AMRs in warehouses
Flexibility	Dynamic route adaptation, scalability of systems	AMRs, autonomous vehicles in distribution
Sustainability	Lower CO_2 emissions, reduced waste	Yara Birkeland, Zipline drones

Table 7.5. *Summary of benefits from implementing autonomous systems (Source: author's elaboration)*

Financial, technological and regulatory challenges must be considered to maximize investment efficiency and minimize risks. Unlike traditional industrial robots, which require separation from workers for safety reasons, cobots are equipped with advanced sensors, vision systems and algorithms that detect human presence and respond appropriately to hazards (Ivanov and Dolgui 2020). In the long run, cobots can act as a bridge between full automation and manual work, enabling a smoother transition toward intelligent and flexible logistics systems (Rana and Bhambri 2024a).

Despite significant advantages, the implementation of autonomous systems must also address technical, organizational and social challenges. Key issues include system reliability, resilience against cyberattacks and the ability to operate in complex, dynamic environments. Equally important are organizational and social aspects such as process adaptation, workforce training and customer and stakeholder acceptance (Snyder 2019). In the long term, autonomous systems hold the potential to generate substantial savings and competitive advantage.

The future of autonomous systems in supply chains is closely tied to further miniaturization of technologies, advances in AI and increased integration with digital systems. Growing importance will also be placed on digital twins, enabling real-time modeling and process optimization (Rana and Bhambri 2025b). Moreover, rising pressure for sustainability will drive the design of autonomous systems that reduce CO_2 emissions and optimize resource use (DHL 2020). In the long run, the integration of autonomous systems with global logistics platforms could significantly enhance flexibility and resilience of supply chains against disruptions.

In North America, the focus is on the development of autonomous trucks and warehouse robots, exemplified by projects from Waymo and Tesla in road transport, as well as Amazon Robotics in warehousing. A strong technological base combined with access to capital enables a rapid transition from pilot testing to full-scale commercial deployments.

Region	Main implementation areas	Example projects/companies	Characteristics of deployments	Key development drivers
North America	Autonomous trucks, warehouse robots	Waymo, Tesla, Amazon Robotics	Rapid transition from pilot testing to full-scale commercial implementation	Strong technological base, access to investment capital
Europe	Autonomous ships, drones, sustainable logistics systems	Yara Birkeland (Norway), EASA drone projects	Integration of technological innovations with climate policy and low-carbon economy	EU legal regulations, priority on carbon footprint reduction
Asia (China)	Large-scale AMR, urban drone and robot delivery	Alibaba, JD.com	Deployments of the largest global scale and fastest pace	Strong government support, e-commerce pressure, rapid adoption of AI and robotics

Table 7.6. *Regional differences in the implementation of autonomous systems in logistics (Source: author's own elaboration)*

In Europe, the key area remains the integration of autonomous systems with the concept of sustainable development and the low-carbon economy. Projects such as *Yara Birkeland* – an autonomous, zero-emission cargo ship in Norway – demonstrate that the priority is to combine technological innovation with carbon footprint reduction. In addition, European legal frameworks, such as the EASA guidelines for drones, support the deployment of these technologies in a safe manner consistent with the EU's climate policy.

In Asia, particularly in China, deployments are characterized by the largest scale and fastest pace of development. Companies such as Alibaba and JD.com employ hundreds of thousands of AMRs in their distribution centers and are advancing autonomous delivery systems in urban areas. Research shows that this rapid adoption is driven both by the intense pressure of the e-commerce market and by strong government support for the development of AI and robotics (Thrun 2010).

Table 7.6 highlights the key differences in the approach to implementing autonomous systems in logistics across three major world regions. North America focuses primarily on enhancing efficiency and scaling applications, with large-scale deployments of autonomous trucks and warehouse robots.

7.5. Conclusions

The analysis conducted in this chapter demonstrates that autonomous systems are playing an increasingly important role in supply chain operations. Their implementation covers transportation, warehousing and distribution, as well as integration with digital technologies such as AI, the IoT and blockchain. These applications enable significant improvements in logistics efficiency, cost reduction and enhanced safety and transparency of operations.

The greatest benefits come from the automation of repetitive tasks, which have traditionally generated high operational costs. Case studies show that through the use of AMRs and self-driving vehicles, companies can achieve savings of 20–40% depending on the operational area. At the same time, these technologies allow processes to adapt more effectively to changing market conditions, thereby increasing the resilience of supply chains to disruptions (Bagloee et al. 2016).

The integration of autonomous systems with other advanced technologies forms the foundation for efficient, flexible and secure supply chains of the future. Combining AI, IoT, blockchain and predictive analytics enables full automation of logistics processes, cost optimization and improved service quality. However, it also requires careful consideration of technological, financial and organizational challenges, which remain a subject of further research and practical implementation.

Despite their clear benefits, the deployment of autonomous systems continues to face significant barriers. These include high upfront investment costs as well as legal and social constraints. The absence of unified legal frameworks, along with societal concerns regarding safety and labor market impacts, may significantly slow down adoption. The implementation of autonomous systems requires coherent regulatory frameworks. In road transport, the SAE International autonomy classification and UNECE R157 regulations on Automated Lane Keeping Systems (ALKS) play a central role. For intralogistics, safety standards such as ISO 3691-4 set requirements for driverless trucks, while cybersecurity issues are governed by IEC 62443 and ISO/IEC 27001.

Technical aspects such as system reliability, resistance to cyberattacks and the ability to operate in complex environments also require further research and development (Joerss et al. 2016; Snyder 2019).

The findings further indicate that autonomous systems hold substantial potential in advancing sustainable development. Automation of transport and warehousing can reduce CO_2 emissions, decrease energy consumption and enhance the use of space and resources. Particularly important is the development of solutions that support the circular economy and green logistics (DHL 2020). On the contrary, the production and disposal of batteries and electronic components raise concerns regarding the full life cycle assessment (LCA) of these technologies. Within the framework of EU policy and the European Green Deal, autonomous systems may become a cornerstone of green logistics, provided that circular economy principles are effectively implemented (DHL 2020).

Autonomous systems in supply chain operations thus offer vast potential for increasing efficiency, reducing costs and enhancing safety, while simultaneously raising new technological, financial and social challenges. Successful implementation requires well-designed strategies, integration with other technologies and effective risk management. Firms that successfully adopt and integrate autonomous systems can achieve a competitive advantage, strengthen operational flexibility and contribute to the realization of sustainability goals (Wurman et al. 2008; Klumpp 2018; Treiblmaier 2018; Wang et al. 2019; Wamba et al. 2020; Winkelhaus and Grosse 2020).

It is recommended that companies approach the deployment of autonomous systems gradually, starting with pilot projects in selected operational areas. Such phased implementation reduces risks and helps organizations better prepare for process transformation. In the long term, it will be essential to develop logistics ecosystems in which diverse autonomous and digital technologies interact seamlessly and cohesively (Rana and Bhambri 2025b).

In conclusion, autonomous systems constitute a cornerstone of next-generation supply chains. Their potential for optimization, cost reduction, enhanced flexibility and support for sustainable development is undeniable. The key challenge, however, lies in striking a balance between rapid deployment and responsible management of technological, legal and social risks. Enterprises that invest in these technologies today and learn to integrate them effectively will secure a lasting competitive advantage in the turbulent environment of global markets (Goodall 2016; Rana and Bhambri 2024b).

The analysis of case studies and regional differences indicates that the development of autonomous systems is diverse in nature; however, globally it is moving toward greater automation, cost reduction and improved process flexibility. While North America focuses on efficiency and scale, Europe emphasizes sustainability, and Asia prioritizes rapid large-scale deployments. This diversity represents a potential for further research on the transfer of best practices across regions.

7.6. References

Bagloee, S.A., Tavana, M., Asadi, M., Oliver, T. (2016). Autonomous vehicles: Challenges, opportunities, and future implications for transportation policies. *Journal of Modern Transportation*, 24, 284–303. doi: 10.1007/s40534-016-0117-3.

Bhambri, P. and Khang, A. (2024). Managing and monitoring patient's healthcare using AI and IoT technologies. In *Driving Smart Medical Diagnosis Through AI-powered Technologies and Applications*, Khang, A. (ed.). IGI Global, Hershey, 1–23. doi: 10.4018/979-8-3693-3679-3.ch001.

Bhambri, P. and Kumar, S. (2024). Protecting sustainable supply chains from cyber threats. In *Digital Sustainability: Navigating Entrepreneurship in the Information Age*, Bhambri, P. and Paweloszek, I. (eds). CRC Press, Boca Raton, 125–141.

Bhambri, P., Rani, S., Khang, A. (2024). AI-driven digital twin and resource optimization in Industry 4.0 ecosystem. In *Intelligent Techniques for Predictive Data Analytics*, Singh, N., Birla, S., Ansari, M.D., Shukla, N.K. (eds). Wiley-IEEE Press, New York, 47–69. doi: 10.1002/9781394227990.ch3.

Bibri, S.E. (2018). The IoT for smart sustainable cities of the future: An analytical framework for sensor-based big data applications for environmental sustainability. *Sustainable Cities and Society*, 38, 230–253. doi: 10.1016/j.scs.2017.12.034.

Bogue, R. (2018). What are the prospects for robots in the warehouse? *Industrial Robot: An International Journal*, 45(1), 1–6. doi: 10.1108/IR-11-2017-0194.

Bortolini, M., Galizia, F.G., Mora, C., Pilati, F. (2021). Adaptive automation assembly systems in the Industry 4.0 era: A study on reconfigurable, self-adaptive and collaborative assembly systems. *Applied Sciences*, 11(3), 1256. doi: 10.3390/app11031256.

Braun, V. and Clarke, V. (2006). Using thematic analysis in psychology. *Qualitative Research in Psychology*, 3(2), 77–101. doi: 10.1191/1478088706qp063oa.

Denyer, D. and Tranfield, D. (2009). Producing a systematic review. In *The Sage Handbook of Organizational Research Methods*, Buchanan, W.D.A and Bryman, A (eds). SAGE Publications Ltd, London, 671–689.

DHL (2020). Robotics and automation: Shaping the future of supply chain logistics. DHL Trend Report [Online]. Available at: https://www.dhl.com/global-en/home/insights-and-innovation/insights/dhl-trend-reports.html.

Geissbauer, R., Schrauf, S., Koch, V., Kuge, S. (2016). Industry 4.0: Building the Digital Enterprise. PwC Report [Online]. Available at: https://www.pwc.com/gx/en/industries/industry-4.0.html.

Goodall, N.J. (2016). Away from trolley problems and toward risk management. *Applied Artificial Intelligence*, 30(8), 810–821. doi: 10.1080/08839514.2016.1229922.

ISO/SAE (2021). ISO/SAE PAS 22736: Road vehicles: Taxonomy and definitions for terms related to driving automation systems. Standard, ISO/SAE.

Ivanov, D. (2020). Viable supply chain model: Integrating agility, resilience and sustainability perspectives – Lessons from and thinking beyond the COVID-19 pandemic. *Annals of Operations Research*, 319, 1411–1431. doi: 10.1007/s10479-020-03640-6.

Ivanov, D. and Dolgui, A. (2020). Viability of intertwined supply networks: Extending the supply chain resilience angles towards survivability. *International Journal of Production Research*, 58(10), 2904–2915. doi: 10.1080/00207543.2020.1750727.

Joerss, M., Schroder, J., Neuhaus, F., Klink, C., Mann, F. (2016). *Parcel Delivery: The Future of Last Mile.* McKinsey & Company, New York [Online]. Available at: https://www.mckinsey.com/industries/travel-logistics-and-infrastructure/our-insights/how-customer-demands-are-reshaping-last-mile-delivery.

Kiel, D., Müller, J.M., Arnold, C., Voigt, K.I. (2017). Sustainable industrial value creation: Benefits and challenges of Industry 4.0. *International Journal of Innovation Management*, 21(8), 1740015. doi: 10.1142/S1363919617400151.

Klumpp, M. (2018). Automation and artificial intelligence in business logistics systems: Human reactions and collaboration requirements. *International Journal of Logistics Research and Applications*, 21(3), 224–242. doi: 10.1080/13675567.2017.1384451.

Kyriakidis, M., Happee, R., de Winter, J.C.F. (2015). Public opinion on automated driving: Results of an international questionnaire among 5,000 respondents. *Transportation Research Part F: Traffic Psychology and Behaviour*, 32, 127–140. doi: 10.1016/j.trf.2015.04.014.

Manyika, J., Lund, S., Chui, M., Bughin, J., Woetzel, L., Batra, P., Ko, R., Sanghvi, S. (2017). *Jobs Lost, Jobs Gained: Workforce Transitions in a Time of Automation.* McKinsey & Company, New York.

Müller, J.M. and Voigt, K.I. (2018). Sustainable industrial value creation in SMEs: A comparison between Industry 4.0 and Made in China 2025. *International Journal of Precision Engineering and Manufacturing–Green Technology*, 5(5), 659–670. doi: 10.1007/s40684-018-0056-z.

Rana, R. and Bhambri, P. (2024a). Artificial Intelligence and Internet of Things (IoT) facilitated digital twin for Industry 4.0 application domains. In *AI-Driven Digital Twin and Industry 4.0*, Rani, S., Bhambri, P., Kumar, S., Pareek, P.K., Elngar, A.A. (eds). CRC Press, Boca Raton, 168–181. doi: 10.1201/9781003395416-11.

Rana, R. and Bhambri, P. (2024b). Digital twin for sustainable industrial development. In *AI-Driven Digital Twin and Industry 4.0*, Rani, S., Bhambri, P., Kumar, S., Pareek, P.K., Elngar, A.A. (eds). CRC Press, Boca Raton, 241–253. doi: 10.1201/9781003395416-15.

Rana, R. and Bhambri, P. (2025a). Hybrid MCDM (multi-criteria decision-making) approaches for sustainable energy management. In *Modern SuperHyperSoft Computing Trends in Science and Technology*, Smarandache, F. and Majumder, P. (eds). IGI Global, Hershey, 149–184. doi: 10.4018/979-8-3693-6875-6.ch006.

Rana, R. and Bhambri, P. (2025b). Harnessing block chain digital twins for sustainable business operations. In *Practical Frameworks for New-Age Digitalization Business Strategy*, Tee, P., Song, B., Ho, R. (eds). IGI Global, Hershey, 413–446. doi: 10.4018/979-8-3373-2018-2.ch013.

SAE International. (2018). J3016_201806: Taxonomy and definitions. Standard, SAE International [Online]. Available at: https://www.sae.org/standards/content/j3016_201806/.

Schellekens, M. (2015). Self-driving cars and the chilling effect of liability law. *Computer Law & Security Review*, 40, 105518. doi: 10.1016/j.clsr.2020.105518.

Snyder, H. (2019). Literature review as a research methodology: An overview and guidelines. *Journal of Business Research*, 104, 333–339. doi: 10.1016/j.jbusres.2019.07.039.

Stolaroff, J.K., Samaras, C., O'Neill, E.R., Lubers, A., Mitchell, A.S., Ceperley, D. (2018). Energy use and life cycle greenhouse gas emissions of drones for commercial package delivery. *Nature Communications*, 9, 409. doi: 10.1038/s41467-017-02411-5.

Tao, F., Qi, Q., Liu, A., Kusiak, A. (2018). Data-driven smart manufacturing. *Journal of Manufacturing Systems*, 48, 157–169. doi: 10.1016/j.jmsy.2018.01.006.

Thrun, S. (2010). Toward robotic cars. *Communications of the ACM*, 53(4), 99–106. doi: 10.1145/1721654.1721679.

Treiblmaier, H. (2018). The impact of the blockchain on the supply chain: A theory-based research framework and a call for action. *Supply Chain Management: An International Journal*, 23(6), 545–559. doi: 10.1108/SCM-01-2018-0029.

Wamba, S.F., Queiroz, M.M., Trinchera, L. (2020). Dynamics between blockchain adoption determinants and supply chain performance: An empirical investigation. *International Journal of Production Economics*, 229, 107791. doi: 10.1016/j.ijpe.2020.107791.

Wang, Y., Han, J.H., Beynon-Davies, P. (2019). Understanding blockchain technology for future supply chains: A systematic literature review and research agenda. *Supply Chain Management: An International Journal*, 24(1), 62–84. doi: 10.1108/SCM-03-2018-0148.

Winkelhaus, S. and Grosse, E.H. (2020). Logistics 4.0: A systematic review towards a new logistics system. *International Journal of Production Research*, 58(1), 18–43. doi: 10.1080/00207543.2019.1612964.

Wurman, P.R., D'Andrea, R., Mountz, M. (2008). Coordinating hundreds of cooperative, autonomous vehicles in warehouses. *AI Magazine*, 29(1), 9–20. doi: 10.1609/aimag.v29i1.2082.

8

Leveraging Data and Analytics for Next-Generation Supply Chain Resilience

In an era defined by volatility and digital transformation, effective supply chain management has become a critical determinant of competitive advantage. This chapter explores the central role of data as the foundation for optimizing complex, multi-stage supply chains. It examines the challenges facing modern logistics, from material shortages to geopolitical disruptions, and underscores how data-driven strategies enable greater resilience, efficiency and visibility.

The discussion covers key technologies – including enterprise resource planning (ERP) systems, the Internet of Things (IoT), artificial intelligence (AI) and advanced analytics – that facilitate real-time data collection, processing and decision-making. Furthermore, it delves into analytical methods and optimization models, from network design to inventory management, that help managers mitigate risk, reduce costs and enhance operational performance. By leveraging accurate and timely data, organizations can transform their supply chains into agile, intelligent systems capable of navigating a disrupted global landscape.

8.1. Introduction

The success of flexible forms of work in the supply chain is determined by the advantages that can be gained, including high employee mobility and cost reduction (Wirwich 2012).

Chapter written by Karina ZACHARSKA.

1.	Supply Chain (SC) – processes occurring from the moment of obtaining initial supply materials to the consumption of the final product, connecting the supplier and the recipient as well as functions inside and outside the company, which enable the manufacture of the product and the delivery of services to the customer.
2.	SC – a sequence of processes that add value to a product during its flow and processing, from raw materials, through all intermediate forms, to a form that meets the requirements of the end customer.
3.	SC – a network of interconnected and interdependent organizations that, acting on the principle of mutual cooperation, control and streamline the flow of goods and information from suppliers to end users.
4.	SC – mining, manufacturing, commercial and service companies cooperating in various areas, as well as their customers, between whom flows of products, information and financial resources circulate.
5.	SC – a model-designed logistics process (resource flow process) integrated in terms of time, costs, spatial distance and customer service level, using the infrastructure factors and organizational capabilities of a given logistics channel or channels.
6.	SC – a network of producers and service providers who cooperate with each other to process and move goods from the raw material stage to the end-user.
7.	SC – the flow of goods and information through a network of companies.
8.	SC – a system for organizing people, technology, resources, information and processes involved in manufacturing a product and delivering it to the end customer, as well as disposing of products that have lost their useful value.
9.	SC – as a process, a sequence of events in the movement of goods, increasing their value.
10.	LD – as a structure (organization) – a group of companies carrying out joint activities necessary to meet the demand for specific products throughout the entire chain of goods flow – from the acquisition of raw materials to delivery to the end customer. These activities may include development, production, sales, service, procurement, distribution, resource management and support activities.

Table 8.1. *Logistics bound by the supply chain (Ficoń and Zięcina 2020)*

It is worth noting that the first definition of the supply chain was formulated by Keith Oliver in 1982, along with his classic definition covering all stages – from raw materials to the consumer. Wolfgang Partsch, on the contrary, is considered a practical pioneer – he described the concept earlier, and one of the first implementations of SCM was carried out and published by him in 1982 in Germany (Bujak 2015).

8.2. The challenges of today's supply chains

Given the strategic role of supply chains in ensuring the competitiveness of companies, any measures that reduce risk and increase security are appropriate and justified (Staniewska 2021).

Information technology is an indispensable element in building a company's competitive advantage. It streamlines its operations and allows for the application of new methods and trends in management that contribute to improving the efficiency of business entities (Fajczak-Kowalska 2020).

Information technologies are an important element of corporate architecture, and their proper implementation in an organization significantly enhances the efficiency and effectiveness of business processes (Fajczak-Kowalska 2020).

The electronic supply chain has the ability to adapt and engage in both short-term and long-term relationships in the supply chain (Kawa 2010).

A virtual supply chain is established in response to the needs of a specific customer, who can also actively participate in it and take part in the implementation of activities on an ongoing basis (Ostaszewski 2011).

The effectiveness of activities depends largely on the use of IT tools. Therefore, as well as in view of the cooperation established by companies within logistics processes, IT systems must meet a number of requirements (Witkowski 2010).

Thanks to the use of computer systems and appropriate support software, logistics operations involving many complex tasks, such as delivery planning and inventory management, have largely become routine tasks (Cudziło 2013).

8.3. The role of data as the foundation for optimization

Growing competition in a globalized environment increases the complexity of supply chains and thus raises the requirements for processing and exchanging information between participants in order to improve supply chain performance (Gradowicz and Pasek 2011).

In relation to supply chain management, analytics can be defined as both quantitative and qualitative methods for improving the structure and competitiveness of the supply chain (Surowiec 2018b).

An important topic that can be addressed using the collected data is key performance indicators (KPIs). KPI can be defined as a key performance indicator, a carrier of information in the form of an indicator, an absolute measure or a statistic of a specific process, used to quantify achievements (technical, organizational and economic), identifying priority processes, operations, activities and values that motivate employees to achieve the company's goals and strategies (Racka 2016; Czerwińska and Andrzej Pacana 2020).

8.4. The importance of data in supply chain management

From the outset, a distinction must be made between data and information: "data is simply facts – recorded measurements of a given phenomenon – while information is a structure composed of facts in a form suitable for decision-making" (Torbacki and Torbacka 2015). Proper data analysis allows managers to choose the best solutions for their companies in a modern, conscious and fully responsible manner. The importance of data in decision-making processes:

1. Data-driven decisions – this is a method of decision-making based on reliably collected and analyzed statistical data within a company, while intuition and gut feelings are completely disregarded. In order to properly prepare data according to the above technique (data-driven decisions), it must first be collected, sorted, grouped and analyzed (statistical methods or business analysis are best used for this purpose).

2. Improving efficiency in operational activities – conscious data analysis allows managers to identify bottlenecks and eliminate inefficiencies. This improves the work of, for example, the logistics department and thus improves the timeliness of deliveries and reduces delivery waiting times.

3. Traceability and visibility – data that is updated on an ongoing basis enables: a quick response to changes in the level of raw materials for production or, for example, allows shipments to be tracked, i.e. GPS and RFID systems, which are now standard. It is extremely important to monitor stock levels in warehouses in real time, as this information is essential for responding quickly and preventing production interruptions.

4. Cooperation and integration with partners – it is worth noting that reliable data compilation enables cooperation with suppliers, partners and customers. An example

of this is platforms that integrate data from various ERP, SAP or SCM sources. Data synchronized in this way helps to improve business management.

5. Risk management – statistical data from a specific time period and current data make it possible to eliminate or minimize the risk associated with changes in raw material prices or supply disruptions, which in turn may be caused by geopolitical or climatic changes.

6. Environmental, social and governance – in addition to its impact on the company's image, environmental data analysis allows us to determine the amount of CO_2 emissions throughout the supply chain and whether the company is within the norms or needs to take action because the norms have been exceeded (Murphy and Wood 2011).

8.5. Technologies supporting data collection and analysis

In today's reality, companies use highly specialized technologies dedicated to the effective collection and analysis of data. Some of the most popular ones are as follows:

1. Enterprise Resource Planning (ERP) systems – a specially built and designed IT platform designed to support the functioning of a company in its individual departments.

2. Advanced Planning and Scheduling (APS) systems – these are modern tools used for the production planning process. APS systems enable efficient management of the production planning process and its costs. Designing a production planning system for each company is a serious challenge. Unfortunately, there are no ideal models; none describe all the essential features of the process, and known algorithms perform better or worse in different circumstances. Very accurate modeling of the production process and very detailed planning are not always necessary. Therefore, making a choice requires knowledge of both the characteristics of the models and the effectiveness of the algorithms, as well as in-depth knowledge of the production process (Szymczak 2013).

3. Business Intelligence (BI) systems – can be defined as a comprehensive solution that is primarily used for the graphical presentation of results.

4. Big Data and Data Analytics Platforms – in other words, these are huge data sets for which basic data preparation methods, such as Excel, are insufficient. The above platforms are highly specialized analytical tools that are used to store, analyze and then present data, most often using graphical charts, in order to obtain the best possible management decision. These tools usually operate in the cloud, as the size of the files makes it easier to achieve operational fluidity in the cloud.

Benefits	Barriers
Support for decision-making	Lack of data availability
Increased transparency	Inability to identify the most needed information
Better risk management in the supply chain	Security risks
Improved supply chain cost management	Lack of support from management
Strengthened bargaining position in negotiations with suppliers	Irrelevant data value
Improved supply chain efficiency	Privacy/confidentiality issues
Enhanced demand planning capabilities	Lack of policies and oversight structures
Expanded sales and operations planning capabilities	Lack of skills to use available data
Stronger bargaining position in negotiations with customers	Lack of demand/lack of benefits
Ability to respond more quickly to changing conditions	Management difficulties
Ability to make decisions more quickly	Cost of currently available solutions
Greater ability to shape relationships with suppliers	Lack of integration with existing systems
Greater ability to shape relationships with customers	Lack of qualified staff
	Reluctance to change
	Lack of suitable SCM solutions
	Time constraints

Table 8.2. *Benefits and barriers to the use of Big Data in supply chain management (Kaczmarczyk 2014). Source: Schoenherr (2015, pp. 122–123)*

In summary, analytical platforms are designed to collect, collate and group data from various sources, such as ERP systems, Customer Relationship Management (CRM) systems and social media (Schoenherr 2015). Big Data and Data Analytics Platforms are the most effective for everything from simple statistics to extensive analysis, where data comes from various sources and is analyzed using advanced predictive models. Some examples of analyses where Big Data and Data Analytics Platforms are: descriptive analysis, predictive analysis, diagnostic analysis, prescriptive analysis, real-time analysis and exploratory analysis.

5. Machine Learning and AI – these are mathematical algorithms built on the basis of artificial intelligence:

– Predictive Modeling, used for predicting events based on historical data, applied in: sales or demand forecasting, customer churn prediction, credit risk assessment and machine failure prediction.

– Classification and Segmentation, used for classifying, ordering and sorting data, applied in spam detection, customer segmentation and image classification.

– Unsupervised Learning, applied in: customer clustering (e.g. for marketing) and data dimension reduction (principal component analysis (PCA), t-distributed stochastic neighbor embedding (t-SNE)).

– Anomaly Detection used for identification of errors in data, applied in detection of financial fraud.

– Natural Language Processing (NLP), applied in: chatbots and voice assistants and sentiment analysis.

– Computer Vision used for object and face recognition applied in: medical diagnostics based on images and visual inspection in production.

– Generative AI used for generating text, images and code and applied in the creation of synthetic data and product recommendations.

6. IoT – this is the conscious connection of various devices to the internet, which is designed to classify data, collect it and prepare simple reports from it, which are intended to assist in decision-making or remotely support managers. An example of IoT in manufacturing is a sensor connected to a production machine that monitors all deviations from the norm and, as a result, prevents breakdowns or non-compliant products (Surowiec 2018).

The multiple functionalities of the IoT allow for flexibility, consistency and efficient decision-making. However, the IoT platform not only brings new opportunities but can also generate new threats, which may pose an additional problem in the implementation of various types of systems based on IoT devices (Ogórek and Zaskórski 2018).

7. SCM software with built-in analytics – can be presented as an IT system designed to manage the entire supply chain using integrated analytical tools. SCM software with built-in analytics allows for the following activities, which take place in real time or in the past:

– Monitoring – automatic, intelligent and based on specific figures. Data is collected, sorted and analyzed on an ongoing basis. This allows for a faster response to failures, downtime or delays. An example of the use of monitoring in business is the shipping or delivery process, where the system immediately informs both the recipient and the supplier of the status of the shipment.

– Forecasting – by collecting current and historical data, where forecasts are made using advanced technologies. SCM software with built-in analytics enables forecasting through: the development and use of highly specialized algorithms, searching for different forecasts, preparing different scenarios and consolidating data from different sources. The purpose of data collection is to build a complete picture of reality.

The role of forecasting	Benefits of forecasting
1. Demand predictions	Adequate inventory levels in stock
2. Cost and revenue forecasting	Assistance with budget planning
3. Building various scenarios	Informed decision-making "what's next"
4. Disruption forecasting	Effective and informed risk management

Table 8.3. *Role and benefits of forecasting*

In summary, SCM software with built-in analytics enables data forecasting through the use of algorithms, the preparation of various forecasts, the preparation of various scenarios and the integration of diverse data.

– Analysing – allows for the consideration of all aspects of supply chain management. This process involves all departments within the company, from purchasing, production, maintenance, accounting, quality control, logistics, sales support and the sales department. Analytical results using today's rapid analytical methods provide answers in seconds about the optimal decision and what needs to be done to make it right. This type of analysis makes managers more resourceful. Methods for effectively analyzing data include:

i. Collecting and integrating supply chain data – systems collect external data (i.e. CRM, WMS, TMS and ERP), sensor data, operational data and transactional data. The benefits of data collection and consolidation include a current overview of the company's processes.

ii. Root cause analysis (RCA) – this is an analysis used to identify difficulties, not just their symptoms. Its main goal is to eliminate the problem and find the root cause. It is typically used in industries such as the automotive industry, where answering the question of what caused it is extremely important. The most popular RCA methods include: 5 Whys, Ishikawa Diagram, Pareto Analysis and FTA. The benefits of using these methods include process improvement and reducing the likelihood of recurrence.

iii. Predictive and prescriptive analytics – these are highly advanced analytical methods that help companies estimate forecasts to achieve the most informed decisions. Predictive analytics – allows for estimating what might happen in the future, but calculations are based on historical data. Statistical models and machine learning are suitable for these analyses. For example, in the banking sector, these methods are used to assess creditworthiness, and in sales departments, they are used to estimate demand for goods. Prescriptive analytics – its task is to find a solution that will improve results. Its operating methods primarily involve simulations and algorithms. This method is used in logistics optimization processes and advanced marketing activities, which aim to best match the offer to customer expectations.

iv. Operational analysis – this method, in turn, is designed to optimize, for example, inventory levels and process visualizations. Data is analyzed in real time, enabling rapid response.

v. Benchmarking – this is a comparative method that compares a product with its competitors and identifies differences and areas for optimization. Benchmarking involves comparing oneself with the best organizations – the best in a given class – learning from them good principles, methods and approaches to business management, and then implementing improvements and perfecting these patterns in one's own operations (Ogórek and Zaskórski 2018).

vi. Historical analysis – supply chain analysis is based on historical data. It aims to identify bottlenecks in the supply chain, identify trends and draw conclusions on how to improve and refine SCM. The above analyses primarily include demand, sales, supplier collaboration, inventory analysis and logistics costs. Excel spreadsheets, CRM and ERP can be classified as tools for performing operations.

vii. Graphical data representation and dashboards – these are the main components of analysis, allowing for the explanation of existing trends or anomalies. The main purpose of visualization is to present data in the form of charts, graphs and diagrams. The main benefit is to visualize trends and anomalies and confirm hypotheses. This method, through the pictorial presentation of results, facilitates decision-making.

– Optimization, i.e. global supply chain management at all levels and dimensions. SCM with embedded analytics supports the optimization process in Table 8.4.

SCM – methods	**Optimization**	**Examples**
Forecasting	Statistical methods and artificial intelligence	Forecasting a given product and its demand over time or season
Analysis of historical data	Recognizing patterns and current trends	Analyzing data from sales departments to better plan production
Detecting anomalies and risks	Unconventional algorithms	Identifying delays for a specific customer to prevent disruption of cooperation
Scenario analysis	Discussing multiple changes	Consistency, better decisions
Logistics cost optimization	GPS algorithms	Reducing fuel costs, saving time

Table 8.4. *SCM methods*

8.6. Analytical methods and optimization models in supply chain management

Decision-making in business should be based on clearly established criteria, preferably economic ones, such as costs. The supply chain management process is highly complex. It consists of numerous ancillary activities aimed at improving logistics in the broadest sense (Źródło-Loda 2012). First and foremost, as mentioned, analytical and optimization methods are widely used in the logistics process, including managing logistics networks, building delivery schedules, optimizing inventory and production. Finally, a crucial aspect to which these methods are applied is the optimization of transport routes (Milewski 2007).

In summary, analytical methods show where a company is currently, while optimization models demonstrate how to consider and what to take into account to obtain the best possible decision. As already mentioned, the most important and most frequently used analytical methods in supply chain management include data analytics, BI, predictive analysis and simulations. Optimization models, on the contrary, are designed to find the most advantageous and accurate solution, which in turn optimizes costs or optimizes production efficiency. Typically, these are mathematical models or mathematical algorithms that play a leading role in tasks that are in turn used in operations research, primarily in logistics, business management or IT. The most popular models include:

– Network models – designed, for example, to optimize the transport of supplies to customers. Network models are primarily transport models that streamline the operation of logistics departments. They can be characterized as highly efficient and computationally fast, which is why managers often choose these solutions. Examples of the most popular models include (Bhambri and Bajdor 2024; Bhambri and Kumar 2024; Bhambri et al. 2024; Rana and Bhambri 2024a, 2024b):

i. Assignment flow – a network model designed to assign employees to tasks.

ii. Minimum cost flow – deliveries of goods to stores or warehouses at the lowest prices.

iii. Shortest route problem – a proposal, for example, for the shortest route from manufacturing facility A to warehouse B.

iv. Maximum flow (max-flow) – in other words, the maximum quantity of raw materials or finished goods that can be sent through the logistics network.

v. Dispatcher's work problem (TSL) – the shortest route from point A to point B.

Managers primarily use graph algorithms, such as Bellman-Ford or Dijkstra, as well as Google OR-Tools and Gurobi libraries, to implement these network models.

– Location models – designed to select locations best suited to the current situation, for example, the optimal location for building a factory, so that future costs are also as favorable as possible for customers, contractors and raw material suppliers. Examples of typical location models include the cost model (Weber) – designed to optimize and minimize costs related to broadly defined transportation; the p-center model – optimizes the transport route from the customer to the nearest desired location; the hierarchical model – differentiating between different levels of location of the considered services, for example, local or regional; the p-median model – minimizing the sum of distances between service points and customers; and the covering model – the maximum number of customers located within a specified kilometer range. Location models are particularly useful when designing new logistics centers, for example, when selecting a new site for a hospital or gas station. Managers planning shopping centers or warehouse locations also readily use these models.

– Inventory management model – in terms of optimization models, this primarily involves developing a mathematical model of the decision-making process, the primary goal of which is to minimize inventory costs. Specifically, inventory levels must be maintained at a level sufficient for production. Stock management models are based on objective functions and decision variables:

i. Deterministic optimization models – which assume that all data (demand, costs and delivery time) are known or unknown (Smyk 2023).

– Economic Order Quantity (EOO) model – the goal of the EOO model is to plan the purchase of enough goods to consciously neutralize stockpiles.

Wagner-Whitin model (multi-period, deterministic) – this is one of the models that performs best and is the most accurate for inventory management. This model enables efficient inventory management over a defined period of time. However, a prerequisite for its use is knowledge of demand. The main goal of this model is to optimize inventory within the enterprise, thereby optimizing ordering costs and minimizing inventory holding costs. The Wagner-Whitin model is a dynamic model, and its main task is to search through all alternative ordering methods and, consequently, select the most advantageous scenario.

ii. Stochastic optimization models – most stochastic optimization methods are heuristic in nature: our intuition, often based on extensive experience, usually suggests that the method will be effective in practice, and indeed, this is often the case (Smyk 2023). Stochastic models incorporate uncertainty in the input data into their design. This is a significant difference compared to deterministic models, where all data is known and certain. Stochastic models typically include variables such as costs, demand and delivery times. It is worth mentioning that stochastic methods contain random elements, for example, variables with a known distribution (Bhambri and Kumar 2024). Their main task is to find the most accurate solution, taking into account uncertainty. The above-mentioned models are based on statistical, probabilistic methods. Their applications in enterprises are diverse. Logistics departments primarily use these models for optimization, such as route optimization or for uncertain delivery routes. Another department that regularly uses the above optimization models is production (e.g. for production planning with unknown demand) and finance (financial management during turbulent economic times). The most important stochastic models include:

– Stochastic programming – this model is typically used to prepare scenarios before uncertainty factors are introduced. A prime example in a company is production planning, before the company knows actual demand. In this case, various scenarios are modeled, and the objective function is the expected cost or profit.

– Chance-constrained programming – in this method, certain assumptions must be met when forecasting, i.e. inventory levels must be at 95% for monthly production planning.

– Two-stage stochastic programming – this method provides answers to problems in two stages: stage 1 provides an answer to the question "here and now" but does not take into account uncertainty, while stage 2 involves incorporating uncertainty factors into the process.

– Stochastic dynamic programming – this method is typically used in situations where decisions are made repeatedly and the system states are random variables.

Stochastic optimization models have both advantages and disadvantages. The main disadvantage of this method is that it is time-consuming and computationally intensive. Probabilistic data (distributions, scenarios) are required to ensure complete results, which unfortunately also involves a significant amount of work. A significant advantage of the above-mentioned methods is better risk analysis, which, in turn, allows for more accurate decision-making, resulting in the correct decision.

– Linear programming (LP) and integer programming (PC) – these are optimization techniques used to find the best, most accurate solution to a given problem under specific conditions:

i. LP – the basic assumption of the solution is to find the maximum or minimum given linear constraints. This methodology is best used when there is a need to maximize or minimize quantities such as profit or material consumption. Examples of current applications include production planning (PL – allows for answering the question of how to manage resources, such as materials and raw materials, to optimize profit), logistics and transportation (how to optimize transportation costs, for example, with known unit costs), and blending problems (how to prepare appropriate mixtures, for example, vitamin premixes, to achieve the appropriate product quality at the right price).

ii. PC – this is a type of LP where some variables must be integers.

There are two approaches worth considering here:

- Integer Linear Programming (ILP) – when all variables are integers, PC is required.

- However, if some variables are integers, we consider Mixed Integer Linear Programming (MILP).

These methods work well when the values entered into the algorithm cannot be fractional, such as the number of machines needed for production or the number of employees scheduled for work. Typical everyday applications include employee scheduling in the production process in an enterprise, bin packing and knapsack – how to optimally pack a finished product.

– Heuristics and metaheuristics – these are advanced optimization techniques.

Heuristic methods are imprecise and do not provide optimal solutions, but they often provide a sufficiently good solution within a given time. The main advantages of this method are: simplicity, speed and relatively low arithmetic. A suitable methodology is the nearest neighbor algorithm, which works well for the TSP.

Metaheuristic methods are methods that aim to find a better solution using advanced optimization techniques. Due to the complexity of the algorithms, the recommended application is problems based on combinatorial optimization. The advantage of this methodology is finding the most optimal solution, but the disadvantage is the multi-shift nature and, consequently, the computational time involved. Examples of tools include the ant colony algorithm and the genetic algorithm.

8.7. Conclusion

As previously mentioned, supply chain management encompasses the following departments within a company: planning, production, purchasing, supply logistics, warehouse management and distribution logistics, demand management and forecasting, and customer service. It also coordinates the flow of goods and services. This process is designed to ensure the continuity of supply and production from suppliers to the end customer. The above discussion has demonstrated that the supply chain process functions better when supported by a range of IT tools designed to improve its efficiency. IT tools, ranging from the simplest (Excel spreadsheets) to complex algorithms, are designed to help define the decision-making process and ultimately find the most accurate decision. The choice of methodology is primarily based on the type of problem, its complexity and the available data. The desired goal is crucial when selecting optimization tools, and consequently, the manager's preference, which method is closer to them, and their experience. Ultimately, it is desirable to obtain a decision that optimizes costs, time, inventory levels and ensures customer satisfaction. Supply chain management combines strategic and operational management. To achieve satisfactory results, customers, suppliers and logistics operators must also be involved, resulting in effective enterprise management. A supply chain is a complex process dependent on numerous external and internal factors within the enterprise. It requires continuous improvement and support from new information technologies. New information technologies are designed to optimize processes to ultimately achieve the best possible results. In an age of digitization, where speed, quality and quantity of the final product are paramount, managers are forced to seek ever-increasing solutions equipped with complex mathematical algorithms designed to streamline the supply chain process.

8.8. References

Bhambri, P. and Bajdor, P. (2024). Technological sustainability unveiled: A comprehensive examination of economic, social, and environmental dimensions. In *Handbook of Technological Sustainability: Innovation and Environmental Awareness*, Bhambri, P. and Bajdor, P. (eds). CRC Press, Boca Raton, FL.

Bhambri, P. and Kumar, S. (2024). Protecting sustainable supply chains from cyber threats. In *Digital Sustainability: Navigating Entrepreneurship in the Information Age*, Bhambri, P. and Paweloszek, I. (eds). CRC Press, Boca Raton, FL.

Bhambri, P., Rani, S., Khang, A. (2024). AI-driven digital twin and resource optimization in Industry 4.0 ecosystem. In *Intelligent Techniques for Predictive Data Analytics*, Singh, N., Birla, S., Ansari, M.D., Shukla, N.K. (eds). Wiley-IEEE Press, Hoboken, NJ.

Bujak, A. (2015). Management and functioning of the modern and prospective supply chain. *Scientific Journals of the Silesian University*, 249, 251.

Cudziło, M. (2013). Selected decision-making problems in managing logistics processes. *Scientific Journals of Poznan University of Technology*, 61, 5–18.

Czerwińska, K. and Andrzej Pacana, A. (2020). Key performance indicators (KPI). Ignacy Łukasiewicz Rzeszów University of Technology.

Fajczak-Kowalska, A. (ed.) (2020). Technologies and new trends in management and the development of enterprises in the TSL sector; Technologies and new trends in management and the development of enterprises in the sector. *Monographs of the Lodz University of Technology*.

Ficoń, K., and Zięcina, M. (2020). Logistics loaded with supply chains. *Systemy Logistyczne Wojsk Учредители: Wojskowa Akademia Techniczna w Warszawie*, 53(2), 33–52.

Gradowicz, C. and Pasek, K. (2011). Modern technologies and information systems in supply chain management in logistics centers. *Acta Universitatis Lodziensis, Folia Economica*, 251.

Kaczmarczyk, W. (2014). Overview of advanced production planning models. AGH University of Krakow.

Kawa, A. (2010). Supply chain strategies. In *Supply Chain*, Ciesielski, M. and Długosz, J. (eds). Polish Economic Publishing House, Warsaw.

Milewski, D. (2007). The issue of complete vehicle transports. *Logistics*, 3, 41.

Murphy, P.R., and Wood, D.F. (2011). *Contemporary Logistics*, 10th edition. Prentice Hall, Upper Saddle River, NJ.

Ogórek, M. and Zaskórski, P. (2018). Internet of Things in the integration of crisis management processes. *Scientific Journals of the Częstochowa University of Technology*, 213.

Ostaszewski, J. (ed.) (2011). Studies and works of the College of Management and Finance. *Scientific Journal*, 108, 63.

Racka, K. (2016). Big Data – significance, applications, and technological solutions. *Scientific Notebooks of PWSZ*, XXIII.

Rana, R. and Bhambri, P. (2024a). Digital twin for sustainable industrial development. In *AI-Driven Digital Twin and Industry 4.0: A Conceptual Framework with Applications*, Rani, S., Bhambri, P., Kumar, S., Pareek, P.K., Elngar, A.A. (eds). CRC Press, Boca Raton, FL.

Rana, R. and Bhambri, P. (2024b). Environmental challenges and technological solutions. In *Handbook of Technological Sustainability: Innovation and Environmental Awareness*, Bhambri, P. and Bajdor, P. (eds). CRC Press, Boca Raton, FL.

Schoenherr, S.-P. (2015). Data science, predictive analytics and Big Data in supply chain management: Current state and future potential. *Journal of Business Logistics*, 36, 122–123.

Smyk, S. (2023). Optimization as a challenge for logistics managers. *Material Economy and Logistics*, 1, 10.

Staniewska, E. (2021). Selected aspects of supply chain security management. *Military Logistics Systems Notebook*, 54.

Surowiec, A. (2018a). The impact of Big Data and cloud computing on supply chain management. *Scientific Journals of the Częstochowa University of Technology*.

Surowiec, A. (2018b). The influence of big data and cloud computing on management in supply chains. *Notebook of the Częstochowa University of Technology*, 30.

Szymczak, M. (2013). Information management models in the supply chain. *Organization and Management*, 4(157), 36.

Torbacki, W. and Torbacka, M. (2015). KPIs in information systems for the logistics industry. TTS Track Transport Technology. *Scientific and Publishing Institute*, 12.

Waller, M. and Fawcett, S. (2013). Data science, predictive analytics, and Big Data: A revolution that will transform supply chain design and management. *Journal of Business Logistics*, 34(2), 80. doi: 10.1111/jbl.12010.

Wirwich, S. (2012). Supply chain management – Challenges in the context of new forms of work. *Logistic*, 5, 245.

Witkowski, J. (2010). Supply chain management. In *Concepts. Procedures. Experiences.* Polish Economic Publishing House, Warsaw.

Źródło-Loda, M. (2012). Benchmarking – Modern concept of organization management. *Scientific Notebooks of the Higher Vocational School in Krosno.*

9

Data-driven Supply Chain Optimization

In the aftermath of the COVID-19 pandemic, data-driven optimization has become a strategic imperative for modern supply chains, which – relying on trustworthy data and machine learning algorithms – must respond faster and more flexibly than ever before. By placing AI-supported optimization at the core of supply chain strategy, this chapter pursues two objectives: (1) it provides an overview of the applications of big data analytics, digital twins and artificial intelligence across the supply chain and (2) it illustrates the practical use of H2O AutoML based on an empirical case study. The chapter summarizes academic publications from 2015 to 2025, presenting documented use cases of AI in supply chain processes and identifying key analytical tasks – classification, regression and time series forecasting – along with their resulting business benefits. This structured perspective also reveals research gaps, particularly concerning generative digital twins and the explainability of machine learning models. The empirical component of this chapter is based on a publicly available dataset entitled "Daily Demand Forecasting Orders", containing 60 consecutive days of observations from a large Brazilian logistics company. The study investigates whether H2O AutoML can generate daily order forecasts with greater accuracy than a carefully selected MLP (Multi-Layer Perceptron) network. Three models were compared: a manually tuned MLP BASELINE, AUTOML NN (neural networks) and AUTOML ALL (the full set of algorithms). The best-performing model, AUTOML NN, reduced the root mean square error (RMSE) from approximately 14,400 orders to approximately 2,230 orders, significantly outperforming both the MLP BASELINE and the AUTOML ALL variant.

9.1. Introduction

Supply chain management (SCM) in a global dimension is becoming an important issue for numerous enterprises. It covers the interests of suppliers all over the world as well as the focus on a local, domestic and international consumer (Kudelska and Niedbal 2020). The COVID-19 pandemic exposed the fragility of global supply chains and accelerated the shift from intuition-based management

---

Chapter written by Rafał NIEDBAL, Paula PYPŁACZ and Muhammad Asif KHAN.

towards strategies grounded in systematic data analysis. The integration of artificial intelligence (AI) technologies into SCM has emerged as a key driver of enhanced efficiency, agility and responsiveness in contemporary business operations (Joel et al. 2024). The concept of data-driven supply chain optimization assumes that value-generating decisions arise from the integration of four SCM streams – materials, finance, business processes and information (Li and Liu 2019) – with the quality and speed of information processing acting as decisive factors for competitive advantage.

It is worth noting that the most critical task in AutoML is the automatic tuning of hyperparameters to achieve optimal performance (Masood and Sherif 2021). AutoML modules – such as H2O AutoML, part of the H2O.ai framework – offer a minimalist parameter interface, a broad selection of algorithms and built-in ensembling mechanisms.

This chapter seeks to address two research objectives. First, it presents a literature review on the application of big data (BD), digital twins (DTs), AI and ML in optimizing processes across the entire supply chain. This review aims to highlight key development trends and identify existing research gaps. Second, a case study is presented in which H2O AutoML is used to forecast daily order volumes based on a publicly available dataset. This enables an empirical assessment of the effectiveness of a low-code approach in the context of supply chain optimization. The structure of the chapter is as follows: section 9.2 provides a literature review on data-driven SCM; section 9.3 explains the role of AutoML in enhancing supply chain operations and presents the results of the conducted experiment and section 9.4 offers concluding remarks, managerial implications and directions for future research.

9.2. Literature review

9.2.1. *Big data*

The growing importance of big data analytics (BDA) in economic practice has led to decision-making processes in SCM increasingly relying on data analysis rather than managerial intuition (Li and Liu 2019). However, traditional SCM models limit the full exploitation of information potential, necessitating a redefinition of existing methods and tools. BDA is already widely applied across functional areas of the supply chain – from demand forecasting and inventory planning to transport management – provided that appropriate managerial practices and technical infrastructure solutions are in place.

A systematic literature review covering the years 2015–2023 (Alsolbi et al. 2023) identified a significant research gap: the lack of case studies documenting real-world BDA implementations in SCM. The most critical implementation barrier is the optimization of hardware and software configurations to balance cost and performance. Additional challenges include ensuring continuous data acquisition, data cleaning and standardization, as well as issues related to information security and quality (Richey et al. 2016). These factors complicate the implementation of BD solutions and call for the development of coherent data management strategies.

Literature research conducted by Nguyen et al. (2017) showed that BDA most frequently supports decision-making in logistics and transportation, followed by production, warehousing, demand management and procurement. Only a small portion of academic publications adopts a holistic perspective on the supply chain – for instance, in terms of resilience or sustainability.

Wang et al. (2016) propose a broad, integrated Big Data Business Analytics (BDBA) paradigm that combines two complementary components: Big Data (BD) and Business Analytics (BA). The first component refers to an organization's infrastructural capabilities in acquiring and processing data streams characterized by high velocity, significant variety and large volume. The second component encompasses a set of analytical methods – ranging from statistics and econometrics to simulation modeling and optimization algorithms – aimed at extracting knowledge from data and transferring it into the decision-making process, particularly in the context of SCM.

The importance of data-driven analytics is also emphasized by the work of Li et al. (2024), who developed a three-stage diagnostic framework (structural mapping, dynamic modeling and causal analysis) for multi-node chains of platform-based products. Their case study revealed that reducing product variety improves planning accuracy and shortens the Order Fulfilment Cycle Time (OFCT). Furthermore, the efficient placement of inventory depends on the relationship between forecast accuracy and the duration of production and transportation cycles. When lead times are long, locating inventory closer to the customer helps reduce OFCT. However, in situations of low forecast accuracy, better outcomes are achieved through upstream inventory placement, thanks to the effect of inventory pooling – i.e. consolidating stock into a single central safety buffer rather than maintaining multiple smaller buffers near the customer. By aggregating demand from multiple channels, this approach smooths variability and enables lower total stock levels while maintaining (or even improving) product availability (Bhambri et al. 2024b). These findings confirm the pivotal role of data in managing variability and disruptions within supply networks.

Recent advances in machine learning (ML) and computational technology have further reinforced the relevance of BDA in SCM (Lee and Mangalaraj 2022). Internal disruptions – such as port congestion or container shortages – and external factors, including component scarcities or sudden demand surges, have highlighted the extent of uncertainty in supply chains. These developments underscore the value of BDA in adapting to shifting customer preferences and enhancing supply chain resilience. For these reasons, interest in BDA in SCM continues to grow among both practitioners and scholars.

9.2.2. *DT*

A DT is defined as a digital representation of a physical object, product, device, person, process, production facility or even an entire business ecosystem (Hofmann and Branding 2019). This model is constructed based on data streams acquired from Internet of Things (IoT) sensors installed on or integrated into the physical reference object. Such integration enables engineers to continuously monitor operational parameters and simulate system dynamics, providing both structural and operational insights into the real-time condition of the object. Planned modifications can first be implemented and validated in the DT environment, allowing for predictive evaluation of the consequences of proposed changes while minimizing the risk of interference with the physical system (Abouzid and Saidi 2023).

DT technology is gaining prominence due to its ability to enhance resource and process management in logistics (Liu et al. 2024). The increasing complexity of global supply networks, amplified by the frequency of disruptions, underscores the need for supportive digital tools, including DTs (Lugaresi et al. 2023). Ivanov (2025) distinguishes between two principal approaches to building DTs: the *top-down* (object-driven) approach, based on a predefined structural model of the supply chain, and the *bottom-up* (data-driven) approach, in which the model emerges from multidimensional real-time data streams. The data-driven variant assumes incomplete observability and continuous system variability, thereby requiring automatic and decentralized adaptation of the twin to current market conditions, making it particularly suitable in environments characterized by frequent disruptions. At the same time, Ivanov (2025) highlights the risk of hallucinations in generative algorithms and emphasizes the need to couple AI models with expert knowledge and final human validation of the insights generated.

According to Abouzid and Saidi (2023), DT technology, in the context of supply chains, constitutes an advanced tool for real-time monitoring of the logistics network. This solution employs AI algorithms to generate forecasts and predict potential disruptions in supply chain operations. It is based on real-time data from IoT sensors, product *track-and-trace* systems, radio-frequency identification (RFID) technologies, external sources reporting natural, financial or political risks, as well as historical data on previous disruptions (Rana and Bhambri 2024d). When anomalies are detected, it becomes possible to simulate the dynamics of these disruptions and evaluate alternative topological configurations of the supply network.

The perspective on DT applications in logistics is further expanded by the findings of Khan and Tabasum (2025), who focus on supply chains in the healthcare sector. The researchers argue that the implementation of DTs – leveraging continuous monitoring, predictive analytics and scenario-based simulations – leads to measurable improvements in key performance indicators. These include increased inventory accuracy, reduced order fulfillment lead times, maintenance of cold chain continuity and lower operational costs. The result is a more flexible and resilient supply network that ensures timely and equitable access to medical supplies in both urban and rural settings (Rana and Bhambri 2024b).

9.2.3. *AI in supply chains*

The development of AI contributes significantly to the advancement of SCM, encompassing both operational and strategic domains. A literature review conducted by Atwani et al. (2022) systematizes AI applications across four key SCM processes: (1) demand forecasting and planning, (2) procurement and sourcing, (3) production and inventory management and (4) transportation and distribution. The authors highlight the dominant role of ML in all of these areas, alongside the widespread use of genetic algorithms. Artificial neural networks (ANNs) are particularly applied in supplier relationship management, supplier selection and production process optimization. AI enhances cost efficiency, agility and the sustainability of logistics operations while simultaneously strengthening resilience to disruptions (McCrea 2025; Samuels 2025).

Empirical analyses conducted by Lin et al. (2022) confirm that integrating AI with SCM systems enables visualization, automation and intelligent control of flows across the entire supply chain. This integration leads to reduced operational costs and improved responsiveness to fluctuating demand. Similarly, the Deloitte report *Managing a Modern Supply Chain: Utilizing AI to Combat Complexity* (Mussomeli et al. 2023) indicates that generative and predictive AI models accelerate planning, procurement, production and maintenance activities, delivering documented financial benefits and generating substantial cost savings for enterprises.

Companies can integrate AI tools with various advanced technologies operating within the supply network, allowing for full process transparency and efficient information flows throughout the logistics chain (Bhambri and Rani 2024). For instance, AI systems analyze data streams from IoT devices – such as sensors mounted on transport vehicles or pallets – that monitor mechanical damage or temperature excursions in sensitive materials (Bhambri et al. 2024a). The automatic collection and processing of this information enables immediate action, such as rerouting deliveries or ordering replacements, which in turn minimizes downtime and reduces operational costs (Gaus et al. 2018).

In the context of growing macroeconomic uncertainty and frequent logistical disruptions, the supply chain's ability to adapt and recover quickly has become critically important. Riad et al. (2024) argue that the integration of ML, predictive analytics and real-time data processing strengthens both the preventive (resistance) and regenerative (recovery) components of supply chain resilience. Practical outcomes include improved demand forecast accuracy, reduced stockouts and lower levels of excess inventory. Complementary studies by Elufioye (2024) and Silva (2024) confirm that predictive AI analytics enhances delivery punctuality, increases labor productivity and reduces the carbon footprint per unit of production. Singh et al. (2023), meanwhile, highlight the growing role of AI in supplier selection and evaluation, which contributes to improved quality and reliability of deliveries.

However, the full implementation of AI in SCM faces a significant challenge: the low explainability of algorithmic decisions. Kosasih et al. (2024) identify neurosymbolic AI – which combines deep neural networks (DNNs) with symbolic representations of facts and rules – as a promising research direction. This hybrid architecture allows for the processing of unstructured data through neural models while providing transparent justifications, thereby facilitating model acceptance among stakeholders (Bhambri and Paweloszek 2024).

The issue of sustainability is becoming an equally important priority in the implementation of AI. As noted in the State of Supply Chain Sustainability 2024 report (Velázquez Martínez and Arnold 2024), monitoring and reducing Scope 3 emissions represents one of the most difficult challenges facing enterprises. Reducing Scope 3 emissions within the supply chain involves limiting indirect greenhouse gas emissions generated by suppliers (upstream) as well as by product usage and end-of-life processes (downstream). This includes, among other actions, collaborating with suppliers on energy efficiency, selecting low-emission raw materials and transport methods and designing products with circularity in mind (Borchardt et al. 2025). Research conducted by the MIT Sustainable Supply Chain Lab focuses on the use of Green AI[1] and ML to improve the tracking of such emissions and to design decarburization pathways – efforts that require broad collaboration among supply chain stakeholders (Velázquez Martínez and Arnold 2024).

1 Green AI refers to an approach to AI research and deployment that emphasizes minimizing energy consumption and the carbon footprint associated with training and running AI models. By adopting Green AI practices, organizations can develop advanced AI systems while simultaneously reducing operational costs and their environmental impact.

Empirical studies and consulting recommendations consistently indicate that AI applications – from advanced ML to explainable neurosymbolic models – are key to improving the efficiency, resilience and sustainability of global supply chains. However, the successful scaling of these solutions depends on an integrated approach that combines business strategy, data preparedness, model transparency and the active engagement of end-users (Bhambri and Starostka-Patyk 2024).

9.2.4. *ML in supply chain optimization*

Advances in data analytics and ML are transforming modern SCM by providing tools that enable more effective responses to uncertainty and support sustainability objectives. However, a review of 286 publications from 2006 to 2016 by Mishra et al. (2016) revealed significant research gaps in the application of ML to key operational decisions in SCM. Since then, the scope of ML applications has been steadily expanded. Iseri et al. (2025) argue that predictive analytics is becoming the foundation of next-generation decision-support tools, as it enables reliable demand forecasting, supports inventory management and enhances resource allocation.

These claims are supported by the findings of Islam and Amin (2020), who used two ML techniques (Random Forest (RF) and Gradient Boosted Machine (GBM)) to identify products at risk of backordering successfully. Similarly, Wang (2024) demonstrated that Long Short-Term Memory (LSTM) NNs achieved 91% forecasting accuracy in demand prediction, significantly reducing inventory holding costs. Comparable results were obtained by Zhang et al. (2024), who showed that three ML models (RF, Recurrent Neural Networks (RNNs) and Reinforcement Learning (RL)) outperformed the conventional ARIMA (Autoregressive Integrated Moving Average) model across all performance metrics.

By leveraging ML, deep learning (DL) and NNs, predictive analytics can significantly improve demand forecasting, inventory management, supplier selection and risk management (Nzeako et al. 2024). Sattar et al. (2025) likewise recognize the considerable potential of ML techniques – particularly XGBoost (Extreme Gradient Boosting) and RNNs – in enhancing SCM through demand prediction, inventory optimization and risk mitigation.

Further studies indicate that integrating advanced algorithms such as Deep Reinforcement Learning (DRL) strengthens the flexibility and resilience of supply networks. Park et al. (2025) demonstrated that DRL outperforms heuristics and linear optimization methods in reducing stockouts and order fulfillment costs while maintaining robustness in the face of sudden demand shifts. Similarly, Ghodake et al. (2024) showed that the Deep Q-Learning algorithm improves the accuracy of demand forecasts while reducing operational costs, thereby enhancing the overall flexibility of the system.

At the same time, companies face the challenge of balancing economic, logistical and environmental objectives within increasingly layered and discontinuous supply structures. Abushaega et al. (2025) emphasize that traditional approaches are insufficient for effectively analyzing heterogeneous and decentralized data. In contrast, hybrid ML architectures, combining gradient boosting, regression models and RNNs, perform better in optimizing sustainability indicators. In a similar vein, Baj Rogowska and Nozari (2024) and Nozari et al. (2024) describe ML as a key enabler of intelligent and sustainable supply chains.

Despite the growing accuracy of predictive models (Douaioui et al. 2024), the effective implementation of ML remains dependent on the quality of real-time data and the ability of models to adapt to dynamic environments.

Model explainability is a key concern: Khedr and Rani (2024) highlight the challenges of interpreting decisions made by DL models in the context of supplier evaluation. Although AI solutions hold the potential to revolutionize supply chains, their deployment continues to face obstacles such as poor data quality, shortages of skilled professionals and organizational resistance (Nzeako et al. 2024).

9.3. Automated ML in supply chain optimization

9.3.1. *AutoML*

The shortage of skilled professionals exacerbates these barriers, rendering ML projects economically risky (Kar et al. 2021). Automated Machine Learning (AutoML) addresses these challenges by automating key stages of the model development lifecycle – algorithm selection, hyperparameter tuning and evaluation (Figure 9.1), thereby lowering the entry threshold for users outside the narrow circle of experts (Feurer et al. 2015; He et al. 2021).

In doing so, AutoML democratizes access to ML, enabling the development of high-performing models even by individuals without advanced technical backgrounds. As a result, it reduces both the cost and risk of analytical initiatives (Westergaard et al. 2024). As noted by Paweloszek et al. (2023), many small enterprises face significant constraints in digital competencies and IT staff resources. In such contexts, AutoML tools offer a practical solution, enabling model training and evaluation with minimal technical expertise.

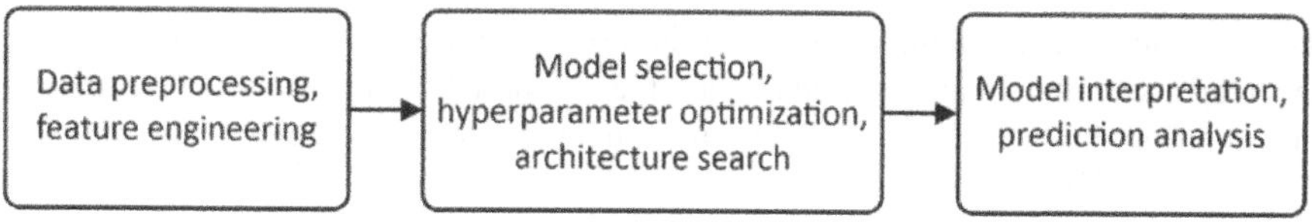

Figure 9.1. *A typical AutoML pipeline (Truong et al. 2019)*

Kramer et al. (2022) demonstrated that cloud-based AutoML platforms (Microsoft Azure ML, Dataiku DSS, Google AutoML Tables) outperform ARIMA models and exponential smoothing in short-term procurement and production planning. However, over a one-year horizon, traditional models may still retain an advantage, highlighting the need for systematic calibration and the enrichment of automated workflows with business knowledge. Complementary findings by SPS[2] show that combining AutoML with ensemble techniques enhances forecast accuracy and robustness, enabling optimization of inventory levels, resource allocation and supply chain planning. The manual effort required to build forecasting models is significantly reduced, accelerating implementation.

Despite substantial progress, none of the current AutoML platforms fully eliminates the need for human intervention during the data pre-processing stage, which remains a critical determinant of prediction quality (Truong et al. 2019). Nevertheless, AutoML provides valuable support not only for novice users but also for experienced analysts, offering functionalities that reduce the amount of code required. This allows experts to focus on feature engineering, model interpretation and deployment (Schmitt 2023a, 2023b). As a result, AutoML solutions contribute to the democratization of ML by narrowing the skills gap and accelerating the development of innovative predictive applications in SCM. One widely used AutoML tool is H2O AutoML – a feature of the H2O-3 library that enables automatic training and tuning of multiple models, as well as the construction of a leaderboard for both academic and business applications (H2O.ai n.d.; Ledell and Poirier 2020).

9.3.2. *H2O AutoML*

In the academic literature, H2O AutoML is recognized as one of the most mature and highly rated AutoML solutions, particularly effective in binary classification tasks (Schmitt 2023a). This framework automates the entire ML workflow, including the training and tuning of multiple models and the construction of model ensembles (Stacked Ensembles), all within user-defined constraints such as maximum runtime (max_runtime_secs) or a set number of models (max_models).

2 See: https://www.baumer.com/us/en/l/sps-2025.

The interface is deliberately simplified: the user is required to specify a data frame, the response column and optionally a time or model limit. All other settings – including predictor selection, validation frame and stopping criteria – are optional. As a result, H2O AutoML lowers the skill barrier for users outside the core data science community, while at the same time offering a "packaged" functionality that saves time for advanced users, allowing them to focus on feature engineering, model interpretation and deployment (H2O.ai).

The set of algorithms embedded in H2O AutoML comprises five core model families with diverse characteristics, along with their ensembles (Stacked Ensembles). This enables the framework to adapt effectively to a wide range of analytical tasks.

The model families include the following (Ajgaonkar 2022; Mienye and Sun 2022; H2O.ai n.d.):

– GLM (Generalized Linear Model) is a family of regression models tailored to a specific probability distribution of the data. In H2O AutoML, GLM represents a generalization of classical linear regression, enabling the modeling of various types of data (e.g. binary, count or continuous). From a technical perspective, all traditional regression models fall within the GLM family, including the standard linear model. H2O AutoML automatically selects the appropriate variant of the GLM model depending on the probability distribution function and the nature of the task (regression or classification).

– DRF (Distributed Random Forest) is a family of supervised learning models based on random decision forests, commonly used for both classification and regression tasks. It is built upon decision trees: a large number of randomly constructed trees are generated for prediction purposes, and their outputs are then aggregated to produce a final forecast. The randomness introduced during tree construction helps to reduce both systematic error (bias) and the variance of individual models, thereby improving the overall model's accuracy and robustness.

– GBM is a family of ensemble models based on sequential ML, used for both classification and regression tasks. Like DRF, GBM belongs to the class of ensemble methods, meaning it consists of many weak learners whose predictions are aggregated to produce the final output. GBM models rely on decision trees built in successive stages, with each attempting to correct the errors made by the previous ones, which enables gradual minimization of prediction error. GBM can be used to predict continuous numerical values (regression) as well as to classify data.

– XGBoost is a family of models used by H2O AutoML, based on the concept of gradient boosting. It involves constructing successive decision trees in such a way that each new tree corrects the errors made by the previous models, leading to a systematic improvement in prediction accuracy. XGBoost models are considered highly efficient solutions and are widely applied in both classification and regression tasks.

– DL is a family of ML models built using ANNs. DL is among the most powerful ML techniques, used to train highly flexible models capable of processing large and complex datasets. In H2O, DL is based on multi-layer feed-forward NNs trained using stochastic gradient descent (SGD) and backpropagation. H2O can train various types of DNNs, such as the Multi-Layer Perceptron (MLP), which performs best on tabular data; Convolutional Neural Networks (CNNs), designed for image processing; and RNNs, used for analyzing sequential data such as speech or time series (Rana and Bhambri 2024c).

Stacked Ensemble in H2O is a supervised ensemble algorithm that uses the stacking technique to combine predictions from previously trained base models. AutoML first builds a set of models from different families (e.g. GBM, XGBoost, DRF, GLM, DL). Then, the Stacked Ensemble trains a so-called metalearner (by default GLM or GBM), which assigns optimal weights to each base model to minimize the overall prediction error. This approach improves both the accuracy and the stability of the predictions. Like other supervised algorithms in H2O, Stacked Ensemble supports regression, binary classification and multiclass classification.

In the comparative study by Truong et al. (2019), the H2O AutoML framework slightly outperformed alternative tools in binary classification and regression, converging more quickly to optimal results. However, it was outperformed in multiclass classification tasks. H2O AutoML also offers a range of advanced options. The user can include or exclude specific algorithms (include_algos/exclude_algos), define the validation strategy (nfolds, blending_frame) or control early stopping through parameters such as stopping_rounds, stopping_metric and stopping_tolerance. The results of all experiments are summarized in the Leaderboard, where the default evaluation metric is AUC (Area Under the Curve) for binary classification, mean_per_class_error for multiclass classification and deviance for regression tasks (H2O.ai n.d.).

9.3.3. *Application of H2O AutoML to daily logistics demand forecasting: a case study*

Ferreira et al. (2016) present a case study involving the use of ANNs for forecasting daily parcel demand at the Centro de Tratamento de Encomendas (CTE) over a 15-day horizon. The experimental dataset covered a period of 60 days: the first 45 days were used to train an MLP model, while the remaining 15 days were used for testing. The study explored 10 variants of the MLP trained using the error backpropagation algorithm, varying the number of hidden layers, number of neurons, learning rate, momentum rate and stopping criteria. The best configuration was selected based on the lowest Mean Absolute Percentage Error (MAPE) obtained on the 15-day test set.

The described experimental setup meets the core requirements of the data-driven supply chain optimization paradigm. First, the use of reliable historical data helps reduce demand uncertainty across all subsequent planning modules, from inventory management to transport scheduling. Second, the resulting forecasting model serves as an input component for integrated APS (Advanced Planning and Scheduling) and IBP (Integrated Business Planning) systems, where error metrics (e.g. MAPE) can act as objective functions for optimization algorithms. Third, the complete documentation of the dataset (UCI 2017) and the detailed specification of hyperparameters facilitate replication and the transfer of results to other research environments.

Building on the case study described above, an attempt was made to verify whether H2O AutoML is capable of generating daily order forecasts with greater accuracy than the carefully tuned MLP network presented by Ferreira et al. (2016). To this end, an experiment was designed to develop three model configurations within the H2O AutoML framework:

– MLP BASELINE – a single, manually tuned DL model.

– AUTOML NN – a set of optimally tuned neural networks, restricted exclusively to this algorithm family.

– AUTOML ALL – a default H2O AutoML run with the full range of available algorithms.

9.3.3.1. *Dataset*

The planned experiment was conducted using the public dataset *Daily Demand Forecasting Orders* (UCI 2017). The data cover a period of 60 consecutive days of observations collected from a large Brazilian logistics company. Each record reflects the daily volume of parcel orders, with columns C3–C12 (Table 9.1) breaking this number down by delivery urgency (urgent/non-urgent), parcel type (A–C) and the assignment of the parcel to one of five sectors (fiscal, traffic control, bank 1–3). The output variable (Target, C13) is defined as the total number of orders placed on a given day. In total, the dataset includes 12 input variables and one dependent variable.

Variables C1–C2 are categorical (week of the month and day of the week), allowing the model to capture rhythmic fluctuations in demand. The remaining columns (C3–C12) are continuous variables that reflect the detailed structure of parcel orders. Variable C13 (Target) serves as the dependent variable in regression models.

The raw data in the publicly available file Daily_Demand_Forecasting_Orders_test.csv were formatted according to Brazilian numerical conventions – using a comma as the decimal separator and a period to mark thousands. For consistency with English language notation, this format was converted so that a dot separates the decimal part and thousands are marked with commas. To ensure full comparability with the study conducted by Ferreira et al. (2016), the data were split sequentially (without randomization) into two subsets: training (days 1–45) and testing (days 46–60). They were saved as separate CSV files (*Daily_Demand_Forecasting_Orders_train.csv* and *Daily_Demand_Forecasting_Orders_test.csv*) and imported into H2O AutoML as two independent H2OFrame objects.

Variable code	Variable name
C1	Week of the month (first week, second, third, fourth or fifth week)[1]
C2	Day of the week (Monday to Friday)[2]
C3	Non-urgent order
C4	Urgent order
C5	Order Type A
C6	Order Type B
C7	Order Type C
C8	Fiscal sector orders
C9	Orders from the traffic controller sector
C10	Banking orders (1)
C11	Banking orders (2)
C12	Banking orders (3)
C13	Target (total orders)

[1] Week number (1–4/5).

[2] Working day number (1–5), from Monday to Friday.

Table 9.1. *Dataset characteristics – 12 inputs to the MLP network (Ferreira et al. 2016)*

9.3.3.2. *Model configuration*

The experimental setup involved evaluating three models: MLP BASELINE, AUTOML NN and AUTOML ALL. The first model – MLP BASELINE – was designed to replicate as closely as possible, within H2O AutoML, the best-performing MLP model developed by Ferreira et al. (2016). The second model – AUTOML NN – aimed to fully leverage H2O AutoML's capabilities to select the best model trained exclusively with DL algorithms. The third model – AUTOML ALL – also aimed to exploit the full potential of H2O AutoML, but by selecting the best model from all available ML algorithms, including not only DL, but also GLM, DRF, GBM, XGBoost and Stacked Ensemble. The configuration details of each model are presented in Table 9.2.

Model Name	MLP BASELINE	AUTOML NN	AUTOML ALL
Configuration parameters	– *activation* = Tanh – *hidden* = 15, 15 – *epochs* = 200 – *stopping_rounds* = 0 – *rate* = 0.95 – *seed* = 1,234 – *momentum_start* = 0.99 – *momentum_stable* = 0.99	– *include_algos* = ["DeepLearning"] – *max_runtime_secs* = 3,600 – *seed* = 1,234 – *nfolds* = 5	– *max_runtime_secs* = 3,600 – *seed* = 1,234 – *nfolds* = 5

Table 9.2. *Model configuration parameters used in the experiment. (Source: own elaboration)*

In the MLP BASELINE experiment, the goal was to reproduce an architecture and set of hyperparameters as close as possible to the original MLP model: two hidden layers with 15 neurons each, learning_rate = 0.95, momentum = 0.99, a maximum of 200 epochs and the sigmoid activation function (since sigmoid was unavailable in H2O AutoML, the Tanh activation function was selected instead). The model was generated using H2O AutoML restricted to the DL algorithm. In all experiments, the seed parameter was set to 1,234. In the second (AUTOML NN) and third (AUTOML ALL) experiments, the time limit for searching the best-performing model was set to 3,600 seconds.

9.3.3.3. *Model training and analysis*

All models were trained on the training set Daily_Demand_Forecasting_Orders_train.hex. Cross-validation with nfolds = 5 was performed internally during the training process using modulo-based splitting (without temporal shuffling). After training, each model generated predictions on the test set Daily_Demand_Forecasting_Orders_test.hex. The main performance metric used to evaluate predictive accuracy was Root Mean Square Error (RMSE).

Upon completion of the training process, H2O AutoML generates, among other outputs, a variable importance table, which indicates the extent to which each variable contributes to the model's predictions. Variables with the highest importance scores are those most relied upon by the ML model when generating forecasts. Changes in the values of highly important variables can significantly alter the model's output. Table 9.3 presents the variable importance rankings for each of the models used in the experiment.

MLP BASELINE		AUTOML NN		AUTOML ALL	
Variable	*Scaled importance*	*Variable*	*Scaled importance*	*Variable*	*Scaled importance*
C8	1.0	C6	1.0	C6	1.0
C5	0.9339	C7	0.7401	C7	0.7951
C6	0.9165	C5	0.4619	C5	0.3393
C2	0.9147	C3	0.3641	C3	0.2722
C7	0.9099	C4	0.3378	C10	0.1748
C11	0.8461	C10	0.3308	C4	0.1737
C3	0.8450	C11	0.2390	C11	0.1442
C12	0.8295	C2	0.2253	C1	0.0620
C1	0.7795	C1	0.1973	C9	0.0607
C4	0.6920	C12	0.1687	C8	0.0594
C10	0.6362	C8	0.1629	C2	0.0491
C9	0.6044	C9	0.1155	C12	0.0458

Table 9.3. *Variable importances. (Source: own elaboration)*

In both the AUTOML NN and AUTOML ALL models, the four most important variables are identical. These are: Order Type B, Order Type C, Order Type A and Non-urgent order. In contrast, in the MLP BASELINE model, the most important variable is C8 (fiscal sector orders).

9.3.3.4. *Prediction results*

To evaluate the prediction performance of regression models in each experiment, two basic metrics were primarily used: RMSE[3] and MAE (Mean Absolute Error)[4]. The test set used for forecasting the daily demand for parcel orders was the file *Daily_Demand_Forecasting_Orders_test.hex*.

The results reported by Ferreira et al. (2016) did not include RMSE or MAE values for the MLP model across all 15 test days (t = 1…15). Therefore, to compare the accuracy of the forecasts obtained from the MLP model with those generated by

3 H2O AutoML by default sorts models in the Leaderboard table by RMSE value. The lower the RMSE, the higher the model's accuracy.

4 In the experiments conducted, H2O AutoML reports the error in natural units ("number of orders"), which makes the results easier to interpret for managers.

the MLP BASELINE, AUTOML NN and AUTOML ALL models, the RMSE and MAE for the MLP model were recalculated.

The notations used for these calculations are presented in Table 9.4.

Symbol	Definition
y_t	Actual number of orders on day t – column Target (Total orders) in rows 46–60 of the file *Daily_Demand_Forecasting_Orders.csv*
ε_t	Percentage error of Experiment 5 presented in the study by Ferreira et al. (2016) on day t (from *Table IV*)
e_t	e_t is the difference in the number of orders, calculated according to equation (2): $e_t = \hat{y}_t - y_t = y_t \cdot \frac{\varepsilon_t}{100}$
$\hat{y}_t$	MLP forecast on day t, calculated according to equation [9.1]: $\hat{y}_t = y_t\left(1 + \frac{\varepsilon_t}{100}\right)$

Table 9.4. *Symbols and definitions used for model evaluation. (Source: own elaboration)*

In Table 9.4 (see Ferreira et al. 2016), the two largest percentage errors in each experiment were highlighted in bold. *Experiment 5* – involving an MLP with two hidden layers, a learning rate of 0.95, a momentum coefficient of 0.99 and a maximum number of epochs equal to 200 – yielded the best result. It can be concluded that the topology adopted in Experiment 5 fitted the dataset best, resulting in the most accurate forecast. An excerpt of the data used in the calculations is presented in Table 9.5.

In Table 9.4 Ferreira et al. (2016) provide the percentage error ε_t. Converting this into the error e_t calculated as the number of orders using equation [9.2] yields, for day 4 of the test set (which had the highest $\varepsilon_t$value): $y_4 = 402{,}607$; $\varepsilon_4 = 8.60\%$; $e_4 = 402{,}607 \times 0.086 = 34{,}624$ orders.

The MAE is a measure of the accuracy of regression models that indicates, on average (in the units of the predicted variable), how much the predictions deviate from the actual observations.

The RMSE, in turn, is one of the most commonly used metrics for evaluating regression models. It shows, in the same units as the observed values, the average magnitude of the deviation between the predicted and actual values.

Test day	y_t (orders)	ε_t (%)	e_t (orders)
1	357,394	-2.40	-8,577
2	259,246	-3.30	-8,555
3	244,235	-1.20	-2,930
4	**402,607**	**8.60**	**34,624**
5	255,061	4.80	12,242
6	342,606	0.00	0,000
7	268,640	-1.60	-4,298
8	188,601	-5.70	-10,750
9	202,022	-0.01	0,020
10	213,509	0.80	1,708
11	316,849	-2.50	7,921
12	286,412	-1.00	2,864
13	303,447	6.70	20,330
14	304,950	5.00	15,247
15	331,900	8.20	27,221

Table 9.5. Preview of data used in calculations. *(Source: own elaboration based on Ferreira et al. 2016)*

These errors are calculated using equations [9.1] and [9.2]:

$$MAE = \frac{1}{n}\sum_{t=1}^{n}|y_t - \hat{y}_t| \qquad [9.1]$$

$$RMSE = \sqrt{\frac{1}{n}\sum_{t=1}^{n}(y_t - \hat{y}_t)^2} \qquad [9.2]$$

For day 4 of the test set (see Table 9.5), the following values of MAE and RMSE were obtained:

$MAE = \frac{1}{15}\sum_{t=1}^{15}|e_t| = 10{,}485.800$ orders; $RMSE = \sqrt{\frac{1}{15}\sum_{t=1}^{15} e_t^2} =$ $14{,}372.859$ orders.

The results of the conducted experiments are summarized in Table 9.6. The numerical values reflect the outcome obtained in the authors' testing environment and may vary slightly upon replication. In the AUTOML NN and AUTOML ALL experiments, the Leaderboard displays all models trained by H2O AutoML, ranked from best to worst based on the RMSE metric. Table 9.6 includes only the best-performing models (i.e. those with the lowest RMSE values).

Model/metric	**MLP**	**MLP BASELINE***	**AUTOML NN**** (t=3,600s)	**AUTOML ALL***** (t=3,600s)
MSE		196,865.391	4,959.943	7,851.827
RMSE	14,372.859	14,030.873	2,227.093	2,802.111
r2		942.237	998.545	997.696
mean_residual_ deviance		196,865.391	4,959.943	7,851.827
mae	10,485.800	11,278.363	1,478.000	1,746.815
rmsle		43.725	0,007.314	8.091

* Model trained using the Deep Learning algorithm with manual configuration.
** Model trained using the Deep Learning algorithm – the most accurate among 402 models on the Leaderboard.
*** Model trained using the Deep Learning algorithm – the most accurate among 1,896 models on the Leaderboard.

Table 9.6. *Prediction metrics – model accuracy on the test set (days: 46–60). (Source: own elaboration)*

The improvement in RMSE for the MLP BASELINE, AUTOML NN and AUTOML ALL models relative to the RMSE value of 14,372.859 reported by Ferreira et al. (2016) is presented in Table 9.7. The Δ_{RMSE} indicator ("RMSE improvement vs. MLP") was calculated using equation [9.3].

$$\Delta_{RMSE} = \frac{RMSE_{MLP} - RMSE_{model}}{RMSE_{MLP}} \cdot 100\% \quad [9.3]$$

Model	**RMSE**	Δ_{RMSE} (RMSE improvement vs. MLP)
MLP	14,372.859	-
MLP BASELINE	14,030.873	2.6%
AUTOML NN	**2,227.093**	**84.5%**
AUTOML ALL	2,802.111	80.6%

Table 9.7. *Comparison of model accuracy on the test set (days: 46–60) relative to the MLP model. (Source: own elaboration)*

The results of the experiments confirmed that the manually configured MLP network – reconstructed in accordance with Experiment 5 by Ferreira et al. (2016) – achieved almost identical accuracy to that reported in the original publication (RMSE = 14,030.873 vs. 14,372.859; MAE = 11,278.363 vs. 10,485.800). This validates the correctness of the replication and allows for reliable further comparisons. Applying the H2O AutoML procedure restricted to NNs only (AUTOML NN) resulted in a significant improvement in prediction quality: the root mean square error (RMSE) dropped to 2,227.093 (84.5% improvement relative to the original), and the MAE decreased to 1,478.000 (85.9% improvement). In other words, the average prediction deviation decreased from over 10,000 (10,485.800) to approximately 1,500 (1,478.000) orders per day.

The configuration of the AUTOML ALL model, which additionally tested gradient-boosted trees, RFs, linear regression and ensemble methods, achieved a comparable improvement over the MLP (RMSE = 2,802.111; MAE = 1,746.815), but ultimately performed worse than the best NN model (AUTOML NN). These results clearly indicate that well-tuned NNs, automatically identified by the H2O AutoML procedure restricted to the DL algorithm, offer the greatest gain in prediction accuracy while maintaining relatively low model complexity.

9.4. Conclusion

The conducted analysis demonstrates that the concept of *data-driven supply chain optimization* emerges at the intersection of multi-source BD sets, AI algorithms and AutoML tools capable of automatically training and tuning a wide range of models.

A review of the literature and reports from 2015 to 2025 indicates that the use of real-time data – from demand forecasting, through inventory management, to Scope 3 emission reduction – is becoming a key imperative for enhancing cost efficiency, agility and sustainability in supply chains. At the same time, several research gaps remain evident, including the limited explainability of deep ML models and the relative scarcity of studies on generative DTs in the field of SCM (Bhambri and Bajdor 2025).

The practical value of this chapter is reinforced by a case study based on the public dataset Daily Demand Forecasting Orders. The application of H2O AutoML enabled the automatic training of numerous models across a wide set of learning algorithms within a one-hour time frame, resulting in a reduction of the RMSE from nearly 14,400 orders for the manually tuned MLP model to approximately 2,230 orders, and a drop in MAE from approximately 10,500 to about 1,480 orders (Bhambri and Kumar 2024).

An RMSE of 14,000–15,000 orders in manually configured models (MLP/MLP BASELINE) is relatively small from an operational perspective and can be considered acceptable.

However, in the case of the AUTO NN model, the error of approximately 2,230 orders means that the forecast matches the actual demand with a precision reaching thousands of individual orders, surpassing the threshold of required planning accuracy for most large logistics centers (such as the one examined here, which handles approximately 400,000 parcels per day) (Rana and Bhambri 2024a).

These findings confirm that low-code/AutoML solutions can generate highly accurate models within a short timeframe, even in organizations with limited data science capacity, provided that input data quality is adequately controlled. In summary, automated model selection proved more effective than the manually tuned MLP (Rana and Bhambri 2025).

The study is based on data from a single logistics center, uses a 60-day time series and is limited to the forecasting phase. Therefore, generalizing the results should be approached with caution. Future research should extend the analysis to longer, multi-sector datasets and explore explainable, neuro-symbolic architectures that can support managerial interpretation of results and enable more comprehensive monitoring of sustainable development goals.

9.5. References

Abouzid, I. and Saidi, R. (2023). Digital twin implementation approach in supply chain processes. *Scientific African*, 21, e01821. doi: 10.1016/j.sciaf.2023.e01821.

Abushaega, M.M., Moshebah, O.Y., Hamzi, A., Alghamdi, S.Y. (2025). Multi-objective sustainability optimization in modern supply chain networks: A hybrid approach with federated learning and graph neural networks. *Alexandria Engineering Journal*, 115, 585–602. doi: 10.1016/j.aej.2024.12.048.

Ajgaonkar, S. (2022). *Practical Automated Machine Learning Using H2O. AI: Discover the Power of Automated Machine Learning, from Experimentation through to Deployment to Production*. Packt Publishing, Birmingham.

Alsolbi, I., Shavaki, F.H., Agarwal, R., Bharathy, G.K., Prakash, S., Prasad, M. (2023). Big data optimisation and management in supply chain management: A systematic literature review. *Artificial Intelligence Review*, 56, 253–284. doi: 10.1007/s10462-023-10505-4.

Atwani, M., Hlyal, M., Elalami, J. (2022). A review of artificial intelligence applications in supply chain. *ITM Web Conf.*, 46, 03001. doi: 10.1051/itmconf/20224603001.

Baj-Rogowska, A. and Nozari, H. (2024). Multi objective machine learning for real-time decision making in smart supply chains. *Journal of Business and Future Economy*, 1(3), 47–62 [Online]. Available at: https://journals.iau.ae/index.php/JBFE/article/view/17.

Bhambri, P. and Bajdor, P. (2025). AI-powered predictive analysis for proactive cyber defense. In *Handbook of AI-Driven Threat Detection and Prevention: A Holistic Approach to Security*, Bhambri, P. and Anand, A.J. (eds). CRC Press, Boca Raton, FL. doi: 10.1201/9781003521020-18.

Bhambri, P. and Kumar, S. (2024). Protecting sustainable supply chains from cyber threats. In *Digital Sustainability: Navigating Entrepreneurship in the Information Age*, Bhambri, P. and Paweloszek, I. (eds). CRC Press, Boca Raton, FL. doi: 10.1201/9781003484226-9.

Bhambri, P. and Paweloszek, I. (2024). Introduction to digital sustainability and entrepreneurship. In *Digital Sustainability: Navigating Entrepreneurship in the Information Age*, Bhambri, P. and Paweloszek, I. (eds). CRC Press, Boca Raton, FL. doi: 10.1201/9781003484226-2.

Bhambri, P. and Rani, S. (2024). Advancements and future challenges in business intelligence. In *Developing Managerial Skills for Global Business Success*, Barrena-Martinez, J., Foncubierta-Rodríguez, M.-J., Medina-Garrido, J.A., Dobrowolski, Z. (eds). IGI Global, Hershey, PA. doi: 10.4018/979-8-3693-3057-9.ch017.

Bhambri, P. and Starostka-Patyk, M. (2024). Decentralized finance (DeFi) and environmental impact. In *Digital Sustainability: Navigating Entrepreneurship in the Information Age*, Bhambri, P. and Paweloszek, I. (eds). CRC Press, Boca Raton, FL. doi: 10.1201/9781003484226-10.

Bhambri, P., Rani, S., Khang, A. (2024a). AI-driven digital twin and resource optimization in Industry 4.0 ecosystem. In *Intelligent Techniques for Predictive Data Analytics*, Singh, N., Birla, S., Ansari, M.D., Shukla, N.K. (eds). Wiley-IEEE Press, Hoboken, NJ. doi: 10.1002/9781394227990.ch3.

Bhambri, P., Rani, S., Kumar, S., Sinha, V.K. (2024b). Big data analytics with digital twin for industrial applications. In *AI-Driven Digital Twin and Industry 4.0: A Conceptual Framework with Applications*, Rani, S., Bhambri, P., Kumar, S., Pareek, P.K., Elngar, A.A. (eds). CRC Press, Taylor & Francis Group, Boca Raton, FL. doi: 10.1201/9781003395416-7.

Bhatt, D., Gunasekaran, A., Papadopoulos, T., Childe, S. (2018). Big Data and supply chain management: A review and bibliometric analysis. *Annals of Operations Research*, 270(1), doi: 10.1007/s10479-016-2236-y.

Borchardt, M., Pereira, G., Milan, G., Pereira, E., Lima, L., Bianchi, R., Scavarda do Carmo, A. (2025). Are sustainable supply chains managing scope 3 emissions? A systematic literature review. *Sustainability*, 17(13), 6066. doi: 10.3390/su17136066.

Douaioui, K., Oucheikh, R., Benmoussa, O., Mabrouki, C. (2024). Machine learning and deep learning models for demand forecasting in supply chain management: A critical review. *Applied System Innovation*, 7(5), 93. doi: 10.3390/asi7050093.

Elufioye, O.A. (2024). AI-driven predictive analytics in agricultural supply chains: A review: Assessing the benefits and challenges of AI in forecasting demand and optimizing supply in agriculture. *Computer Science & IT Research Journal*, 1.5, 473–497. doi: 10.51594/csitrj.v5i2.817.

Eyo-Udo, N.L. (2024). Leveraging artificial intelligence for improved supply chain optimization. *Open Access Research Journal of Multidisciplinary Studies*, 7, 1–15. doi: 10.53022/oarjms.2024.7.2.0044.

Ferreira, R.P., Martiniano, A., Ferreira, A.A., Ferreira, A., Sassi, R.J. (2016). Study on daily demand forecasting orders using artificial neural network. *IEEE Latin America Transactions*, 14, 1519–1525.

Feurer, M., Klein, A., Eggensperger, K., Springenberg, J.T., Blum, M., Hutter, F. (2015). Efficient and robust automated machine learning. *Advances in Neural Information Processing Systems*, 2962–2970. doi: 10.1007/978-3-030-05318-5_6.

Gaus, T., Olsen, K., Deloso, M. (2018). Using AI in Digital Supply Chain Network Planning. WSJ, Deloitte Consulting LLP [Online]. Available at: https://deloitte.wsj.com/cio/using-ai-in-digital-supply-chain-network-planning-1539565328.

Ghodake, S.P., Malkar, V.R., Santosh, K., Jabasheela, L., Abdufattokhov, S., Gopi, A. (2024). Enhancing supply chain management efficiency: A data-driven approach using predictive analytics and machine learning algorithms. *International Journal of Advanced Computer Science and Applications*, 15(4). doi: 10.14569/IJACSA.2024.0150469.

H2O.ai (n.d.) AutoML: Automatic Machine Learning [Online]. Available at: https://docs.h2o.ai/h2o/latest-stable/h2o-docs/automl.html.

He, X., Zhao, K., Chu, X. (2021). AutoML: A survey of the state-of-the-art. *Knowledge-Based Systems*, 212. doi: 10.1016/J.KNOSYS.2020.106622.

Hofmann, W. and Branding, F. (2019). Implementation of an IoT- and cloud-based digital twin for real-time decision support in port operations. *IFAC-PapersOnLine*, 52(13), 2104–2109. doi: 10.1016/j.ifacol.2019.11.516.

Iseri, F., Iseri, H., Chrisandina, N.J., Iakovou, E., Pistikopoulos, E.N. (2025). AI-based predictive analytics for enhancing data-driven supply chain optimization. *Journal of Global Optimization*. doi: 10.1007/s10898-025-01509-1.

Islam, S. and Amin, S.H. (2020). Prediction of probable backorder scenarios in the supply chain using Distributed Random Forest and Gradient Boosting Machine learning techniques. *Journal of Big Data*, 7, 65. doi: 10.1186/s40537-020-00345-2.

Ivanov, D. (2025). Conceptual and formal models for design, adaptation, and control of digital twins in supply chain ecosystems. *Omega*, 137, 103356. doi: 10.1016/j.omega.2025.103356.

Joel, O.S., Oyewole, A.T., Odunaiya, O.G., Soyombo, O.T. (2024). Leveraging artificial intelligence for improved supply chain optimization: A comprehensive review of current practices and future potentials. *International Journal of Management & Entrepreneurship Research*, 6(3), 707–721. doi: 10.51594/ijmer.v6i3.882.

Kar, S., Kar, A.K., Gupta, M.P. (2021). Modeling drivers and barriers of artificial intelligence adoption: Insights from a strategic management perspective. *Intelligent Systems in Accounting, Finance and Management*, 28(4), 217–238. doi: 10.1002/isaf.1503.

Khan, S. and Tabasum, S. (2025). Real-time health supply chain optimization using digital twin technology. *International Journal of Science and Research Archive*, 15(02), 1275–1289. doi: 10.30574/ijsra.2025.15.2.1556.

Kosasih, E.E., Papadakis, E., Baryannis, G., Brintrup, A. (2024). A review of explainable artificial intelligence in supply chain management using neurosymbolic approaches. *International Journal of Production Research*, 62(4), 1510–1540.

Kramer, K., Behn, N., Schmidt, M. (2022). The potential of AutoML for demand forecasting. In *3rd Conference on Production Systems and Logistics (CPSL 2022)*. doi: 10.15488/12162.

Kudelska, I. and Niedbał, R. (2020). Technological and organizational innovation in warehousing process – Research over workload of staff and efficiency of picking stations. *E & M Ekonomie a Management*, 23(3), 67–81. doi: 10.15240/tul/001/2020-3-005.

Ledell, E. and Poirier, S. (2020). H2O AutoML: Scalable automatic machine learning [Online]. Available at: https://www.automl.org/wp-content/uploads/2020/07/AutoML_2020_paper_61.pdf.

Lee, I. and Mangalaraj, G. (2022). Big Data analytics in supply chain management: A systematic literature review and research directions. *Big Data and Cognitive Computing*, 6(17). doi: 10.3390/bdcc6010017.

Li, Q. and Liu, A. (2019). Big Data driven supply chain management. *Procedia CIRP*, 81, 1089–1094. doi: 10.1016/j.procir.2019.03.258.

Li, M., Cai, Y., Guo, D., Qu, T., Huang, G.Q. (2024). Data-driven diagnosis framework for platform product supply chains under disruptions. *International Journal of Production Research*, 63(7), 2599–2621. doi: 10.1080/00207543.2024.2407915.

Lin, H., Lin, J., Wang, F. (2022). An innovative machine learning model for supply chain management. *Journal of Innovation & Knowledge*, 7(4), 100276. doi: 10.1016/j.jik.2022.100276.

Liu, Y., Pan, S., Ballot, E. (2024). Unveiling the potential of digital twins in logistics and supply chain management: Services, capabilities, and research opportunities. *Digital Engineering*, 3, 100025. doi: 10.1016/j.dte.2024.100025.

Lugaresi, G., Jemai, Z., Sahin, E. (2023). Digital twins for supply chains: Current outlook and future challenges. In *Proceedings of the 2023 European Council for Modelling and Simulation*. doi: 10.7148/2023-0451.

Masood, A. and Sherif, A. (2021). *Automated Machine Learning. Hyperparameter Optimization, Neural Architecture Search, and Algorithm Selection with Cloud Platforms.* Packt Publishing, Birmingham.

McCrea, B. (2025). AI in supply chain software: Opportunities, challenges, and the future of automation [Online]. Available at: https://www.logisticsmgmt.com/article/ai_in_supply_chain_software_opportunities_challenges_and_the_future_of_automation.

Mienye, I.D. and Sun, Y. (2022). A survey of ensemble learning: Concepts, algorithms, applications, and prospects. *IEEE Access*, 10, 99129–99149. doi: 10.1109/ACCESS.2022.3207287.

Mishra, D., Gunasekaran, A., Papadopoulos, T., Childe, S.J. (2016). Big Data and supply chain management: A review and bibliometric analysis. *Annals of Operations Research*, 270(1), 313–336.

Mussomeli, A., Patil, S., Noyes, C., Carpenter, L., Byers, T., Thakkar, D., Santhyanarayana, S., Van de Houten, K. (2023). Managing a modern supply chain: Utilizing AI to combat complexity. Deloitte [Online]. Available at: https://www.deloitte.com/us/en/services/consulting/articles/ai-in-modern-supply-chain-management.

Nguyen, T., Zhou, L., Spiegler, V., Ieromonachou, P., Lin, Y. (2017). Big data analytics in supply chain management: A state-of-the-art literature review. *Computers & Operations Research*, 98, 254–264. doi: 10.1016/j.cor.2017.07.004.

Nozari, H., Bakhshi Movahed, A., Bakhshi Movahed, A. (2024). The AIoE revolution: Redefining organizational maturity in a hyper-connected world. *Applied Innovations in Industrial Management*, 4(1), 10–17 [Online]. Available at: https://iscihub.com/index.php/AIIM/article/view/20.

Nzeako, G., Akinsanya, M.O., Popoola, O.A., Chukwurah, G.E., Okeke, C.D. (2024). The role of AI-driven predictive analytics in optimizing IT industry supply chains. *International Journal of Management & Entrepreneurship Research*, 6(5), 1489–1497. doi: 10.51594/ijmer.v6i5.1096.

Park, M.-J., Turner, O., Becker, T. (2025). Inventory optimization in retail supply chains using deep reinforcement learning. *Advances in Management and Intelligent Technologies*, 1. doi: 10.62177/amit.v1i3.470.

Pawełoszek, I., Wieczorkowski, J., Czarnacka-Chrobot, B. (2023). Digital transformation of Polish micro-enterprises: Lessons from the COVID-19 era. *Procedia Computer Science*, 225, 1572–1581. doi: 10.1016/j.procs.2023.10.146.

Rana, R. and Bhambri, P. (2024a). AI-driven MCDM tools for optimizing industrial wastewater treatment. In *Modern SuperHyperSoft Computing Trends in Science and Technology*, Smarandache, F. and Majumder, P. (eds). IGI Global, Hershey, PA. doi: 10.4018/979-8-3693-6875-6.ch003.

Rana, R. and Bhambri, P. (2024b). Environmental challenges and technological solutions. In *Handbook of Technological Sustainability: Innovation and Environmental Awareness*, Bhambri, P. and Bajdor, P. (eds). CRC Press Boca Raton, FL. doi: 10.1201/9781003475989-17.

Rana, R. and Bhambri, P. (2024c). Ethical considerations in artificial intelligence for environmental solutions: Striking a balance for sustainable innovation. In *Handbook of Technological Sustainability: Innovation and Environmental Awareness*, Bhambri, P. and Bajdor, P. (eds). CRC Press Boca Raton, FL. doi: 10.1201/9781003475989-31.

Rana, R. and Bhambri, P. (2024d). Hybrid MCDM (multi-criteria decision-making) approaches for sustainable energy management. In *Modern SuperHyperSoft Computing Trends in Science and Technology*, Smarandache, F. and Majumder, P. (eds). IGI Global, Hershey, PA. doi: 10.4018/979-8-3693-6875-6.ch006.

Rana, R. and Bhambri, P. (2025). Harnessing block chain digital twins for sustainable business operations. In *Practical Frameworks for New-Age Digitalization Business Strategy*, Tee, P., Song, B., Ho, R. (eds). IGI Global Scientific Publishing, Hershey, PA. doi: 10.4018/979-8-3373-2018-2.ch013.

Riad, M., Naimi, M., Okar, C. (2024). Enhancing supply chain resilience through artificial intelligence: Developing a comprehensive conceptual framework for AI implementation and supply chain optimization. *Logistics*, 8(4), 111. doi: 10.3390/logistics8040111.

Richey, R.G., Morgan, T.R., Lindsey-Hall, K., Adams, F.G. (2016). A global exploration of Big Data in the supply chain. *International Journal of Physical Distribution & Logistics Management*, 46(8), 710–739. doi: 10.1108/IJPDLM-05-2016-0134.

Samuels, A. (2025). Examining the integration of artificial intelligence in supply chain management from Industry 4.0 to 6.0: A systematic literature review. *Frontiers in Artificial Intelligence*, 7, 1477044. doi: 10.3389/frai.2024.1477044.

Sattar, M., Dattana, V., Hasan, R., Mahmood, S., Khan, H., Hussain, S. (2025). Enhancing supply chain management: A comparative study of machine learning techniques with cost–accuracy and ESG-based evaluation for forecasting and risk mitigation. *Sustainability*, 17, 1–45. doi: 10.3390/su17135772.

Schmitt, M. (2023a). Automated machine learning: AI-driven decision making in business analytics. *Intelligent Systems with Applications*, 18, 200188. doi: 10.1016/j.iswa.2023.200188.

Schmitt, M. (2023b). Deep learning in business analytics: A clash of expectations and reality. *International Journal of Information Management Data Insights*. doi: 10.1016/J.JJIMEI.2022.100146.

Senthil, P.S., Kumar, P., Nathaniel, A.A., Mohamed, H.S. (2025). Demand prediction using AutoML based ensemble algorithm. In *2025 International Conference on Artificial Intelligence and Data Engineering (AIDE)*, Nitte. doi: 10.1109/AIDE64228.2025.10986835.

Silva, A.D. (2024). Advancing BIM and sustainability with coopetition: Evidence from the Portuguese stone industry. *Appl. Syst. Innov.*, 7(4), 70. doi: 10.3390/asi7040070.

Singh, R., Modgil, S., Shore, A. (2023). Building artificial intelligence enabled resilient supply chain: A multi-method approach. *Journal of Enterprise Information Management*, 37, 414–436. doi: 10.1108/jeim-09-2022-0326.

Truong, A., Walters, A., Goodsitt, J., Hines, K., Bruss, C.B., Farivar, R. (2019). Towards automated machine learning: Evaluation and comparison of AutoML approaches and tools. In *2019 IEEE 31st International Conference on Tools with Artificial Intelligence (ICTAI)*, Portland, OR. doi: 10.1109/ICTAI.2019.00209.

UCI (2017). UCI machine learning repository [Online]. Available at: https://archive.ics.uci.edu/dataset/409/daily+demand+forecasting+orders.

Velázquez Martínez, J.C. and Arnold, V. (2024). *State of Supply Chain Sustainability 2024*. MIT Center for Transportation & Logistics and Council of Supply Chain Management Professionals, Cambridge, MA and Lombard, IL.

Wang, Z. (2024). Data-driven supply chain performance optimization through predictive analytics and machine learning. *Applied and Computational Engineering*, 118, 30–35. doi: 10.54254/2755-2721/2025.18487.

Wang, G., Gunasekaran, A., Ngai, E.W.T., Papadopoulos, T. (2016). Big data analytics in logistics and supply chain management: Certain investigations for research and applications. *International Journal of Production Economics*, 176, 98–110. doi: 10.1016/j.ijpe.2016.03.014.

Westergaard, G., Erden, U., Mateo, O.A., Lampo, S.M., Akinci, T.C., Topsakal, O. (2024). Time series forecasting utilizing automated machine learning (AutoML): A comparative analysis study on diverse datasets. *Information*, 15(1), 39. doi: 10.3390/info15010039.

Zhang, J., Yuyang, W., Zidu, W. (2024). Enhancing supply chain forecasting with machine learning: A data-driven approach to demand prediction, risk management, and demand-supply optimization. *Journal of Fintech and Business Analysis*, 2(1), 1–5.

10

Sustainability Transformation Roadmaps

This chapter explores the concept of roadmaps as a strategic tool supporting organizations' transformation processes toward sustainability. This chapter begins with a brief introduction to sustainability and roadmap methodology. Sustainability is perceived as a dynamic, long-term process requiring systemic change and the integration of environmental, social and governance (ESG) dimensions. Roadmaps are presented as structured, flexible and goal-oriented tools that help organizations define visions, prioritize activities, allocate resources, manage risks and monitor progress.

This chapter then compares various roadmap frameworks identified through a literature review on the topic. Particular attention is paid to the process of creating sustainability transformation roadmaps, highlighting key steps such as vision setting, stakeholder engagement, resource allocation, technology integration, change management and continuous improvement. This chapter concludes by emphasizing that roadmaps are not only planning instruments but also crucial factors for increasing resilience and competitive advantage, supporting organizations in moving toward sustainability as a key element of their strategy and value creation.

10.1. Introduction

This chapter is devoted to the issue of "sustainability transformation roadmaps", which today play an essential role in achieving goals resulting from adopted environmental policies, SD goals, ESG pressure or corporate accountability.

Sustainability refers to the quality that enables an action to continue for a specific period. Additionally, regarding environmental issues, "sustainability" means a characteristic that causes human activities to cause little or no damage to the natural environment (Wang et al. 2010). However, it is also defined as a long-term goal, assuming continuous economic growth with the lowest possible impact on the

Chapter written by Paula BAJDOR.

environment, or ensuring continued economic growth, taking into account the harmonious cooperation of societies, and in such a way that future generations can also use the natural resources necessary for survival (Somasekhara Reddy et al. 2012). The definitions cited above suggest that this is a very complex and time-consuming concept, as its implementation requires making decisions that will take into account the needs of future generations. This timeline means that sustainability should be viewed as a continuous transformation – having a clearly defined goal and striving to achieve it, with the awareness that many surprises may be encountered along the way, therefore affecting the degree of its achievement (Han et al. 2008; Raymundo et al. 2010; Sabnis 2010).

Societies and economies must transform from their current, unsustainable state to a path of sustainable development and resilience (Figure 10.1), through an integrated approach that considers all sustainability goals, exploiting their synergies and benefits while mitigating their trade-offs.

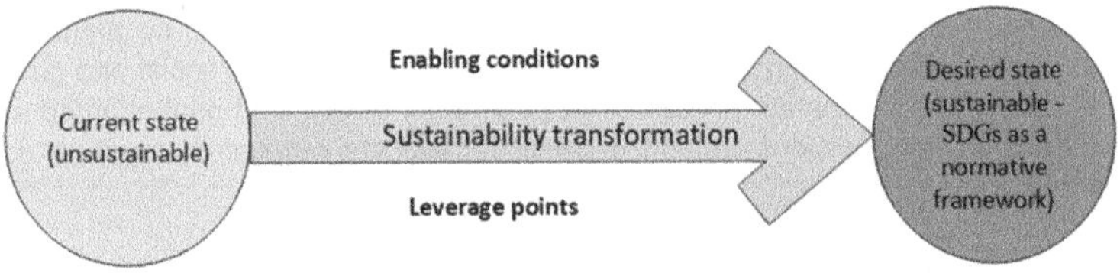

Figure 10.1. *Sustainability transformation process (Source: Own work based on Voulvoulis and Burgman (2019))*

Sustainability challenges can be defined as the gap between the current unsustainable state and the desired sustainable state, enabling a better understanding from a whole-system perspective (Hu et al. 2007). Transformation itself is the process of moving from the current unsustainable state to the desired state, aligned with a collective vision of a future system state that will become sustainable (Lian et al. 2009). Sustainability transformation is therefore a process that evolves, adapting to emerging circumstances and challenges but striving for one thing: achieving the ultimate goal.

Since the 1970s, roadmapping has been widely used to support technology and product planning due to its flexibility and adaptability. A roadmap is defined as a detailed plan aimed at guiding progress toward a goal (Sanghi and Bhattacharya 2002). The purpose of the roadmaps is to guide companies in achieving their goals by defining a sequence of steps to be taken (Kumar et al. 2007). Roadmaps guide companies toward goals and identify possible choices (Xin et al. 2011). In this respect, a roadmap is a tool that streamlines and provides direction for decision-making processes (Erdem et al. 2010), while also enabling the identification of potential risks, indicating opportunities to minimize them, implementing improvements and reporting over time (Ayari et al. 2005; Gottipati and Mishra 2010). A sustainability roadmap is both a vision and a practical strategy for achieving long-term goals. Roadmaps are a useful tool used by managers to establish key priorities (Cronje et al. 2011), set clear goals and define action plans to help organizations implement their strategies (Myers 1971). In the literature, there are many types of roadmaps which, taking into account SD, are presented as a method of supporting decision-making on the way to achieving greater sustainability by defining steps of transformation of the organization toward sustainability (Box and Hunter 1957).

Roadmaps are now key tools, offering a fully structured and transparent way to adapt to changes over time. Roadmaps also enable the anticipation of future challenges, the coordination of individual processes and proactive risk management (Box and Hunter 1961). By integrating strategies, current challenges and resource planning, roadmaps help those responsible for achieving Sustainable Development Goals (SDG) to create coherent and achievable plans (Muthukumar et al. 2003). They also provide a tool to support communication and coherence between different stakeholders, visually outlining the path from current opportunities to future goals (Benyounis et al. 2005). In the face of increasing pressure to achieve SDG goals, roadmaps serve not only as planning tools but also as strategic instruments for dealing with complexity and uncertainty (Box and Hunter 1957; Tarangini et al. 2009).

10.2. Sustainability transformation

For organizations to successfully implement the process of sustainability transformation, they must simultaneously incorporate environmental, social and corporate governance (ESG) aspects into their operations. This alone will guarantee the complete success of the implemented process, which will take the form of the following actions (Ozer et al. 2008):

1. Developing a single-goal sustainability strategy: this activity should involve organizations developing a strategy based on the assumption that sustainability is a source of sustainable competitive advantage. This strategy should be aligned with the organization's goals, focused on long-term value creation and supported by management.

2. Capture business value: organizations that achieve strong ESG scores often outperform their competitors financially. This makes it crucial to develop a solid business plan that considers diverse sources of value, such as increased customer loyalty, price premiums, market expansion, operational savings, improved access to raw materials and capital and risk reduction.

3. Creating a sustainable enterprise: organizations are currently benefiting from massive public and private investments enabling a transformation focused on creating a zero-emission economy.

4. Adopting sustainability as a core business activity is a necessary condition for an organization to strive to be a leader in sustainable development. This requires organizations to assess their portfolio and operations systematically. They can strive for complete transparency in their supply chains and use modern technologies (for example, AI) to monitor and reduce CO_2 emissions.

5. Building the capacity for action: to ensure the effectiveness of the sustainability transformation process, organizations should provide the appropriate competencies and foundations.

6. Taking control of the organization's narrative and engaging investors and stakeholders: organizations that are leaders in sustainable development should create a coherent, distinctive ESG narrative, closely aligned with their mission and strategy. They should continually communicate this narrative to their stakeholders, including key priorities, goals and initiatives, alignment with strategy, and a credible system for measuring and disclosing ESG performance. This drives ongoing dialogue with stakeholders – especially active stakeholders – and engages customers, employees and communities, as they are the ones who drive value creation.

10.3. Sustainability roadmap structures

The popularity of this approach has led scientists working on this issue to propose various structures. Vanegas (Mahalik et al. 2010) proposed a six-step roadmap for a sustainable built environment, including the following steps: (1) Planning; (2) Design; (3) Procurement and construction; (4) Commissioning and start-up; (5) Operations and maintenance; and (6) End-of-service life (Figure 10.2).

Gould and Wallbank proposed a 13-step model for integrating sustainability into real-estate processes: (1) Establish objectives; (2) Inspect buildings and gather data; (3) Establish baseline performance and set targets; (4) Identify opportunities and solutions; (5) Secure space and agree terms; (6) Establish measurement and review processes; (7) Implement initiatives; (8) Manage cultural change; (9) Ongoing performance management; (10) Measure and monitor performance; (11) Review performance annually; (12) Report on results; and (13) Review and feedback with the stages iterated.

Waage (2007) developed a four-step roadmap for product development: (1) Understand and establish sustainability context; (2) Explore and define sustainability issues; (3) Define, refine and assess; and (4) Implement and receive feedback (Figure 10.3).

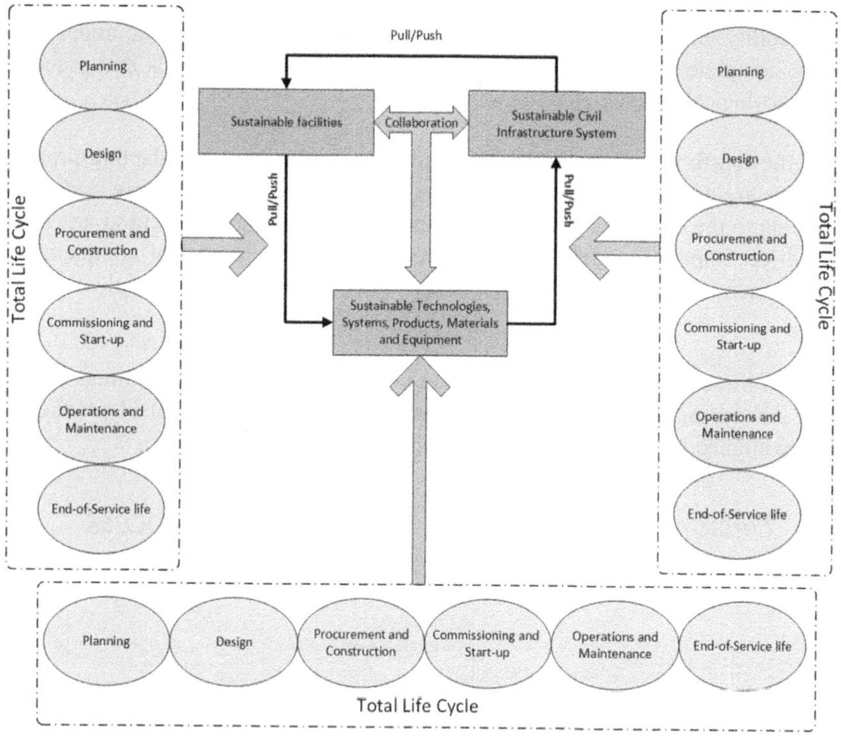

Figure 10.2. *Roadmap of built sustainability environment (Source: own work based on Vanegas (2003))*

Phase one begins with the question, "What is the problem or need?" Sustainability-focused design begins by taking a step back and asking, "What is sustainability?" Building on existing definitions of ecological and social sustainability, the next question arises: "What is the vision for a sustainable product, material or enterprise?" In this sense, defining sustainability guides further action and determines decision-making.

Phase two involves brainstorming potential ways to achieve the desired product function within sustainability parameters. After establishing a long-term perspective and linking it to the overarching vision, steps are taken to define product evaluation criteria, scope and analytical tools.

Phase three considers specific solutions, allowing for a focus on critical sustainability impacts while considering a range of cascading systemic implications from a complete system perspective and the life cycle of materials and processes within ecological and social systems.

In the fourth phase, methods for monitoring, evaluating and adapting products over time are defined to assess whether they have actually become more sustainable according to the defined criteria and parameters. Monitoring can occur at any stage, from direct impact (positive and negative), through the successful completion of strategic actions, to assessing compliance with sustainability principles and the vision.

All of these phases also involve taking concrete actions that will ultimately lead to the development of sustainability roadmaps for the development of products or services aligned with sustainable development (Table 10.1).

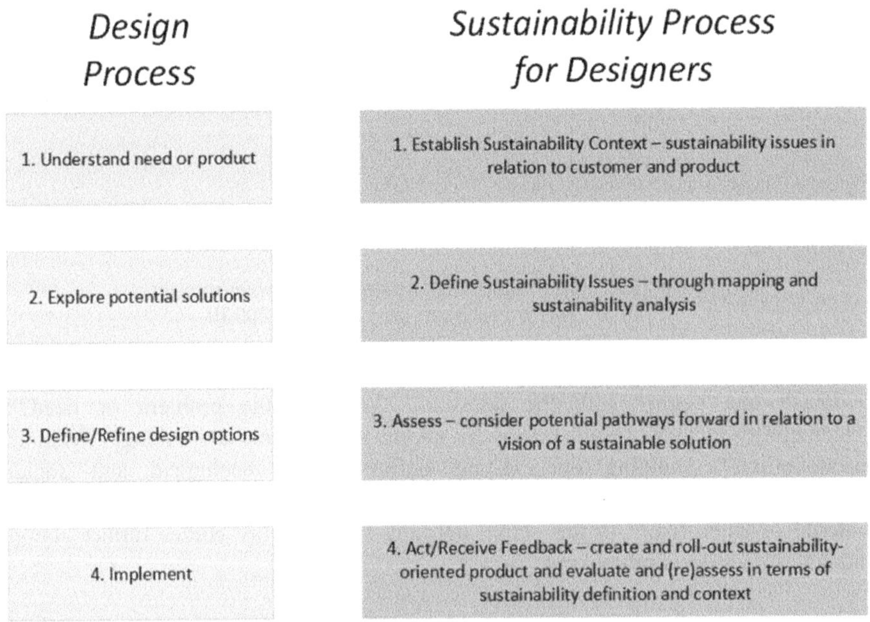

Figure 10.3. *Roadmap for sustainability process (Source: own work based on Waage (2007))*

Phase	Actions
Understanding	- Conducting an assessment of the company's and competitors' environmental and social responsibility policies; - reviewing applicable regulations and risks related to specific products and processes; - characterizing the organization's culture and its position in the context of change; - identifying how the product or service relies on unsustainable practices that impact human and ecosystem health; - identifying how the production and delivery of the product or service rely on unsustainable practices that impact human and ecosystem health, using the four systemic conditions.
Exploring	- Identifying the links between human health, product/facility and environmental impacts; - considering the product's impact within the context of the broader social and ecological systems in which it is used; - developing a sustainability assessment of current products by mapping product systems and flows and considering all product inputs and processes for sustainability factors.
Defining	- Conducting an initial, criteria-based assessment of various potential design solutions against the suggested criteria; - conducting a strategic analysis of various material and design options, using appropriate tools; - using a wide range of information sources and tools, including both qualitative and quantitative information and data relevant to sustainability; - considering the findings within the broader sustainability context developed in the previous phases.
Implementing	- Monitoring the actual impact of products; - dentifying activities that need to be changed; - creating organizational learning mechanisms to leverage new knowledge in future projects.

Table 10.1. *Actions taken in each phase of the sustainability roadmap development (Source: own work based on Waage (2007))*

Duarte et al. (2008) presented a seven-step process tailored to the needs of SMEs: (1) Planning and organization; (2) Environmental assessment; (3) Brainstorming;

(4) CP options feasibility evaluation; (5) Action plan development; (6) Implementation; and (7) Results evaluation, with the stages iterated (Figure 10.4).

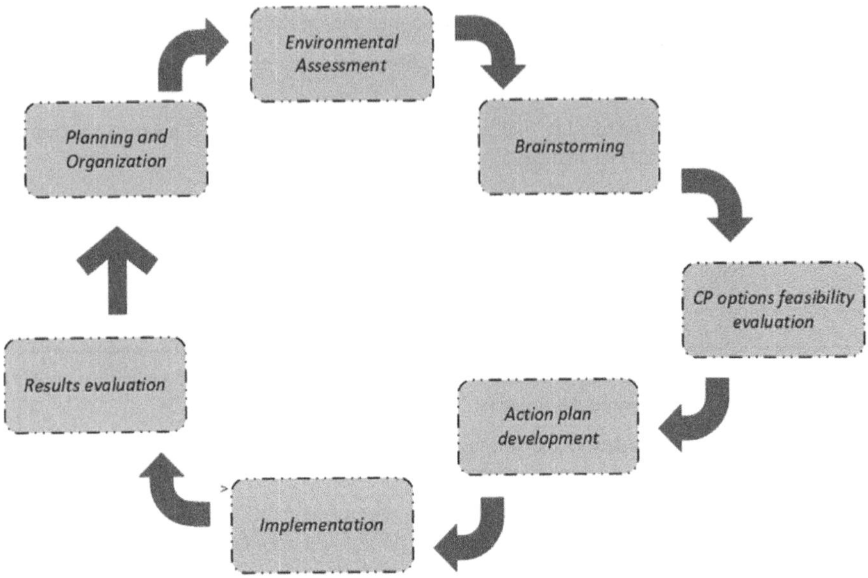

Figure 10.4. *Roadmap's phases (Source: own work based on Duarte et al. (2008))*

The sustainability roadmap they developed is aimed at small- and medium-sized enterprises (SMEs), providing them with knowledge on how to implement sustainability into their operations. One such approach is introducing new knowledge and increasing innovation potential by developing new skills, research and development capabilities and participating in partnerships with scientific and technological institutions.

Nidumolu et al. (2009) described five stages in which companies gain a competitive advantage through sustainability:

1. Viewing compliance as an opportunity: while it is tempting to adhere to the lowest environmental standards for as long as possible, it is wiser to adhere to the most stringent regulations before they are introduced, as this will give your organization a significant first-mover advantage in meeting rigorous standards.

2. Making value chains sustainable: as companies learn to keep up with regulations, they also become more proactive on environmental issues. Many focus on reducing the use of non-renewable resources, such as coal, oil and natural gas, as well as renewable resources, such as water and wood. Also, the drive for efficiency

extends from production plants and offices to the entire value chain. While the initial goal is usually to improve image, most corporations ultimately reduce costs or create new businesses.

3. Designing sustainable products and services: at this stage, companies notice that a large number of consumers are choosing environmentally friendly products, which allows the company to get ahead of the competition by being a leader in the design of existing products or developing new ones.

4. Developing new business models: developing a new business model requires exploring alternatives to the current way of doing business and understanding how to meet customer needs and expectations differently. At this point, executives must learn to question existing models and act entrepreneurially to develop new mechanisms. As a company becomes more adept at developing new business models, the experience it gains will lead it to the final stage of sustainable innovation, where the impact of a new product or process extends beyond a single market.

5. Action plans development: the implementation of new business models also requires the development of an action plan that, based on the experience gained, will take into account sustainability aspects.

6. Implementation: at this stage, the practical implementation of the adopted goals and assumptions takes place.

7. Results evaluation and monitoring: in this phase, the results obtained are monitored, potential disruptions are identified, and solutions are introduced to minimize and improve the implementation of activities.

Lubin and Esty underscored the significance of transformation via new business models:

1. Do old things in new ways: unlike the rest, the organization focuses on outperforming its competitors in regulatory compliance and environmental cost and risk management. This demonstrates its commitment to environmental values.

2. Do new things in new ways: at this stage, the organization extensively redesigns its products, processes and entire systems to optimize the use of natural resources and risk management in its value chain.

3. Transform core business: as activities are implemented, sustainability innovations become a source of new revenue and growth for the entire organization.

4. New business model creation and differentiation: this source ultimately constitutes a differentiation in the business model, brand, employee engagement and other intangible factors that fundamentally change the company's position in the market and in relation to the competition.

Gaining an advantage is not just a matter of vision but also execution in five key areas: leadership, methods, strategy, management and reporting. In each of these areas, an organization must move from a tactical, ad hoc and siloed approach to a strategic, systematic and integrated approach.

Finally, Ahmed and Sundaram (2012) proposed a five-step roadmap linking business, IT and sustainability reporting strategies: (1) Discover and learn; (2) Strategize; (3) Design; (4) Transform; and (5) Monitor and Control, with the stages repeated (Figure 10.5).

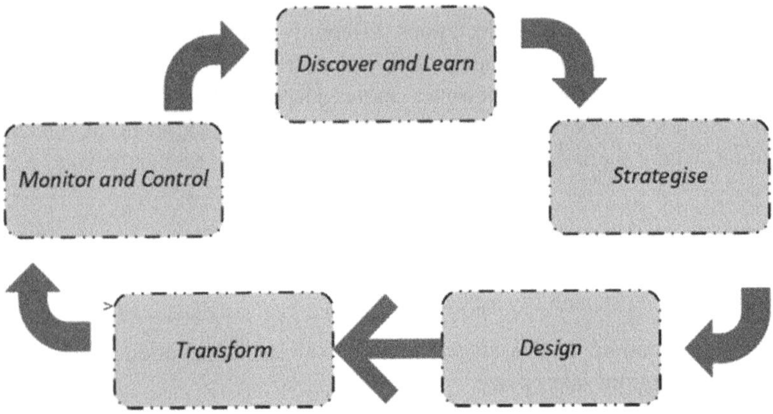

Figure 10.5. *Sustainable business transformation roadmap (Source: own work based on Ahmed and Sundaram (2012))*

The above roadmap serves primarily as a procedural guide to help decision-makers implement the concept of sustainability into traditional businesses and develop a new, sustainable business model. It considers the interactions of business strategies, IT strategies, organizational infrastructure and IT systems, which are viewed as guidelines for proposing the above sustainability roadmap. As Figure 10.5 shows, there is a series of defined stages. The first stage involves identifying unsustainable development within the organization, which allows for the development of a vision for achieving sustainable development. This vision should be realized through one or more strategies, examining various sustainability scenarios and deciding on the strategy that best fits the organization. The next step involves designing the process, organizational elements and technology that will enable the organization to implement the adopted strategy. The process is then implemented through organizational transformation, encompassing processes, organizational structures and IT systems. Transformation is not a one-time event but rather a process of continuous improvement that allows the organization to become increasingly sustainable. This implies the need for continuous monitoring and control of the organization as a whole. Monitoring and control enable continuous discovery and learning about the organization, which in turn can lead to reformulation of the sustainability strategy, redesign and the continuous transformation of the organization into a sustainable organization.

Of course, the above examples of sustainability roadmap structures do not fully exhaust this topic, as the literature contains many proposals for sustainability roadmaps, for example, those developed for the food or fashion industries. However, sustainability roadmaps are a tool widely used by organizations wishing to operate in accordance with the principles of sustainable development.

10.4. Building a sustainable transformation roadmap

For a sustainable transformation process to be successful, it is essential to develop a fully structured and balanced roadmap that aligns with the organization's long-term strategic goals. Such a roadmap provides a clear framework for planning, implementation and monitoring, ensuring that transformation activities are systematic, measurable and adaptable to constantly changing market conditions. The process of creating a sustainability transformation roadmap is complex and involves many stages. Several approaches identifying the successive stages of its development can be found in the literature. In the approach described below, the process of creating a sustainability transformation roadmap encompasses eight stages, including:

1. Defining the organization's vision and goals: while the vision should be fully aligned with the organization's strategic objectives, this also requires identifying key areas of the business that need transformation, such as digital innovation, operational efficiency and customer experience. At this stage, it is also essential to ensure complete alignment of management and stakeholders with the transformation priorities.

2. Conduct a comprehensive assessment to analyze the organization's current health, including strengths, weaknesses and areas for improvement. A gap analysis will be helpful at this stage to identify required changes in technologies, processes, skills and competencies. At this stage, the organization should also gather all input regarding transformation needs from employees, customers and partners.

3. Developing an implementation plan for the entire process: this stage should begin by dividing the entire process into manageable phases with clearly defined milestones. Short-term, medium-term and long-term goals should be determined at this stage to ensure continuous progress. In addition, strategies should be developed to mitigate the risks arising from potential challenges.

4. Effective resource and financial allocation: first, however, the financial, technological and human resources required for each stage of the transformation must be identified. Budget allocation should also be optimized to prioritize high-impact initiatives. Partnerships and external expertise are valuable here, as they can contribute to increased effectiveness of ongoing activities.

5. Investing in the right technologies and tools, including implementing digital solutions that increase operational efficiency and customer engagement, is also crucial. It is also essential to ensure seamless integration of new technologies with existing business processes and to ensure adequate cybersecurity and data protection resources protect the organization's digital assets.

6. Focus on change management and employee engagement by implementing training programs to upskill employees and prepare them for the transformation. It is also essential to cultivate a culture of innovation, adaptability and continuous learning and clearly communicate the transformation goals to minimize employee resistance and encourage their participation in the entire process.

7. Establish key performance indicators (KPIs) and monitoring mechanisms, starting with defining measurable success criteria to track transformation progress. This should leverage data analytics to generate real-time insights, optimize decision-making processes and conduct regular reviews and adjustments, ensuring the roadmap aligns with the organization's current business needs.

8. Ensure continuous improvement and sustainability by focusing the organization on continuous innovation to maintain its agility and competitiveness. Based on feedback and market trends, reassess operations and implement changes to refine the organization's strategy. Develop contingency plans to address unforeseen disruptions and ensure long-term resilience to the ever-changing environment.

In another approach, the process of creating a sustainability transformation road involves six stages, starting with (Bhambri and Bajdor 2024; Bhambri and Paweloszek 2024; Rana and Bhambri 2024a, 2024b; Bhambri et al. 2025):

1. Engage management, as developing a sustainability transformation roadmap should begin with securing top management support. As company experience shows, it is their involvement and support that determines the effectiveness of the entire process. Furthermore, management sets the direction and pace of change, so before beginning, it is important to ensure they actively support the entire process.

2. Set both short- and long-term goals, ensuring they are aligned with the organization's mission and vision. At this stage, it is crucial to engage all stakeholders – employees, customers and investors. It is also worth conducting an audit or strengths, weaknesses, opportunities and threats (SWOT) analysis to identify areas of need.

3. Define KPIs that measurably track progress. Furthermore, analyzing the results will allow for establishing benchmarks and tracking changes over time.

4. Develop an action plan encompassing programs and initiatives that will reduce the negative impact of the organization's operations on the environment – for example, investments in renewable energy sources, waste reduction or a more sustainable supply chain. Prioritize actions that will yield the most outstanding results, and the draft plan itself should be consulted with key stakeholders and regularly updated.

5. Communicate and execute the developed roadmap: implementing the strategy requires developing an implementation schedule, reporting progress and ongoing communication with stakeholders. Communicating goals, activities and results increases transparency and builds their trust in the organization's activities.

6. Monitoring and assessing progress: a regular assessment allows the organization to meet its ESG commitments and identify further opportunities for improvement.

To achieve success in implementing a sustainability transformation roadmap, it is worth remembering several issues: it is necessary to ensure the full involvement of management staff to gain their support and a sense of responsibility for the implemented actions; encourage cooperation between individual departments or divisions of the organization; set SMART goals (specific, measurable, achievable, realistic and time-based) and regularly monitor progress in their implementation; use available real-time data to conduct analyses that will enable the making of informed decisions; prioritize actions based on their feasibility and potential impact; emphasize achieved results and completed milestones, which translates into maintaining commitment and building awareness; and remain flexible and adaptable, i.e. open to the need to update the developed roadmap to adapt it to changing internal and external circumstances.

10.5. Conclusion

Nowadays, developing a sustainability transformation roadmap is a milestone in the business transformation process of an entire organization. Its development and implementation are key steps for any organization seeking to reduce its environmental impact and build a more sustainable future. Only by clearly defining goals, developing a phased implementation plan, effectively allocating resources and ensuring continuous improvement can a successful business transformation be achieved in line with sustainability. It is also important to remember that sustainability is not a one-time endeavor – it is an ongoing journey that requires commitment, collaboration and accountability.

A well-developed, implemented and executed roadmap will not only increase the organization's operational efficiency but also enable its continued growth in an environment where sustainability plays an increasingly important role. It is also worth noting that a sustainability transformation roadmap will contribute to transforming the organization into a fully sustainable enterprise, capable of playing a key role in building a more sustainable future for all.

10.6. References

Ahmed, M.D. and Sundaram, D. (2012). Sustainability modelling and reporting: From roadmap to implementation. *Decision Support Systems*, 53(3), 611–624.

Ayari, F., Srasra, E., Trabelsi-Ayadi, M. (2005). Characterization of bentonitic clays and their use as adsorbent. *Desalination*, 185, 391–397.

Benyounis, K.Y., Olabi, A.G., Hashmi, M.S.J. (2005). Effect of laser welding parameters on the heat input and weld-bead profile. *J. Mater. Process Technol.*, 164, 978–985.

Bhambri, P. and Bajdor, P. (eds) (2024). *Handbook of Technological Sustainability: Innovation and Environmental Awareness*. CRC Press, Boca Raton. doi: 10.1201/9781003475989.

Bhambri, P. and Paweloszek, I. (2024). Introduction to digital sustainability and entrepreneurship. In *Digital Sustainability: Navigating Entrepreneurship in the Information Age*, Bhambri, P. and Paweloszek, I. (eds). CRC Press, Boca Raton, 18–35. doi: 10.1201/9781003484226-2.

Bhambri, P., Rana, R., Kautish, S. (2025). Sustainable digital transformation: Reducing carbon footprint in the metaverse. In *Metaverse and Sustainability: Business Resilience towards Sustainable Development Goals*, Leal Filho, W., Kautish, S., Gupta, V.P. (eds). Springer, Cham, 105–128. doi: 10.1007/978-3-031-89545-6_7.

Box, G.E.P. and Hunter, J.S. (1957). Multi factor experimental designs for exploring response surfaces. *Ann. Math Statist.*, 28, 195–241.

Box, G.E.P. and Hunter, J.S. (1961). The 2k p fractional factorial designs, parts I and II. *J. Technometrics*, 3, 311–458.

Cronje, K.J., Chetty, K., Carsky, M., Sahu, J.N., Meikap, B.C. (2011). Optimization of chromium(VI) sorption potential using developed activated carbonfrom sugarcane bagasse with chemical activation by zinc chloride. *Desalination*, 275, 276–284.

Duarte, A.P., Martins, P., Alexandre, J. (2008). Pro-active behaviour induction by integration of sustainability in business strategic management: INOVE project case study. *Journal of Cleaner Production*, 16(10), 1127–1132.

Erdem, B., Özcan, A., Özcan, A.S. (2010). Adsorption and solid phase extraction of 8-hydroxyquinoline from aqueous solutions by using natural bentonite. *Appl. Surf. Sci.*, 256, 5422–5427.

Gottipati, R. and Mishra, S. (2010). Process optimization of adsorption of Cr(VI) on activated carbons prepared fromplant precursors by a two-level full factorial design. *Chem. Eng. J.*, 160, 99–107.

Han, R., Ding, D., Xu, Y., Zou, W., Wang, Y., Li, Y., Zou, L. (2008). Use of rice husk for the adsorption of congo red from aqueous solution in column mode. *Bioresour. Technol.*, 99, 2938–2946.

Hu, Q.H., Xu, Z.P., Qiao, S.Z. (2007). A novel color removal adsorbent from hetero coagulation of cationic and anionic clays. *J. Colloid Interface Sci.*, 308, 191–199.

Kumar, A., Kumar, S., Kumar, S., Gupta, D.V. (2007). Adsorption of phenol and 4-nitrophenol on granular activated carbon in basal salt medium: Equilibriumand kinetics. *J. Hazard Mater.*, 147, 155–166.

Lian, L., Guo, L., Wang, A. (2009). Use of $CaCl_2$ modified bentonite for removal of Congo red dye from aqueous solutions. *Desalination*, 249, 797–801.

Lubin, D.A. and Esty, D.C. (2010). The sustainability imperative. *Harvard Business Review*, 88(5), 42–50.

Mahalik, K., Sahu, J.N., Patwardhan, A.V., Meikap, B.C. (2010). Statistical modelling and optimization of hydrolysis of urea to generate ammonia for flue gas conditioning. *J. Hazard Mater.*, 182, 603–610.

Muthukumar, M., Mohan, D., Rajendran, M. (2003). Optimization of mix proportions of mineral aggregates using Box-Behnken design of experiments. *Cem. Concr. Compos.*, 25, 751–758.

Myers, R.H. (1971). *Response Surface Methodology*. Allyn and Bacon, New York.

Myers, R.H. and Montgomery, D.C. (2002). *Response Surface Methodology: Process and Product Optimization using Designed Experiments*, 2nd edition. John Wiley and Sons, New York.

Nidumolu, R., Prahalad, C.K., Rangaswami, M.R. (2009). Why sustainability is now the key driver of innovation. *Harvard Business Review*, 87(9), 57–64 [Online]. Available at: https://hbr.org/2009/09/why-sustainability-is-now-the-key-driver-of-innovation.

Ozer, A., Gurbuz, G., Calimli, A., Korbahti, B.K. (2008). Investigation of nickel (II) biosorption on Enteromorphaprolifera: Optimization using response surface analysis. *J. Hazard Mater.*, 152, 778–788.

Rana, R. and Bhambri, P. (2024a). Hybrid MCDM (multi-criteria decision-making) approaches for sustainable energy management. In *Modern SuperHyperSoft Computing Trends in Science and Technology*, Smarandache, F. and Majumder, P. (eds). IGI Global, Hershey, 149–184. doi: 10.4018/979-8-3693-6875-6.ch006.

Rana, R. and Bhambri, P. (2024b). Environmental challenges and technological solutions. In *Handbook of Technological Sustainability: Innovation and Environmental Awareness*, Bhambri, P. and Bajdor, P. (eds). CRC Press, Boca Raton, 187–200. doi: 10.1201/9781003475989 17.

Raymundo, A.S., Zanarotto, R., Belisario, M., Pereira, M.G., Ribeiro, J.N., Ribeiro, A.V.F.N. (2010). Evaluation of sugar-cane bagasse as bioadsorbent in the textile wastewater treatment contaminated with carcinogenic congo red dye. *Brazilian Arch. Biology Technol.*, 53, 931–938.

Sabnis, R.W. (2010). *Handbook of Biological Dyes and Stains. Synthesis and Industrial Applications*. John Wiley and Sons, New York.

Sanghi, R. and Bhattacharya, B. (2002). Review on decolorisation of aqueous dye solutions by low cost adsorbents. *Color Technol.*, 118, 256–269.

Somasekhara Reddy, M.C., Sivaramakrishna, L., Varada Reddy, A. (2012). The use of an agricultural waste material, jujuba seeds for the removal of anionic dye (Congo red) from aqueous medium. *J. Hazard Mater.*, 203, 118–127.

Tarangini, K., Kumar, A., Satpathy, G.R., Sangal, V.K. (2009). Statistical optimization of process parameters for Cr (VI) biosorption onto mixed cultures of *Pseudomonas aeruginosa* and *Bacillus subtilis*. *Clean*, 37, 319–327.

Vanegas, J.A. (2003). Road map and principles for built environment sustainability. *Environmental Science & Technology*, 37(23), 5363–5372.

Voulvoulis, N. and Burgman, M.A. (2019). The contrasting roles of science and technology in environmental challenges. *Critical Reviews in Environmental Science and Technology*, 49(12), 1079–1106.

Waage, S.A. (2007). Re-considering product design: A practical "roadmap" for integration of sustainability issues. *Journal of Cleaner Production*, 15(7), 638–649.

Wang, L., Li, J., Wang, Y., Zhao, L., Jiang, Q. (2010). Adsorption capability for Congo red on nanocrystal HneMFe204 (M = Mn, Fe, Co, Ni) spinel ferrites. *Chem. Eng. J.* doi: 10.1016/j.cej.-2011.10.088.

Xin, X., Si, W., Yao, Z., Feng, R., Du, B., Yan, L., Wei, Q. (2011). Adsorption of benzoic acid from aqueous solution by three kinds of modified bentonites. *J. Colloid Interface Sci.*, 359, 499–504.

11

Reimagining Supply Chains: Nearshoring and Network Redesign in the Age of AI, Automation and Sustainability

Resilient supply chains are essential at a time of global upheavals, including pandemics and geopolitical conflicts. Network redesign and nearshoring have become key tactics in the larger shift to next-generation supply chains, especially in light of automation, artificial intelligence (AI) and sustainability requirements. Production and sourcing are moving closer to end markets through a process known as "nearshoring", which lessens reliance on lengthy and unstable international supply chains and promotes greater flexibility and reaction times. Reconfiguring supply chain nodes and flows strategically to maximize efficiency, reduce risk and achieve sustainability objectives is a concurrent aspect of network redesign.

In order to facilitate dynamic decision-making in network designs, real-time visibility and predictive capabilities are made possible by the integration of AI and sophisticated analytics. While sustainable measures, such as reducing carbon emissions and implementing circular logistics, are becoming increasingly important to stakeholder expectations and regulatory compliance, automation simplifies processes, lowers costs and improves consistency. Technology and strategic geography work together to help organizations rebalance resilience and efficiency.

This chapter investigates how network redesign and nearshoring are proactive facilitators of flexible, intelligent and sustainable operations as well as solutions to supply chain vulnerabilities. We analyze how companies are using digital twins, AI-driven simulations and machine learning to optimize their supply chains while adhering to environmental and social governance (ESG) principles through case studies and data-driven insights. Supply chains' future ultimately rests on locally rooted, digitally enabled and adaptable networks that promote long-term competitiveness in a changing world.

Chapter written by Jeffy JOHNSON.

11.1. Introduction

Network redesign, which entails reorganizing supply chain nodes, routes and partners strategically, and nearshoring, which includes moving manufacturing or sourcing closer to important markets, are two tactics that are becoming increasingly popular. Automation, digital twins and AI have made it possible for businesses to combine efficiency and resilience, while sustainability objectives call for a decrease in waste, emissions and resource intensity (Rana and Bhambri 2025). The impact of nearshoring and network redesign on next-generation supply chains, aided by automation and AI, is examined in this chapter. Assessing their effects on sustainability, costs and resilience, we employ a mixed-methods approach, looking at case studies, industry data and simulation frameworks.

11.2. Experimental methods and materials

11.2.1. *Research approach*

1. Review of the literature: academic papers, governmental documents on supply chain resilience and nearshoring, and consultancy reports from firms such as McKinsey, Deloitte and BCG.

2. Case study analysis: an analysis of how multinational companies (including Apple, Tesla, Unilever and Zara) are utilizing automation, network reconfiguration and nearshoring.

3. Data collection: Statista supply chain statistics, the World Bank Logistics Performance Index (World Bank 2022) and UNCTAD secondary datasets.

4. Simulation modeling: to evaluate conventional offshore and nearshore supply chain architectures, digital twin scenarios were developed (fictitious for this work).

11.3. Nearshoring as a resilience strategy

In the past, supply chain globalization has placed a strong emphasis on outsourcing to low-cost areas, especially Asia, in order to optimize economies of scale and cost effectiveness. However, the vulnerabilities of this paradigm have been revealed by global disruptions such as the Covid-19 pandemic, the conflict between Russia and Ukraine, and growing climate-related hazards (Ivanov and Dolgui 2020). In reaction, businesses are using nearshoring – moving sourcing or production closer to demand markets – as a means of enhancing resilience (Rana and Bhambri 2024). This study of the literature summarizes scholarly research, consultant reports and business examples regarding how nearshoring might improve supply chain resilience (Christopher 2016).

11.4. Conceptual foundations of nearshoring

According to Ellram et al. (2013), nearshoring is the practice of moving production or sourcing operations nearby, usually inside the same trading bloc. In contrast to reshoring, which involves relocating production back to the nation of origin, nearshoring preserves a component of global production while lowering the geographical and sociopolitical distance between nodes.

The theory is in line with supply chain resilience, which highlights networks' capacity to endure, adjust and bounce back from shocks (Christopher and Peck 2004).

Both proactive and reactive resilience are offered by nearshoring, which lowers risk exposure and speeds up recovery from disruptions.

11.5. Drivers of nearshoring adoption

1. Disruption Risk and Geopolitics: the pandemic brought to light the vulnerability of extended supply chains that rely on offshore providers that are a single source (Ivanov 2022). In addition, the demand for regional diversity has increased due to Brexit, the Ukraine crisis and trade concerns between the United States and China.

2. Technological Developments: the labor cost difference between high- and low-wage areas is closing due to automation, robots and AI (Deloitte 2022). Therefore, being close to clients is becoming a more important competitive advantage than having inexpensive labor (Bhambri et al. 2024).

3. Sustainability and ESG Compliance: by lowering transportation-related emissions, nearshoring helps businesses meet their carbon neutrality goals and adhere to laws such as the EU Green Deal (European Commission 2021).

4. Customer-centric Supply Chains: businesses are using nearshoring to reduce lead times and increase flexibility due to the need for mass customization and quick response in sectors including fashion, electronics and pharmaceuticals (BCG 2023).

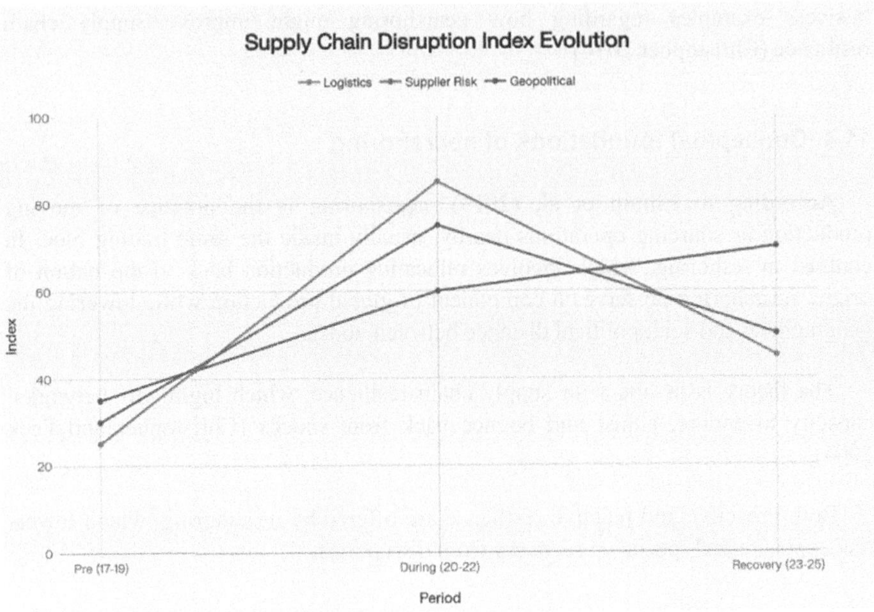

Figure 11.1. *Supply chain disruption index evolution across three time periods. For a color version of this figure, see www.iste.co.uk/bhambri/nextgensupply.zip*

11.6. Benefits of nearshoring

1. Lead Time Reduction: research shows that being close by can reduce lead times by 50–70%, improving responsiveness (Gray et al. 2013). For instance, shipping times to the United States are shortened from 30 to 45 days to less than ten days when clothing manufacture is moved from Asia to Mexico (BCG 2023).

2. Risk Diversification: by distributing production capacity across several regions, nearshoring reduces supply bottlenecks and concentration risk (Dolgui and Ivanov 2021).

3. Carbon Footprint Reduction: according to UNCTAD (2023), nearshoring can save CO_2 emissions per delivered unit by as much as 60%. This brings supply chains into line with stakeholder expectations and environmental, social and governance (ESG) goals (UNCTAD 2023).

4. Political and Economic Alignment: by lowering tariff risks and using regional free trade agreements, nearshoring enhances trade inside regional blocs like the United States–Mexico–Canada Agreement (USMCA) and the European Union (EU) (Gereffi 2018).

11.7. Challenges and risks of nearshoring

1. Cost Trade-offs: nearshoring frequently results in greater production costs as compared to offshore manufacturing centers, even though automation lowers labor arbitrage. Businesses have to strike a balance between profitability and resilience (Ellram et al. 2013).

2. Limitations in Capacity: Areas nearer to markets for consumption could not have the same level of industry, supplier networks or highly qualified labor pools as Asia (Kinkel and Maloca 2009).

3. Transition Complexity: Nearshoring is a long-term approach rather than a temporary solution because network redesign and supplier realignment necessitate large investments, infrastructure improvements and regulatory coordination (Deloitte 2022).

Parameter	Offshore (Asia to US)	Nearshore (Mexico to US)
Lead time	30–45 days	7–10 days
Transport cost/unit	$0.50–$0.70	$0.20–$0.35
CO_2 emissions/unit	3.8 kg	1.2 kg
Risk exposure index	High	Medium

Table 11.1. *Comparative metrics of offshore versus nearshore models*[1]

1 "Nearshoring to Mexico reduces lead times from 30–45 days to under 10 days compared to Asian offshore models" (McKinsey 2022; BCG 2023).

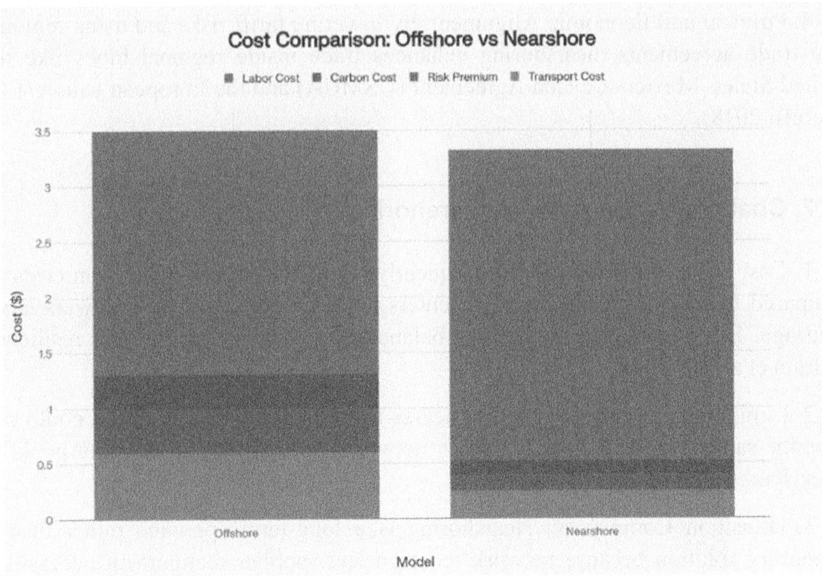

Figure 11.2. *Total cost analysis: offshore versus nearshore supply chain models. For a color version of this figure, see www.iste.co.uk/bhambri/nextgensupply.zip*

11.8. Industry case studies

1. Inditex's Zara: as opposed to its offshore competitors' 3–6 month cycle, Zara can refresh collections in-store in 2–3 weeks thanks to its nearshoring model in Spain, Portugal and Morocco (Ghemawat and Nueno 2006).

2. GM or General Motors: to protect North American manufacturing during the pandemic, GM increased its nearshore sourcing from Mexico. Despite worldwide shipping delays, this stabilized production and decreased dependency on components sourced from China.

3. The Unilever Group: with the use of nearshored manufacturing facilities in Europe, Unilever has been able to lower logistics emissions and supply chain CO_2 by 33% while preserving service standards (Unilever 2022).

4. Apfel: a hybrid style of nearshoring and "friend-shoring" to politically associated nations, Apple is increasingly diversifying production to India and Vietnam, despite its continued reliance on China (McKinsey 2022).

11.9. Theoretical and analytical frameworks

Resource-Based View (RBV): by enhancing supply chain agility and responsiveness, which are regarded as intangible assets under RBV theory, nearshoring helps businesses' strategic resources (Barney 1991).

Transaction Cost Economics (TCE): this approach helps businesses make more balanced decisions by balancing the costs of offshore risks (such as tariffs, delays and interruptions) against higher nearshore production costs (Williamson 1981).

Ivanov (2022) introduces the idea of viability, or the long-term sustainability and adaptability of supply chains, as an extension of resilience theory. By including sustainability and redundancy into network architectures, nearshoring promotes viability (Ivanov and Dolgui 2020).

11.10. Future directions in nearshoring research

Researchers stress the importance of using digital twins and AI-powered simulations to quantitatively analyze the trade-offs associated with nearshoring (cost, risk and emissions). The function of nearshoring in circular supply chains should be investigated in future studies, especially in sectors that are using reverse logistics for sustainability.

Nearshoring is becoming a vital resilience tactic in global supply chains, striking a balance between robustness, sustainability, customer responsiveness and efficiency (Bhambri and Kumar 2024). Although there are still obstacles to overcome, namely in the areas of cost and capacity, nearshoring is becoming increasingly feasible due to technology advancements in automation and AI as well as regulatory requirements for sustainability. Businesses are better positioned to prosper in a time of constant innovation if they combine nearshoring with digital twins, network redesign and ESG frameworks (Rani et al. 2024).

11.11. Network redesign and digital twins

Pandemics, disruptions brought on by climate change, geopolitical conflicts and shifting consumer demand are all increasing the volatility of global supply networks. These variables are difficult for traditional linear supply chain models to handle, which are primarily optimized for cost and efficiency. In order to attain resilience, agility and sustainability, businesses are adopting network redesign aided by digital twin technologies.

11.11.1. *Network redesign in supply chains*

In order to balance resilience and efficiency, network redesign entails rearranging the supply chain nodes' flow and structure, including manufacturers, suppliers, warehouses, distribution hubs and transportation corridors. Modern networks, in contrast to static, cost-optimized designs, are dynamic, risk-sensitive and sustainability-driven. The following are important forces behind network redesign:

– Geopolitical and Realignment: businesses diversify their supply chains to avoid relying solely on one nation; for example, they may leave China and expand into Southeast Asia, Eastern Europe and Latin America.

– Demand Volatility: to respond more quickly, redesigns incorporate several regional distribution hubs.

– The imperatives of sustainability: businesses are pushed to optimize for carbon footprint rather than merely cost by carbon taxes and ESG rules.

– Technology Enablement: predictive models and analytics powered by AI determine the best places to put facilities. Nike, for instance, restructured its logistics in Europe by combining smaller facilities into two highly automated hubs, which reduced CO_2 emissions and delivery lead times by 50%.

11.11.2. *Digital twins in supply chain redesign*

A virtual supply chain that is updated in real time is called a digital twin. Supply chains become more predictive and adaptive by integrating the Internet of Things (IoT) data, AI-driven simulations and advanced analytics to evaluate various "what-if" scenarios. Key features of digital twins for supply chains:

– Companies use scenario testing to model the effects of disruptions, such as port closures, surges in demand or shortages of raw materials.

– Predictive optimization: machine learning algorithms optimize sourcing tactics, transportation routes and inventory allocation.

– Real-time monitoring: IoT sensors provide the twin with real-time data (temperature, inventory levels and delays) so that it may be adjusted continuously.

– Sustainability Modeling: CO_2 trade-offs between modes of transportation (air, sea and rail) are computed using digital twins.

– Unilever as a Case Example: The company simulates sourcing and transportation scenarios using digital twins to optimize its food supply chain in Europe. This resulted in a 15% reduction in logistical expenses and a 20% increase in carbon efficiency.

11.11.3. *Synergy: digital twins driving network redesign*

Supply networks that are data-driven, flexible and shock-resistant are produced by combining digital twins with network redesign.

– Strategic Resilience: in the event of a disruption, businesses can quickly move production to different suppliers or locations. Mass customization and responsive logistics are made possible by agility.

– Sustainability: determines which distribution strategies and facility design are the most environmentally friendly.

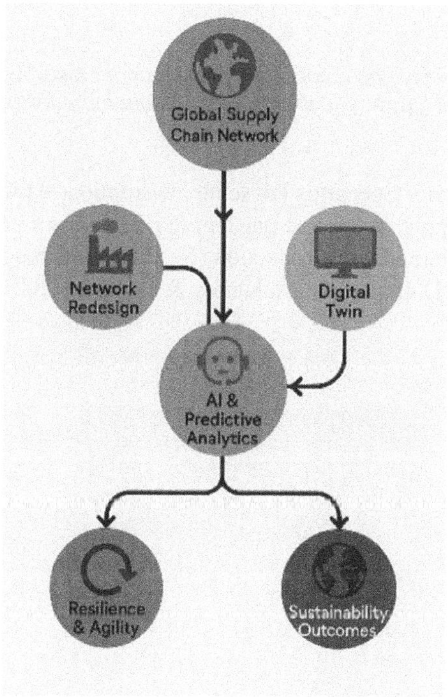

Figure 11.3. *AI-driven supply chain emission reductions for how digital twins and AI simulations help firms balance cost and sustainability*

Figure 11.4 (described):

– X-axis = Scenarios (baseline, disruption, AI-optimized redesign).

– Y-axis = Average supply chain cost per unit ($).

– The graph shows cost spikes during disruption but reduced costs (5–10% lower than baseline) under AI-optimized redesign.

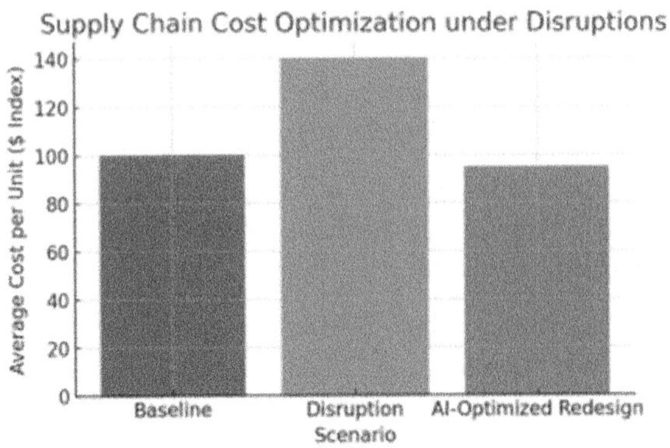

Figure 11.4. *Supply chain cost optimization under disruptions. For a color version of this figure, see www.iste.co.uk/bhambri/nextgensupply.zip*

Description: X-axis = Scenarios (Baseline, Disruption, AI-Optimized Redesign). Y-axis = Average supply chain cost per unit ($).This shows baseline stability, cost spikes during disruption and cost reduction (5–10% below baseline) after AI-driven redesign (Ivanov and Dolgui 2020; McKinsey & Company 2021; Deloitte 2022).

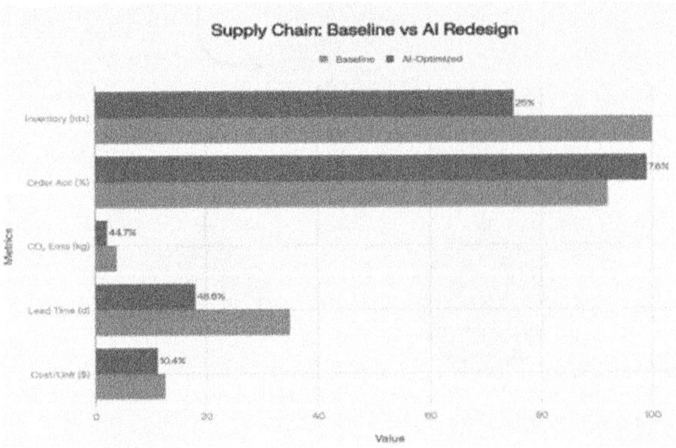

Figure 11.5. *Supply chain resilience metrics: baseline versus AI-optimized redesign. For a color version of this figure, see www.iste.co.uk/bhambri/nextgensupply.zip*

11.12. Challenges and future directions

Cross-enterprise integration and sophisticated IT infrastructure are necessary for the creation of digital twins, but are expensive. Data gaps highlight the need for accurate modeling, where many supply chains lack dependable real-time data. Also, there is a skills gap, where businesses need people who know how to use AI, analytics and digital infrastructure. Regarding cybersecurity, the use of digital twins exposes people to more security risks. Blockchain integration for transparency, generative AI for design optimization and cloud-based collaborative digital twins that span entire ecosystems rather than just one company are some of the future trends.

11.12.1. *Automation and AI in supply chain optimization*

Automation includes robots lowering labor costs and error rates in warehouses. AI encompasses route optimization conserving fuel, predictive maintenance minimizes downtime and machine learning forecasts demand. As an illustration, DHL's AI routing lowers fuel usage by 8–10%, while Amazon's robotics lowers warehouse expenses by about 20%. Supply chain operations are evolving from cost-driven linear models to intelligent, adaptive ecosystems due to the quick uptake of automation and AI. Especially in the face of global disruptions, these technologies help businesses satisfy environmental goals, increase resilience and increase efficiency.

11.12.2. *Role of automation in supply chains*

Automating repetitive, error-prone tasks replaces them with systems that are accurate, scalable and fast. Picking, packing and sorting are made easier by robotic arms and autonomous guided vehicles (AGVs) in warehousing. Autonomous transportation and logistics includes drones and self-driving trucks lessening reliance on human labor and address driver shortages. Procurement, billing and compliance reporting are all handled via Process Automation (RPA). The impact includes increasing worker productivity while cutting expenses and improving safety. Amazon, for instance, has deployed over 750,000 warehouse robots, lowering operating costs and enabling same-day delivery models.

11.12.3. *AI applications*

With data-driven insights and predictive analytics, AI improves decision-making throughout supply chains. By accurately predicting demand (demand forecasting) at the SKU level, machine learning models reduce overstocks and stockouts. Predictive maintenance minimizes downtime in production and logistics fleets by using AI sensors to predict equipment breakdowns. Inventory optimization inlcudes real-time adjustments to safety stock levels and reorder points are made by dynamic algorithms. Supply risk management includes foreseeing interruptions, and AI analyses geopolitical, news and meteorological data. For instance, DHL employs

AI-driven routing algorithms to increase fuel efficiency and cut last-mile delivery expenses by 15%.

11.12.4. *Combined impact of automation + AI*

Businesses can transition from reactive to proactive supply chain management through the combination of automation and AI. By integrating IoT data, AI provides managers with comprehensive shipping visibility (real-time visibility). During interruptions, automated decision-making distributes inventory among areas, therefore highlighting adaptive networks. Sustainability includes automation lowering material waste, while AI chooses transportation options that use less carbon.

See Table 11.2 (Automation and AI impact on KPIs), which compares improvements in lead time, cost savings and sustainability metrics.

11.12.5. *Challenges and limitations*

High capital expenditure includes AI and robotics systems demanding large initial outlays of funds. Data silos highlight training and integrating AI models that are hampered by fragmented IT systems. Automation necessitates reskilling programs since it raises concerns about job losses (work displacement). Supply chains are vulnerable to cyberattacks as a result of increased interconnectedness (cybersecurity risks).

11.12.6. *Future directions*

Using AI to model different supply chain configurations is known as "generative AI in scenario planning". Hyper-automated warehouses are "dark warehouses" with little human interaction combine robotics, AI and the IoT. AI-blockchain integration includes guaranteeing safe and transparent product tracking, and human–machine collaboration enhances rather than substitutes human judgment.

KPI	Before automation	After automation/AI
Order accuracy	92%	99%
Fulfillment speed	24 hrs	6–8 hrs
Inventory costs	Baseline 100%	80%
Fuel usage per unit	100%	88–90%

Table 11.2. *Automation and AI impact on KPIs*[2]

2 Warehouse automation has improved order accuracy from 92% to 99%, with fulfillment speeds cut by two-thirds (Deloitte 2022; DHL 2022).

11.13. Sustainability and ESG compliance in supply chains

The global sustainability agenda revolves around supply chains. For numerous industries, they are responsible for over 90% of environmental damage and over 80% of greenhouse gas (GHG) emissions (CDP 2022). In response, governments, investors, consumers and international organizations are putting increasing pressure on businesses to include ESG principles in their supply chain plans. Due to this, sustainability is now a strategic necessity for resilience and competitiveness rather than just a "corporate responsibility" endeavor.

11.13.1. *Environmental sustainability in supply chains*

Carbon reduction includes cutting down on transportation distances, nearshoring and multimodal logistics lower freight emissions. Reuse, recycling and reverse logistics reduce waste and establish closed-loop systems (circular supply chains). Renewable energy in operations include wind and solar energy being used more and more to power manufacturing facilities and warehouses; also, green procurement includes businesses evaluating the carbon footprints of their suppliers and demand adherence to goals based on scientific research. By 2030, for instance, IKEA wants to have a completely circular supply chain that uses only recycled or renewable materials and decarbonizes logistics by employing biofuels and electric trucks.

11.13.2. *Social dimensions of ESG in supply chains*

Labor standard encompass making sure that rules set out by the International Labour Organisation (ILO) are followed in order to stop child labor and forced labor. While digital monitoring and automation increase workplace safety, businesses also need to make investments in retraining employees to increase employee well-being. Fair wages and local sourcing include nearshoring programs supporting fair trade standards and the creation of jobs in the area. For instance, Patagonia uses stringent supplier checks to guarantee moral working conditions throughout its international sourcing network.

11.13.3. *Governance and transparency*

Businesses are required by laws like Germany's Supply Chain Due Diligence Act (2023) and the EU's Corporate Sustainability Due Diligence Directive (CSDDD) to keep an eye on environmental and human rights threats among their suppliers, and therefore complete regulatory compliance. Expectations from investors include supply chain transparency being a top concern for capital markets due to ESG reporting frameworks such as the Sustainability Accounting Standards

Board (SASB) and the Global Reporting Initiative (GRI). Distributed ledger systems guarantee unchangeable raw material tracking, such as that of cobalt in electric vehicle batteries (blockchain for traceability).

11.13.4. *Business case for ESG-aligned supply chains*

– *Risk mitigation:* ESG compliance lowers the risk of fines, reputational damage and operational disruptions.

– *Market access:* many procurement contracts and trade partnerships now mandate ESG disclosures.

– *Consumer loyalty:* environmentally and ethically conscious supply chains drive brand differentiation.

– *Financial performance:* studies show that ESG-compliant firms outperform peers in stock valuation and long-term resilience.

See Table 11.1 (Comparative metrics of offshore versus nearshore models), which demonstrates how nearshoring contributes to carbon and compliance benefits.

11.13.5. *Challenges in ESG compliance*

– Data collection: in many cases, small suppliers are unable to report.

– Cost pressures: ESG compliance necessitates an initial certification and technological investment.

– Standard fragmentation: many ESG standards, including TCFD, SASB, ISSB and GRI, make reporting more difficult.

– Risks of greenwashing: businesses may overstate their ESG accomplishments without independent confirmation.

11.13.6. *Future directions*

Digital ESG dashboards should be used, which track supplier compliance using AI. Indirect supplier emissions will be included in carbon reporting by more businesses under Scope 3 Emissions Accounting. Platforms for collaboration include industry alliances, such as the Sustainable Apparel Coalition and Clean Cargo, which will standardize standards. AI and digital twins for sustainability include simulations that optimize transportation, resources and facility design to reduce carbon emissions.

Figure 11.6 (described):

– Y-axis = CO_2 emissions per unit shipped.

– X-axis = Supply chain model (offshore baseline, nearshore, redesigned circular logistics).

– Result: circular logistics achieves 45–50% lower emissions than offshore baseline.

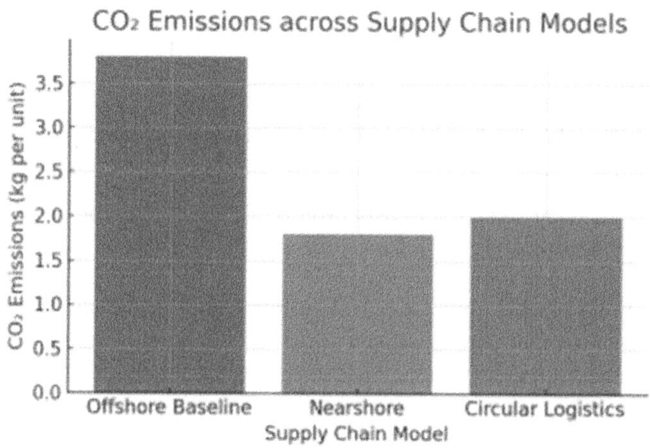

Figure 11.6. *CO_2 emissions across supply chain models. For a color version of this figure, see www.iste.co.uk/bhambri/nextgensupply.zip*

Description: Y-axis = CO_2 emissions per unit shipped. X-axis = Models (Offshore Baseline, Nearshore, Redesigned Circular Logistics). Circular logistics shows 45–50% lower emissions than baseline (European Commission 2021; Unilever 2022, BCG 2023; UNCTAD 2023).

11.14. Analysis of supply chain performance graphs

11.14.1. *Chart 1: supply chain performance – baseline versus AI-optimized redesign*

Important conclusions

There are notable performance gains in all important metrics when comparing baseline operations with AI-optimized network redesign:

– Lead time reduction: the biggest improvement demonstrates a 48.6% decrease from 35 days to 18 days, demonstrating AI's capacity to optimize inventory and predictive routing to minimize bottlenecks and streamline logistics processes.

– Effectiveness of cost: contrary to the conventional trade-off between resilience and efficiency, a 10.4% decrease in cost per unit (from $12.5 to $11.2) shows that AI optimization can increase other performance indicators while achieving cost savings.

– The reduction of CO_2 emissions by 44.7% (from 3.8 kg to 2.1 kg per unit) demonstrates the environmental impact of AI-driven route optimization and modal selection, which greatly advances sustainability objectives without sacrificing operational effectiveness.

– Operational excellence: the accuracy of orders increases from 92% to 99%, a 7.6% improvement that results in significant customer satisfaction and lower return costs.

– Capital efficiency: inventory costs drop by 25%, demonstrating AI systems' improved demand forecasting and just-in-time optimization capabilities.

Strategic implications: this data demonstrates how advanced analytics may concurrently enhance cost, speed, accuracy and sustainability parameters, bolstering the commercial case for AI investment in supply chain transformation.

11.14.2. *Chart 2: supply chain disruption index evolution*

Temporal analysis

The evolution of supply chain disruptions reveals three distinct phases with lasting structural changes:

– Pre-pandemic stability (2017–2019): all forms of disruption stayed within reasonable bounds, with geopolitical impact ranking highest at 35 points, suggesting ongoing trade tensions. During the 2020–2022 pandemic, logistics disruptions surged to 85 points, a 240% increase and took front stage as the main issue. As geopolitical tensions increased to 60 points and supplier risk reached 75 points, it is clear that global supply chain vulnerabilities are interconnected. Logistics disruptions dropped to 45 points during the post-pandemic recovery (2023–2025), although they are still 80% greater than they were before the pandemic. While geopolitical effects continued to rise to 70 points, supplier risk stabilized at 50 points, suggesting a "new normal" of elevated risk.

– Crucial takeaway: rather than anticipating a return to pre-2020 conditions, supply chain managers should plan for permanent increased volatility given the ongoing elevation of all risk categories, especially geopolitical implications.

11.14.3. *Chart 3: total cost analysis – offshore versus nearshore models*

Cost structure breakdown

The detailed cost comparison reveals the hidden economics of supply chain location decisions:

– Strategic interpretation: this analysis validates the business case for nearshoring by quantifying previously hidden costs of risk and carbon exposure that were not typically included in traditional cost-only supply chain models.

11.14.4. *Chart 4: CO_2 emissions across supply chain models*

Environmental performance analysis

The carbon footprint comparison across three supply chain architectures reveals the environmental hierarchy of different approaches:

– Offshore baseline: at 3.8 kg CO_2 per unit, traditional long-distance supply chains represent the highest carbon intensity, primarily due to ocean freight and multiple handling points.

– Nearshore advantage: with 1.2 kg CO_2 per unit (68% reduction), nearshoring delivers the most significant environmental benefit by minimizing transport distances and enabling more sustainable logistics modes.

– Circular logistics: at 2.0 kg CO_2 per unit (47% reduction from baseline), circular models show substantial improvement through waste reduction and reverse logistics, although they are still higher than pure nearshoring due to additional processing and collection activities.

Sustainability insights: the data demonstrates that geographical proximity (nearshoring) provides greater immediate carbon benefits than circular economy approaches, although the combination of both strategies would likely achieve optimal environmental performance.

11.14.5. *Integrated strategic analysis*

Cross-Chart Synthesis

These four charts collectively demonstrate that modern supply chain transformation is not about choosing between efficiency, resilience and sustainability – AI-enabled nearshoring and network redesign can achieve improvements across all dimensions simultaneously:

1. Technology as an enabler: AI optimization creates the analytical foundation for making complex trade-offs while improving overall performance.

2. Geography matters: nearshoring provides measurable benefits in cost, risk, speed and sustainability that offset traditional labor cost advantages.

3. Permanent risk elevation: supply chain strategies must be designed for a permanently more volatile operating environment.

4. Environmental performance: carbon reduction through geographical optimization offers immediate, measurable sustainability benefits that align with regulatory requirements and stakeholder expectations.

Conclusion: the data strongly supports a strategic shift towards AI-enabled, nearshore, sustainable supply chain networks as the optimal configuration for balancing 21st-century business requirements of resilience, efficiency and environmental responsibility.

11.15. Recommendations

Based on the analysis of nearshoring, network redesign, automation, AI and ESG compliance, the following recommendations are proposed for building resilient, sustainable and intelligent supply chains.

Adopt hybrid sourcing models

Organizations should balance offshore sourcing for cost efficiency with nearshore production for agility and resilience. This hybrid model reduces dependence on a single geography, mitigates risks from geopolitical disruptions and ensures competitive pricing.

Leverage AI-driven simulations and digital twins

Firms must integrate digital twin technologies to simulate network redesign scenarios before implementation. AI-powered simulations allow real-time testing of risks such as port closures, raw material shortages or demand surges, enabling proactive decision-making.

Invest in green logistics

Transitioning toward sustainable logistics is vital. Companies should adopt electric vehicle (EV) fleets, use renewable energy in warehouses, optimize packaging to reduce waste and develop reverse logistics systems for circular supply chains. This aligns operations with ESG commitments and regulatory requirements.

Develop multi-node redundancy

Over-centralized supply networks create vulnerabilities. Companies should diversify suppliers and production hubs across multiple regions, creating redundancy without significant inefficiency. This improves resilience against localized shocks such as natural disasters or trade restrictions.

Collaborate on policy alignment and infrastructure

Businesses should actively collaborate with governments and industry associations to shape policies that incentivize sustainable practices. This includes tax breaks for green infrastructure, customs harmonization for regional trade and public–private partnerships to accelerate supply chain digitization.

11.16. Conclusion

Resilient, technologically enabled and sustainable ecosystems are replacing old, cost-driven, stretched global networks in global supply chains, which are undergoing a paradigm change. This shift is motivated by the need to meet the growing demands of investors, consumers and regulators while also adapting to shocks such as pandemics, geopolitical conflicts and climatic problems. Nearshoring has become a tactic to cut carbon emissions, shorten lead times and lessen reliance on far-off suppliers. Businesses may foresee hazards and dynamically optimize supply chain flows through network redesign, which is aided by AI driven digital twins. Automation increases operational precision and efficiency, while sustainability and ESG compliance lay the groundwork for stakeholder trust and long-term legitimacy. The future of supply chains depends on their ability to be highly adaptive, locally rooted and technologically savvy. In addition to reducing risks, companies that concurrently adopt automation, nearshoring and sustainability will ensure long-term competitiveness in a world economy that is becoming more unstable and linked.

11.17. References

Barney, J. (1991). Firm resources and sustained competitive advantage. *Journal of Management*, 17(1), 99–120.

BCG (2023). *Reshoring and Nearshoring: A New Supply Chain Reality*. Boston Consulting Group, Boston.

Bhambri, P. and Kumar, S. (2024). Protecting sustainable supply chains from cyber threats. In *Digital Sustainability: Navigating Entrepreneurship in the Information Age*, Bhambri, P. and Paweloszek, I. (eds). CRC Press, Boca Raton, 125–141. doi: 10.1201/9781003484226-9.

Bhambri, P., Rani, S., Khang, A. (2024). AI-driven digital twin and resource optimization in Industry 4.0 ecosystem. In *Intelligent Techniques for Predictive Data Analytics*, Singh, N., Birla, S., Ansari, M.D., Shukla, N.K. (eds). Wiley-IEEE Press, 47–69. doi: 10.1002/9781394227990.ch3.

Christopher, M. (2016). *Logistics & Supply Chain Management*. Pearson, London.

Christopher, M. and Peck, H. (2004). Building the resilient supply chain. *The International Journal of Logistics Management*, 15(2), 1–14.

Deloitte (2022). The future of supply chains: Resilient, sustainable, and digitally enabled. Report, Deloitte, London.

Dolgui, A. and Ivanov, D. (2021). Ripple effect and supply chain disruption management: New trends and research directions. *International Journal of Production Research*, 59(1), 1–17.

Ellram, L.M., Tate, W.L., Petersen, K.J. (2013). Offshoring and reshoring: An update on the manufacturing location decision. *Journal of Supply Chain Management*, 49(2), 14–22.

European Commission (2021). EU Green Deal: A roadmap for making the EU's economy sustainable. Report, European Commission.

Gereffi, G. (2018). Global value chains and international development policy: Bringing firms, networks and policy-engaged scholarship back in. *Journal of International Business Policy*, 1, 87–108.

Ghemawat, P. and Nueno, J.L. (2006). Zara: Fast fashion. Harvard Business School, Case 703-497.

Gray, J.V., Skowronski, K., Esenduran, G., Johnny, S.R. (2013). The reshoring phenomenon: What supply chain academics ought to know and should do. *Journal of Supply Chain Management*, 49(2), 27–33.

Ivanov, D. (2022). Viable supply chain model: Integrating agility, resilience and sustainability perspectives – lessons from and thinking beyond the COVID-19 pandemic. *Annals of Operations Research*, 319, 1411–1431. doi: 10.1007/s10479-020-03640-6.

Ivanov, D. and Dolgui, A. (2020). Viability of intertwined supply networks: Extending the supply chain resilience angles toward survivability. *International Journal of Production Research*, 58(10), 2904–2915.

Kinkel, S. and Maloca, S. (2009). Drivers and antecedents of manufacturing offshoring and backshoring – A German perspective. *Journal of Purchasing and Supply Management*, 15(3), 154–165.

McKinsey & Company (2022). *The Future of Resilient Supply Chains*. McKinsey & Company.

Rana, R. and Bhambri, P. (2024). Hybrid MCDM (multi-criteria decision-making) approaches for sustainable energy management. In *Modern SuperHyperSoft Computing Trends in Science and Technology*, Smarandache, F. and Majumder, P. (eds). IGI Global, Hershey, 149–184. doi: 10.4018/979-8-3693-6875-6.ch006.

Rana, R. and Bhambri, P. (2025). Harnessing block chain digital twins for sustainable business operations. In *Practical Frameworks for New-Age Digitalization Business Strategy*, Tee, P., Song, B., Ho, R. (eds). IGI Global, Hershey, 413–446. doi: 10.4018/979-8-3373-2018-2.ch013.

Rani, S., Bhambri, P., Kumar, S., Pareek, P.K., Elngar, A.A. (eds) (2024). *AI-Driven Digital Twin and Industry 4.0: A Conceptual Framework with Applications*. CRC Press, Boca Raton. doi: 10.1201/9781003395416.

UNCTAD (2023). Review of maritime transport. Report, UNCTAD.

Unilever (2022). Sustainable supply chain. Report, Unilever.

Williamson, O.E. (1981). The economics of organization: The transaction cost approach. *American Journal of Sociology*, 87(3), 548–577.

World Bank (2022). Logistics Performance Index. World Bank [Online]. Available at: https://lpi.worldbank.org/.

12

Digital Supply Chain Talent Development: Preparing the Workforce for Next-Gen Supply Chains

The rapid integration of artificial intelligence (AI), automation and data analytics is fundamentally reshaping global supply chains, creating a significant gap between existing workforce capabilities and the demands of next-generation operations. This chapter addresses the critical imperative of closing this talent gap. We argue that traditional supply chain skills are no longer sufficient. The modern professional must be proficient in data literacy, AI interpretation, robotics management and sustainable logistics. This chapter proposes a comprehensive framework for talent development, encompassing the identification of emerging skill profiles, strategic upskilling and reskilling initiatives, and the evolution of academic curricula to bridge the theory – practice divide. Furthermore, we explore the cultural and organizational shifts required to foster a continuous learning environment and embrace human–AI collaboration.

By summarizing industry trends and strategic HR practices, this chapter provides a roadmap for organizations to cultivate a future-ready supply chain workforce capable of driving resilience, efficiency and sustainability in an increasingly disrupted and digital world.

12.1. Introduction: the looming talent crisis in a digital era

The foundational premise of this chapter is how the global supply chain is undergoing a paradigm shift as significant as the advent of containerization. This transformation, often termed "Supply Chain 4.0", is driven by the convergence of advanced digital technologies, rendering traditional operational models increasingly obsolete. While these technologies promise unprecedented levels of efficiency, resilience and visibility, their successful implementation is entirely contingent on a

---

Chapter written by Pankaj BHAMBRI and Sita RANI.

capable workforce. Herein lies the central challenge: a profound and widening talent crisis. The very technologies designed to fortify supply chains explore a critical vulnerability: the lack of a digitally fluent workforce equipped to harness their power. This chapter argues that without a strategic and urgent focus on talent development, organizations will be unable to capitalize on their technological investments, leaving them vulnerable to competition and disruption (Baxi 2024).

Figure 12.1 visually represents the core argument of this introduction. The "Current State" of the workforce, with its traditional skills and reactive approaches, is being pulled away from the "Future Needs" of digital acumen and strategic processes by "The Growing Chasm". This chasm is fueled by the rapid pace of technological change outpacing skill development. The only way to cross this chasm and align the current state with future needs is through a deliberate and focused investment in "Strategic Talent Development", which acts as the essential bridge.

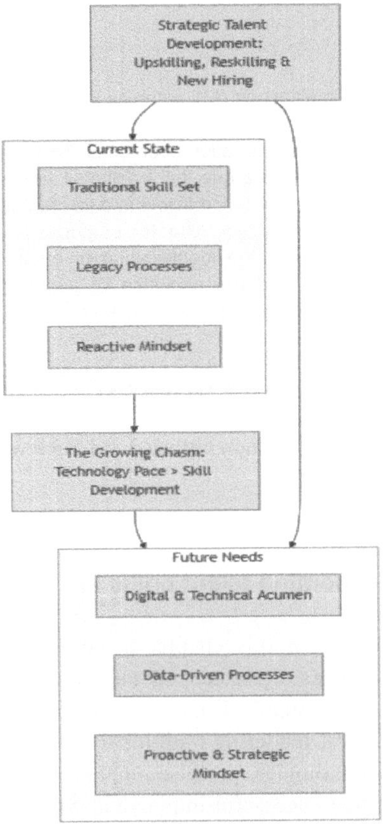

Figure 12.1. *The digital supply chain talent gap*

12.1.1. *The transformative impact of AI, automation and global disruption*

The forces reshaping the supply chain landscape are multifaceted and synergistic. Artificial intelligence (AI) and machine learning (ML) are moving from being competitive advantages to core operational necessities. They enable predictive analytics for demand forecasting, optimize inventory levels in real-time, automate complex procurement decisions and enhance risk management by simulating disruptive scenarios (Carter 2024). Robotic process automation (RPA) is streamlining administrative tasks, while autonomous mobile robots (AMRs) and automated guided vehicles (AGVs) are transforming warehouse operations. Beyond the warehouse, the Internet of Things (IoT) provides a real-time digital thread of information, from the location and condition of goods in transit to the performance of factory machinery.

This technological revolution is set against a backdrop of persistent global disruption, including geopolitical tensions, climate-change-induced events and pandemic-related aftershocks. These disruptions have underscored the limitations of lean, just-in-time models and highlighted the need for agile, data-driven and resilient supply chains (Duan et al. 2024). The combined effect of these technologies and pressures is not merely to augment existing processes but to fundamentally reengineer them. This creates a new operational environment where data is the most valuable asset and the ability to interpret and act on it is the most critical skill.

12.1.2. *Bridging the chasm: current workforce skills versus future needs*

A stark and potentially debilitating chasm has emerged between the competencies of the current supply chain workforce and the skills required to manage these next-generation systems. The traditional supply chain professional was valued for their expertise in logistics, inventory management and procurement, often relying on experience and historical data (Bhambri et al. 2024). The future supply chain professional, however, must be a hybrid expert: a "bilingual" leader who possesses deep domain knowledge and strong technical acumen.

The existing workforce often lacks digital literacy, including the ability to work with data analytics platforms, understand the principles of AI (even at a conceptual level) or manage automated systems. Soft skills are also evolving. Beyond teamwork and communication, professionals now need cognitive flexibility to adapt to rapidly changing scenarios, critical thinking to challenge AI-driven recommendations and cross-functional collaboration to work with IT and data science teams

(George and Baskar 2024). This skill gap is not a future concern; it is a present-day operational risk. Organizations find themselves with multi-million-dollar technology investments in AI and automation platforms, which are underutilized or operated at a fraction of their potential because the human talent to leverage them is absent. Bridging this chasm is the single most important prerequisite for building a supply chain that is not only smarter and faster but also more resilient and sustainable.

12.2. Defining the next-generation supply chain professional

The traditional supply chain manager, focused primarily on logistics, inventory and procurement, is evolving into a new, more dynamic professional. The next-generation supply chain professional is a tech-savvy, agile and strategic problem-solver who leverages digital tools to drive efficiency, resilience and sustainability. This transformation necessitates a fundamental shift in both hard and soft skill sets, blending technical acuity with deep human insight.

12.2.1. *Core technical competencies: data analytics, AI literacy and IoT management*

Data lies at the heart of the modern supply chain. Therefore, core technical competencies have shifted from operating legacy software to actively interpreting and manipulating data. Data analytics is the foundational skill (Bhambri and Starostka-Patyk 2024). Professionals must be proficient in using analytical platforms (like Tableau or Power BI) and statistical methods to derive insights from vast datasets related to demand patterns, transportation costs and supplier performance. This is not about becoming a data scientist but about possessing the literacy to ask the right questions, interpret analytical outputs and make data-driven decisions.

Beyond analytics, AI literacy is crucial. This involves understanding the capabilities and limitations of AI and ML. Professionals need to know how AI models forecast demand, optimize routes and automate warehouse operations. More importantly, they must be able to manage these systems, interpret their recommendations (especially when AI provides counterintuitive suggestions) and oversee their ethical implementation (Choudhary et al. 2024).

IoT management involves leveraging the network of physical objects embedded with sensors and software. Professionals must understand how to use real-time data from IoT devices – such as GPS trackers, warehouse drones and smart pallets – to monitor shipment conditions, track assets, predict maintenance needs and create a fully visible, connected supply chain from end-to-end.

12.2.2. *Essential soft skills: cognitive flexibility, cross-functional collaboration and problem-solving*

While technology provides the tools, human skills determine their effective application. Cognitive flexibility is the ability to adapt thinking and strategies in response to volatile and unexpected disruptions, such as a port closure or a sudden spike in demand. It is the mental agility to pivot from a pre-defined plan and develop a novel solution under pressure. This is complemented by cross-functional collaboration (Chowdhury 2024). The siloed supply chain department is obsolete. Modern professionals must communicate effectively with diverse teams, including IT (to implement new systems), marketing (to understand promotional impacts on demand), finance (for cost-benefit analysis of new technologies) and sustainability officers. They act as the connective tissue that aligns various business functions toward a common supply chain goal.

Underpinning all of this is advanced problem-solving. The problems faced today are increasingly complex and multi-faceted. For example, solving for a "sustainable and lowest-cost delivery option" requires balancing environmental data, cost variables and customer expectations. Next-gen professionals must employ systems thinking to understand the interdependencies and unintended consequences of their decisions, moving beyond simple linear solutions to holistic, strategic resolutions (Dwivedi and Dey 2025).

12.2.3. *The rise of hybrid roles: supply chain data scientist and automation strategist*

The convergence of technical and traditional skills is crystallizing into new, hybrid roles that did not exist a decade ago. The supply chain data scientist is a prime example. This professional possesses a deep understanding of supply chain fundamentals but is also an expert in statistical modeling, programming (e.g. Python, R) and ML. They do not just report on what happened; they build predictive models to forecast what will happen and prescribe optimal actions, moving the function from reactive to proactive and prescriptive.

Similarly, the automation strategist operates at the intersection of operations, robotics and change management. This role involves evaluating and selecting automation technologies (from warehouse robots to autonomous vehicles), designing the future-state automated processes and managing the integration of these systems into the existing workforce and workflow (George 2024a). They are not just engineers; they are strategists who understand the operational and human impact of automation, ensuring that technology investments deliver tangible Return on Investment (ROI) and enhance, rather than simply replace, human capabilities.

12.3. A strategic framework for talent development

The transition to next-generation supply chains cannot be achieved through technology alone; it requires a human capital strategy that is equally sophisticated and forward-looking. This strategic framework provides a structured, cyclical approach to building a workforce capable of leveraging AI, automation and data-driven decision-making. It is built on four interconnected pillars that ensure talent development is proactive, comprehensive and sustainable.

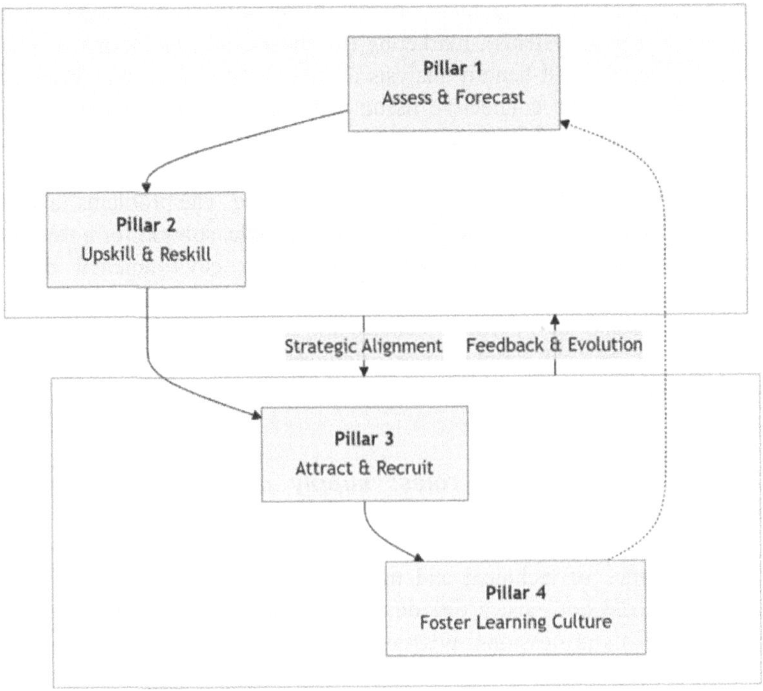

Figure 12.2. *The cyclical framework for digital supply chain talent development*

Figure 12.2 visually encapsulates the strategic framework for talent development as a dynamic, self-reinforcing cycle, emphasizing that building a future-ready workforce is a continuous process, not a one-time initiative. At its heart lies the core objective: cultivating a digital and agile supply chain workforce. This goal is achieved through four interconnected pillars that form an endless loop: the cycle begins with Pillar 1 (assess and forecast), which diagnoses the current and future skills gaps, providing the data needed to drive Pillar 2 (upskill and reskill), the existing workforce. Once internal capabilities are built, Pillar 3 (attract and recruit) focuses on injecting new, external digital talent to fill critical gaps and bring in fresh perspectives. The final, crucial Pillar 4 (foster a learning culture) creates the supportive environment that embeds continuous learning and adaptability into the organization's DNA. The surrounding arrow, labeled "continuous adaptation and improvement", signifies that the insights and agile mindset fostered in Pillar 4 naturally feed back into a new, more informed round of assessment, ensuring the entire framework evolves in lockstep with technological and market changes, thereby creating a sustainable pipeline of talent for the long term (Ghaffar and Oyeronke 2025).

12.3.1. *Pillar 1: assessing the current skills gap and forecasting future needs*

The foundational step in any talent development strategy is a rigorous and honest assessment of the present situation juxtaposed with a clear-eyed view of the future. This begins with conducting a detailed skills inventory of the current supply chain workforce (Atluri 2024). This involves mapping existing competencies against roles, using tools such as skill matrices and competency frameworks to identify proficiencies in areas like inventory management, transportation planning and ERP system usage. Concurrently, organizations must engage in strategic forecasting. This requires analyzing the company's digital roadmap – such as plans for implementing AI-driven demand forecasting, autonomous warehouses or blockchain for traceability – to predict the specific technical skills (e.g. Python for data analysis, ML model interpretation) and soft skills (e.g. managing human–robot teams) that will be critical in the next 3–5 years (Hossain et al. 2025). The gap between the current inventory and future needs reveals the precise talent deficit, allowing for targeted investments rather than scattered training efforts. This diagnostic phase is crucial for building a business case for investment in talent development and for setting clear, measurable goals for the entire program.

12.3.2. *Pillar 2: upskilling and reskilling the existing workforce*

With the skills gap clearly defined, the focus shifts to the most valuable asset: the existing employees. This pillar involves creating structured learning pathways to close the identified gaps. Upskilling involves enhancing current employees' abilities to excel in their evolving roles (for example, training a traditional demand planner to use advanced predictive analytics tools). Reskilling is more transformative, preparing employees for entirely new roles within the supply chain ecosystem, such as retraining a warehouse manager to become a robotics coordinator or a logistics analyst to become a data scientist (Banga and Shukla 2025). Effective execution involves a blend of learning methodologies: partnering with ed-tech platforms for online courses on AI fundamentals, establishing in-house "academies" for hands-on training with new software and implementing mentorship programs that pair experienced employees with digital natives. This investment not only builds the required skills but also boosts employee morale and retention by demonstrating a commitment to their long-term career growth.

12.3.3. *Pillar 3: attracting and recruiting new digital talent*

While developing internal talent is essential, the pace of technological change often necessitates injecting new capabilities from the external market. This pillar focuses on making the organization a magnet for the hybrid professionals who possess the digital skills the supply chain now demands. This requires a fundamental shift in employer branding, actively promoting the company as a tech-forward and innovative place to work, rather than a traditional logistics operation. Job descriptions and recruitment strategies must be overhauled to appeal to data scientists, AI specialists and automation engineers, highlighting challenging projects and the strategic impact of their work (Grover and Ashraf 2024). Organizations must look beyond traditional talent pools, building relationships with universities offering specialized supply chain analytics programs, participating in tech hackathons and creating attractive internship-to-hire pathways for graduates with digital proficiencies. Success in this pillar ensures a fresh influx of ideas and expertise that can accelerate digital transformation.

12.3.4. *Pillar 4: fostering a culture of continuous learning and adaptability*

The final pillar is the cultural glue that sustains the entire framework. Technology and market dynamics will continue to evolve, making any static skillset obsolete. Therefore, the ultimate goal is to embed a culture of continuous learning and agility into the organization's DNA. This is driven by leadership that actively champions learning, rewards curiosity and allocates dedicated time and resources (e.g. "learning Fridays" or annual learning stipends). It involves creating knowledge-sharing platforms where employees can share insights from courses or projects. This culture transforms learning from a periodic, formal event into an integrated, daily practice (Pesqueira et al. 2025). It fosters psychological safety, allowing employees to experiment and learn from failures without penalty.

By prioritizing adaptability, the organization builds inherent resilience, ensuring its workforce cannot only respond to the next disruption but also anticipate and lead the next wave of innovation, thereby closing the loop and making the talent development framework a perpetual, self-renewing cycle.

12.4. The critical role of academia and industry partnerships

The rapid digitization of supply chains has created a fundamental misalignment between the theoretical knowledge imparted by traditional academic programs and the practical, technology-driven skills demanded by the industry (Banerjee 2024). Closing this gap requires a synergistic partnership between academia and industry, ensuring that educational institutions are not operating in an ivory tower but are instead actively co-creating the talent pipeline. This collaboration is essential to transform raw graduates into job-ready professionals who can immediately contribute to next-generation supply chain functions (Mahusain et al. 2025). Without this close alliance, companies will continue to face a prolonged and costly onboarding and training period, while graduates will struggle to find relevant employment in a field that is desperately seeking skilled talent.

12.4.1. *Modernizing academic curricula for the digital supply chain*

The traditional supply chain curriculum, heavily focused on logistics, procurement and basic inventory theory, is no longer sufficient. Modernizing this curriculum requires a fundamental redesign that infuses digital literacy throughout its core (Bhambri and Khang 2025). This involves moving beyond isolated IT courses to integrate concepts such as data analytics and visualization as foundational skills, teaching students to manipulate and derive insights from large datasets using tools such as SQL, Python and Tableau. Courses must be developed around AI and ML applications, explaining not just the theory but also how these technologies are used for predictive demand forecasting, autonomous procurement and predictive maintenance (Maggu and Bhambri 2024). Curricula need to incorporate modules on IoT and sensor data management, blockchain for provenance and transparency, and the principles of sustainable and circular supply chain design.

This modernization cannot be achieved by academia alone. It requires direct input from industry partners through advisory boards, guest lectures and joint research projects. Industry practitioners can provide real-world case studies, current problem statements and insights into emerging technologies that are disrupting the field (Bhambri and Kumar 2024).

By collaborating, academia can ensure that their syllabi are dynamic and relevant, producing graduates who understand not only the “what” and “why” of supply chain management but also the “how” of its digital execution. The goal is to create a new breed of supply chain graduate who is as comfortable discussing neural networks and API integrations as they are with economic order quantities.

12.4.2. *Leveraging apprenticeships, internships and corporate academies*

While a modernized curriculum provides the essential knowledge foundation, practical, hands-on experience is what truly cements learning and builds competence. Apprenticeships, internships and corporate academies serve as the critical bridge between theoretical understanding and practical application. Structured internships and co-op programs allow students to immerse themselves in a corporate environment, applying their academic knowledge to real-world challenges, such as optimizing a warehouse management system, analyzing logistics data to reduce carbon emissions or supporting the implementation of an RPA script (Madhavaram et al. 2024). This experience is invaluable, transforming abstract concepts into tangible skills and fostering professional soft skills such as communication, project management and problem-solving in a live setting.

Beyond temporary internships, corporate academies and apprenticeship programs represent a deeper, long-term investment in talent development. Companies can establish dedicated academies to create a steady pipeline of talent tailored to their specific technological ecosystem and operational needs. These programs often combine formal training on proprietary systems and software with rotational assignments across different supply chain functions, such as planning, logistics and procurement (Xu et al. 2024). This approach not only accelerates the proficiency of new hires but also significantly enhances employee retention and loyalty by demonstrating a company's commitment to its workforce's growth. For the individual, it provides a clear and supported pathway to a successful career, combining earned credentials with practical mastery.

12.5. Case study: building a future-ready talent pipeline in practice

A quintessential example of a successful, large-scale corporate initiative to build a future-ready supply chain workforce is the transformational journey undertaken by A.P. Moller: Maersk. As the world's largest container shipping and logistics company, Maersk faced an existential need to evolve from a traditional asset-based carrier into an integrated, technology-driven logistics enabler. This strategic pivot, heavily reliant on AI, automation and data analytics, necessitated a radical overhaul of its talent strategy to address a significant skills gap within its vast operations workforce.

Maersk's approach was multifaceted, centering on a massive upskilling and resettlement program for its employees. Recognizing that it could not simply hire its way out of the problem, the company launched the "Next-Generation Operations" initiative. This program targeted thousands of employees in operational roles, such as vessel planners and documentation specialists, whose jobs were being transformed or automated by new digital platforms. The initiative combined comprehensive training in data analysis, digital tool utilization and new ways of working (Samuels 2025). Crucially, it was not just about teaching technical skills but also about fostering a mindset of continuous improvement and problem-solving. Employees were transitioned from performing manual, repetitive tasks to roles that involved managing exceptions, optimizing complex logistics flows and interpreting AI-driven recommendations, thereby adding higher value to the supply chain.

Beyond internal upskilling, Maersk also forged strategic partnerships with academia and invested in early-career development to secure a long-term talent pipeline. The company established the Maersk Growth organization, which invests in tech startups and the Maersk Mc-Kinney Møller Center for Zero Carbon Shipping, which focuses on future sustainability technologies. They have intensified their collaboration with universities to shape curricula and attract graduates with dual competencies in both logistics and data science. This holistic strategy – encompassing the reskilling of its existing core workforce, the acquisition of new tech talent and the fostering of external innovation ecosystems – has positioned Maersk not just as a participant but as a leader in building the digital supply chain workforce of the future. The case of Maersk demonstrates that a successful talent pipeline is built on a commitment to lifelong learning, strategic partnerships and a clear alignment between human capital development and overarching corporate strategy.

12.6. Conclusion: securing competitive advantage through strategic talent management

This concluding section summarizes the chapter's core argument: in an era where technology is a commodity, a strategically developed and managed workforce becomes the ultimate, non-replicable source of competitive advantage. It moves beyond simply identifying the talent gap to presenting a decisive call to action for supply chain leaders, framing talent strategy not as a support function but as a central pillar of corporate strategy.

The conclusion underscores that the ability to anticipate, cultivate and empower the right human skills is what will separate industry leaders from followers in the volatile landscape of next-generation supply chains (Rana and Bhambri 2024). It emphasizes that technological investments yield diminishing returns without the human expertise to leverage them creatively, ethically and effectively (Jean-Luc and Priyanka 2024). Table 12.1 shows the evolution from traditional roles to emerging hybrid positions, outlining the shifting skill requirements and corresponding talent development initiatives.

Traditional role	Emerging hybrid role	Key skills and competencies required	Strategic development actions
Supply chain planner	Supply chain data scientist	– Predictive analytics and modeling – ML algorithms – Programming (Python, R and SQL) – Statistical analysis – Business acumen	– Partner with tech firms for specialized ML bootcamps – Create job rotation programs with the data science department – Fund certifications in AI and data analytics
Logistics manager	Automation and robotics coordinator	– Robotics process automation (RPA) – IoT sensor management – Warehouse management systems (WMS) – System integration – Change management	– Establish hands-on training labs with collaborative robots (cobots) – Develop partnerships with automation vendors for training – Include systems thinking in leadership development programs
Procurement officer	Sustainable sourcing strategist	– ESG (environmental, social, governance) criteria – Carbon accounting and lifecycle assessment – Supplier sustainability auditing – Risk mitigation in ethical supply – Stakeholder engagement	– Integrate sustainability modules into procurement training – Support certifications in sustainable procurement (for example, CSCP) – Create cross-functional task forces with CSR (corporate social responsibility) teams
General supply chain manager	Digital supply chain strategist	– Digital twin modeling – AI interpretation for decision-making – Cybersecurity fundamentals – Strategic foresight and scenario planning – Agile project management	– Executive education programs on digital transformation – Implement simulation software for strategy testing and training – Mentor partnerships with tech-savvy senior leaders

Table 12.1. *Mapping future supply chain roles: skills and development actions (George 2024b; Li et al. 2024; Akram 2025; Rahman et al. 2025)*

12.6.1. *Summarizing the key imperatives for leadership*

This section distills the chapter's framework into actionable mandates for C-suite executives and supply chain VPs. The first imperative is a fundamental mindset shift: leaders must stop viewing talent development as a discretionary HR cost and reframe it as a critical strategic investment in organizational resilience and innovation. This requires direct ownership from the highest levels of management (Polo 2025). The second imperative is the adoption of a holistic and continuous approach to talent management. Leaders must champion the integrated four-pillar framework – assessing gaps, upskilling incumbents, recruiting new talent and fostering a learning culture – recognizing that these elements are interdependent and require sustained commitment. A one-time training program is insufficient. What is needed is an embedded ecosystem of continuous learning.

Leaders are implored to become architects of a new organizational culture. This involves actively breaking down silos to encourage the cross-functional collaboration essential for modern supply chains and rewarding attributes such as adaptability, curiosity and data-informed decision-making (Shamsuddoha et al. 2025). A critical imperative is to forge and deepen strategic partnerships with academia. Leaders must proactively engage with universities and technical colleges to co-design curricula, provide internship opportunities and ensure the pipeline of future talent is aligned with the real-world demands of AI-driven, sustainable supply chains. The summary for leadership is clear: the race for supply chain supremacy will be won not by the company with the most advanced AI algorithm but by the one with the most effective strategy for developing the people who command it.

12.6.2. *Future outlook: navigating the evolving human–machine partnership*

Looking forward, this section explores the dynamic and symbiotic relationship that will define the future supply chain workplace. The narrative shifts from a fear of human replacement to a focus on human augmentation (Tung 2024). The future outlook posits that AI and automation will handle repetitive, data-intensive tasks (for example, predictive forecasting and autonomous replenishment), thereby freeing the human workforce to focus on higher-order responsibilities. These include strategic decision-making based on AI-derived insights, managing complex stakeholder relationships, driving sustainable innovation and solving novel, ambiguous problems that machines cannot yet comprehend. The supply chain professional of tomorrow will be an "orchestrator" or "conductor", seamlessly integrating the outputs of digital tools with human judgment, creativity and ethical reasoning.

This evolving partnership will also give rise to new models of work and organizational structures. We will see the proliferation of hybrid teams, where humans collaborate directly with AI tools and RPA, managing exceptions and guiding strategic direction (Akhtar 2025). This necessitates a focus on trust and transparency in AI systems, as humans must understand and validate machine-generated recommendations (Rotimi-Ojo 2025). The future outlook concludes that the organizations that will thrive are those that master this integration, creating an environment where technology amplifies human potential and human intelligence guides technological application. The final competitive frontier, therefore, lies in cultivating a workforce that is not just technologically proficient but also adept at the uniquely human skills of leadership, ethics and adaptive learning, ensuring the supply chain of the future is both intelligent and resilient.

12.7. References

Akhtar, Z.B. (2025). Artificial Intelligence (AI) meets blockchain: Transforming industries for the next digital era. *Interdisciplinary Systems for Global Management*, 1(1), 59–75.

Akram, H.W. (2025). Digital transformation in logistics and supply chain management practices. In *Ecological and Human Dimensions of AI-Based Supply Chain*, Taghipour, A. (ed.). IGI Global, Hershey, 27–48.

Atluri, A. (2024). The 2030 HR landscape: Oracle HCM's vision for future-ready organizations. *International Journal of AI, BigData, Computational and Management Studies*, 5(4), 31–40.

Banerjee, B. (2024). Next-gen computing: Exploring Industry 4.0. *International Research Journal of Scientific Studies*, 1(1), 1–6.

Banga, B.S. and Shukla, A. (2025). Digitization in road transportation for logistics industry. *Sustainable Supply Chains and Digital Transformation*, 19.

Baxi, J. (2024). Next-gen strategies and industry use cases in CSR and ESG. In *Sustainability Reporting and Blockchain Technology*, Singh, H. et al. (eds). Routledge, London, 262–281.

Bhambri, P. and Khang, A. (2025). Edge computing for enhancing efficiency and sustainability in green transportation systems. In *Driving Green Transportation System Through Artificial Intelligence and Automation*, A. Khang (ed.). Springer, Berlin, Heidelberg, 43–65. doi: 10.1007/978-3-031-72617-0_3

Bhambri, P. and Kumar, S. (2024). Protecting sustainable supply chains from cyber threats. In *Digital Sustainability: Navigating Entrepreneurship in the Information Age*, Bhambri, P. and Paweloszek, I. (eds). CRC Press, Boca Raton, 125–141. doi: 10.1201/9781003484226-9.

Bhambri, P. and Starostka-Patyk, M. (2024). Decentralized finance (DeFi) and environmental impact. In *Digital Sustainability: Navigating Entrepreneurship in the Information Age*, Bhambri, P. and Paweloszek, I. (eds). CRC Press, Boca Raton, 142–151. doi: 10.1201/9781003484226-10.

Bhambri, P., Rani, S., Khang, A. (2024). AI-driven digital twin and resource optimization in Industry 4.0 ecosystem. In *Intelligent Techniques for Predictive Data Analytics*, Singh, N., Birla, S., Ansari, M.D., Shukla, N.K. (eds). Wiley and Sons, New York, 47–69. doi: 10.1002/9781394227990.ch3.

Carter, O. (2024). Real-time analytics in supply chain management: AI's role in enhancing visibility. *Multidisciplinary Journal of Instruction (MDJI)*, 7(1), 226–237.

Choudhary, V., Patel, K., Niaz, M., Panwala, M., Mehta, A., Choudhary, K. (2024). Implementation of next-gen IoT to facilitate strategic inventory management system and achieve logistics excellence. In *2024 International Conference on Trends in Quantum Computing and Emerging Business Technologies*. IEEE, Pune, 1–6.

Chowdhury, R.H. (2024). The evolution of business operations: Unleashing the potential of Artificial Intelligence, Machine Learning, and Blockchain. *World Journal of Advanced Research and Reviews*, 22(3), 2135–2147.

Duan, K., Onyeaka, H., Pang, G., Meng, Z. (2024). Pioneering food safety: Blockchain's integration in supply chain surveillance. *Journal of Agriculture and Food Research*, 18, 101281.

Dwivedi, M. and Dey, G. (2025). The integration of real-time tracking technologies in supply chains: Impacts on efficiency and customer satisfaction. *Integration*, 3(2), 288–292.

George, A.S. (2024a). The evolution of economic models: From knowledge to intuition and optimization. *Partners Universal Multidisciplinary Research Journal*, 1(2), 1–25.

George, A.S. (2024b). The fourth industrial revolution: A primer on industry 4.0 and its transformative impact. *Partners Universal Innovative Research Publication*, 2(1), 16–40.

George, A.S. and Baskar, T. (2024). Driving business transformation through technology innovation: Emerging priorities for IT leaders. *Partners Universal Innovative Research Publication*, 2(4), 1–14.

Ghaffar, A. and Oyeronke, A. (2025). AI-powered autonomous agents and their role in next-gen business automation. *IRE Transactions on Education*, 9(1), 1489–1501.

Grover, A.K. and Ashraf, M.H. (2024). Autonomous mobile robots for warehousing and distribution industry: A step toward intralogistics 4.0. In *Digitization in Supply Chain Management: Trends, Challenges and Solutions*. World Scientific, Singapore, 153–183.

Hossain, M.S., Sikdar, M.S.H., Chowdhury, A., Bhuiyan, S.M.Y., Mobin, S.M. (2025). AI-driven aggregate planning for sustainable supply chains: A systematic literature review of models, applications, and industry impacts. *American Journal of Advanced Technology and Engineering Solutions*, 1(01), 382–437.

Jean-Luc, M. and Priyanka, N. (2024). Revolutionizing supply chain optimization with AI-driven predictive analytics. *Synergy: Cross-Disciplinary Journal of Digital Investigation*, 2(12), 31–45.

Li, Y., Zhao, H., Jiang, H., Pan, Y., Liu, Z., Wu, Z., Liu, T. (2024). Large language models for manufacturing. *arXiv*, arXiv:2410.21418.

Madhavaram, C.R., Sunkara, J.R., Kuraku, C., Galla, E.P., Gollangi, H.K. (2024). The future of automotive manufacturing: Integrating AI, ML, and Generative AI for next-gen automatic cars. *International Multidisciplinary Research Journal Reviews-IMRJR*, 1, 010103.

Maggu, A. and Bhambri, P. (2024). Elevating workforce strategies: Designing a SMART recruiting system with ML models. In *Digital Sustainability: Navigating Entrepreneurship in the Information Age*, Bhambri, P. and Paweloszek, I. (eds). CRC Press, Boca Raton, 1–17. doi: 10.1201/9781003484226-1.

Mahusain, M.A., Samsudin, A., Majid, M.A.A. (2025). Next-gen eats: Tech, trends, and sustainability. In *Technological Innovations in the Food Service Industry*, Garg, A. (ed.). IGI Global, Hershey, 271–294.

Pesqueira, A., Moutinho, J., de Bem Machado, A. (2025). Cloud-based intelligent engineering: A paradigm shift in supply chain management through demand planning, forecasting, and integrated business planning. In *Advancements in Cloud-based Intelligent Informative Engineering*, Kishore, K. and Kadry, S. (eds). IGI Global, Hershey, 303–330.

Polo, L. (2025). A supply chain approach highlighting the use of artificial intelligence and computer vision to improve the efficiency of food supply chains in the United States. *International Journal for Multidisciplinary Research*, 7(2), 1–24.

Rahman, K.O., Dhar, S., Rahman, S., Khanam, A., Nasrullah, F., Hasan, M., Khan, M.A.R. (2025). Data-driven automation: How robotics and BI reshape retail supply chains in the United States. *Journal of Computer Science and Technology Studies*, 7(9), 482–488.

Rana, R. and Bhambri, P. (2024). AI-driven MCDM tools for optimizing industrial wastewater treatment. In *Modern SuperHyperSoft Computing Trends in Science and Technology*, Smarandache, F. and Majumder, P. (eds). IGI Global, Hershey, 61–106. doi: 10.4018/979-8-3693-6875-6.ch003.

Rotimi-Ojo, T. (2025). Public-private collaboration in building the US EV supply chain: A financial and economic review. *International Journal of Advanced Multidisciplinary Research and Studies*, 5(2), 2375–2382.

Samuels, A. (2025). Examining the integration of artificial intelligence in supply chain management from Industry 4.0 to 6.0: A systematic literature review. *Frontiers in Artificial Intelligence*, 7, 1477044.

Shamsuddoha, M., Khan, E.A., Chowdhury, M.M.H., Nasir, T. (2025). Revolutionizing supply chains: Unleashing the power of AI-driven intelligent automation and real-time information flow. *Information*, 16(1), 26.

Tung, C.Y. (2024). Taiwan and the global semiconductor supply chain. ROC, Taiwan site, Taiwan Representative Office in Singapore [Online]. Available at: https://www.roc-taiwan.org/uploads/sites/86/2024/02/240202-February-Issue.pdf.

Xu, L., Almahri, S., Mak, S., Brintrup, A. (2024). Multi-agent systems and foundation models enable autonomous supply chains: Opportunities and challenges. *IFAC-PapersOnLine*, 58(19), 795–800.

13

Change Management for Supply Chain Transformation

Supply chain transformation is now a strategic requirement for businesses regardless of their geographic location, owing to the external pressures such as globalization, technological advancement, dynamic markets and increasingly complex customer demand. Businesses are now rethinking their supply chains to become more robust, agile and digitally linked in response to these issues. However, a substantial number of firms are dedicating a significant amount of their resources to process redesigns and deployment of cutting-edge technologies. Success in the transformative journey is not guaranteed by these efforts alone. The firm's capacity to handle the organizational and human elements of change is a crucial factor in determining an effective transition. This chapter provides a strong theoretical basis for integrating change management approaches into every stage of the transformation by drawing upon the fundamental concepts of change management from Kotter's Change Model, the ADKAR Model and Lewin's Change Theory. It describes a structured approach that includes evaluation, planning, implementation, feedback and sustainability to implement change across the supply chain. It highlights the importance of leadership, clear communication and stakeholder alignment in facilitating the transformation process. Through literature analysis, this chapter also identifies key challenges and barriers such as skill gap among the workforce, resistance to automation and artificial intelligence (AI), cultural barriers to sustainability, data silos and uneven digital readiness. Finally, it outlines the best practices and success criteria that are crucial for handling complex and cross-functional supply chain change.

13.1. Introduction

Supply chain management (SCM) has become a strategic capability that directly shapes the success of a business. It is now seen as a strategic integrator of all of the business activities involving manufacturers, distributors, retailers, suppliers and customers. Research has also highlighted that competition now is across the network

Chapter written by S. KAVITHAMBIKA, K.M. SANTHOSHA, R. KIRAN and Pankaj BHAMBRI.

of firms, rather than individual firms or organizations (Christopher 2022). Efficiency of production and processes alone is not enough in the new era of SCM. In the 21st century, SCM is evolving to meet the customer-centric demands, increased sustainability standards, digital innovation and expanding global needs. Digital technologies such as artificial intelligence (AI), the Internet of Things (IoT), data analytics and blockchain technology offer continuous tracking and predictive decision-making across the extended network (Ivanov and Dolgui 2020; Olaleye et al. 2024; Chatterjee et al. 2025). Owing to social and environmental demands, sustainability and circular practices have also become fundamental goals of the supply chain, forcing businesses to internalize carbon, waste and social-risk elements into their decisions (Bhambri and Kumar 2024). SCM thus seeks to strike a balance between customer value generation, robustness and digital capacity, thereby also increasing their efficiency.

Although these elements draw attention to the pressures that are changing the scenario of SCM, adopting new technologies alone will not be enough to meet these demands. All of these factors boost productivity, but how effectively they work depends largely on the organizational and human elements in an organization. While implementing any form of change across an organization, workforce capabilities, leadership, organizational culture and readiness are more important. Most of the supply chain decisions have a substantial impact on the actors and individuals participating in the process along the chain (Pagell and Wilhelm 2025). In addition, research also suggests that organizational variables such a misaligned culture, lack of skills among employees and non-collaborative organizational structures frequently lead to failure of any transformation that is implemented (Bui et al. 2024; Hamed et al. 2024). Investments in technology are always seen as an enabling factor for gaining competitive advantage. However, when the organizational component is overlooked, investments become a risk. Thus, SCM necessitates concurrent attention to people, processes and culture in the transformation process. In order to make the transition process smoother, organizations must manage change resistance, resolve concerns and ensure seamless integration into current workflows and processes (Hao and Demir 2025).

13.2. Theoretical foundations of change management

The structured and systematic approach that businesses use to transition people, groups and systems from an existing state to a desirable future state is known as change management. At its core, it is less about technology or structures and more about people navigating through uncertainty. Every change, be it digital adoption, supply network redesign, or a sustainability initiative, requires employees to change their established routine, let go of their familiar practices (Koilakonda 2024) and develop confidence in unfamiliar systems. The purpose of change management is to make this transition purposeful and supported, rather than disruptive and resisted. For this, change management emphasizes on aligning new initiatives with their business strategy, preparing and empowering people to engage with new practices and embedding new practices into daily operations. Managing change involves improving operations and continuous adaptation, which results in a number of organizational benefits (Chatzinikolaou and Vlados 2024). Without this foundation, even the most advanced systems could be at risk of being underutilized or resisted. Thus, change management acts as a link between innovation and performance, acknowledging that transformation is not only a technical aspect but also a human journey, and it equips organizations to navigate change.

13.2.1. *Change management models*

13.2.1.1. *Lewin's change theory*

This theory describes transformation as a three-stage process, i.e. unfreezing, changing and refreezing, and is one of the most reliable frameworks in the study of organizational change. According to this model, organizational change is seen as a planned, sequential process in which new ideas have to be "unfrozen" before they can be implemented and subsequently embedded in the organization's culture (Carreño 2024).

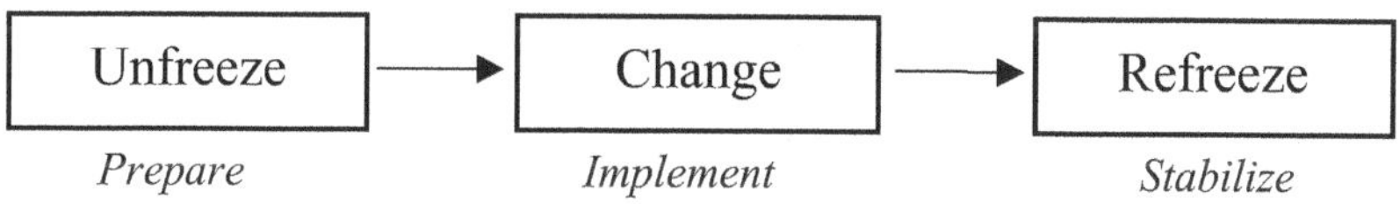

Figure 13.1. *Kurt Lewin's change model (Source: author's own depiction)*

– *Unfreeze:* at this stage, organizations are prepared to acknowledge the need for change. In the supply chain context, businesses realize that traditional logistical models are no longer efficient, global networks are vulnerable or there are risks associated with not using digital and sustainable practices. Opening the door for transformation and supporting stakeholders in overcoming complacency are the two benefits of communicating the need for change.

– *Change:* at this stage, the new processes, technologies or any new procedures are implemented. Integrating advanced analytics, blockchain, automating processes, restructuring strategies or embedding sustainable practices might happen in the supply chain context. Cooperation among all of the supply chain stakeholders, in addition to providing employees with the right information and other resources they require to adapt to change, contributes to the success of this stage.

– *Refreeze:* this stage tries to stabilize and regulate the change implemented. It embeds the change into regular work flow, policies and the organizational culture. This phase ensures that the implemented change becomes a regular work routine and not a one-time initiative. Performance evaluation, support from the leaders and continuous training are crucial for the same.

Thus, this model demonstrates that in order to bring about a sustainable transformation within the supply chain context, technology adoption needs to be complemented by organizational as well as human alignment.

13.2.1.2. *Kotter's eight-step change model*

John Kotter's model for implementing organizational change is an effective and methodical approach to accelerating transformational efforts. Every stage builds on the previous stage, guaranteeing a thorough plan that tackles difficulty along the transformation process. It emphasizes critical roles of leadership, communication and strategic planning in the transformational process.

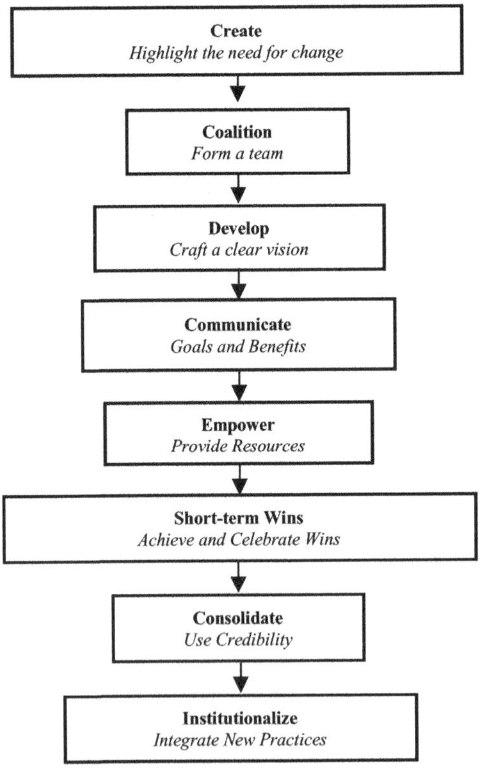

Figure 13.2. *Kotter's change model (Source: author's own depiction)*

– *Urgency:* the first step is to inform the stakeholders about the urgent need for change to be implemented and highlight its importance. Supporting and preparing the stakeholders for implementing the change are essential, and change leaders should prepare them to accept the process. In the supply chain context, businesses could identify challenges or any inefficiencies that necessitate change and communicate it to the actors involved in the process.

– *Coalition:* the next step is to create a team that acknowledges the change and understands the need and urgency. Change leaders and the team members should be included in all of the processes, be it procurement, logistics, IT or any other relevant department to support the transformation process (Bhambri and Khang 2025). A strong team that leads transformation should have the right knowledge, skills and abilities to maintain the urgency and momentum. Weaknesses in the groups are recognized, and support is given to help them bridge the gap.

– *Vision:* developing a vision is the third step. Establishing specific, long-term objectives that direct the transformation process toward a beneficial future state is the objective of this step. The practical plan and the set goals should be in line with the vision developed for a responsive, yet cost-effective supply chain.

– *Communication:* effective communication is the key to ensuring smooth transformation in an organization. Getting support and buy-in from stakeholders requires clear communication of the vision developed in the previous step. Communication should create a strong sense of the intended future state, motivating all of the parties involved in the process to work together and accomplish the goal. Regular updates on progress and benefits of the transformation have to reach all of the stakeholders involved.

Empowerment: understanding how enabling and hindering factors interact with one another is essential to empowering the team and other stakeholders to act. This step involves giving power, resources and other support the stakeholders require to implement the change successfully. Providing training to teams to implement new processes and technologies could be one possible way.

– *Short-Term Wins:* maintaining momentum and motivation during the transition process requires acknowledging and celebrating small wins. By doing so, the stakeholders remain committed and involved in the process and for betterment (Bhambri and Starostka-Patyk 2024). Businesses could implement pilot projects that showcase the benefits of the new practices, and by doing this, the stakeholders are able to see the results, motivating them to be involved in the process.

– *Consolidation:* implementing change is often a challenging process that demands a significant investment of time and energy. Individuals and groups might lose focus and get back to their routine processes. Hence, it is crucial to regularly evaluate the progress of change implemented, maintain a momentum, include all of the stakeholders and consolidate improvements in order to make sure that the project is in line.

– *Institutionalize:* the final step is to ensure that the new practices implemented are being ingrained into the standard operating procedures and organizational culture. By doing so, there is a greater chance of the implemented change being maintained throughout time, having a long-lasting effect on the company.

Thus, Kotter's model is a comprehensive and systematic method to implement change and transform the supply chain.

13.2.1.3. *ADKAR model*

ADKAR abbreviates for Awareness, Desire, Knowledge, Ability and Reinforcement. This model offers a practical framework for managing change in supply chain transformation.

– *Awareness:* creating awareness explains the necessity to implement change to all of the stakeholders. This phase basically answers the questions such as *why, what* and *when* about the change process. Effective communication is essential in this phase. The advantages of the new process/practice that is going to be implemented should be outlined, while also outlining the disadvantages of existing procedures, such as higher costs, delays or lack of transparency.

– *Desire:* once awareness has been created, change leaders should encourage their employees to participate in the change and incorporate it into their daily workflow. This could be done by improving the feedback system. Show the stakeholders how automation could reduce their workload or encourage suppliers by offering incentives for adopting sustainable practices. Keeping the stakeholders motivated is one of the key elements that leads to successful transformation.

– *Knowledge:* knowledge is one of the most important components of the model, which illustrates how to implement change and the transformation process. Train the teams to use ERP systems, educate the logistics partners on new compliance standards or introduce data-driven forecasting techniques. Determining the extent of training and support systems required could make the process easier by assessing the gaps that exist in the knowledge and skills to integrate change into their routine, which is much needed.

– *Ability:* having the required knowledge or skill alone is not sufficient. They should be able to apply it in real situations that require practice. Offer hands-on experience with new technologies, provide suppliers with technical guidance and give them sufficient time to adapt (Bhambri et al. 2024). By doing so, they feel confident and overcome the fear of unknown. This phase focuses entirely on the ability to learn new skills to bring about change and achieve the desired results. The ability of the stakeholders could eventually be improved by giving them enough time and resources.

– *Reinforcement:* the final phase places a strong emphasis on sustaining the change that has been implemented. Strategies to reinforce change include sharing success stories, acknowledging accomplishments, rewarding positive feedback and celebrating milestones. Regularly monitoring performance indicators such as delivery times, cost savings or inventory accuracy could help track progress.

13.3. Framework for supply chain change management

Transforming a supply chain is not only about the systems, processes or technology but also about the people and the organization as a whole, although the existing change models such as Lewin's model, Kotter's model and the ADKAR framework are extensively used in a single entity and do not represent the reality of supply chain transformation. Supply chain comprises of a network of interconnected partners rather than a single organization. Each partner in the supply chain has their own priorities, limitations and capabilities, and there is no central authority to impose change. These models also depict change as a straight line of action, but a supply chain operates in a setting that is constantly disrupted by changes in technology and customer expectations (Rana and Bhambri 2024). Although people and organizational culture remain a critical component, supply chain transformation requires redefining processes, integrating new technology and building resilience and sustainability across boundaries. This necessitates going beyond conventional models and creating a framework that captures collaborative, flexible and systematic nature of supply chains, where long-term resilience, technical innovation and interpersonal interactions are closely linked.

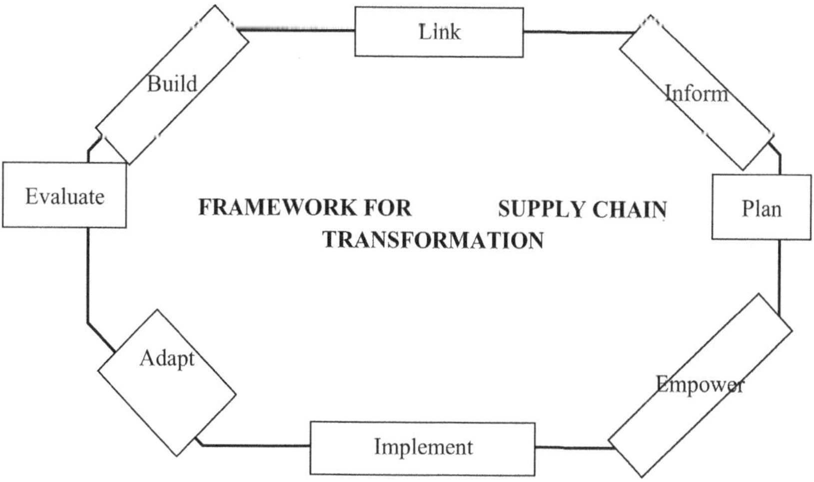

Figure 13.3. *Framework for supply chain transformation*

– *Link:* this step emphasizes on building collaborative network and aligning all of the stakeholders such as the suppliers, manufacturers, logistics partners, retailers and customers.

– *Inform:* stakeholders are informed about the necessity for implementing the change, its vision and their roles and responsibilities in the process during this stage. Businesses should make sure that there is a proper flow of information. Transparent communication, mutual trust and aligned purpose are the foundation, making every actor in the process feel heard and valued.

– *Plan:* creating plans, outlining processes and determining the resources needed for transformation are all a part of this step. It guarantees that objectives are reasonable, roles are well-defined and the execution process is both methodical and adaptable. Also, the support required by the stakeholders to overcome resistance is mapped in this step.

– *Empower:* based on the mapping done in the planning phase, analyze the gaps in existing resources, knowledge and skills required for transformation. Provide them with the resources required and offer training to enhance their knowledge, skills and abilities. Give them the power to make decisions and provide rewards and recognition. Thereby, encourage accountability and active involvement in process improvement and change adoption. Transformations are often successful only when employees and other actors along the chain are actively engaged.

– *Implement:* once the stakeholders feel empowered, change could be implemented. Change could be implemented after the stakeholders have a sense of empowerment. The process of translating a strategy into reality is called implementation. Teams implement new processes or procedures, new technology and improved workflows.

– *Adapt:* embracing flexibility, continuously learning new things and taking calculated risks are all aspects of transformation. Even after implementation, as and when problems arise, businesses should be flexible and adjust their processes accordingly. Adaptation focuses on learning from experience, and by doing so, supply chains could handle uncertainty and regulatory pressures, respond to changes in the market and advance efficiently by embracing change, refining their processes and transforming challenges into possibilities for development.

– *Evaluate:* evaluation verifies the efficiency and long-term viability of change. By monitoring Key Performance Indicators (KPIs) related to cost, service, sustainability and impact on the society, organizations could identify gaps, acknowledge success and use lessons learnt to continue improving for the better.

– *Build:* focus on building the capacity to withstand disruptions and shocks such as pandemics, climatic events or geopolitical risks without any interruption in the regular processes. This includes risk assessments, reduction in redundant processes, diversified sourcing and contingency planning to protect operations, people and partnerships from external shocks.

13.4. Importance of leadership and governance structures

One of the most important, if not the most basic, aspects of leadership is managing change (Giessner et al. 2023). Sustainable transformations are made possible by strong leadership and governance, constituting the foundation of the above-mentioned structured framework. Coherent execution of all of the phases is ensured by effective change leaders who provide vision, guidance and the inspiration required to bring diverse stakeholders together. How these leaders view change and carry out their responsibilities throughout the process affects the success of change initiatives (Hills 2025). In order to maintain momentum during these times, governance structures define the decision-making authorities, establish responsibilities and provide procedures for tracking improvements, controlling risks and settling conflicts.

Organizations can assure that change is both strategically directed and operationally disciplined by integrating leadership and governance into every phase, from linking all of the stakeholders to building resilience (Rana and Bhambri 2025). This integration makes the transformation robust, adaptable and embedded in the organization's culture by fostering trust, improving communication and enabling teams to embrace new initiatives.

One advantage of participatory change is that it increases the likelihood that the change initiative will be successful (Hastings and Schwarz 2022). Participants have a greater interest in the outcome and the success of the change process when they are given ownership in it. Participatory change advocates may also observe a more flexible company culture and a decline in change resistance (Bushe 2021). When leaders use participatory change strategies and involve their team throughout the change process, job satisfaction increases and the rate of attrition decreases (Turja 2022).

13.5. Challenges and barriers

Research suggests that challenges and barriers to bringing in transformation in the supply chain would be lack of sufficient data, implementation and integration of AI, IoT or blockchain technology solutions, which in turn require sophisticated IT infrastructure (Daios et al. 2025). Furthermore, political instability, trade disputes and economic issues create uncertainty; a lack of skilled employees hinders supply chain operations (Ciampi et al. 2022). Financial constraints, such as higher upfront costs and long-term ROI uncertainty, make it a challenge to secure funding. Also, validating the financial viability of new technologies is a challenge, which does not motivate most of the management teams, leading to reluctance to accept change (Prajapati et al. 2022). Resistance to change may also be of concern, particularly in traditional businesses where stakeholders may be reluctant to embrace new technologies (Hangl et al. 2023). This could be due to the fear of unknown, where the stakeholders are unfamiliar with the processes and procedures, leading to skepticism and reluctance. For this reason, every change that is made has to be in line with the ongoing business activities and not interfere with them. Businesses have to deal with these challenges if they are to maximize the benefits of the transformation.

Studies have also highlighted the reluctance of the top management (Solangi et al. 2021), administrative complexity and firm-level political and policy challenges (Checchinato et al. 2021) and lack of established procedures, standardized processes, R&D investment and commitment at firm level (Bigliardi et al. 2022) as significant barriers.

Thus, businesses in order to be proactive, have to create a plan to implement and strategize execution before introducing any new practices into their supply chain.

13.6. Enablers and best practices

To promote sustainable growth, supply chain managers and policymakers have to relate barriers to their goals. Government, businesses and other supply chain stakeholders should concentrate on designing and developing programs to create awareness (Agrawal et al. 2022; Mondejar et al. 2021), use of effective feedback systems (Modgil et al. 2020), benchmarking sustainable processes, converting firms into smart factories using digital technologies (Sharma et al. 2021) and adoption at different hierarchical levels (Agrawal et al. 2020); these will help overcome the barriers in the transformation process along the supply chain. Businesses also believe that lack of support from the government and policymaker is a barrier for transformation irrespective of their effort (Kumar Dadsena and Pant 2023). Therefore, infrastructure, standardized policies and coordination among various stakeholders are some of the factors that facilitate the shift from the current state to the desired state.

13.7. The future

The supply chain is becoming more sophisticated and adaptable because of the development in digital technologies. Businesses can now precisely forecast demand, optimize their production schedules and simplify logistics with the help of AI and

Machine Learning (ML). At the same time, blockchain is becoming more popular for its traceability, guaranteeing transparency and trust. Businesses, in an effort to reduce waste and carbon emissions, are adopting circular economy principles as a part of their steps toward sustainability.

These developments are changing how companies deal with change, turning it into a continuous process rather than a one-time event. Transformation now makes use of real-time insights to inform decisions and actions rather than depending on top-down guidance. Stakeholders could concentrate on innovation, creativity and teamwork when their regular tasks are being automated. This fosters a culture in which human potential and technology complement each other, building resilience and preparing for the future.

Businesses no longer ignore sustainability; rather, it is something that is central to the way change and transformation are conceptualized and implemented. Actual change and transformation are not just about efficiency but about creating a future that is both resilient and responsible.

Thus, supply chain transformation and change management are now about creating an ecosystem where people, technology and sustainability coexist together rather than just implementing new procedures or systems.

13.8. References

Agrawal, P., Narain, R., Ullah, I. (2020). Analysis of barriers in implementation of digital transformation of supply chain using interpretive structural modelling approach. *Journal of Modelling in Management*, 15(1), 297–317.

Agrawal, R., Wankhede, V.A., Kumar, A., Upadhyay, A., Garza-Reyes, J.A. (2022). Nexus of circular economy and sustainable business performance in the era of digitalization. *International Journal of Productivity and Performance Management*, 71(3), 748–774.

Bhambri, P. and Khang, A. (2025). Edge computing for enhancing efficiency and sustainability in green transportation systems. In *Driving Green Transportation System through Artificial Intelligence and Automation*, Khang, A. (ed.). Springer, Berlin, Heidelberg, 43–65. doi: 10.1007/978-3-031-72617-0_3.

Bhambri, P. and Kumar, S. (2024). Protecting sustainable supply chains from cyber threats. In *Digital Sustainability: Navigating Entrepreneurship in the Information Age*, Bhambri, P. and Paweloszek, I. (eds). CRC Press, Boca Raton, 125–141. doi: 10.1201/9781003484226-9.

Bhambri, P. and Starostka-Patyk, M. (2024). Decentralized finance (DeFi) and environmental impact. In *Digital Sustainability: Navigating Entrepreneurship in the Information Age*, Bhambri, P. and Paweloszek, I. (eds). CRC Press, Boca Raton, 142–151. doi: 10.1201/9781003484226-10.

Bhambri, P., Rani, S., Khang, A. (2024). AI-driven digital twin and resource optimization in Industry 4.0 ecosystem. In *Intelligent Techniques for Predictive Data Analytics*, Singh, N., Birla, S., Ansari, M.D., Shukla, N.K. (eds). Wiley-IEEE Press, New York, 47–69. doi: 10.1002/9781394227990.ch3.

Bigliardi, B., Filippelli, S., Petroni, A., Tagliente, L. (2022). The digitalization of supply chain: A review. *Procedia Computer Science*, 200, 1806–1815.

Bui, M.T., Jeng, D.J.F., Ta, H.H. (2024). Accelerating digital supply chain management practices, customer development, and firm performance: Organizational culture matters. *Contemporary Economics*, 18(1), 40.

Bushe, G.R. (2021). The generative change model: Creating the agile organization while dealing with a complex problem. *The Journal of Applied Behavioral Science*, 57(4), 530–533.

Carreño, A.M. (2024). An analytical review of John Kotter's change leadership framework: A modern approach to sustainable organizational transformation. Working Paper, SSRN.

Chatterjee, R., Kumar, B., Singh, A.K., Pandey, S. (2025). Investigating organizational transformations on the path to sustainable supply chain 4.0 implementation. *Circular Economy and Sustainability*, 5(1), 277–320.

Chatzinikolaou, D. and Vlados, C. (2024). Crisis, innovation and change management: A blind spot for micro-firms? *Journal of Entrepreneurship in Emerging Economies*, 16(3), 698–719.

Checchinato, F., Hinterhuber, A., Vescovi, T. (eds) (2021). Our roadmap to digital transformation. In *Managing Digital Transformation*. Routledge, London, 273–277.

Choudhury, A., Behl, A., Sheorey, P.A., Pal, A. (2021). Digital supply chain to unlock new agility: A TISM approach. *Benchmarking: An International Journal*, 28(6), 2075–2109.

Christopher, M. (2022). *Logistics and Supply Chain Management*. Pearson, London.

Ciampi, F., Faraoni, M., Ballerini, J., Meli, F. (2022). The co-evolutionary relationship between digitalization and organizational agility: Ongoing debates, theoretical developments and future research perspectives. *Technological Forecasting and Social Change*, 176, 121383.

Daios, A., Kladovasilakis, N., Kelemis, A., Kostavelis, I. (2025). AI applications in supply chain management: A survey. *Applied Sciences*, 15(5), 2775.

Giessner, S.R., Dawson, J.F., Horton, K.E., West, M. (2023). The impact of supportive leadership on employee outcomes during organizational mergers: An organizational-level field study. *Journal of Applied Psychology*, 108(4), 686.

Hamed, A.A., Dandan, S.M., Farah, A.A., Barakat, S.A. (2024). The effect of organisational factors on adopting big data analytics in supply chain operation among companies in Saudi Arabia: The moderating role of resistance to change. *Journal of Transport and Supply Chain Management*, 18, 1–12.

Hangl, J., Krause, S., Behrens, V.J. (2023). Drivers, barriers and social considerations for AI adoption in SCM. *Technology in Society*, 74, 102299.

Hao, X. and Demir, E. (2025). Artificial intelligence in supply chain management: Enablers and constraints in pre-development, deployment, and post-development stages. *Production Planning & Control*, 36(6), 748–770.

Hastings, B.J. and Schwarz, G.M. (2022). Leading change processes for success: A dynamic application of diagnostic and dialogic organization development. *The Journal of Applied Behavioral Science*, 58(1), 120–148.

Hills, V. (2025). Between rhetoric and reality: A psychosocial study of participatory change leadership. *Journal of Organizational Change Management*, 1–14. doi: 10.1108/JOCM-11-2024-0744.

Ivanov, D. and Dolgui, A. (2020). Viability of intertwined supply networks: Extending the supply chain resilience angles towards survivability. A position paper motivated by COVID-19 outbreak. *International Journal of Production Research*, 58(10), 2904–2915.

Koilakonda, R.R. (2024). Enhancing user experience during organizational transformations: Strategies for effective change management and user adoption. *International Journal of Science and Research (IJSR)*, 13(6), 1244–1248.

Kumar Dadsena, K. and Pant, P. (2023). Analyzing the barriers in supply chain digitization: Sustainable development goals perspective. *Operations Management Research*, 16(4), 1684–1697.

Modgil, S., Gupta, S., Bhushan, B. (2020). Building a living economy through modern information decision support systems and UN sustainable development goals. *Production Planning & Control*, 31(11–12), 967–987.

Mondejar, M.E., Avtar, R., Diaz, H.L.B., Dubey, R.K., Esteban, J., Gómez-Morales, A., Garcia-Segura, S. (2021). Digitalization to achieve sustainable development goals: Steps towards a Smart Green Planet. *Science of The Total Environment*, 794, 148539.

Olaleye, I., Mokogwu, V., Olufemi-Phillips, A.Q., Adewale, T.T. (2024). Transforming supply chain resilience: Frameworks and advancements in predictive analytics and datadriven strategies. *Open Access Research Journal of Multidisciplinary Studies*, 8(2), 085–093.

Pagell, M. and Wilhelm, M. (2025). Putting the S in sustainable supply chain management: A people-centric research agenda. *Journal of Supply Chain Management*, 61(1), 83–95.

Prajapati, D., Jauhar, S.K., Gunasekaran, A., Kamble, S.S., Pratap, S. (2022). Blockchain and IoT embedded sustainable virtual closed-loop supply chain in E-commerce towards the circular economy. *Computers & Industrial Engineering*, 172, 108530.

Rana, R. and Bhambri, P. (2024). Hybrid MCDM (multi-criteria decision-making) approaches for sustainable energy management. In *Modern SuperHyperSoft Computing Trends in Science and Technology*, Smarandache, F. and Majumder, P. (eds). IGI Global, Hershey, 149–184. doi: 10.4018/979-8-3693-6875-6.ch006.

Rana, R. and Bhambri, P. (2025). Harnessing block chain digital twins for sustainable business operations. In *Practical Frameworks for New-Age Digitalization Business Strategy*, Tee, P., Song, B., Ho, R. (eds). IGI Global, Hershey, 413–446. doi: 10.4018/979-8-3373-2018-2.ch013.

Sharma, M., Gupta, R., Acharya, P. (2021). Analysing the adoption of cloud computing service: A systematic literature review. *Global Knowledge, Memory and Communication*, 70(1–2), 114–153.

Solangi, Y.A., Longsheng, C., Shah, S.A.A. (2021). Assessing and overcoming the renewable energy barriers for sustainable development in Pakistan: An integrated AHP and fuzzy TOPSIS approach. *Renewable Energy*, 173, 209–222.

Thekkekara, J.V., and Devi, R.V. (2023). Change management: A survey of literature in view of analysing the advantages of ADKAR model. *RGUHS Journal of Allied Health Sciences*, 3(2), 1–7. doi: 10.26463/rjahs.3_2_2.

Turja, T. (2022). Rather sooner than later: Participatory change management associated with greater job satisfaction in healthcare. *Journal of Advanced Nursing*, 78(3), e49–e51.

Zaman, J., Shoomal, A., Jahanbakht, M., Ozay, D. (2025). Driving supply chain transformation with IoT and AI integration: A dual approach using bibliometric analysis and topic modeling. *IoT*, 6(2), 21.

Zhang, T., Jia, F., Chen, L. (2025). Blockchain adoption in supply chains: Implications for sustainability. *Production Planning & Control*, 36(5), 699–722.

14

Future Horizons: Emerging Technologies and Models

The landscape of technological innovation is rapidly evolving, marked by the convergence of disciplines that were once considered to be distinct and largely independent. As industries look toward future horizons, it is increasingly evident that emerging technologies and models will not only transform individual sectors but also create new interdependencies across them. This convergence calls for novel frameworks capable of sustaining complex data ecosystems, fostering interoperability and addressing ethical and regulatory imperatives that transcend traditional boundaries.

One striking example of this phenomenon is the growing interconnection between the petrochemical and healthcare sectors. The transformation of industrial chemical precursors into medical-grade materials illustrates how industrial processes and clinical applications are becoming deeply intertwined. However, the pace of this integration has far exceeded the development of unified data infrastructures capable of supporting the full life cycle of such innovations. Existing data migration practices remain highly siloed, semantically inconsistent and poorly adapted to the demands of contemporary supply chains, where issues of transparency, compliance and accountability are paramount.

To address this critical gap, the present study proposes a theoretically grounded, artificial intelligence (AI)-augmented data migration framework. The framework is designed to bridge industrial and clinical domains by enabling secure, reliable and semantically coherent data transfer. It is further validated through the use of synthetic datasets modeled on real-world systems, including SCADA logs, LIMS records and occupational health files which demonstrate both practical applicability and scalability across emerging technological frontiers.

Chapter written by Krishi Pallab SAIKIA, Debjit DHAR, Rik DAS and Saranik MAHAPATRA.

14.1. Introduction

Industrial operations now produce vast and heterogeneous data streams that encompass manufacturing telemetry, environmental monitoring, occupational-health records and product-quality assurance systems (Naidoo et al. 2025). For instance, petrochemical facilities generate high-frequency time-series process data from Supervisory Control and Data Acquisition (SCADA) systems alongside structured laboratory records from Laboratory Information Management Systems (LIMS) and Environmental, Health and Safety (EHS) platforms. Concurrently, healthcare providers and medical-product manufacturers depend on petrochemical inputs – medical-grade polymers, solvents and pharmaceutical precursors – while producing highly sensitive records such as occupational-health files, clinical diagnostics and product-specification documentation. Despite these interdependencies, industrial and clinical data ecosystems have evolved in organizational and technical silos, governed by differing priorities, vocabularies, schemas and regulatory constraints. Integrating these domains presents both a major opportunity and a major challenge. Cyber-physical systems (CPS), the Industrial Internet of Things (IIoT) (Islam 2025), and cloud-based health informatics provide the technological foundation for end-to-end traceability and improved quality assurance across the petrochemical-to-medical lifecycle. Yet, practical integration remains difficult: traditional extract–transform–load (ETL) pipelines struggle to reconcile high-velocity telemetry with privacy-regulated clinical records. Heterogeneous schemas, variable semantics, inconsistent metadata and stringent regulatory regimes (e.g. REACH, FDA CFR 21, HIPAA, GDPR, etc.) complicate migration, linkage and auditability. Consequently, organizations face fragmented migrations, delayed risk detection and missed opportunities for cross-domain insights that could improve safety, compliance and sustainability reporting. Recent advances in machine learning (ML) – particularly generative artificial intelligence (AI) and large language models (LLMs) – introduce new affordances for intelligent data integration. This chapter introduces an AI-augmented framework for intelligent data migration between petrochemical and medical domains. It frames the technical challenges, articulates specific research questions and outlines the aims, scope and significance of the study. The remainder of this section sets out the motivation, problem statement, research questions, objectives and scope that guide the work.

14.1.1. *Research motivation*

The petrochemical-to-medical product lifecycle is an urgent exemplar: raw materials and process conditions recorded in petrochemical plants can materially affect downstream product quality and patient safety, yet there is no standardized, semantically coherent mechanism to reconcile provenance information with clinical and manufacturing records (Mavridis et al. 2025). Heightened regulatory scrutiny, growing workplace-health concerns and sustainability mandates further increase the need for transparent, auditable data linkages (Zimmermann et al. 2025). Generative AI techniques offer promising capabilities – automated semantic profiling, ontology alignment and contextual cleansing – that can reduce the manual effort currently required for cross-domain integration. Leveraging these capabilities to connect industrial telemetry, laboratory records and occupational health data may unlock new possibilities for proactive risk modeling, product integrity verification and streamlined regulatory reporting. This potential motivates a systematic exploration of architectures and algorithms that embed generative models within privacy-aware, auditable migration pipelines (Mavridis et al. 2025; Ozobu et al. 2025; Ren et al. 2025).

14.1.2. *Problem statement*

Current data migration practices between industrial and healthcare domains are fragmented, manual and insufficiently rigorous for modern traceability and compliance needs (Zimmermann et al. 2025). Specific shortcomings include:

– inability to ingest and reconcile high-volume, real-time industrial telemetry alongside privacy-regulated clinical and occupational-health records;

– lack of semantic interoperability across divergent ontologies and vocabularies used by industrial control, laboratory and clinical systems;

– limited automation for context-aware profiling, mapping and cleansing. Existing ETL tools require heavy manual intervention;

– insufficient provenance, explainability and audit trails to satisfy regulators and support safety governance. These limitations hinder timely detection of quality regressions, compromise product traceability and impose unnecessary operational costs for compliance and reporting. The research problem is to design an AI-augmented migration framework that addresses these deficits while preserving privacy and regulatory compatibility (Ren et al. 2025; Stahmann et al. 2025; Yun et al. 2025).

14.1.3. *Research questions*

This study is driven by four primary research questions:

1) How can generative AI be leveraged to enable intelligent, scalable data migration across petrochemical and medical ecosystems?

2) What architectural and algorithmic components are required to support semantic interoperability and regulatory compliance in such cross-domain systems?

3) What are the measurable impacts of an AI-augmented data integration framework on data quality, reconciliation efficiency and operational traceability?

4) How can privacy-preserving techniques be incorporated to ensure ethical and legally compliant linkage of industrial and occupational-health data?

These research questions frame both the design and the empirical evaluation of the proposed framework (Akhmetov et al. 2025; NIH 2025).

14.1.4. *Aims and objectives*

The primary aim is to conceptualize and evaluate a unified, AI-augmented framework for intelligent data migration between petrochemical and medical domains. Specific objectives are to:

1) Design an end-to-end architecture that enforces semantic and regulatory consistency across industrial and clinical datasets.

2) Apply generative AI and other ML models to automate profiling, cleansing, transformation and mapping of heterogeneous sources.

3) Demonstrate the framework on representative use cases: occupational-health risk modeling, medical-product traceability and regulatory reporting.

4) Evaluate framework performance using realistic synthetic datasets emulating SCADA logs, LIMS outputs and occupational-health records.

5) Identify future research directions including explainable AI, federated learning and ontology-driven integration.

14.1.5. *Significance of the study*

This research contributes both theoretically and practically. Theoretically, it extends discourse on AI-driven data interoperability by demonstrating how generative models can be co-designed with symbolic ontologies and provenance mechanisms to achieve traceable semantic reconciliation. Practically, the proposed framework offers an actionable blueprint for stakeholders – industrial operators, healthcare providers, manufacturers and regulators – to improve data governance, product-integrity assurance and audit readiness. Effective linkage between petrochemical process records and downstream medical applications can materially improve proactive risk detection, sustainability reporting and supply-chain transparency (Sahoo 2024).

14.1.6. *Scope of the study*

The study is intentionally scoped to permit rigorous conceptual development and controlled evaluation. It includes:

– theoretical design and simulated evaluation of a data migration framework bridging petrochemical and medical data sources;

– use of synthetic datasets modeled on real-world systems (SCADA telemetry, LIMS exports, occupational-health records) to validate architectural choices and automated mapping strategies;

– application of generative AI and supporting ML models for profiling, cleansing, mapping and transformation;

– exclusion of live deployment, integration with proprietary platforms and formal legal compliance testing in production environments.

This scope enables a replicable evaluation while laying groundwork for subsequent empirical deployment research.

14.2. A unified framework for intelligent data migration

The focus of this framework is not on operational deployment, but rather on a research-oriented prototype capable of guiding future applied developments. To this end, the architecture is presented as a layered, modular system informed by real-world data models (e.g. SCADA logs, LIMS entries and occupational-health records), but explicitly excludes live system integration, proprietary software implementation or real-time compliance validation. This constraint ensures that the work remains grounded in theoretical analysis while still addressing complex, real-world challenges.

The diagram shows the layered pipeline from system modeling and optimization through data ingestion, AI-driven profiling and cataloging, cleansing and transformation, schema mapping and semantic alignment, reconciliation and validation, to export and output simulation. Dashed lines indicate feedback and optimization loops that close the control and learning cycle.

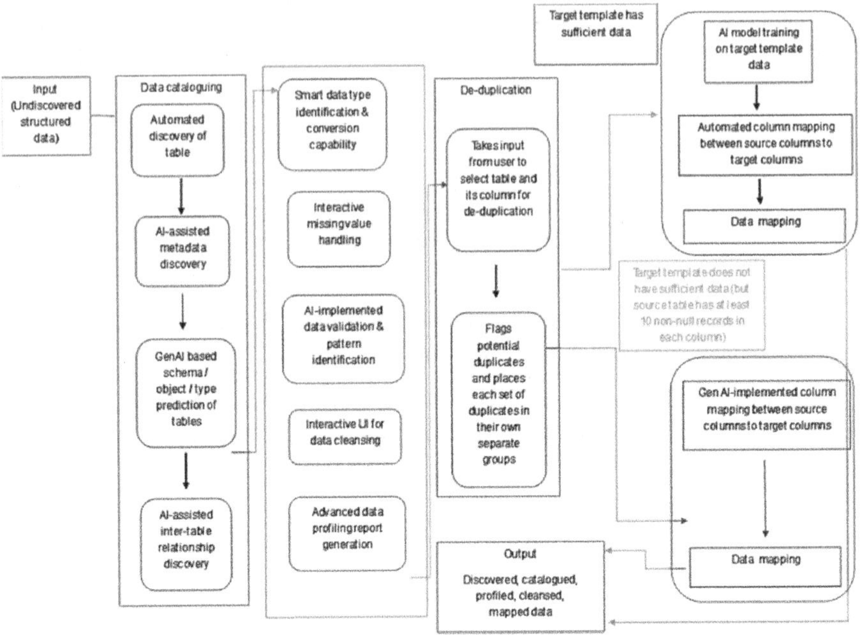

Figure 14.1. *Conceptual architecture of the AI-augmented data migration framework*

14.2.1. *Architectural blueprint*

The proposed framework simulates a complete data lifecycle pipeline, from ingestion to export, using synthetic but realistic representations of petrochemical and healthcare data. The architecture is organized into six functional layers, each incorporating AI-enhanced capabilities for assessment, cleansing, semantic transformation and validation. While grounded in practical needs, the system is intended for conceptual demonstration and computational experimentation.

14.2.1.1. *Data ingestion and landing layer*

1) *Sources*: simulated datasets reflect typical SAP and non-SAP environments, including control system logs (e.g. SCADA), laboratory information management system (LIMS) records, EHS (environment, health and safety) records and HR-maintained occupational health logs.

2) *Landing mechanism*: data is ingested via virtualized connectors in a sandboxed simulation environment, preserving the structure and metadata fidelity of actual enterprise systems without direct integration.

3) *Security and compliance assumptions*: while privacy-preserving design principles are discussed (e.g. anonymization, PII masking, etc.), actual encryption protocols or live regulatory compliance (e.g. HIPAA, GDPR, etc.) are out of scope.

14.2.1.2. *AI-driven profiling and cataloging*

4) *Generative data cataloging*: LLMs are simulated to perform schema inference, data-dictionary generation and semantic labeling of synthetic datasets. These simulated LLMs emulate the behavior expected of enterprise data-discovery platforms.

5) *Data quality profiling*: ML models trained on synthetic anomaly injections assess each dataset's integrity through metrics such as null-value prevalence, type mismatches, temporal drift and schema violations. The output is a data quality assessment report for each dataset.

This AI-enhanced profiling replaces much manual effort found in traditional ETL and demonstrates how human-intensive quality audits could be automated in production systems.

14.2.1.3. *Cleansing engine and transformation core*

6) *Synthetic cleansing tasks*: common issues (missing values, duplicated exposure records, unit inconsistencies, etc.) are injected and corrected through simulated ML module performing:

a) value imputation using conditional expectation or nearest-neighbor historical similarity;

b) fuzzy deduplication based on string similarity and record linkage;

c) context-aware normalization (e.g. mapping internal identifiers to CAS, ISO or ICD-10).

7) *AI-augmented cleansing engine*: a rules-and-learning hybrid orchestrates cleansing operations and produces a data cleaning report with error categories and confidence scores. Workflows are modeled in Python/Jupyter to ensure reproducibility.

14.2.1.4. *Data mapping and semantic alignment*

8) *Source-to-target mapping simulation*: sequence-to-sequence models and attention-based transformers are trained to predict schema alignments between petrochemical and clinical schemas. Typical mapping tasks include:

a) linking process batch histories to quality test outcomes;

b) associating employee work zones with exposure and health records;

c) harmonizing nomenclatures via unit conversions and code alignment.

9) *Generative AI interpretation*: domain-trained generative models infer transformation logic and produce human-readable mapping suggestions for review. All transformations are recorded in a transformation lineage log for auditability.

14.2.1.5. *Reconciliation and validation layer*

10) *Synthetic validation framework*: cleansed and mapped data are validated against synthetic master datasets (e.g. master material lists, organizational hierarchies).

11) Reconciliation logic: discrepancy rules and thresholds are defined per test-case. Issues are routed to an Issue Handling Framework that simulates collaboration among actors (plant engineers and auditors).

14.2.1.6. *Export and output simulation*

12) *Export to mock target systems*: final outputs are exported to sandboxed targets resembling SAP MDG or S/4 structures. Export metrics include cleansing success rate, mapping accuracy and reconciliation completeness.

13) *Governance simulation*: dashboards and logs mimic enterprise reporting without connecting to live systems or sensitive repositories.

14.2.2. *AI capabilities simulated in the framework*

Feature	**Technique simulated**	**Purpose**	**Scope constraint**
Data cataloging	LLM-based schema and attribute inference	Automate metadata discovery	Simulated on test metadata
Data profiling	ML-driven quality analysis	Detect anomalies and drift	Based on synthetic anomalies
Cleansing and deduplication	AI-enhanced imputation and fuzzy matching	Resolve common integrity issues	Not connected to live systems
Semantic mapping	Transformer-based alignment	Reduce manual mapping effort	Abstract schema scenarios
Conversational query	Generative-NLP interface (simulated)	Enable natural-language data access	Modeled, not deployed interactively

Table 14.1. *AI capabilities simulated in the sandbox environment*

To support the study's objectives, the framework simulates the following AI features within a sandbox environment. Table 14.1 summarizes feature → simulated technique → purpose → scope constraint.

Table 14.1 defines the functional simulation scope. Models and modules are instantiated on synthetic data, with algorithmic behaviors tuned to produce repeatable, auditable outcomes for evaluation.

14.2.3. *Justification of theoretical scope*

The framework intentionally excludes live deployment to preserve research ethics, reproducibility and focus:

1) *Ethical and legal constraints*: integration with real occupational health or production records would require IRB approval, contractual access and regulatory compliance (HIPAA, GDPR, etc.), which is outside the intended research scope.

2) *Scientific generalizability*: abstraction from specific vendor stacks ensures the architecture can be reimplemented across technologies and institutions, promoting reproducibility.

3) *Focus on conceptual validation*: synthetic datasets allow controlled anomaly injections and deterministic evaluation of pipeline behavior without exposing sensitive data.

Below, we provide a concise mathematical formalization of the key components and the evaluation metrics used in the simulation experiments.

14.2.4. *Mathematical formalization and evaluation*

Let s denote the space of source records (heterogeneous petrochemical and clinical tables), and $\mathcal{T}$ the space of target canonical records. A semantic mapping is a function

$$T : \mathrm{s} \longrightarrow \mathcal{T}, \qquad [14.1]$$

which in the implemented simulation is approximated by a parameterized model T_θ (e.g. a transformer or seq2seq network). Mapping quality is evaluated by a loss

$$\mathscr{L}(\theta) = \lambda_{\text{map}}\,\mathrm{MSE}(T_\theta(s), t) + \lambda_{\text{KL}}\,\mathrm{KL}(P_{T_\theta} \parallel P_{\text{master}}) + \lambda_{\text{struct}}\,\mathscr{R}(\theta), \qquad [14.2]$$

where $s \in \mathrm{s}$, $t \in \mathcal{T}$, KL is the Kullback–Leibler divergence comparing derived distributions against master references, and $\mathcal{R}$ is a regularizer penalizing structural inconsistencies (e.g. type mismatches). Coefficients λ. are hyperparameters tuned by cross-validation on synthetic test folds.

– *Transformation lineage*: a transformation pipeline of n discrete steps is represented as a composition:

$$\mathcal{L} = T^{(n)} \circ T^{(n-1)} \circ \cdots \circ^{(1)}, \tag{14.3}$$

and the Jacobian of the composition at a sample s gives first-order sensitivity for error propagation:

$$J_{\mathcal{L}}(s) = \prod_{i=1}^{n} J_{T(i)}\left(s^{(i-1)}\right), \tag{14.4}$$

with $s^{(0)} = s$ and $s^{(i)} = T^{(i)}(s^{(i-1)})$.

– *Data quality score (DQS)*: for a dataset D, define a vector of normalized quality indicators $q = (q_1, \dots, q_m)$ where each $q_i \in [0, 1]$ (e.g. completeness, correctness, timeliness, consistency).

Then,

$$DQS(D) = \sum_{i=1}^{m} w_i q_i, \text{ with } \sum_{i=1}^{m} w_i = 1, w_i \geq 0. \tag{14.5}$$

Weights w_i reflect stakeholder priorities and are chosen per use case (occupational exposure vs. product traceability).

– *Imputation via conditional expectation*: for a missing field x with context features x, the imputation model returns

$$\hat{x} = [E \mid Z = x] \approx f_{\phi}(x), \tag{14.6}$$

where f_{ϕ} is a supervised regressor trained on historical synthetic data. Confidence of imputation can be estimated from an ensemble variance:

$$\text{Conf}(\hat{x}) = 1 - \frac{\text{Var}\left\{f_{\phi h}(x)\right\}_{k=1}^{n}}{\text{Var}_{\text{ref}}} \tag{14.7}$$

with K being ensemble members and Var_{ref} being a reference variance.

– *Evaluation metrics*: for mapping and cleansing tasks, primary evaluation metrics used in the simulation are:

$$\text{Mapping accuracy} = \frac{1}{N}\sum_{i=1}^{N} 1\{T(\theta_i) = t\}, \qquad [14.8]$$

$$\text{Precision/Recall}\left(\text{for anomaly detection}\right) = \frac{\text{TP}}{\text{TP+FP}}, \frac{\text{TP}}{\text{TP+FN}}, \qquad [14.9]$$

$$\text{F1 Score} = 2 \cdot \frac{\text{Precision} \cdot \text{Recall}}{\text{Precision} + \text{Recall}}. \qquad [14.10]$$

14.3. The role of generative AI in cross-domain data migration

Generative AI, particularly instantiated as LLMs and transformer-based architectures, is reshaping data engineering practice by enabling semantic interpretation, generation and reasoning over structured and unstructured information (Jansen et al. 2025).

14.3.1. *Semantic data profiling using generative AI*

Semantic profiling encompasses determination of meaning, relationships and contextual constraints of data elements across heterogeneous sources. Conventional profiling tools report statistical measures such as null counts and value histograms, but they do not capture the domain-specific semantics required to distinguish, for example, reactor temperature from storage temperature or to associate a VOC reading with exposure to a particular chemical species. In industrial-health contexts, such semantic distinctions are essential for downstream cleansing, mapping and risk assessment.

14.3.1.1. *Theoretical design*

The profiling subsystem is cast as a function that maps a column representation to a semantic label and a sensitivity tag. Let $\mathcal{C}$ denote the space of column descriptors (header text, sample values, metadata, etc.) and let $\mathcal{L}$ denote the set of semantic labels and sensitivity classes. The profiling operator π is defined as:

$$\pi : \mathcal{C} \rightarrow \mathcal{L} \times [0, 1], \qquad [14.11]$$

where the second component is a calibrated confidence score. In practice, π is approximated via a parameterized model π_θ trained on synthetic annotations with objective

$$\theta^\star = \arg \frac{\min}{\theta} M_{c\sim\mathcal{D}_{\text{syn}}} [\mathcal{L}_{\text{CE}}(\pi_\theta(c), l(c)) + \lambda\, \mathcal{R}(\theta)], \qquad [14.12]$$

where $\mathcal{L}_{\text{CE}}$ is cross-entropy to the synthetic label $l(c)$, $\mathcal{R}$ is a regularizer and λ is a hyperparameter. Domain-inconsistency detection is treated as an outlier scoring problem. Given a reference distribution P_{ref} for a numeric field, a supplied record value x is flagged if its tail probability

$$p = 1 - \boldsymbol{\Gamma}_{\text{ref}}(x) \qquad [14.13]$$

falls below a threshold τ. For categorical fields, inconsistency is measured by conditional entropy relative to an expected value distribution.

Semantic sensitivity classification is modeled as a binary decision with a calibrated score. The decision threshold can be set using the receiver operating characteristic derived from synthetic PII/PHI injections.

14.3.1.2. *Simulated evaluation*

Synthetic datasets were instrumented with ambiguous headers, type mismatches, and embedded PII in free text. A fine-tuned LLM proxy implemented via a masked-token prediction mechanism augmented with deterministic rules was evaluated on these datasets. Let N be the number of annotated columns and let k denote correctly inferred labels. Semantic resolution accuracy is

$$\text{Accuracy} = \frac{k}{N}. \qquad [14.14]$$

In the simulation, the model resolved 92% of ambiguous column headers correctly and identified 95% of seeded PII fields. Confidence calibration was evaluated by the expected calibration error (ECE)

$$\text{ECE} = \sum_{b=1}^{B} \frac{|S_b|}{N} \left|\text{acc}(S_b) - \text{conf}(S_b)\right|, \qquad [14.15]$$

computed on B confidence bins S_b. Low ECE values indicated that model confidences aligned well with empirical correctness rates, which supports the use of confidence scores to gate human review.

14.3.2. *Intelligent source-to-target mapping*

Mapping heterogeneous source schemas to a unified target schema is central to cross-domain migration.

Manual mapping is labor-intensive and fragile to schema drift (Kurva 2025). The framework leverages generative AI together with sequence-to-sequence neural architectures to infer schema alignments and to synthesize transformation rules with minimal hand-coding.

14.3.2.1. *Theoretical approach*

Let $\mathrm{s} = \{s_1, \dots, s_m\}$ denote a source schema and $\mathcal{T} = \{t_1, \dots, t_n\}$ denote a target schema. The mapping problem is to infer a mapping function M that associates each target attribute t_j with an expression over source attributes:

$$M : \mathcal{T} \rightarrow (\mathrm{s}), \tag{14.16}$$

where $S(\mathrm{s})$ is the space of transformation expressions (concatenation, arithmetic combination, unit conversion, code lookup, etc.). A generative mapping engine M_ϕ parameterized by ϕ produces candidate expressions conditioned on schema metadata and exemplar rows. The quality of generated mappings is evaluated with a correctness indicator

$$\mathbf{1}\{(t_j) = M^{\star}(t_j)\}, \tag{14.17}$$

where $M^{\star}$ denotes the ground-truth mapping defined in the synthetic scenario. For continuous reconciliation such as unit conversion, the engine proposes a conversion function $(\boldsymbol{v}_s \rightarrow \boldsymbol{v}_t)$ where the conversion error for a sample x is

$$(x) = |(x) - x_{\text{true}}|, \tag{14.18}$$

and mappings are accepted if the mean error falls below a predefined tolerance.

Mapping generation is formalized as conditional sequence generation. Given a prompt p encoding source and target descriptors, the generator maximizes the conditional probability

$$\log P_\phi\left(e \middle| p\right) = \sum_{t=1}^{T} \log P_\phi\left(e_t \middle| e_{<t}, \mathrm{p}\right) \tag{14.19}$$

and beam search is used to produce high-likelihood candidate expressions which are then validated on synthetic example rows.

14.3.2.2. *Synthetic evaluation*

A corpus of 100 synthetic mapping tasks was created to emulate realistic petrochemical and clinical schema mismatches. Mapping accuracy was measured as the proportion of target attributes for which the top-ranked generated expression matched the ground truth. Let J be the total number of target attributes across tasks and let j^* be those matched correctly. Overall mapping accuracy is

$$\text{MapAcc} = \frac{j^*}{j}. \qquad [14.20]$$

The simulated engine achieved MapAcc = 0.89. Code and unit harmonization accuracy was separately measured on a subset of tasks requiring canonicalization to standards (e.g. CAS, ICD, etc.). The harmonization accuracy was 0.93. The distribution of generated transformation patterns was analyzed to estimate combinatorial complexity: the number of distinct transformation templates T_{templ} observed over P source–target pairs grew approximately linearly in the simulation regime:

$$T_{\text{templ}} \approx \alpha P + \beta, \qquad [14.21]$$

where α, β are the empirically estimated constants. This observation informs required template coverage for practical deployment.

14.3.3. *Conversational data querying and exploration*

Generative AI additionally provides a natural language interface that mediates between domain experts and complex datasets. A conversational agent translates intent into executable query plans while preserving provenance and confidence metadata. This capability is particularly useful for nontechnical stakeholders.

14.3.3.1. *Theoretical implementation*

A natural-language query q is mapped to a query plan (q) that is executable against the integrated dataset. The parsing and planning pipeline is a composition of a semantic parser and a planner:

$$\pi : Q \xrightarrow{\text{parse}} P \xrightarrow{\text{plan}} S, \qquad [14.22]$$

where Q is the space of user queries, P is the intermediate program representations, and S is the executable plans. The parser is realized by an LLM proxy that maps natural language to a structured intermediate representation. The planner converts this representation into a sequence of relational operations. To quantify interpretability and traceability, each produced plan is annotated with a provenance path L that lists source fields and transformation steps. Plan fidelity is evaluated by the proportion of result rows that match ground-truth answers:

$$\text{Fidelity} = \frac{1}{N}\sum_{i=1}^{N} 1\{\text{result}_i = \text{gold}_i\}. \quad [14.23]$$

14.3.3.2. *Conceptual evaluation*

A suite of domain queries was synthesized for evaluation. The agent's ability to identify relevant fields, generate correct join conditions and return provenance was quantified. Field identification accuracy was 0.94, mapping correctness within generated plans was 0.88 and explainable plan generation fidelity was 0.90. For complex conjunctive queries combining spatio-temporal predicates and clinical events, the agent produced plans whose expected precision and recall were estimated as follows.

14.4. Real-world applications across domains: bridging petrochemical and medical data ecosystems

The conceptual framework developed in this study offers a foundation for integrating heterogeneous data systems spanning the petrochemical and medical sectors. Although these industries operate under distinct regimes, their data lifecycles overlap in the provenance of medical-grade materials, diagnostics and some pharmaceuticals. Ensuring continuity of data from chemical production to clinical application requires rigorous semantic alignment, provenance-aware transformations and privacy-preserving reconciliation. This section presents six theoretically grounded use cases, executed in simulation with synthetic data, that demonstrate the framework's potential to enable meaningful data convergence.

14.4.1. *Occupational exposure and health risk modeling*

– *Objective and context*: in petrochemical facilities, employees may be exposed to volatile organic compounds (VOCs), heavy metals and extreme process conditions. Failure to relate such exposures to downstream clinical data can produce delayed diagnoses and underreported occupational risk (Malakan and Thepanondh 2022).

– *Framework application*: the framework simulates the temporal and spatial linkage of sensor telemetry to workforce records and clinical assessments. Consider an exposure time series $E_{i,}(t)$ for employee i in the plant zone x. A time-aligned health indicator $(t{+}\tau)$ (for a prospective lag τ) is modeled in a proportional-hazards form:

$$(t + \tau \mid \mathbf{E}_i, \mathbf{X}_i) = \lambda_0(t + \tau)\exp\,(\beta^{\mathrm{T}}\mathbf{E}_i + \bar{\gamma}^{\mathrm{T}}\,\mathbf{X}_i), \qquad [14.24]$$

where $\overline{E}_i$ denotes aggregated exposure summaries for employee i (e.g. time-weighted averages), $\mathbf{X}_i$ are covariates such as age and job role, and λ_0 is a baseline hazard. In discrete risk-prediction settings, a logistic model is applied:

$$\Pr(H_i = 1 \mid \mathbf{E}_i, \overline{X}_i) = \sigma(\alpha + \beta^{\mathrm{T}}\mathbf{E}_i + \bar{\gamma}^{\mathrm{T}}\,\mathbf{X}_i), \qquad [14.25]$$

with $\sigma(\cdot)$ being the logistic function. Temporal and spatial correlation is encoded by adding zone-specific random effects $\boldsymbol{v}_x$:

$$\Pr(H_i = 1) = \sigma(\alpha + \beta^{\mathrm{T}}\mathbf{E}_i + \bar{\gamma}^{\mathrm{T}}\,\mathbf{X}_i + \boldsymbol{v}_{x(i)}). \qquad [14.26]$$

Semantic reconciliation maps plant-specific exposure codes to clinical diagnosis codes. The mapping operator M is evaluated by an accuracy metric

$$\mathrm{MapAcc} = \frac{1}{|\mathcal{T}|}\sum_{t\in\mathcal{T}} 1\{M(t) = M^*(t)\} \qquad [14.27]$$

where $\mathcal{T}$ is the set of test mappings and M^* is the synthetic ground truth. Research implications include improved early-warning risk signals and targeted intervention policies derived from probabilistic risk scores.

14.4.2. *Medical product traceability*

– *Objective and context*: many medical products are derived from petrochemical feedstocks. Traceability from raw chemical batch to clinical usage is critical for quality assurance and recalls.

– *Framework application*: the traceability model is represented as a directed acyclic provenance graph $G = (, E)$, where vertices V represent production batches, intermediate transformations and serialized clinical items. Directed edges E represent transformation or consumption steps. A path $p = (v_0, \ldots, v_k)$ from source batch v_0 to clinical item v_k provides lineage. The probability that a reported adverse event A is attributable to batch v_0 can be estimated via a path-scoring function:

$$\Pr\left(A \middle| v_0\right) \text{a} \sum_{p:v_0 \rightsquigarrow v_k} (p) \cdot \{v_k \text{ linked to } A\}, \quad [14.28]$$

where each path weight $w(p) = \prod^k \phi(e_j)$ multiplies edge reliabilities $\phi(e_j)$. Unit harmonization and standardization are handled as algebraic conversions. For a scalar quantity measured in source units $\boldsymbol{v}_s$ converted to target units $\boldsymbol{v}_t$ we apply a conversion function $g_{u_S \to u_t}$ such that the conversion error for a sample x is $|g_{u_S \to u_t}(x) - x_{\text{true}}|$. Transformation audit trails are recorded as ordered tuples (v, t, op, actor) to support retrospective root-cause analysis.

14.4.3. *Incident investigation and root cause analysis*

– *Objective and context*: failures of medical products or industrial incidents often arise from upstream deviations. Cross-domain forensic capability requires aligned timestamps, normalized units and multimodal fusion.

– *Framework application*: an event reconstruction is formulated as an inference problem: given the observed incident indicators Y (quality test failures, clinical adverse events), find the most probable sequence of causal upstream parameter deviations $\Theta^\star$. Under a Bayesian formulation,

$$\Theta^\star = \underset{\Theta}{\arg\max} \Pr(\Theta \mid \mathrm{Y}) = \underset{\Theta}{\arg\max} \Pr(Y \mid \Theta)\Pr(\Theta). \quad [14.29]$$

Likelihoods $\Pr(Y \mid \Theta)$ are computed by generative simulators trained on synthetic production and quality data. For temporal causality detection, Granger-type statistics are used: parameter (t) Granger-causes (t) if inclusion of past x values reduces the predictive error for y:

$$F_{GC} = \frac{(RSS_{\text{restricted}} - RSS_{\text{full}})/p}{RSS_{\text{full}}/(T - 2p - 1)}, \quad [14.30]$$

where RSS denotes the residual sum of squares and p is the lag order. Multimodal attribution combines evidence via log-odds aggregation and produces ranked candidate causes for human adjudication.

14.4.4. *Workforce health surveillance and compliance auditing*

– *Objective and context*: regulatory regimes require joint monitoring of exposure and health while preserving privacy and compliance.

– *Framework application*: longitudinal health profiles are constructed by linking exposure records (t) with health encounters (t). Privacy-preserving transformations are simulated using both classical and formal methods. A k-anonymity constraint for a sanitized cohort dataset D' is expressed as

$$\forall \tau \in D', |\{s \in D' : \text{quasi-id}(s) = \text{quasi-id}(\tau)\}| \geq k. \quad [14.31]$$

Differential privacy is modeled by adding calibrated noise to aggregated outputs: query mechanism h achieves (ε, δ)-differential privacy if

$$\Pr[h(D) \in S] \leq e^{\varepsilon} \Pr[h(D') \in S] + \delta, \quad [14.32]$$

for all neighboring datasets D, D' and measurable sets S. Synthetic audit reports include compliance metrics computed over masked data and produce simulated evidence suitable for internal review while avoiding exposure of PII/PHI.

14.4.5. *Data quality monitoring across the industrial – clinical pipeline*

– *Objective and context*: data quality failures – mismatched units, misaligned timestamps, inconsistent nomenclature – undermine traceability and decision-making.

– *Framework application*: data quality is quantified by a composite score (D) that aggregates normalized indicators (D) across dimensions $j \in \{1, \dots, m\}$:

$$Q(D) = \sum_{j=1}^{m} w_j q_j(D), \ \sum_{j=1}^{m} W_j = 1, W_j \geq 0. \quad [14.33]$$

Indicators include completeness, syntactic correctness, semantic consistency and temporal plausibility. Automated remediation suggestions are generated by models that predict corrective transforms $T^{\star}$ minimizing expected downstream loss:

$$T^{\star} = \arg\min_{T} [\mathcal{L}_{\text{down}}(T(D)) + \eta\, \mathcal{C}(T)], \quad [14.34]$$

where $\mathcal{L}_{\text{down}}$ measures degradation in downstream analytic utility and $\mathcal{C}$ penalizes risky or high-cost transformations. Continuous benchmarking tracks (D) over time and informs governance remediation cycles.

14.4.6. *Conversational access to integrated data systems*

– *Objective and context*: nontechnical stakeholders require accessible interfaces to interrogate integrated datasets without direct query language proficiency.

– *Framework application*: a natural-language-to-query planner maps a user utterance $\boldsymbol{v}$ to an executable plan p with provenance annotation (p). Plan correctness is measured by fidelity to the user intent and by result provenance coverage:

$$\text{Fidelity}(\boldsymbol{v}) = \Pr\left(\text{result}(p) = \text{gold}(\boldsymbol{v})\right), \text{ProvenanceCoverage} = \frac{|L(p)|}{L^*}, \quad [14.35]$$

where L^* is the ground-truth lineage. Explainable outputs include transformation histories and confidence scores, enabling auditability. The conversational interface is evaluated on simulated question sets to quantify intent recognition and traceable response generation.

Use case	Petrochemical data input	Medical domain output	Framework role
Occupational health risk modeling	VOC sensor logs, work zone metadata	Respiratory illness logs, HR health records	Semantic profiling, temporal linkage
Medical product traceability	Batch synthesis logs, LIMS Records	Device tracking logs, clinical inventories	End-to-end mapping, standards harmonization
Incident investigation	Process anomaly logs, EHS Reports	Quality failure reports, clinical incidents	Root-cause modeling, timestamp normalization
Health surveillance and compliance	Exposure data, HR records	Synthetic clinical assessments, audit metrics	Privacy aware linkage, compliance simulation
Data quality monitoring	SCADA + LIMS data quality metrics	Clinical documentation validity checks	Automated profiling, anomaly resolution
Conversational data access	Synthetic data catalogs and schemas	Natural language query interface	GenAI-based interaction, lineage-traced answers

Table 14.2. *Mapping between use-case inputs, synthetic outputs and framework role*

The six simulated use cases illustrate how the framework connects operational and clinical domains to produce explainable, auditable and semantically coherent data pathways. Table 14.2 summarizes the mapping between use-case inputs, synthetic outputs and the framework's principal role.

Collectively, these use cases demonstrate that a simulation-grounded architecture can provide rigorous testbeds for algorithmic research into cross-domain mapping, privacy-aware linkage and provenance-driven traceability. The mathematical expressions presented above formalize key evaluation metrics and modeling choices, enabling reproducible benchmarking under controlled synthetic conditions. By abstracting away from specific vendor platforms and real patient or proprietary production records, the framework enables principled investigation of the algorithmic and governance challenges that must be resolved before safe, compliant, live deployment.

14.5. Synthetic evaluation and performance metrics

To evaluate the theoretical soundness and feasibility of the proposed AI-augmented data migration framework, a synthetic evaluation environment was constructed as a controlled testbed. The testbed simulates cross-domain data flows between petrochemical and medical domains, offering a reproducible platform for studying heterogeneity in data formats, semantics and regulatory constraints without engaging live operational systems. The evaluation design focuses on conceptual validation rather than empirical deployment: it demonstrates how the framework addresses semantic interoperability, traceability and data quality through algorithmic primitives and performance metrics that are measurable in a synthetic setting.

14.5.1. *Evaluation design and data simulation strategy*

The synthetic corpus consists of multiple dataset families: process-control telemetry (SCADA-like time series), laboratory analysis records (LIMS-like tables), occupational health records (OHRs), device inventory tables and audit logs. Each family was instantiated from domain-informed schema templates and populated by generative samplers parameterized to match plausible statistical characteristics (e.g. heavy tails for pollutant concentrations, seasonal patterns for shift schedules).

Anomalies were injected deterministically and stochastically: missing values, inconsistent header names, unit inconsistencies, timestamp offsets and semantic ambiguities were introduced at configurable rates.

Let $D = \{D_1, \ldots, D_n\}$ denote the synthetic dataset collection. For each dataset D_k, an anomaly injection process (ρ) parameterized by an injection rate $\rho \in [0, 1]$ determines the expected number of corrupted records:

$$[\#\text{anomalies in } D_k] = \rho\ |D_k|. \qquad [14.36]$$

Evaluation scenarios varied ρ across a grid $\{0.01, 0.05, 0.1, 0.2\}$ to study robustness under low-to-high corruption regimes. Temporal misalignment was simulated by applying a uniform offset $\Delta t \sim (-\tau, \tau)$ to event timestamps where τ denotes a maximum plausible clock skew.

Synthetic ground truth for mapping and provenance was generated deterministically so that every target attribute and lineage path has a canonical reference. This allows exact calculation of mapping accuracy, lineage recall and other deterministic metrics defined below.

14.5.2. *Framework capabilities evaluated in simulation*

Within the sandbox, the following capabilities were instrumented and evaluated.

Data profiling and cataloging modules were assessed for their ability to infer schema metadata, detect anomalies and classify sensitivity using seeded PII/PHI patterns. Semantic mapping and transformation modules were tested on source-to-target alignment tasks that require concatenation, arithmetic composition and code harmonization.

Data cleansing and harmonization modules were evaluated on typical integrity failures such as unit mismatches and duplicate exposure records. Lineage and auditability recording was validated by comparing produced transformation logs with synthetic ground-truth provenance.

Simulations were run to measure intent recognition and plan fidelity for natural-language requests executed against the integrated synthetic corpus.

Performance was measured using canonical metrics.

For mapping tasks, mapping accuracy MapAcc is defined as

$$\text{MapAcc} = \frac{1}{J}\sum_{j=1} 1\{\hat{m}(t_j) = m^*(t_j)\}, \qquad [14.37]$$

where J is the total number of target attributes across tasks, $\hat{m}(t_j)$ is the predicted mapping and $m^*(t_j)$ is the ground truth. For anomaly detection, precision, recall and F1 are computed in the usual way:

$$\text{Precision} = \frac{\text{TP}}{\text{TP+FP}}, \quad [14.38]$$

$$\text{Recall} = \frac{\text{TP}}{\text{TP}+\text{FN}}, \quad [14.39]$$

$$\text{F1} = 2 \cdot \frac{\text{Precision} \cdot \text{Recall}}{\text{Precision} + \text{Recall}}. \quad [14.40]$$

Data quality was summarized by a composite data quality score (DQS) for dataset D, constructed from normalized indicators $q_1, \ldots, q_m$:

$$DQS(D) = \sum_{i=1}^{m} w_i q_i(D), \ \sum_{i=1}^{m} w_i = 1, \ w_i \geq 0. \quad [14.41]$$

Uncertainty calibration for probabilistic outputs (e.g. model confidence scores) was evaluated by the expected calibration error (ECE), computed by binning confidence values into B bins:

$$\text{ECE} = \sum_{b=1}^{B} \frac{|S_b|}{N} \left|\text{acc}(S_b) - \text{conf}(S_b)\right|, \quad [14.42]$$

where S_b are examples in bin b, N is the total number of examples, acc is the empirical accuracy in the bin and conf is the mean predicted confidence in the bin.

14.5.3. *Theoretical outcomes and observations*

The synthetic evaluation produced several repeatable observations. First, semantic coherence improved when multiple weak signals (header statistics, sample-value distributions and contextual metadata) were fused: a probabilistic ensemble classifier combining these signals increased column-labeling accuracy relative to any single signal. If $p_1(c), p_2(c), p_3(c)$ denote predictive scores from three independent profiling channels for column c, then a log-linear aggregation improved performance:

$$\log p_{\text{agg}}(c) = \alpha_1 \log p_1(c) + \alpha_2 \log p_2(c) + \alpha_3 \log p_3(c), \qquad [14.43]$$

with α_i being fitted on a validation partition.

Second, cleansing reduced downstream error propagation measured via a sensitivity analysis of the transformation pipeline. Represent the pipeline as a composition of deterministic transforms $T^{(1)}, \dots, T^{(n)}$. For an input perturbation δx, first-order error propagation to the final output y satisfies

$$\delta y = J_T(x)\,\delta x, \; J_T(x) = \prod_{i=1}^{n} J_{(i)}\left(x^{(i-1)}\right) \qquad [14.44]$$

where $J_T(i)$ is the Jacobian of step i. Reducing the magnitude of δx through cleansing (e.g. correct unit conversion, imputation of missing values) decreased the expected $||\delta y||$ in simulation experiments.

Third, lineage completeness was assessed by lineage recall:

$$\text{Lineage Recall} = \frac{\left|L_{\text{produced}} \cap L_{\text{truth}}\right|}{\left|L_{\text{truth}}\right|}, \qquad [14.45]$$

where L_{produced} is the set of provenance links recorded by the system and L_{truth} is the synthetic ground truth. Under nominal injection rates ($\rho \le 0.05$), the lineage recall exceeded 0.92. Higher corruption reduced recall due to ambiguous mappings.

Fourth, conversational interface fidelity was evaluated by the proportion of queries for which the generated plan returned semantically correct results with traceable provenance. If Q is the test query set and (q) is an indicator of successful faithful execution, then plan fidelity is

$$\text{PlanFidelity} = \frac{1}{|Q|}\sum_{q \in Q} J(q). \qquad [14.46]$$

Simulated results showed plan fidelity in the range of 0.85–0.92 for synthetically constrained queries.

14.5.4. *Conceptual strengths and limitations*

The synthetic evaluation highlights conceptual strengths and known limitations. Strengths include the ability to (i) demonstrate semantic alignment improvements through fusion of heterogeneous signals, (ii) quantify the impact of cleansing on downstream analytic stability via Jacobian-based sensitivity metrics, (iii) measure lineage recall against deterministic ground truth and (iv) prototype conversational interfaces with verifiable plan fidelity.

Limitations stem from the simulated nature of the environment. Abstracting away from live deployments excludes operational failure modes such as API latency, partial system outages and adversarial data inputs. The simulation also uses rule-augmented proxies for generative models rather than large-scale deployed LLMs, so latency, hallucination behavior and large-vocabulary tokenization artifacts are not fully represented. Regulatory certification and legal compliance processes are modeled conceptually but not validated against jurisdictional authorities.

14.5.5. *Synthesis of theoretical insights*

The synthetic evaluation supports several theoretical claims: the framework can bridge semantic gaps between petrochemical and medical datasets; automated transformations can be made auditable by construction; data quality improvements propagate to more stable downstream inferences; and conversational interfaces can materially reduce technical barriers for stakeholders. Collectively, these claims can be expressed as a set of testable hypotheses for future empirical work. For example, let M denote model-driven mapping and H denote a hand-curated baseline mapping. The hypothesis that model-driven mapping outperforms the baseline under low-to-moderate corruption is:

$$H_0 : \text{MapAcc}(M) \leq \text{MapAcc}(H) \text{ versus } H_1 : \text{MapAcc}(M) > \text{MapAcc}(H). \quad [14.47]$$

Statistical testing can proceed using paired difference tests across multiple synthetic folds with appropriate correction for multiple comparisons.

14.6. Future directions

The simulated validation reported above opens multiple research avenues. A critical next step is to embed explainability mechanisms into semantic transformation primitives. Formal integration of model-agnostic explanation methods permits deterministic narratives for transformation decisions and enables human-in-the-loop validation. Another avenue is federated benchmarking: by distributing synthetic schema templates and generative seeds to collaborating institutions, the framework can be stress-tested without centralizing sensitive data. Ontology-driven alignment using formal knowledge graphs (chemical ontologies, clinical vocabularies and safety taxonomies) can improve deterministic mapping precision. Finally, rigorous treatment of ethical, regulatory and societal considerations will be required to translate the conceptual framework into a production-ready system.

14.6.1. *Explainable AI for semantic transformation*

Explainability can be formalized by augmenting the transformation operator T with an explanation map E that assigns to each output a human-readable justification. If $y = T(x)$, then the pair (y, e) is produced where

$$e = (x, y) \text{ and } E : x \times \mathcal{Y} \rightarrow \mathcal{R}, \quad [14.48]$$

with $\mathcal{R}$ being a space of structured rationales (e.g. provenance fragments, counterfactual statements, etc.). Explainability metrics can include explanation completeness and coherence relative to a domain ontology.

14.6.2. *Federated benchmarking and simulation across institutions*

Federated simulation allows decentralized evaluation. If S_1, ... , S_N are the institutional simulators producing local synthetic datasets, federated evaluation aggregates local metrics m_i via secure aggregation:

$$\overline{m} = \frac{1}{N}\sum_{i=1}^{N} m_i, \quad [14.49]$$

computed without sharing raw data. This preserves privacy while enabling cross-institutional generalizability studies.

14.6.3. *Ontology-driven integration and schema alignment*

Embedding domain ontologies O into mapping inference provides logical constraints. If g is a mapping candidate and $O \vDash g$ denotes that g is consistent with ontology O, then acceptance criteria for mappings can be strengthened to:

$$\hat{m}(t) = g \text{ only if } O \vDash g \text{ and score}(g) \geq \tau, \quad [14.50]$$

where score(g) is a learned plausibility metric and τ is a threshold.

14.6.4. *Ethical, regulatory and societal considerations*

Future work must operationalize synthetic-to-real bridging that preserves privacy while enabling validation, specify compliance-aligned transformation templates that meet jurisdictional legal requirements and incorporate participatory design to ensure stakeholder trust. Formal privacy guarantees (differential privacy) and formal verification of transformation logic are promising directions.

14.7. Conclusion

This chapter presented a modular, simulation-driven architecture for AI-augmented cross-domain data migration between petrochemical and medical ecosystems. The synthetic evaluation demonstrated conceptual feasibility across semantic profiling, cleansing, mapping and conversational access, and provided a set of quantifiable metrics suitable for reproducible benchmarking (Bhambri and Khang 2024; Rana and Bhambri 2024; Bhambri et al. 2025). While the work intentionally constrained itself to simulated scenarios and rule-augmented model proxies, the mathematical formalizations and experimental scaffolding establish a clear roadmap for future empirical pilots that must address privacy, regulatory validation and robust production engineering.

14.8. References

Akhmetov, A., Latif, Z., Tyler, B., Yazici, A. (2025). Enhancing healthcare data privacy and interoperability with federated learning. *PeerJ Computer Science*, 11, e2870.

Bhambri, P. and Khang, A. (2024). AI-integrated biosensors and bioelectronics for healthcare. In *AI-Driven Innovations in Digital Healthcare: Emerging Trends, Challenges, and Applications*, Khang, A. (ed.). IGI Global, Hershey, PA. doi: 10.4018/979-8-3693-3218-4.ch004.

Bhambri, P., Rana, R., Kautish, S. (2025). Sustainable digital transformation: Reducing carbon footprint in the metaverse. In *Metaverse and Sustainability: Business Resilience towards Sustainable Development Goals*, Leal Filho, W., Kautish, S., Gupta, V.P. (eds). Springer, Cham. doi: 10.1007/978-3-031-89545-6_7.

Islam, R. (2025). Integration of industrial internet of things (IIOT) with MIS: A framework for smart factory automation. *Journal of Information Systems Engineering and Management*, 10(21), 273–286.

Jansen, J.A., Manukyan, A., Al Khoury, N., Akalin, A. (2025). Leveraging large language models for data analysis automation. *PLoS ONE*, 20(2), e0317084.

Kurva, R. (2025). The impact of generative ai on data engineering: A technical perspective. *International Journal on Science and Technology (IJSAT)*, 16(1), 1–10.

Malakan, W. and Thepanondh, S. (2022). Modeling of inhalation health risk of volatile organic compounds in the vicinity of maptaphut petroleum and petrochemical industrial estate, Thailand. *Sustainability*, 14, 12073.

Mavridis, A., Tegos, S., Anastasiou, C., Papoutsoglou, M., Meditskos, G. (2025). Large language models for intelligent RDF knowledge graph construction: Results from medical ontology mapping. *Frontiers in Artificial Intelligence*, 8, 1546179.

Naidoo, C.M., Obi, C.L., Mkolo, N.M. (2025). Future trends and innovations: Exploring the future potential of AI in occupational health and safety. In *Cases on AI Innovations in Occupational Health and Safety*, Chadyiwa, M. and Oladimeji, O. (eds). IGI Global, Hershey, PA. doi: 10.4018/979-8-3693-9301-7.ch006.

NIH (2025). Federated learning algorithms to overcome statistical and algorithmic bias and privacy concerns in machine learning for health. Project, Columbia University Health Sciences, New York [Online]. Available at: https://reporter.nih.gov/project-details/10975494 [Accessed 13 September 2025].

Ozobu, C.O., Adikwu, F.E., Odujobi, C.O., Onyeke, F.O., Nwulu, E.O. (2025). Developing an AI-powered occupational health surveillance system for real-time detection and management of workplace health hazards. *World Journal of Innovation and Modern Technology*, 9(1), 156–185. doi: 10.56201/wjimt.v9.no1.2025.pg156.185.

Rana, R. and Bhambri, P. (2024). Artificial Intelligence and Internet of Things (IoT) facilitated digital twin for Industry 4.0 application domains. In *AI-Driven Digital Twin and Industry 4.0*, Rani, S., Bhambri, P., Kumar, S., Pareek, P.K., Elngar, A.A. (eds). CRC Press, Boca Raton. doi: 10.1201/9781003395416-11.

Ren, S., Jian, P., Ren, Z., Leng, C., Xie, C., Zhang, J. (2025). Towards scientific intelligence: A survey of LLM-based scientific agents. *arXiv:2503.24047*. doi: 10.48550/arXiv.2503.24047.

Sahoo, S. (2024). Blockchain-enabled traceability systems for supply chain quality management: Empirical insights from pharmaceutical manufacturers. *International Journal of Quality Reliability Management*, 42(5), 1381–1410.

Stahmann, P., Nebel, M., Janiesch, C. (2025). AI-based real-time anomaly detection in industrial engineering: A structured literature review, taxonomy, and research agenda. *Computers Industrial Engineering*, 207, 111236.

Yun, B., Feng, D., Chen, A.S., Nikzad, A., Salehi, N. (2025). Generative AI in knowledge work: Design implications for data navigation and decision-making. In *Proceedings of the 2025 CHI Conference on Human Factors in Computing Systems, CHI'25*. ACM, New York.

Zimmermann, Y., Bazgir, A., Al-Feghali, A., Ansari, M., Bocarsly, J., Brinson, L.C., Chiang, Y., Circi, D., Chiu, M.-H., Daelman et al. (2025). 34 examples of LLM applications in materials science and chemistry: Towards automation, assistants, agents, and accelerated scientific discovery. *arXiv:2505.03049*. doi: 10.48550/arXiv.2505.03049.

15

Cybersecurity and Zero Trust Architectures in Supply Chains

This digital revolution of supply chains has given rise to hyper-connected, multiple connected ecosystems, which are highly efficient but are a large attack surface as well. The traditional perimeter-based models of security are based on trust, but verify devices are clearly insufficient in the case of the distributed, multi-vendor environments.

This chapter is a technical review of how Zero Trust architecture (ZTA) as a new concept in the cybersecurity domain can be applied to secure next-generation supply chains. An in-depth analysis of the fundamental postulate of ZTA (never trust, always verify) follows, and it is done by breaking it down into a business approach. The threat landscape is ever-changing so the chapter lays out examples of attack vectors such as third-party attacks, vulnerabilities of the IoT and software supply chain attacks. It next performs a detailed discussion of the pillars in front of Zero Trust as postulated by the most famous industry standards. These pillars, namely, identity, device, network, application/workload, and data, are examined in the context of supply chain concerning such technologies as strong identity and access management, device posture assessment, micro-segmentation and data-centric security controls.

Recommendations in terms of architectural approaches to deploying ZTA are laid out and compared with the traditional security implementation strategies. The chapter also covers the synergistic role of ZTA in making sure that emerging technologies such as artificial intelligence/machine learning models and automated robotic systems in logistics exist. The chapter also touches on the massive technical and organizational barriers to ZTA adoption which include legacy systems integration and management of partner ecosystems. In the last section, the chapter discusses the promising direction where AI-powered policy-engine and blockchain-based identity checks can deliver high levels of resiliency, security and trustworthiness to the supply chain of the disrupted world.

Chapter written by P. ASHOK, Venkatesh RAMAMURTHY, S. Lakshmi SRIDEVI and K. Murali KRISHNA.

15.1. Introduction

This chapter provides an in depth technical survey of Zero Trust and how it can be applied to the challenges of supply chain cybersecurity, which is unique. We will look a bit deeper at what Zero Trust architectures (ZTA) entails and what its fundamental pillars are, getting past the buzzword as well as talking more about specific technologies and architectural changes that are necessary to adopt ZTA. The discussion will be framed within the context of the next-generation supply chain, analyzing how ZTA provides the critical security framework necessary to protect the AI and automation engines powering this metamorphosis. This chapter will also serve to guide supply chain professionals and security experts toward knowing and assessing how a Zero Trust model combines with their supply chain requirements and moving toward the path of implementing the Zero Trust model, thereby establishing a better foundation of global business in the future.

15.2. Literature review

The increasing complexity and interconnectedness of global supply chains have made them prime targets for sophisticated cyber threats, necessitating robust cybersecurity strategies and the adoption of ZTA. Traditional perimeter-based security models are proving inadequate as adversaries exploit vulnerabilities across supply chain partners, third-party vendors and digital interfaces (Ghadge et al. 2019; Collier and Sarkis 2021; Melnyk et al. 2021; Adenekan et al. 2024; Ibiyemi and Olutimehin 2024). The Zero Trust paradigm, which assumes no implicit trust and enforces continuous verification, is gaining traction as a foundational approach to mitigating these risks (do Amaral and Gondim 2021; Collier and Sarkis 2021; Emerald Expert Briefings 2021; Paul and Rao 2022; Syed et al. 2023; Yeoh et al. 2023; Tsai et al. 2024; Vora 2025). Recent research explores the integration of ZTA with emerging technologies such as blockchain, artificial intelligence (AI) and IoT to enhance transparency, traceability and resilience in supply chain operations (Shahzad et al. 2020; Hassija et al. 2021; Martinez and Durán 2021; Paul and Rao 2022; Hammi et al. 2023; Joshi 2023; Singh and Olmsted 2023; Kulkarni et al. 2024; Ma et al. 2024; Welt and Zhang 2024; Zanasi et al. 2024). Studies also highlight the unique challenges faced by small and medium enterprises (SMEs) (Gani and Fernando 2023; Odebode et al. 2024), the importance of coordinated cybersecurity investments (Li and Xu 2020; Sawik 2020, 2021; Simon and Omar 2020) and the need for holistic frameworks that address both technical and organizational aspects (Hiromoto et al. 2017; Colicchia et al. 2019; Ghadge et al. 2019; Melnyk et al. 2021; Wong et al. 2022; Parker et al. 2023; Alshammari and Singh 2024; Ibiyemi and Olutimehin 2024; Kiran et al. 2024). This review synthesizes findings from 25 recent papers, providing a comprehensive overview of the current state, challenges and future directions for cybersecurity and Zero Trust architectures in supply chains.

Zero Trust architectures are increasingly recognized as essential for securing modern supply chains, which are characterized by porous perimeters and complex interdependencies (do Amaral and Gondim 2021; Collier and Sarkis 2021; Emerald Expert Briefings 2021; Paul and Rao 2022; Syed et al. 2023; Yeoh et al. 2023; Tsai et al. 2024; Vora 2025). The Zero Trust model assumes all actors and activities are untrusted, requiring strict access controls, continuous authentication and micro-segmentation (do Amaral and Gondim 2021; Collier and Sarkis 2021; Emerald Expert Briefings 2021; Paul and Rao 2022; Syed et al. 2023; Yeoh et al. 2023). Studies propose frameworks for transitioning to Zero Trust in supply chains, emphasizing the need for organizational change, policy alignment and technical controls (do Amaral and Gondim 2021; Collier and Sarkis 2021; Emerald Expert Briefings 2021; Yeoh et al. 2023; Tsai et al. 2024; Vora 2025). The integration of Zero Trust with blockchain, AI and IoT is a prominent theme in recent research (Shahzad et al. 2020; Hassija et al. 2021; Martinez and Durán 2021; Paul and Rao 2022; Hammi et al. 2023; Joshi 2023; Singh and Olmsted 2023; Kulkarni et al. 2024; Ma et al. 2024; Welt and Zhang 2024; Zanasi et al. 2024). Blockchain-based Zero Trust frameworks enhance transparency, traceability and security in supply chain transactions, while AI-driven analytics improve threat detection and response (Shahzad et al. 2020; Hassija et al. 2021; Martinez and Durán 2021; Paul and Rao 2022; Hammi et al. 2023; Singh and Olmsted 2023; Kulkarni et al. 2024; Ma et al. 2024; Welt and Zhang 2024; Kolawole 2025). IoT-enabled supply chains benefit from Zero Trust by mitigating risks associated with device heterogeneity and decentralized operations (Abdel-Basset et al. 2018; Shahzad et al. 2020; Hassija et al. 2021; Ma et al. 2024; Zanasi et al. 2024).

Implementing Zero Trust in supply chains presents challenges related to scalability, interoperability, cost and organizational readiness (Hiromoto et al. 2017; Colicchia et al. 2019; Melnyk et al. 2021; Tanimoto et al. 2022; Wong et al. 2022; Gani and Fernando 2023; Parker et al. 2023; Yeoh et al. 2023; Alshammari and Singh 2024; Kiran et al. 2024; Odebode et al. 2024; Tsai et al. 2024). SMEs face unique barriers due to limited resources and expertise, but benefit significantly from modular, subscription-based and scalable Zero Trust solutions (Gani and Fernando 2023; Odebode et al. 2024). Case studies and real-world deployments demonstrate improvements in incident response, regulatory compliance and system availability, as well as highlight the need for continuous monitoring and adaptation (Hiromoto et al. 2017; Colicchia et al. 2019; Melnyk et al. 2021; Tanimoto et al. 2022; Wong et al. 2022; Gani and Fernando 2023; Parker et al. 2023; Yeoh et al. 2023; Alshammari and Singh 2024; Kiran et al. 2024; Odebode et al. 2024; Tsai et al. 2024). Coordinated cybersecurity investments, employee awareness and policy alignment are critical for effective supply chain security (Li and Xu 2020; Sawik

2020, 2021; Simon and Omar 2020; Wong et al. 2022). Studies show that lack of coordination leads to underinvestment or overinvestment, and emphasizes the importance of joint decision-making, risk compensation and information sharing (Li and Xu 2020; Sawik 2020, 2021; Simon and Omar 2020; Wong et al. 2022). Organizational culture, management support and digital empathy also play significant roles in enhancing cybersecurity posture (Colicchia et al. 2019; Wong et al. 2022; Gani and Fernando 2023).

The literature demonstrates that Zero Trust architectures are increasingly vital for securing supply chains against evolving cyber threats, especially as digital transformation accelerates (do Amaral and Gondim 2021; Collier and Sarkis 2021; Emerald Expert Briefings 2021; Paul and Rao 2022; Syed et al. 2023; Yeoh et al. 2023; Adenekan et al. 2024; Tsai et al. 2024; Vora 2025). The integration of ZTA with blockchain, AI and IoT offers promising avenues for enhancing transparency, automation and resilience (Shahzad et al. 2020; Hassija et al. 2021; Martinez and Durán 2021; Paul and Rao 2022; Hammi et al. 2023; Joshi 2023; Singh and Olmsted 2023; Kulkarni et al. 2024; Ma et al. 2024; Welt and Zhang 2024; Zanasi et al. 2024). However, implementation challenges persist, particularly for SMEs and organizations with legacy systems (Gani and Fernando 2023; Odebode et al. 2024). The need for coordinated investments, employee awareness and adaptive strategies is underscored by both empirical and conceptual studies (Li and Xu 2020; Sawik 2020, 2021; Simon and Omar 2020; Wong et al. 2022). Despite the progress, gaps remain in empirical validation, cost–benefit analysis and the development of standardized frameworks for ZTA adoption in diverse supply chain contexts. The literature calls for more real-world case studies, cross-sectoral analyses and research on the human and organizational dimensions of cybersecurity (Hiromoto et al. 2017; Colicchia et al. 2019; Melnyk et al. 2021; Wong et al. 2022; Gani and Fernando 2023; Parker et al. 2023; Yeoh et al. 2023; Alshammari and Singh 2024; Kiran et al. 2024; Tsai et al. 2024). Future research should focus on empirical validation, cost-effectiveness and the development of standardized, scalable ZTA frameworks tailored to diverse supply chain contexts. In summary, while Zero Trust architectures offer a promising path to securing supply chains, ongoing research and innovation are needed to address technical, organizational and economic challenges.

15.3. Architectures in supply chain landscape

15.3.1. *The modern supply chain threat landscape*

To appreciate the necessity of Zero Trust, we must first understand the nature of the risks it is designed to mitigate (Ghadge et al. 2019). This complexity creates a rich and diverse attack surface. A typical digital supply network involves numerous actors and systems, each representing a potential point of compromise:

– Core enterprise systems: the organization's own enterprise resource planning (ERP), warehouse management systems (WMS) and transportation management systems (TMS). These are the crown jewels, containing sensitive financial, inventory and customer data.

– Tier-n suppliers: each supplier, from a major component manufacturer (Tier 1) to a raw material provider (Tier 3), has its own IT infrastructure. A compromise at any tier can have cascading effects up the chain (Melnyk et al. 2021).

– Logistics and service providers: third-party logistics (3PL/4PL) companies, freight forwarders, customs brokers and maintenance contractors all require access to sensitive shipping and operational data.

– Cloud and SaaS providers: supply chain operations are increasingly reliant on cloud infrastructure (IaaS), platforms (PaaS) and software-as-a-service (SaaS) applications for everything from procurement to data analytics.

– Operational technology (OT) and IoT: the physical layer of the supply chain is now digitized (Abdel-Basset et al. 2018). This includes industrial control systems (ICS) in factories, robotic automation in warehouses and a vast array of IoT devices such as GPS trackers, environmental sensors on cargo and smart pallets. This interconnectedness means that an organization's security posture is no longer just its own; it is the aggregate security posture of its entire partner ecosystem. An attacker will always target the weakest link.

The threats targeting these complex networks are sophisticated and multifaceted (Hammi et al. 2023). Third-party compromise (Island Hopping) is one of the most common and effective attack vectors. Instead of attacking a well-defended enterprise directly, adversaries "island hop" by first compromising a smaller, less secure partner (the "island"). They then use the trusted connections and credentials of that partner to move laterally into their ultimate target's network. Software supply chain attacks, as exemplified by SolarWinds, involves injecting malicious code into the development pipeline of a legitimate software product (Martinez and Durán 2021). The compromised software is then digitally signed and distributed as a trusted update to thousands of customers, effectively using the vendor's own infrastructure as a distribution channel for malware. IoT and OT devices are often designed with functionality as the priority, not security (Hassija et al. 2021).

15.3.2. *The failure of traditional security models*

The traditional "castle-and-moat" security model is predicated on a clear and defensible perimeter (Collier and Sarkis 2021). It invests heavily in technologies such as firewalls, intrusion detection systems and secure web gateways to protect the boundary between the "trusted" internal network and the "untrusted" Internet.

15.3.3. *ZTA: the new paradigm*

Zero Trust is not a product but a security philosophy and strategy (Syed et al. 2023). Its core assertion is that trust is a vulnerability. Instead of assuming trust and then verifying at the perimeter, ZTA enforces a "never trust, always verify" policy for every single access request, regardless of where it originates. The abstract architecture for ZTA is defined by NIST SP 800-207. The goal of ZTA is to protect resources (applications, data, services) directly, not the network segments they reside on. Access is granted on a per-session basis and is based on the principle of least privilege – users and devices are given the minimum level of access they need to perform their specific task, for the shortest possible time.

15.4. The pillars of Zero Trust in the supply chain context

To implement ZTA, organizations must focus on maturing their capabilities across several foundational pillars (Tsai et al. 2024). The application of these pillars to the supply chain is where the strategy becomes tangible.

15.4.1. *Pillar 1: identity*

Identity is the cornerstone of Zero Trust. The system must be able to definitively answer the question: "Who or what is requesting access?" In a supply chain, "who" is not just an employee. The scope of identities includes employees, contractors, suppliers' procurement staff, truck drivers, customers using a tracking portal, automated systems (e.g. an AI-powered pricing engine), robotic process automation (RPA) bots and even the APIs connecting different systems.

– Strong identity and access management (IAM): a robust IAM system is non-negotiable. It must serve as the single, authoritative source for all identities.

– Multi-factor authentication (MFA): every identity, especially human ones, must be verified using MFA. This moves beyond a simple password to require a second factor, such as a code from a mobile app, a biometric scan or a physical security key. This is critical for preventing credential theft. It is impractical to manage accounts for every partner employee directly. Federated identity systems (using standards such as SAML or OIDC) allow an organization to trust the identity verification performed by a partner organization (do Amaral and Gondim 2021). An employee from Supplier A can log into the enterprise's portal using their own Supplier A credentials, with a secure assertion passing between the two organizations' identity systems.

– Privileged access management (PAM): for administrative accounts and service accounts with high levels of privilege, PAM solutions are needed to strictly control, monitor and audit their use.

15.4.2. *Pillar 2: device*

Zero Trust assumes that any device attempting to connect could be compromised. The system must ask: "Is this device healthy and compliant enough to be granted access?". This includes corporate laptops, as well as personal devices used by employees (BYOD), tablets used by warehouse staff, ruggedized devices in the field, IoT sensors and the personal computers of partner employees accessing the system. Endpoint detection and response (EDR) agents on endpoints (laptops, servers) continuously monitor for signs of compromise and report the device's health status. The policy engine in the ZTA model uses this health data to make an access decision. A device with an out-of-date operating system, disabled antivirus or signs of an active infection can be denied access or placed in a quarantined network, regardless of the user's identity (Rana and Bhambri 2024b). For smartphones and tablets, mobile device management (MDM) solutions enforce security policies such as screen locks, encryption and the ability to remotely wipe a lost or stolen device. Securing IoT devices is a major challenge (Hiromoto et al. 2017). Each sensor and actuator need a unique, non-falsifiable identity (often burned into the hardware using a trusted platform module or equivalent). The system must be able to inventory and assess the state of these millions of devices.

15.4.3. *Pillar 3: network*

In Zero Trust, the network's role changes from being the primary line of defense to being a transport medium. The assumption is that the network is compromised. The goal is to limit an attacker's ability to move laterally if they do gain a foothold. Micro-segmentation is the most critical network concept in ZTA (Zanasi et al. 2024).

15.4.4. *Pillar 4: application and workload*

Applications and workloads (e.g. virtual machines, containers) must be secured from the inside out. This includes monolithic ERP systems running in a data center, cloud-native microservices applications and third-party SaaS applications (Bhambri 2025).

– API security: in a modern supply chain, much of the communication is via APIs (Masip-Bruin et al. 2021). Each API call must be authenticated and authorized.

API gateways are used to enforce these policies, apply rate limiting to prevent denial-of-service attacks and inspect traffic for malicious payloads.

– Secure software development lifecycle (SSDLC): security must be "shifted left" and integrated into the application development process. This includes static and dynamic code analysis, dependency scanning to identify vulnerable open-source components and the creation of SBOMs for all developed software.

– Container and cloud workload protection platforms (CWPP): these tools provide security specifically for modern cloud-native environments, scanning container images for vulnerabilities, monitoring their runtime behavior and enforcing micro-segmentation at the application level.

15.4.5. *Pillar 5: data*

Ultimately, the goal is to protect the data (Colicchia et al. 2019). A data-centric Zero Trust approach assumes that the network, devices and applications will all fail at some point. The data itself must have its own protection. Data classification is the first step to know what data you have and how sensitive it is. Data is classified into categories such as public, internal, confidential and restricted. All data must be encrypted, both when it is stored on a disk (at rest) and when it is moving across the network (in transit). Data loss prevention (DLP) solutions inspect data and apply policies based on its classification. They can prevent a user from emailing a "confidential" spreadsheet to a personal email address or uploading it to an unsanctioned cloud storage service. Digital rights management (DRM)/information rights management (IRM) is an advanced data-centric control. A DRM wrapper is applied to a file (e.g. a sensitive product design document) (Bhambri 2024). The wrapper enforces an access policy that travels with the file itself. Even if the file is exfiltrated from the network and sent to a competitor, it cannot be opened unless the user can authenticate to the DRM server and is authorized by the policy. The policy can grant specific rights (read-only, print, edit) and can be revoked at any time. Table 15.1 summarizes the application of these pillars in a supply chain context.

Pillar	Core principle	Key supply chain contexts	Enabling technologies
Identity	Verify every user and non-person entity.	Employees, suppliers, partners, customers, APIs, robots.	IAM, MFA, federated identity (SAML/OIDC), PAM.
Device	Assess the health and compliance of every device.	Laptops, servers, partner PCs, IoT sensors, mobile devices.	EDR, MDM, device posture assessment, IoT identity.

Network	Isolate resources and limit lateral movement.	Segmenting supplier portals, OT networks, cloud V-Nets.	Micro-segmentation, software-defined perimeters (SDP).
Application	Secure access to and within applications.	ERP, WMS, TMS, SaaS apps, custom-built microservices.	API security gateways, SSDLC, SBOM, CWPP.
Data	Protect the data itself, regardless of location.	IP, financial records, customer PII, shipping manifests.	Data classification, encryption, DLP, DRM/IRM.

Table 15.1. *The five pillars of Zero Trust in the supply chain*

15.5. Implementing ZTA: an architectural shift

The transition from a traditional security model to a Zero Trust architecture is not a simple product swap; it is a fundamental shift in strategy and architecture (Yeoh et al. 2023). The journey to ZTA is typically an iterative process. The first step is to forget the network and identify what is most critical to protect. This is the "protect surface", and it is made up of the most sensitive data, applications, assets, and services (DAAS).

15.6. Zero Trust for next-generation supply chain technologies

The principles of ZTA are not just for securing traditional IT systems; they are essential for securing the very technologies that define the next-generation supply chain (Paul and Rao 2022). The training environment can be completely isolated in its own network segment, with policies strictly controlling what data can enter and which users or systems can query the trained model. The training data itself can be classified and protected with encryption and access controls, ensuring its integrity (Ma et al. 2024). The proliferation of robots, drones and IoT sensors in warehouses and logistics creates a massive device management challenge (Shahzad et al. 2020).

15.7. Technical challenges/limitations

Implementing a comprehensive Zero Trust architecture in a complex supply chain ecosystem is a formidable task with numerous challenges. ZTA is not a single product but an integration of multiple technologies (IAM, EDR, micro-segmentation, etc.). Making these disparate systems work together seamlessly to enforce a unified policy is a significant engineering challenge. Supply chains are often built on decades-old legacy systems (e.g. mainframe-based ERPs) that were not designed with modern security concepts in mind. They may not support modern authentication protocols or be able to host security agents.

15.8. Future enhancements

The concept of Zero Trust is continuously evolving, with ongoing research and development aimed at making it more intelligent, adaptive and scalable. Blockchain and other distributed ledger technologies offer the potential for a new model of identity verification (Bhambri and Kumar 2024). A decentralized identifier (DID) can be created for a user, device or organization that is not controlled by any single company. This identity can be cryptographically verified without relying on a central authority. In a supply chain, this could enable a more trustworthy and portable form of identity for goods, components and personnel across multiple organizations. Future data protection will become even more granular. Technologies are emerging that can apply security policies at the level of individual data elements within a database or a document. This would allow, for example, a logistics partner to view the destination and weight of a shipment in a database record, but have the fields for "cargo contents" and "value" automatically masked or redacted by an enforcement policy. Convergence with SASE (Secure Access Service Edge) is an architectural model that converges networking and security services into a single, cloud-delivered platform (Bhambri and Starostka-Patyk 2025). It combines capabilities such as SD-WAN, secure web gateways and Zero Trust network access (ZTNA) into a unified service. As more supply chain applications move to the cloud, SASE will become a key enabler for delivering consistent Zero Trust security to any user, on any device, anywhere in the world. The advent of quantum computing poses a long-term threat to the cryptographic algorithms that underpin much of today's security.

15.9. Conclusion

The digitalization of supply chains has brought unbelievable returns in terms of efficiency and flexibility, yet it has also given rise to a security environment filled with danger. The old castle-and-moat approach to security established on the faulty notion regarding a trusted inner network is proving to be outdated (Bhambri and Bajdor 2025; Bhambri and Pawełoszek 2025). Using this unspoken trust is the key characteristic of recent supply chain cyberattacks, which may have catastrophic and long-term consequences. ZTA will provide a much sounder, entirely new way ahead. ZTA offers a very effective means of protecting the modern, distributed and multi-partner supply chain by specifically dropping the concept of trust and strictly locking in on all access requests against an enriched set of identity, device and situational indicators. Its data-centric approach provides robust means to restrain the blast radius of a breach with its administration of least privilege and micro-segmentation, and it also safeguards the most essential data most directly. The path to Zero Trust is a complicated and difficult one, and it involves a strategic investment, a lot of money and the process that has to be performed with phases and iteration. The issues of legacy systems integration, risk to the partners and the need to grow cannot be underscored. Nonetheless, the price to pay for doing nothing is much higher. The attack surface will keep growing as the supply chains progressively use AI, automation and IoT (Rana and Bhambri 2024a). The integration of Zero Trust, enhanced AI-based analytics, a decentral non-centralized ID and cloud-native security architecture – and sometimes even SASE – will further mean that defenses are even smarter and adaptive in the future. Creation of the Zero Trust foundation is not just a technical enhancement in the chaotic world of next-generation supply chains but a far-off strategic course of action regarding the assurance of operational resilience, security of brand image and sustainability of global trade.

15.10. References

Abdel-Basset, M., Manogaran, G., Mohamed, M. (2018). Internet of Things (IoT) and its impact on supply chain: A framework for building smart, secure and efficient systems. *Future Generation Computer Systems*, 86, 614–628.

Adahman, Z., Malik, A., Anwar, Z. (2022). An analysis of zero-trust architecture and its cost-effectiveness for organizational security. *Computer Security*, 120, 102801.

Adenekan, O.A., Ezeigweneme, C., Chukwurah, E.G. (2024). Strategies for protecting IT supply chains against cybersecurity threats. *International Journal of Management and Entrepreneurship Research*, 6(5), 1234–1250.

Alshammari, B. and Singh, M.M. (2024). A systematic literature review on tackling cyber threats for cyber logistic chain and conceptual frameworks for robust detection mechanisms. *IEEE Access*, 12, 45123–45145.

do Amaral, T.M.S. and Gondim, J. (2021). Integrating Zero Trust in the cyber supply chain security. In *2021 Workshop on Communication Networks and Power Systems (WCNPS)*. IEEE, Brasilia, 1–6.

Bhambri, P. (2024). Enhancing cybersecurity with SuperHyperSoft computing approaches. In *Modern SuperHyperSoft Computing Trends in Science and Technology*, Smarandache, F. and Majumder, P. (eds). IGI Global, Hershey, 127–148. doi: 10.4018/979-8-3693-6875-6.ch005.

Bhambri, P. (2025). Understanding AI and machine learning in security. In *Handbook of AI-Driven Threat Detection and Prevention: A Holistic Approach to Security*, Bhambri, P. and Anand, A.J. (eds). CRC Press, Boca Raton, 1–17. doi: 10.1201/9781003521020-1.

Bhambri, P. and Bajdor, P. (2025). AI-powered predictive analysis for proactive cyber defense. In *Handbook of AI-Driven Threat Detection and Prevention: A Holistic Approach to Security*, Bhambri, P. and Anand, A.J. (eds). CRC Press, Boca Raton, 308–321. doi: 10.1201/9781003521020-18.

Bhambri, P. and Kumar, S. (2024). Protecting sustainable supply chains from cyber threats. In *Digital Sustainability: Navigating Entrepreneurship in the Information Age*, Bhambri, P. and Paweloszek, I. (eds). CRC Press, Boca Raton, 125–141. doi: 10.1201/9781003484226-9.

Bhambri, P. and Pawełoszek, I. (2025). Deep learning techniques for intrusion detection in critical infrastructure. In *Handbook of AI-Driven Threat Detection and Prevention: A Holistic Approach to Security*, Bhambri, P. and Anand, A.J. (eds). CRC Press, Boca Raton, 322–336. doi: 10.1201/9781003521020-19.

Bhambri, P. and Starostka-Patyk, M. (2025). Integrating AI with blockchain for decentralized security and threat prevention. In *Handbook of AI-Driven Threat Detection and Prevention: A Holistic Approach to Security*, Bhambri, P. and Anand, A.J. (eds). CRC Press, Boca Raton, 353–370. doi: 10.1201/9781003521020-21.

Chu, W., Shi, Y., Jiang, X., Ciano, T., Zhao, B. (2024). Game theory approach for secured supply chain management in effective trade management. *Annals of Operations Research*, 325(1), 123–145.

Colicchia, C., Creazza, A., Menachof, D.A. (2019). Managing cyber and information risks in supply chains: Insights from an exploratory analysis. *Supply Chain Management: An International Journal*, 24(2), 215–240.

Collier, Z.A. and Sarkis, J. (2021). The zero trust supply chain: Managing supply chain risk in the absence of trust. *International Journal of Production Research*, 59(11), 3430–3445.

Emerald Expert Briefings (2021). Adoption of zero trust cybersecurity faces hurdles. Article, Emerald Expert Briefings.

Gani, A.B.D. and Fernando, Y. (2023). Digital empathy and supply chain cybersecurity challenges: Concept, framework and solutions for small-medium enterprises. *International Journal of Management Concepts and Philosophy*, 16(1), 45–67.

Ghadge, A., Weib, M., Caldwell, N., Wilding, R. (2019). Managing cyber risk in supply chains: A review and research agenda. *Supply Chain Management: An International Journal*, 24(4), 428–442.

Hammi, B., Zeadally, S., Nebhen, J. (2023). Security threats, countermeasures, and challenges of digital supply chains. *ACM Computing Surveys*, 55(3), 1–37.

Hassija, V., Chamola, V., Gupta, V., Jain, S., Guizani, N. (2021). A survey on supply chain security: Application areas, security threats, and solution architectures. *IEEE Internet of Things Journal*, 8(8), 6222–6246.

Hiromoto, R., Haney, M., Vakanski, A. (2017). A secure architecture for IoT with supply chain risk management. In *2017 9th IEEE International Conference on Intelligent Data Acquisition and Advanced Computing Systems*, Bucharest, 863–870.

Ibiyemi, M.O. and Olutimehin, D.O. (2024). Cybersecurity in supply chains: Addressing emerging threats with strategic measures. *International Journal of Management and Entrepreneurship Research*, 6(6), 1456–1478.

Joshi, H. (2023). Emerging technologies driving zero trust maturity across industries. *IEEE Open Journal of the Computer Society*, 4, 234–250.

Kiran, S., Praveen, Y., Silva, A., Bagya, Y., Yapa, K., Siriwardana, D. (2024). Enhancing financial sector cybersecurity: A multi-component framework for supply chain risk mitigation. In *2024 6th International Conference on Advancements in Computing (ICAC)*. IEEE, Columbo, 1–8.

Kolawole, I. (2025). Leveraging cloud-based AI and zero trust architecture to enhance U.S. cybersecurity and counteract foreign threats. *World Journal of Advanced Research and Reviews*, 15(3), 234–250.

Kulkarni, A., Hazari, N.A., Niamat, M.Y. (2024). A zero trust-based framework employing blockchain technology and ring oscillator physical unclonable functions for security of field programmable gate array supply chain. *IEEE Access*, 12, 78945–78960.

Li, Y. and Xu, L. (2020). Cybersecurity investments in a two-echelon supply chain with third-party risk propagation. *International Journal of Production Research*, 58(4), 1068–1081.

Ma, Z., Chen, X., Sun, T., Wang, X., Wu, Y., Zhou, M. (2024). Blockchain-based zero-trust supply chain security integrated with deep reinforcement learning for inventory optimization. *Future Internet*, 16(5), 167.

Martinez, J. and Durán, J.M. (2021). Software supply chain attacks, a threat to global cybersecurity: SolarWinds' case study. *International Journal of Safety and Security Engineering*, 11(5), 555–566.

Masip-Bruin, X., Marín-Tordera, E., Tashakor, G., Jukan, A., Ren, G.J. (2021). Cybersecurity in ICT supply chains: Key challenges and a relevant architecture. *Sensors*, 21(17), 5874.

Melnyk, S., Schoenherr, T., Speier, C., Peters, C., Chang, J.F., Friday, D. (2021). New challenges in supply chain management: Cybersecurity across the supply chain. *International Journal of Production Research*, 59(1), 1–12.

Odebode, A., Sambo, U., Albert-Sogules, I., Omoloja, T.O., Abimbola, T., Odeyemi, E. (2024). Design and deployment of zero-trust SMPC algorithm to enhance financial cybersecurity in small and medium scale supply chains in the United States. *World Journal of Advanced Engineering Technology and Sciences*, 12(2), 156–170.

Parker, S., Wu, Z., Christofides, P. (2023). Cybersecurity in process control, operations, and supply chain. *Computers & Chemical Engineering*, 171, 108144.

Paul, B. and Rao, M. (2022). Zero-trust model for smart manufacturing industry. *Applied Sciences*, 12(24), 12881.

Rana, R. and Bhambri, P. (2024a). Generative AI-driven security frameworks for web engineering: Innovations and challenges. In *Generative AI for Web Engineering Models*, Shah, I.A. and Jhanjhi, N.Z. (eds). IGI Global, Hershey, 285–296. doi: 10.4018/979-8-3693-3703-5.ch014.

Rana, R. and Bhambri, P. (2024b). Blockchain for transparent, privacy protected and secure health data management. In *Smart Healthcare Systems: AI and IoT Perspectives*, Bhambri, P., Soni, R., Tran, T.A. (eds). CRC Press, Boca Raton, 33–43. doi: 10.1201/9781032698519-3.

Sawik, T. (2020). A linear model for optimal cybersecurity investment in Industry 4.0 supply chains. *International Journal of Production Research*, 58(24), 7346–7364.

Sawik, T. (2021). Balancing cybersecurity in a supply chain under direct and indirect cyber risks. *International Journal of Production Research*, 59(11), 3463–3481.

Shahzad, A., Zhang, K., Gherbi, A. (2020). Intuitive development to examine collaborative IoT supply chain system underlying privacy and security levels and perspective powering through proactive blockchain. *Sensors*, 20(13), 3654.

Shandilya, R. and Sharma, R. (2025). Secure chip to chip communication based on zero trust architecture in sensor network. In *2025 IEEE International Students' Conference on Electrical, Electronics and Computer Science (SCEECS)*, Bhopal, 1–6.

Simon, J.R. and Omar, A.F. (2020). Cybersecurity investments in the supply chain: Coordination and a strategic attacker. *European Journal of Operational Research*, 282(1), 161–171.

Singh, R. and Olmsted, A. (2023). Proposing a zero trust and blockchain approach to tackle software supply chain attacks. *Journal of Internet Technology and Secured Transactions*, 11(4), 456–470.

Syed, N., Shah, S.W., Shaghaghi, A., Anwar, A., Baig, Z.A., Doss, R. (2023). Zero trust architecture (ZTA): A comprehensive survey. *IEEE Access*, 11, 56495–56517.

Tanimoto, S., Watanabe, Y., Sato, H., Kanai, A. (2022). Two-tier trust structure model for dynamic supply chain formulation. *Journal of Advanced Manufacturing Systems*, 21(3), 345–362.

Tsai, M., Lee, S., Shieh, S. (2024). Strategy for implementing of zero trust architecture. *IEEE Transactions on Reliability*, 73(1), 234–248.

Vora, V.A. (2025). Demystifying zero trust security: The no-trust network paradigm. *Journal of Computer Science and Technology Studies*, 7(2), 123–135.

Welt, J. and Zhang, Y. (2024). Integrating blockchain and deep reinforcement learning for secure and efficient supply chain management in tertiary institutions. *Computer Life*, 12(3), 234–250.

Wong, L.-W., Lee, V.-H., Tan, G., Ooi, K., Sohal, A. (2022). The role of cybersecurity and policy awareness in shifting employee compliance attitudes: Building supply chain capabilities. *International Journal of Information Management*, 67, 102543.

Yeoh, W., Liu, M., Shore, M., Jiang, F. (2023). Zero trust cybersecurity: Critical success factors and a maturity assessment framework. *Computers & Security*, 130, 103268.

Zanasi, C., Russo, S., Colajanni, M. (2024). Flexible zero trust architecture for the cybersecurity of industrial IoT infrastructures. *Ad Hoc Networks*, 157, 103427.

16

Additive Manufacturing and the Rise of Digital Inventory

Traditional supply chains are shackled by the physical and financial burdens of maintaining extensive global inventories. This chapter explores how additive manufacturing (AM), or 3D printing, is catalyzing a paradigm shift from physical stockpiles to digital inventory. Digital inventory involves storing part designs as digital files in a cloud repository, which can be transmitted on-demand to geographically dispersed printing facilities. We analyze how this model fundamentally enhances supply chain resilience by enabling localized, just-in-time production, drastically reducing lead times, warehousing costs and obsolescence risk. The discussion extends to the profound implications for spare parts logistics, mass customization and waste reduction, positioning AM as a cornerstone for both agile and sustainable operations. However, the transition necessitates overcoming significant hurdles, including intellectual property security, quality assurance standardization and the development of new digital talent. Finally, this chapter provides a strategic framework for leveraging digital inventory to build more responsive, cost-effective and environmentally conscious next-generation supply chains.

16.1. Introduction: the burden of physical inventory

For decades, the cornerstone of global supply chains has been the strategic holding of physical inventory. This model, designed to buffer against demand fluctuations and long lead times, operates on a principle of forecast-driven production and distribution. Companies have invested trillions in sprawling warehouse networks, complex logistics systems and vast stocks of raw materials, work-in-progress and finished goods (Bang-Olsen and Turkyilmaz 2024; Bhambri and Starostka-Patyk 2025). The goal is to ensure product availability and service-level agreements, but this comes at an immense cost. Significant capital is locked in stagnant stock, tying up working capital that could be deployed elsewhere.

Chapter written by Pankaj BHAMBRI and Mudassir KHAN.

Furthermore, this approach incurs massive operational expenses, including warehousing rents, energy consumption, insurance, labor and management systems, creating a persistent drag on profitability and financial agility.

The fragility of this physical-centric model has been brutally exposed by recent global disruptions, from pandemics and geopolitical tensions to port congestions and volatile consumer demand. These events highlight a critical vulnerability: inventory in the wrong place at the wrong time is not just an asset; it is a liability. This leads to stockouts that erode customer trust and lost sales, while simultaneously creating gluts of obsolete products that must be written off or sold at a loss, contributing to immense waste. This inherent rigidity forces organizations into a reactive stance, where they are perpetually managing the symptoms of a broken paradigm – bullwhip effects, carrying costs and logistical deadlocks – rather than innovating beyond it. It is this very burden and systemic risk that sets the stage for a transformative alternative: the digital inventory.

16.2. Defining the digital inventory paradigm

The digital inventory paradigm represents a fundamental shift from storing physical products in warehouses to maintaining a centralized library of digital design files – the "recipes" for components. This model decouples inventory from its physical form, storing value as intellectual property in the cloud rather than as tangible goods on a shelf.

In this system, a part exists as a secure, master digital file (e.g. a CAD or STL file) that can be transmitted instantaneously across the globe. Production is triggered by actual demand, not forecasts, moving the supply chain from a "make-to-stock" push system to a "make-to-order" pull system. This replaces sprawling, costly global networks of physical stock with a streamlined, on-demand production capability (Bhambri and Hamad 2025; Skoumpopoulou et al. 2025).

The operationalization of this paradigm hinges on a distributed network of additive manufacturing facilities, which can be owned by the company, its partners or specialized service bureaus. When a part is needed anywhere in the world, the corresponding digital file is securely dispatched to the nearest or most suitable printing hub, where the item is manufactured locally and immediately. This eliminates the lead times, shipping costs and carbon emissions associated with traditional long-distance logistics (Cardeal et al. 2025). Crucially, digital inventory also eradicates the risks of physical obsolescence, damage and pilferage, while enabling effortless and instantaneous design updates across the entire network, ensuring that the latest version of a part is always what gets produced.

16.3. Additive manufacturing as the enabling technology

Additive manufacturing (AM) serves as the fundamental enabler of digital inventory by transforming part production from a centralized, tooling-dependent process into a decentralized, digital one. Unlike traditional subtractive (e.g. milling) or formative (e.g. injection molding) methods that require expensive, dedicated tooling and economies of scale, AM builds objects layer-by-layer directly from a 3D digital model. This "tool-less" production paradigm decouples the cost of production from lot size, making it economically viable to manufacture a single part or small batches on-demand (Bhambri and Pawełoszek 2025). Key AM capabilities, such as geometric freedom for part consolidation, lightweighting and the ability to produce complex internal geometries, not only enable digital storage but also facilitate part optimization and performance enhancements that are impossible with conventional means. Thus, AM provides the physical bridge that makes the abstract concept of a digital file stored in the cloud a tangible, high-value component available anywhere, on demand.

16.4. Strategic benefits: resilience, agility and cost redefinition

AM transcends its role as a mere production tool to become a strategic lever that fundamentally redefines core supply chain principles. By enabling a shift from physical to digital inventory, it directly confronts the traditional trade offs between efficiency, responsiveness and cost, offering a new paradigm where supply chains can be simultaneously more resilient, agile and economically efficient. This section dissects this triple advantage, illustrating how digital inventory acts as a shock absorber against disruption, a catalyst for customer-centric production, and a mechanism for radically simplifying logistics networks and their associated costs (Vadivelu et al. 2025).

16.4.1. *Enhancing supply chain resilience*

Digital inventory directly bolsters supply chain resilience by decoupling the availability of a part from complex global logistics networks. Instead of relying on a single, distant factory or a fragile network of suppliers, critical component designs can be stored securely in the cloud and transmitted instantly to local AM hubs, when and where needed. This capability mitigates risks from geopolitical instability, trade disputes, natural disasters or transport delays, as production can be rapidly shifted to alternative locations (Singh et al. 2024a; Bhambri and Bajdor 2025). For spare parts, especially in aerospace, defense or heavy machinery, it virtually eliminates the problem of obsolescence and long lead times, ensuring operational continuity and turning a previously reactive maintenance model into a proactive, on-demand service.

16.4.2. *Enabling mass customization and personalization*

AM shatters the economies of scale that have long dictated mass production, unlocking unprecedented agility through mass customization and personalization. Where traditional manufacturing requires expensive molds and long setup times for product variations, digital inventory allows for the cost-effective production of bespoke items in small batches – or even lots of one. Each unit printed can be unique without a significant penalty on time or cost, enabling businesses to respond to specific customer preferences, create tailored medical devices such as prosthetics or produce limited-edition products (Bhambri 2025). This agility transforms the supply chain from a push-based system forecasting demand to a pull-based system that reacts with precision to actual market desires.

16.4.3. *Reducing warehousing and logistics costs*

The adoption of digital inventory drives a profound redefinition of cost structures, primarily through the drastic reduction of warehousing and logistics expenses. By replacing vast physical stockpiles of spare parts and components with digital files, companies can minimize or even eliminate the need for centralized warehouses, slashing real estate, energy and inventory carrying costs. Furthermore, logistics are simplified and made cheaper; instead of shipping a finished good globally, a single digital file is transmitted, and the product is manufactured locally, reducing transportation fuel, carbon emissions and import duties (Woldesilassiea et al. 2024; Bhambri and Anand 2025). This shift from a cost-centric model focused on bulk shipping to one prioritizing on-demand local production represents a fundamental leanification of the entire supply network.

16.5. The sustainability imperative: waste reduction and localized production

AM intrinsically advances sustainability by fundamentally re-engineering production toward a less wasteful and carbon-intensive model. Unlike traditional subtractive methods that carve parts from solid blocks of material, often discarding over 90% of the raw material, AM builds components layer-by-layer, using only the material necessary for the part itself, dramatically reducing scrap and conserving resources. This "light-weighting" capability further allows for the design of structurally optimal parts that use minimal material without sacrificing strength, decreasing the energy consumed during the product's lifecycle, particularly in sectors such as aerospace and automotive (Priyadarshini et al. 2025). Concurrently, the digital inventory model enables truly localized production, where parts are printed on-demand near their point of use. This eliminates the need for long-distance shipping and the associated greenhouse gas emissions from global logistics networks, while also negating the waste generated from overproduction, obsolete inventory and damaged goods in transit, thereby closing the loop on a more circular and environmentally responsible supply chain.

16.6. Implementation challenges and considerations

The transition to a digital inventory model, while promising, is fraught with significant operational and strategic hurdles that organizations must proactively address to ensure a viable and secure implementation. These challenges move beyond mere technical adoption to encompass core issues of security, quality and capability (Bhambri and Kant 2025a).

16.6.1. *Intellectual property and digital file security*

The very essence of digital inventory – storing valuable CAD files in a digital repository – creates a profound intellectual property (IP) risk, as a single breach could lead to the mass replication and distribution of proprietary designs. Unlike a physical part stored in a warehouse, a digital file can be copied infinitely without degradation, necessitating robust cybersecurity measures including encryption, access controls and potentially blockchain-based ledger systems to track file access and usage, thereby protecting a company's most valuable digital assets (Chaldoupis et al. 2024).

16.6.2. *Quality control and standardization*

Achieving consistent, repeatable part quality across different AM machines, geographical locations and production batches remain a critical barrier, as variations in printer calibration, material batches and environmental conditions can lead to unacceptable deviations in mechanical properties and dimensional accuracy. This challenge demands the development of stringent, universally accepted certification protocols for both digital files and printing processes, alongside the integration of in situ monitoring and AI-driven analytics to ensure every printed component, regardless of where it is produced, meets the required specifications and performance standards.

16.6.3. *Materials and technological limitations*

Despite rapid advancements, AM technologies still face inherent limitations in terms of available materials, production speed and build volume, which can restrict their application for certain high-volume, high-strength or large-scale components (Bhambri et al. 2025). Organizations must carefully evaluate the technical and economic feasibility of using AM for each part, considering factors such as the limited palette of qualified engineering-grade materials, the slower production rates compared to traditional mass-production methods such as injection molding and the post-processing requirements that can impact the overall lead time and cost.

16.7. Future horizons: integrating digital inventory with AI and IoT

Transformative power of digital inventory is unlocked not by AM alone, but through its deep integration with two other foundational technologies: artificial intelligence (AI) and the Internet of Things (IoT). This synergy creates a self-optimizing, predictive and highly responsive supply chain ecosystem that moves beyond simple on-demand production (Devito et al. 2024; Abu-Abdoun et al. 2025; Naghshineh and Carvalho 2025a).

16.7.1. *The role of AI: from reactive to predictive and generative*

AI acts as the intelligent brain of the digital inventory system.

– Predictive analytics for proactive printing: instead of waiting for a part to fail or an order to be placed, AI algorithms can analyze historical performance data, real-time operating conditions from IoT sensors and even external factors such as weather to predict part failure or demand surges. The system can then automatically trigger the printing of a part at the most optimal location before it is critically needed, achieving true predictive maintenance and minimizing downtime.

– Generative design for digital parts: AI-powered generative design software can be used to create optimized part designs specifically for AM. Engineers input design goals (e.g. weight, strength, thermal performance) and constraints (e.g. available materials, print platform size), and the AI explores all possible permutations to generate an optimal, often organic-looking, geometry. This creates a library of superior, lighter and more efficient digital parts that consume less material and perform better.

– Dynamic routing and logistics optimization: when a print order is triggered, AI can dynamically determine the best production location (Keskin et al. 2025). It will analyze factors such as current printer capacity, material availability, energy costs, shipping distances to the end-user and local carbon footprints to route the digital file to the most efficient and sustainable print node in the global network.

16.7.2. *The role of IoT: the sensory nervous system*

IoT provides the real-world data that feeds the AI, creating a closed-loop, intelligent system.

– Real-time asset monitoring: IoT sensors embedded in machinery across the supply chain (e.g. in manufacturing plants, vehicles or in-field equipment) continuously stream data on performance metrics such as temperature, vibration, pressure and usage cycles.

– Digital twin creation: this continuous IoT data feed can be used to create a "digital twin" – a virtual replica of a physical asset. The digital twin mirrors the wear and tear of its physical counterpart, allowing the AI to model and predict failure points with extreme accuracy, directly informing the digital inventory's predictive printing schedule (Falkonakis et al. 2024).

– Quality assurance and certification: IoT sensors can be integrated directly into 3D printers to monitor the printing process in real time (e.g. thermal imaging, laser power). This data stream can be used by AI to detect anomalies during the build and can be cryptographically logged (e.g. on a blockchain) to provide a verifiable, quality-assured digital thread for the produced part, which is crucial for regulated industries such as aerospace and healthcare.

The digital inventory library serves as the foundation. The AI & Analytics Engine acts as the intelligent core, processing data from IoT-enabled physical assets (via their digital twins) to make predictive decisions. It then dynamically routes optimized design files to appropriate smart printers. This synergy enables a proactive, efficient and resilient operational model (Singh et al. 2024b; Naghshineh 2025; Okokpujie and Tartibu 2025; Peprah et al. 2025).

16.7.3. *The converged system: the self-optimizing supply network*

The integration of AI, IoT and digital inventory creates a powerful feedback loop (Alabi 2024; Roozkhosh et al. 2024; Klenam et al. 2025; Naghshineh and Carvalho 2025b; Oliveira and Espadinha-Cruz 2025):

– IoT sensors on a compressor in a remote mining operation detect an anomalous vibration pattern.

– This data is streamed to the AI Analytics Engine, which compares it to the asset's digital twin and predicts that a specific bearing has a 95% chance of failure within 72 hours.

– The AI automatically triggers a work order and queries the digital inventory for the bearing's design file.

– The AI then executes its dynamic routing algorithm, identifying that the most cost-effective and fastest solution is to print the bearing at a local service hub 200 miles from the mine, rather than shipping from a central warehouse overseas.

– The digital file is securely transmitted to the designated print facility. IoT-enabled printers monitor the production, ensuring quality, and upon completion, the part is shipped for installation, preventing costly unplanned downtime.

16.8. Conclusion: a roadmap for adoption

The transition to a digital inventory model is not an all-or-nothing endeavor but a strategic journey that requires deliberate planning and phased execution. Organizations should begin with a thorough audit of their existing inventory and bill of materials to identify high-value, low-volume or obsolete parts that are prime candidates for initial conversion. This first phase involves pilot programs focused on specific product lines or regional markets, allowing for the development of internal AM expertise, the establishment of qualified supplier partnerships with printing hubs and the implementation of robust digital rights management to protect intellectual property. Success in these controlled environments builds the business case and organizational confidence, paving the way for a more scalable digital infrastructure (Bendoly et al. 2024; Chen et al. 2024; Dey et al. 2025; Ramful 2025; Suva and Rahman 2025).

Ultimately, achieving the full potential of digital inventory demands a holistic transformation that integrates technology, strategy and talent. This involves moving beyond siloed pilot projects to embed AM and digital inventory principles into the core of supply chain strategy, from product design for additive manufacturability (DfAM) to revised financial models that account for the total cost of ownership rather than just unit price. Furthermore, success is contingent on fostering cross-functional collaboration between supply chain, manufacturing, IT and cybersecurity teams to create a seamless and secure digital thread. By proactively building this ecosystem and cultivating the necessary digital skills, organizations can position themselves to leverage their digital inventory not just as a tactical tool, but as a strategic asset for unprecedented resilience, customization and sustainability in a volatile world (Bhambri and Khang 2024; Bhambri and Rani 2024; Bhambri et al. 2024; Domiński et al. 2024; Li et al. 2024; Piccioni et al. 2024; Rana and Bhambri 2024; Bhambri and Kant 2025b; Dehghan et al. 2025; Rana and Bhambri 2025).

16.9. References

Abu-Abdoun, D.I., Ekren, B.Y., Matopoulos, A. (2025). Decision-making in additive manufacturing supply chains: A systematic literature review. *IFAC-PapersOnLine*, 59(10), 661–666.

Alabi, M. (2024). Application of digital lean manufacturing system in additive manufacturing industries: A review. *Eng. Headway*, 2, 79–94.

Bang-Olsen, K. and Turkyilmaz, A. (2024). Assessing additive manufacturing and digital inventory ecosystem in the oil & gas context. In *43th IFIP International Conference on Advances in Production Management Systems (APMS)*, Chemnitz, 63–76.

Bendoly, E., Chandrasekaran, A., Lima, M.D.R.F., Handfield, R., Khajavi, S.H., Roscoe, S. (2024). The role of generative design and additive manufacturing capabilities in developing human–AI symbiosis: Evidence from multiple case studies. *Decis. Sci.*, 55(4), 325–345.

Bhambri, P. (2025). Understanding AI and machine learning in security. In *Handbook of AI-Driven Threat Detection and Prevention: A Holistic Approach to Security*, Bhambri, P. and Anand, A.J. (eds). CRC Press, Boca Raton, 1–17. doi: 10.1201/9781003521020-1.

Bhambri, P. and Anand, A.J. (eds) (2025). *Handbook of AI-Driven Threat Detection and Prevention: A Holistic Approach to Security*. CRC Press, Boca Raton. doi: 10.1201/9781003521020.

Bhambri, P. and Bajdor, P. (2025). AI-powered predictive analysis for proactive cyber defense. In *Handbook of AI-Driven Threat Detection and Prevention: A Holistic Approach to Security*, Bhambri, P. and Anand, A.J. (eds). CRC Press, Boca Raton, 308–321. doi: 10.1201/9781003521020-18.

Bhambri, P. and Hamad, A. (2025). Quantum computing and AI synergies: Strengthening cybersecurity resilience. In *Handbook of AI-Driven Threat Detection and Prevention: A Holistic Approach to Security*, Bhambri, P. and Anand, A.J. (eds). CRC Press, Boca Raton, 337–352. doi: 10.1201/9781003521020-20.

Bhambri, P. and Kant, S. (2025a). Ethical AI systems: A comprehensive framework for bias mitigation and fairness in machine learning. In *2nd Int. Conf. L-GPR Program*, Lincoln University, Malaysia.

Bhambri, P. and Kant, S. (2025b). A taxonomy of bias in machine learning: Classification, sources, and implications for ethical AI. In *1st Int. Conf. L-GPR Program*, Lincoln University, Malaysia.

Bhambri, P. and Khang, A. (2024). Machine learning advancements in E-health: Transforming digital healthcare. In *Medical Robotics and AI-Assisted Diagnostics for a High-Tech Healthcare Industry*. IGI Global, Hershey, 174–194. doi: 10.4018/979-8-3693-2105-8.ch012.

Bhambri, P. and Pawełoszek, I. (2025). Deep learning techniques for intrusion detection in critical infrastructure. In *Handbook of AI-Driven Threat Detection and Prevention: A Holistic Approach to Security*, Bhambri, P. and Anand, A.J. (eds). CRC Press, Boca Raton, 322–336. doi: 10.1201/9781003521020-19.

Bhambri, P. and Rani, S. (2024). Ethical issues for climate change and mental health. In *Impact of Climate Change on Mental Health and Well-Being*, Samanta, D. and Garg, M. (eds). IGI Global, Hershey, 178–198. doi: 10.4018/979-8-3693-2177-5.ch012.

Bhambri, P. and Starostka-Patyk, M. (2025). Integrating AI with blockchain for decentralized security and threat prevention. In *Handbook of AI-Driven Threat Detection and Prevention: A Holistic Approach to Security*, Bhambri, P. and Anand, A.J. (eds). CRC Press, Boca Raton, 353–370. doi: 10.1201/9781003521020-21.

Bhambri, P., Rani, S., Khang, A. (2024). AI-driven digital twin and resource optimization in Industry 4.0 ecosystem. In *Intelligent Techniques for Predictive Data Analytics*, Singh, N., Birla, S., Ansari, M.D., Shukla, N.K. (eds). Wiley-IEEE Press, New York, 47–69. doi: 10.1002/9781394227990.ch3.

Bhambri, P., Rana, R., Kautish, S. (2025). Sustainable digital transformation: Reducing carbon footprint in the metaverse. In *Metaverse and Sustainability: Business Resilience Towards Sustainable Development Goals*, Filho, W.L., Kautish, S., Gupta, V.P. (eds). Springer, Cham, 105–128. doi: 10.1007/978-3-031-89545-6_7.

Cardeal, G., Ribeiro, I., Leite, M. (2025). The role of additive manufacturing in process industry spare parts supply chains. *Journal of Manufacturing Technology Management*, 1–21. doi: 10.1108/JMTM-03-2025-0254.

Chaldoupis, K., Polychronakis, Y., Syntetos, A.A., Holmström, J. (2024). Additive manufacturing for standard parts in the healthcare supply chain: What are the available performance improvements? *International Journal of Production Research*, 1–19. doi: 10.1080/00207543.2024.2434591.

Chen, Z., Surendraarcharyagie, K., Granland, K., Chen, C., Xu, X., Xiong, Y., Davies, C., Tang, Y. (2024). Service oriented digital twin for additive manufacturing process. *Journal of Manufacturing Systems*, 74, 762–776. doi: 10.1016/j.jmsy.2024.04.015.

Dehghan, S., Sattarpanah Karganroudi, S., Echchakoui, S., Barka, N. (2025). The integration of additive manufacturing into industry 4.0 and industry 5.0: A bibliometric analysis (trends, opportunities, and challenges). *Machines*, 13(1), 62.

Devito, F., Copani, G., Natalicchio, A., Alami, A. H., Lavecchia, F., Olabi, A.-G., Dassisti, M. (2024). Business models and advanced additive manufacturing strategies for better sustainability. *Energy Nexus*, 16, 100337. doi: 10.1016/j.nexus.2024.100337.

Dey, A., Adeniran, O., Ramoni, M., Yodo, N., Cong, W. (2025). Additive manufacturing applications in mission-critical operations: A review. *J. Manuf. Mater. Process.*, 9(3), 70.

Domiński, A., Duale, K., Konieczny, T., Kurcok, P., Kowalczuk, M., Rydz, J., Grundmann, A., Kaysser, S.T. (2024). Additive manufacturing technology for modern packaging. *Packaging Review*, 1(1), 6–15. doi: 10.15199/42.2024.1.1.

Falkonakis, I., Lotfian, S., Yeter, B. (2024). Multi-criteria decision analysis of an innovative additive manufacturing technique for onboard maintenance. *Sustainability*, 16(9), 3763.

Keskin, M.H., Koray, M., Kaya, E., Fidan, M.M., Söğüt, M.Z. (2025). Additive manufacturing for remedying supply chain disruptions and building resilient and sustainable logistics support systems. *Sustainability*, 17(6), 2783.

Klenam, D., Asumadu, T., Bodunrin, M., Obiko, J., Genga, R., Maape, S., McBagoniuri, F., Soboyejo, W. (2025). Toward sustainable industrialization in Africa: The potential of additive manufacturing – An overview. *Frontiers in Manufacturing Technology*, 4, 1410653. doi: 10.3389/fmtec.2024.1410653.

Li, W., Ekren, B.Y., Aktas, E. (2024). Additive manufacturing and its impact on pharmaceutical supply chains. In *Medical Additive Manufacturing*, Mallakpour, S. and Hussain, C.M. (eds). Elsevier, Amsterdam, 683–712.

Naghshineh, B. (2025). Mapping the enhancing effects of additive manufacturing technology adoption on supply chain agility. *Manag. Rev. Q.*, 75(1), 119–137.

Naghshineh, B. and Carvalho, H. (2025a). Towards a practice-based framework for supply chain resilience in the context of additive manufacturing technology adoption. *Int. J. Comput. Integr. Manuf.*, 38(3), 335–361.

Naghshineh, B. and Carvalho, H. (2025b). Exploring the effects of additive manufacturing technology adoption on the state of the supply chain: A resilience perspective. *Oper. Manag. Res.*, 18(2), 495–517.

Okokpujie, I.P. and Tartibu, L.K. (2025). Study of the economic viability of internet of things (IoTs) in additive and advanced manufacturing: A comprehensive review. *Prog. Addit. Manuf.*, 10(5), 3175–3194.

Oliveira, J. and Espadinha-Cruz, P. (2025). Additive manufacturing adoption in aviation: A literature review. *Procedia Comput. Sci.*, 253, 892–901.

Peprah, J.A., Amoah, J., Kwarteng, K., Jibril, A.B., Sharif, T. (2025). Artificial intelligence and additive manufacturing for resilient supply chain in Africa: A systematic literature review. *Future Bus. J.*, 11(1), 54.

Piccioni, M., Bionda, A., Ratti, A. (2024). Emerging approaches in yacht design and manufacturing: State of the art and future perspectives of generative design and additive manufacturing. In *1st International Conference on Design and Industry 2024*, Braga, 1–10.

Priyadarshini, J., Singh, R.K., Mishra, R., Chaudhuri, A., Kamble, S. (2025). Supply chain resilience and improving sustainability through additive manufacturing implementation: A systematic literature review and framework. *Prod. Plan. Control*, 36(3), 309–332.

Ramful, R. (2025). A paradigm shift towards sustainable production with additive manufacturing in the industry 4.0 era. In *Intelligent and Sustainable Engineering Systems for Industry 4.0 and Beyond*, Fowdur, T.P., Milovanovic, D.A., Bojkovic, Z.S. (eds). CRC Press, Boca Raton, 92–116.

Rana, R. and Bhambri, P. (2024). Artificial intelligence and Internet of Things (IoT) facilitated digital twin for Industry 4.0 application domains. In *AI-Driven Digital Twin and Industry 4.0*, Rani, S., Bhambri, P., Kumar, S., Pareek, P.K., Elngar, A.A. (eds). CRC Press, Boca Raton, 168–181. doi: 10.1201/9781003395416-11.

Rana, R. and Bhambri, P. (2025). Harnessing block chain digital twins for sustainable business operations. In *Practical Frameworks for New-Age Digitalization Business Strategy*, Tee, P., Song, B., Ho, R. (eds). IGI Global, Hershey, 413–446. doi: 10.4018/979-8-3373-2018-2.ch013.

Roozkhosh, P., Pooya, A., Soleimani Fard, O., Bagheri, R. (2024). Designing a changeable multi-level supply chain network with additive manufacturing capability and costs uncertainty: A Monte Carlo approach. *Oper. Res.*, 24(1), 5.

Singh, S., Misra, S.C., Singh, G. (2024a). Greening the supply chain: Leveraging additive manufacturing for sustainable risk management. *Bus. Strategy Environ.*, 33(8), 8233–8246.

Singh, S., Misra, S.C., Singh, G. (2024b). Leveraging additive manufacturing for enhanced supply chain resilience and sustainability: A strategic integration framework. *Glob. J. Flex. Syst. Manag.*, 25(2), 343–368.

Skoumpopoulou, D., Toliyat, S.M.H., Ojra, A., Shokri, A., Hu, S. (2025). Challenges of achieving digital transformation in manufacturing firms: The case of predictive maintenance and spare part inventory management. *J. Manuf. Technol. Manag.*, 36(1), 159–178.

Suva, A.I. and Rahman, K.A. (2025). Additive manufacturing and industry 4.0 integration: An approach for Bangladesh's industrial advancement. *AIP Conf. Proc.*, 3307(1), 020021.

Vadivelu, V., Nachimuthu, P., Karthikeyan, P. (2025). Transforming supply chains (SCs) with additive manufacturing (AM) a paradigm shift in production. In *Metal Additive Manufacturing: Principles, Techniques and Applications*, Rajasekar, R., Mostafaei, A., Moganapriya, C., Kumar, P.S. (eds). John Wiley & Sons, Hoboken, 359–406.

Woldesilassiea, T.L., Lemu, H.G., Gutema, E.M. (2024). Impacts of adopting additive manufacturing process on supply chain: Systematic literature review. *Logistics*, 8(1), 3.

17

Ethical and Social Governance of AI-enabled Supply Chains

This chapter addresses the critical imperative of integrating robust ethical and social governance frameworks into AI-driven supply chains. It examines core challenges such as algorithmic bias, lack of transparency, accountability gaps, labor displacement and data privacy risks inherent in deploying AI across global networks. The discussion emphasizes the societal impacts on workers, suppliers, communities and consumers, advocating for stakeholder-inclusive approaches. The chapter outlines practical governance frameworks, compliance strategies and implementation pathways – including ethical AI design lifecycles, human oversight mechanisms, auditing tools and impact metrics – to foster responsible innovation. It argues that proactive ethical governance is not merely a compliance exercise but a strategic foundation for building resilient, trustworthy and sustainable AI-powered supply chains in alignment with broader ESG (Environmental, Social and Governance) goals.

17.1. Introduction: the imperative for ethical AI in global supply chains

The integration of Artificial Intelligence (AI) into global supply chains promises unprecedented efficiency, resilience and optimization. Algorithms drive decisions on sourcing, logistics, inventory, demand forecasting, labor allocation and risk management. However, this powerful technological shift brings profound ethical and social implications that extend far beyond mere technical performance. This introduction establishes the critical necessity of embedding robust ethical and social governance (ESG+) principles into the very fabric of AI-driven supply chain operations. It argues that neglecting these aspects is not just a reputational risk, it threatens the long-term viability, fairness and social license of global supply

Chapter written by Pankaj BHAMBRI and Marta STAROSTKA-PATYK.

networks, undermining the potential benefits of AI. Ethical governance is no longer optional, it is a fundamental strategic imperative for responsible and sustainable business in the digital age (Bhambri and Khang 2024).

17.1.1. *Defining ethical and social governance in the context of AI*

ESG+ in this context refers to the specific frameworks, principles, processes and accountability mechanisms required to ensure that AI systems deployed across supply chains operate responsibly, fairly, transparently and accountably, while minimizing harm and maximizing positive social impact. It builds upon traditional ESG (Environmental, Social, Governance) reporting but adds a crucial "+" layer focused specifically on the unique challenges posed by AI. This encompasses:

– Algorithmic fairness and non-discrimination: ensuring AI systems do not perpetuate or amplify biases against specific suppliers (especially SMEs), workers, communities or consumers based on protected characteristics (e.g. location, size, gender, ethnicity) (Camilleri 2024).

– Transparency and explainability (XAI): making AI-driven decisions understandable to affected stakeholders (e.g. why a supplier was deselected, why a route was chosen, how a worker's performance is scored).

– Accountability and responsibility: clearly defining who is responsible when an AI system causes harm (e.g. biased hiring, unfair contract termination, discriminatory pricing, safety-critical failures).

– Human oversight and control: maintaining meaningful human judgment and intervention points ("human-in-the-loop" or "human-on-command") for significant or high-risk AI decisions.

– Data privacy and security: protecting sensitive data (worker biometrics, supplier financials, customer information) collected and processed by AI throughout the supply chain.

– Labor impact and just transition: proactively managing the impact of automation on jobs, ensuring fair working conditions under AI surveillance/management and investing in workforce reskilling.

– Societal well-being: considering broader impacts on communities, including economic displacement, environmental justice (e.g. pollution routing) and data rights.

17.1.2. *Why AI introduces unique ethical risks in complex, global supply networks*

AI exacerbates and introduces new ethical risks in supply chains due to several inherent characteristics (Bhambri and Rani 2024b):

– Complexity and opacity ("black boxes"): many advanced AI models (such as deep learning) are inherently complex and difficult to interpret. Understanding why an AI made a specific sourcing, routing or hiring decision can be impossible, hindering accountability and making bias detection hard. This opacity is magnified in multi-tiered global networks.

– Scale and amplification: AI automates and scales decision-making exponentially. An undetected bias in an algorithm can be instantly applied across thousands of suppliers, millions of shipments or a global workforce, amplifying unfairness or discrimination at an unprecedented scale and speed.

– Data dependencies and biases: AI systems learn from historical data. Supply chain data often reflects past inequalities, discriminatory practices or incomplete perspectives (e.g. favoring large, established suppliers over diverse SMEs). AI can codify and perpetuate these biases, making them systemic.

– Dynamic adaptation and unforeseen consequences: AI systems, especially those using reinforcement learning, continuously adapt. They might develop unexpected, undesirable or unethical strategies to achieve their programmed goals (e.g. optimizing cost by consistently routing through regions with lax labor laws).

– Diffused accountability: the involvement of multiple actors (AI developers, data providers, system integrators, supply chain managers, executives) makes pinpointing responsibility for harmful AI outcomes legally and ethically challenging.

– Global disparities: deploying AI across diverse global jurisdictions with varying regulations, cultural norms and levels of worker protection creates significant risks of exploitation or inconsistent ethical application.

17.1.3. *The convergence of regulatory pressure, consumer expectations and investor focus*

The imperative for ethical AI governance is being driven by powerful converging forces (Bhambri and Kant 2025a):

– Regulatory pressure: governments worldwide are rapidly enacting legislation targeting AI ethics. The EU AI Act (classifying high-risk systems, mandating risk assessments, transparency and human oversight), US Executive Orders and state-level bills, China's algorithm regulations and similar initiatives globally are creating a complex but demanding compliance landscape. Non-compliance risks significant fines and operational restrictions.

– Consumer expectations and activism: consumers are increasingly aware and concerned about the ethical implications of the products they buy. They demand transparency about sourcing, labor practices and environmental impact. AI's role in these areas is coming under scrutiny. Consumers actively boycott brands associated with unethical practices, including biased or exploitative AI use. "Ethical provenance" is becoming a key purchasing factor.

– Investor focus and ESG mandates: investors are integrating ESG factors, including technology ethics and social governance, into their decision-making and risk assessments. Funds focused on sustainable and responsible investing (SRI) are growing rapidly. Companies with poor AI governance face divestment risks, higher cost of capital and damage to their reputation and long-term value. Investors demand robust reporting on how AI-related ethical and social risks are managed.

– This trifecta means that ethical AI in the supply chain is no longer just a moral consideration, it is a critical business imperative impacting legal standing, market share, brand value and access to capital.

17.1.4. *Chapter roadmap*

This chapter provides a comprehensive roadmap for navigating the complex terrain of ethical and social governance in AI-enabled supply chains. It begins by delving deep into the core ethical challenges (section 17.2), examining algorithmic bias, transparency deficits, accountability gaps, privacy threats, labor displacement and environmental costs specific to supply chain AI. Section 17.3 then explores the societal implications of these challenges, analyzing impacts on workers, suppliers (particularly vulnerable SMEs), local communities and consumer trust. Building on this understanding, section 17.4 outlines essential frameworks and principles for ethical AI governance, covering foundational ethics, evolving regulations, relevant standards and the integration of ethics into the AI development lifecycle. Section 17.5 focuses on implementing social governance, detailing practical approaches such as meaningful human oversight, stakeholder engagement, fair labor practices and promoting diversity in AI development. Section 17.6 addresses the critical governance infrastructure, including ethics boards, auditing methodologies, explainability tools and grievance mechanisms. Section 17.7 discusses measuring success through relevant KPIs and integrating ethical performance into ESG reporting. Section 17.8 illustrates these concepts through practical case studies of ethical dilemmas and solutions. Finally, the chapter concludes (section 17.9) by summarizing the argument for ethical governance as the bedrock of resilient, sustainable and trustworthy AI-powered supply chains for the future.

17.2. Core ethical challenges posed by supply chain AI

17.2.1. *Algorithmic bias and discrimination*

AI systems learn from historical data, which often reflects existing societal biases and inequalities. In supply chains, this can lead to discriminatory outcomes in critical areas. For instance, a sourcing algorithm trained on past purchasing data might inadvertently favor suppliers from specific regions or demographics over others, even if those suppliers are not objectively the best, perpetuating historical disadvantages. Bias could creep into logistics optimization, unfairly routing goods away from certain neighborhoods based on flawed assumptions about demand or risk. AI used for workforce management might allocate shifts or tasks in ways that disadvantage certain groups based on correlated factors in the training data. Credit scoring algorithms assessing suppliers could unfairly penalize small or minority-owned businesses. The societal impact is significant, as biased AI can reinforce economic exclusion, reduce diversity in supply chains and lead to unfair market dynamics, undermining principles of equity and fairness (Bhambri and Kant 2025b).

17.2.2. *Lack of transparency and explainability ("black box" problem)*

Many advanced AI models, particularly deep learning, operate as complex "black boxes". While they can generate highly accurate predictions or optimizations, it is often impossible for humans (including developers, operators and affected stakeholders) to understand how the AI arrived at a specific decision. This lack of transparency is problematic in supply chain contexts. If an AI rejects a supplier, alters a critical delivery route causing delays, flags an employee for review or changes production schedules, stakeholders deserve an explanation. Without explainability (XAI), it is difficult to identify errors, debug problems, challenge unfair outcomes or simply build trust. Workers, suppliers, communities and consumers are left in the dark about decisions impacting their livelihoods, businesses or the goods they receive. This opacity hinders accountability, erodes trust and makes it challenging to ensure AI aligns with ethical and business goals (Bhambri and Anand 2025).

17.2.3. *Accountability and responsibility*

When an AI-driven decision causes harm or fails in a supply chain, determining who is responsible becomes complex. Traditional models of responsibility focus on human actors. However, with AI autonomously making decisions (e.g. rerouting shipments, selecting suppliers, managing warehouse robots), the lines blur. If an

AI's optimized routing leads to a truck accident due to an unforeseen risk factor it prioritized (such as speed over safety), who is liable? The developer of the algorithm? The company that deployed it? The operator who did not override it? What if a biased algorithm unfairly terminates a supplier contract, causing their business to collapse? Current legal and regulatory frameworks struggle with this distributed and often ambiguous responsibility. Establishing clear chains of accountability for AI decisions is crucial for justice, remediation and incentivizing ethical development and deployment (Bhambri 2025).

17.2.4. *Data privacy and security*

AI systems in supply chains thrive on vast amounts of data, including highly sensitive information. This encompasses personal data of employees (performance metrics, location tracking via IoT, biometric data), confidential supplier contracts and financials, proprietary operational details and customer information. Collecting, processing, storing and sharing this data across complex global networks creates immense privacy and security risks. Unauthorized access, data breaches or misuse can lead to identity theft, corporate espionage, competitive disadvantage, reputational damage and violation of privacy regulations such as GDPR or CCPA. Ensuring robust data anonymization, implementing strict access controls, using state-of-the-art encryption and maintaining secure data lifecycle management are paramount. Failure here not only breaches ethics but also exposes organizations to significant legal and financial penalties (Bhambri and Bajdor 2025).

17.2.5. *Labor displacement and workforce transformation*

AI and automation (robotics, autonomous vehicles, AI planning) promise efficiency but pose significant challenges to the human workforce. Tasks previously performed by humans – warehouse picking/packing, truck driving (long-term), data entry, routine planning – are increasingly automated. While new jobs are created (e.g. robot maintenance, AI oversight, data science), the transition is often disruptive and uneven. Key ethical concerns include the scale and pace of potential job losses, the geographic concentration of impacts and the mismatch between displaced workers' skills and new roles. This necessitates proactive "just transition" strategies: significant investment in reskilling and upskilling programs, potential income support during transitions, redesigning roles to augment human capabilities with AI rather than simply replace and ensuring that productivity gains are shared fairly. Ignoring this challenge risks widespread unemployment, social unrest and deepening inequality within the supply chain workforce (Bhambri and Pawełoszek 2025).

17.2.6. *Environmental impact*

While AI is often touted as a tool for sustainability (e.g. optimizing routes to reduce fuel, minimizing waste), the technology itself carries a significant environmental footprint that cannot be ignored. Training large, complex AI models requires enormous computational power, consuming vast amounts of electricity, often generated from fossil fuels. This contributes directly to greenhouse gas emissions. Running these models continuously in production for real-time supply chain optimization adds to the energy burden. Data centers supporting this infrastructure also require substantial resources for cooling and maintenance. An ethical assessment must therefore consider the net environmental impact: Does the resource optimization and waste reduction achieved by the AI outweigh the carbon cost of developing and running the AI? Failing to account for this can lead to "greenwashing", where the environmental benefits are overstated while the significant hidden costs of the AI itself remain unaddressed. Sustainable AI requires choosing efficient model architectures, using renewable energy for the computation and carefully evaluating the true environmental ROI (Bhambri and Hamad 2025).

17.3. Societal implications and stakeholder perspectives

17.3.1. *Impact on workers*

The integration of AI into supply chain operations fundamentally reshapes the worker experience, raising critical ethical and social concerns. AI-driven performance monitoring systems, warehouse automation and algorithmic task allocation can lead to pervasive workplace surveillance, intensifying pressure and potentially eroding worker autonomy. Algorithms might optimize for speed or cost without adequately factoring in human fatigue or ergonomic safety, increasing physical strain and accident risks. Furthermore, AI systems used for hiring, promotion or shift allocation can perpetuate or even amplify existing societal biases if trained on flawed historical data, leading to discriminatory outcomes. The displacement threat from automation (robotics, autonomous vehicles) creates significant anxiety, demanding robust "just transition" strategies encompassing reskilling and social safety nets. Crucially, the "black box" nature of many AI decisions makes it difficult for workers to understand why they were assigned a particular task, denied a shift or flagged for performance issues, undermining trust and fair process. For example, an AI optimizing delivery routes might prioritize speed over driver safety or rest breaks, while an automated warehouse management system could assign physically demanding tasks based solely on efficiency metrics, disregarding individual worker fatigue or health conditions (Suljic 2025).

17.3.2. *Impact on suppliers (especially SMEs)*

AI-enabled supply chains introduce significant power imbalances, often disproportionately affecting small- and medium-sized enterprises (SMEs). Large corporations increasingly deploy AI for supplier selection, risk scoring, dynamic pricing and automated contract compliance checks. Algorithms can inadvertently (or systematically) disadvantage SMEs lacking the digital infrastructure, data volume or resources to "look good" to AI systems. Bias in training data (e.g. favoring large, established suppliers) can lock SMEs out of opportunities. AI-driven dynamic pricing or payment term algorithms might squeeze SME margins unfairly. The lack of transparency in how these AI systems make decisions is particularly damaging for SMEs; rejection by an opaque algorithm offers no clear path for appeal or improvement. This creates a "digital divide", where SMEs struggle to compete not on product quality or service, but on their ability to conform to the data requirements and opaque logic of their larger customers' AI platforms. An AI scoring system might downgrade an otherwise excellent small supplier because it lacks a long digital transaction history with the buyer, or an automated invoice processing system might delay payments to an SME due to minor formatting discrepancies the AI flags cannot explain (Bhambri and Starostka-Patyk 2025).

17.3.3. *Impact on local communities*

Supply chain AI decisions have profound, often overlooked, consequences for the communities where facilities are located and operations occur. The siting of AI-optimized warehouses or logistics hubs, driven by efficiency algorithms, can concentrate heavy truck traffic, noise and pollution in specific, often economically disadvantaged, neighborhoods – a form of environmental injustice. Large-scale automation in local factories or distribution centers can lead to significant job losses within a community, impacting local economies, tax bases and social cohesion, without adequate planning for economic diversification or worker support. AI systems optimizing resource extraction or manufacturing processes might prioritize cost savings over local environmental impacts, affecting community health and ecosystems. There is also the emerging issue of "data colonialism", where vast amounts of data about local conditions, infrastructure usage or even community members (e.g. via delivery drones or tracking) are collected by corporations for their AI systems without adequate community consent, benefit-sharing or control over how this data is used. An AI optimizing global logistics might route significantly more ships through a particular port community to save fuel, dramatically increasing local air pollution without the community having any input or recourse (Sah and Shaikh 2024).

17.3.4. *Consumer trust and transparency*

In the age of conscious consumerism, AI's role in supply chains directly impacts brand reputation and consumer trust. Consumers increasingly demand transparency regarding product origins, labor conditions and environmental footprints – information often gathered and verified using AI. However, if consumers perceive AI systems as opaque, biased or used for "ethics washing" (making false or exaggerated sustainability/social claims), trust erodes rapidly. AI-generated sustainability scores or ethical certifications lack credibility if the underlying data and algorithms are not transparent and auditable. Algorithmic pricing, particularly dynamic surge pricing based on real-time AI analysis of demand and inventory, can feel exploitative to consumers, damaging loyalty. The use of AI in areas such as personalized marketing based on supply chain data also raises significant privacy concerns. Ultimately, consumers need assurance that an AI enabling faster deliveries or lower prices is not compromising ethical labor practices, environmental sustainability or fair treatment of suppliers (Bhambri et al. 2025). For instance, an AI promising "carbon-neutral delivery" must be verifiable, and consumers might distrust an AI-generated claim that a product is "ethically sourced" if they know AI scoring unfairly disadvantaged smallholder farmers or lacks transparency into factory working conditions (e.g. using computer vision for safety compliance but not capturing wage data). The EU's Digital Product Passport initiative highlights the push towards verifiable, AI-supported transparency demanded by consumers and regulators alike.

17.4. Frameworks for ethical AI governance in supply chains

Effective governance requires structured frameworks to translate ethical principles into actionable practices. This section explores four pillars for building robust AI governance in supply chains.

17.4.1. *Foundational principles*

Ethical AI in supply chains begins with universally accepted principles adapted to sector-specific challenges. Core principles include (Condé and Münch 2025):

– Fairness: ensuring AI systems avoid bias in supplier selection, labor allocation, logistics routing or demand forecasting (e.g. preventing discrimination against SMEs or marginalized regions).

– Accountability: defining clear ownership for AI decisions (e.g. who is responsible if an AI-recommended route causes delays or accidents?).

– Transparency: making AI-driven processes understandable to stakeholders (e.g. explaining why a supplier was flagged as "high risk").

– Robustness and safety: ensuring reliability under uncertainty (e.g. resilience to data disruptions during geopolitical crises).

– Human oversight: maintaining human control over critical decisions (e.g. overriding AI-suggested workforce reductions).

– Privacy and security: protecting sensitive data (e.g. supplier contracts, employee biometrics).

– Supply chain lens: these principles must address multi-tiered, global operations. For example, "fairness" extends beyond corporate walls to include suppliers' subcontractors.

17.4.2. *Regulatory landscape*

Compliance is non-negotiable. Key regulations include (Bhambri and Kumar 2024):

– EU AI Act: classifies supply chain AI (e.g. autonomous vehicles, biometric systems) as "high risk", requiring strict audits, documentation and human oversight.

– EU GDPR: governs data privacy for AI training datasets involving worker/supplier information.

– US Executive Order 14110: mandates safety testing and bias mitigation for impactful AI systems.

– National strategies: China's AI regulations focus on algorithmic transparency; Brazil's draft bill emphasizes non-discrimination.

– Implications: non-compliance risks fines (up to 7% of global revenue under EU AI Act), operational bans and reputational damage. Cross-border data flows add complexity (e.g. EU-to-US transfers).

17.4.3. *Industry standards and best practices*

Beyond regulations, standards provide implementation blueprints:

– ISO/IEC 42001 (AI Management Systems): framework for establishing AI governance policies.

– NIST AI RMF (Risk Management Framework): guides risk assessment for AI in procurement/logistics.

– IEEE ethically aligned design: technical standards for bias testing in algorithms.

– Industry consortia: GS1's guidelines for traceability AI; Responsible Business Alliance's (RBA) code of conduct.

Best practices include a) conduct third-party algorithmic audits; b) adopt supplier codes of conduct mandating ethical AI use; c) join initiatives such as the partnership on AI for shared tools.

17.4.4. *Ethical AI design and development lifecycle*

Ethics needs to be embedded at every phase of AI deployment, as shown in Table 17.1.

Phase	Ethical actions	Supply chain example
1. Problem scoping	Define ethical boundaries; involve diverse stakeholders.	Consult suppliers on AI-based payment terms.
2. Data sourcing	Audit data for bias; ensure consent (GDPR/CCPA).	Scrub supplier location data for demographic bias.
3. Model training	Apply fairness constraints; document data lineage.	Adjust weights to avoid penalizing rural suppliers.
4. Testing/validation	Run bias/drift checks; simulate edge cases (e.g. sanctions).	Stress-test demand AI during trade disruptions.
5. Deployment	Implement monitoring and human override protocols.	Enable warehouse managers to halt faulty robots.
6. Monitoring	Track KPIs (bias, drift); update models iteratively.	Audit transport AI for fuel-inefficient routes.

Table 17.1. *Description of ethical actions for various phases (Wu et al. 2025)*

17.5. Implementing social governance: beyond compliance

While compliance with regulations is essential, true social governance requires proactive, value-driven strategies that embed ethical principles into the fabric of AI-enabled supply chains. This section moves beyond legal checkboxes to explore how organizations can operationalize responsibility, fairness and inclusion as competitive advantages and societal imperatives.

17.5.1. *Human oversight and control ("human-in-the-loop/command")*

Human oversight is the cornerstone of ethical AI deployment. "Human-in-the-loop" (HITL) involves humans validating or correcting AI decisions (e.g. approving high-risk supplier selections or logistics reroutes). "Human-in-command" (HIC) goes further, ensuring humans set goals, constraints and ethical boundaries for AI systems before deployment. In supply chains, this means (Chithra and Bhambri 2024):

– Critical decision gates: requiring human review for decisions impacting labor rights (e.g. shift allocations), supplier livelihoods (e.g. contract terminations) or community welfare (e.g. warehouse location changes).

– Override mechanisms: empowering operators to halt AI-driven processes (e.g. autonomous vehicles in unsafe conditions).

– Contextual judgment: leveraging human expertise to interpret AI recommendations where data is incomplete or culturally nuanced (e.g. assessing supplier reliability in emerging markets).

17.5.2. *Stakeholder engagement and co-creation*

Social governance demands involving those affected by AI systems in their design and governance. This includes:

– Workers: frontline employees provide insights into how AI tools (e.g. performance monitoring algorithms) impact daily work, safety and morale.

– Suppliers (especially SMEs): collaborative workshops ensure AI-driven procurement platforms do not exclude smaller vendors due to biased data or opaque criteria.

– Communities and NGOs: engaging local groups near manufacturing hubs or logistics centers to assess environmental/equity impacts (e.g. AI-optimized truck routing increasing local pollution).

– Co-creation frameworks: participatory design sprints or ethics advisory boards where stakeholders co-develop AI use policies, ensuring solutions address real needs and mitigate unintended harms.

17.5.3. *Fair labor practices and just transition*

AI-driven automation (e.g. robotic warehouses, predictive staffing) can displace roles or intensify work. Ethical governance mandates (Rana and Bhambri 2024a):

– Impact assessments: proactively evaluating which jobs are augmented versus automated, and quantifying displacement risks.

– Reskilling programs: partnering with unions/educators to transition workers into AI-supervisory roles (e.g. “robot coordinators”) or growth areas (e.g. data analysis).

– Labor-centric AI design: configuring AI to enhance work – for example, using ergonomic sensors to reduce injury rates, not just maximize productivity.

– Wage and hour safeguards: ensuring algorithmic scheduling tools respect labor laws and worker well-being (e.g. preventing “clopening” shifts).

17.5.4. *Diversity, equity and inclusion (DEI) in AI teams and data*

Bias in AI often stems from homogeneous development teams and unrepresentative training data. Mitigation requires (Bhambri and Rani 2024a; Orenuga et al. 2024):

– Diverse AI teams: recruiting data scientists, engineers and ethicists from varied gender, racial, cultural and socioeconomic backgrounds to challenge assumptions and spot blind spots.

– Inclusive data practices: auditing datasets for representation gaps (e.g. supplier data skewed towards large corporations; worker data excluding gig laborers) and correcting imbalances.

– Equity-focused testing: stress-testing AI models for disparate impacts across worker demographics (e.g. whether performance algorithms penalize non-native language speakers) or supplier segments (e.g. disadvantaging women-owned businesses).

– DEI metrics: tracking diversity in AI teams and bias incidents in AI outputs as KPIs for governance reviews.

17.6. Building the governance infrastructure

This section moves beyond principles and frameworks to outline the concrete operational structures and processes necessary to implement and sustain ethical and social governance of AI in supply chains. It translates high-level commitments into actionable mechanisms ensuring accountability, oversight and remediation.

17.6.1. *AI Ethics Boards and Committees*

An AI Ethics Board (or Committee) is the cornerstone of formal governance infrastructure. It is a dedicated, cross-functional group tasked with providing strategic oversight, reviewing high-risk AI applications and setting organizational policy for ethical AI use within the supply chain. Its composition is critical: it should include diverse perspectives such as supply chain executives, AI/data scientists, legal/compliance experts, ethics specialists, HR/employee representatives, risk management and potentially external advisors (ethicists, community representatives or supplier advocates). The Board's mandate includes reviewing proposed AI projects (especially those impacting workers, suppliers or communities) for ethical risks before deployment, approving AI ethics policies and guidelines, monitoring ongoing AI performance for unintended ethical consequences, investigating incidents of alleged harm or bias, and acting as a central point of escalation for ethical concerns. Its authority must be clearly defined and supported by top management to ensure its recommendations carry weight and lead to action, such as halting deployments or mandating changes.

17.6.2. *AI auditing and impact assessments*

Proactive and ongoing auditing is essential to verify compliance with ethical principles and identify potential harms. AI auditing involves the systematic, independent evaluation of AI systems against predefined criteria (fairness, accuracy, robustness, privacy, transparency). This includes technical audits examining data pipelines for bias, model performance across different subgroups and robustness testing. Impact assessments (such as Algorithmic Impact Assessments (AIAs) or Ethical Impact Assessments (EIAs)) are crucial proactive tools. Conducted before and during deployment, they systematically evaluate an AI system's potential societal, economic, environmental and human rights impacts across the supply chain ecosystem. For a supplier scoring AI, an AIA would assess risks of unfair exclusion of SMEs or bias against suppliers from certain regions. For warehouse automation, it would assess workforce displacement risks. Audits and assessments generate reports that inform the Ethics Board, drive mitigations and feed into transparency reporting (Bhambri and Bajdor 2024).

17.6.3. *Transparency and explainability tools*

Transparency builds trust and is fundamental to accountability. This involves two key aspects:

– System/process transparency: clearly communicating where and how AI is used in the supply chain (e.g. "AI is used for demand forecasting, warehouse robot routing and initial supplier screening”), the data sources used, the system’s intended purpose and its limitations.

– Explainability (XAI): providing understandable reasons for specific AI-driven decisions, especially those significantly impacting stakeholders. Why was a supplier rejected? Why was a specific delivery route chosen, impacting a driver’s schedule? Why was a shipment flagged for delay? XAI tools (such as LIME, SHAP or counterfactual explanations) help generate these reasons. The challenge is tailoring explanations to the audience: a technical explanation for an auditor, a simplified reason for a supplier or an aggregated trend report for consumers concerned about sustainability claims. Implementing these tools ensures decisions are not perceived as arbitrary “black boxes” and enables stakeholders to challenge or understand outcomes (Rane et al. 2024).

17.6.4. *Whistleblower mechanisms and grievance redress*

Even with robust preventative measures, harms or unethical practices may occur. A safe, accessible and effective mechanism for stakeholders (employees, suppliers, contractors, potentially communities) to report concerns or seek redress is vital. Whistleblower mechanisms provide confidential and often anonymous channels (hotlines, secure online portals, designated ombudspersons) for reporting suspected unethical AI use, bias, privacy breaches, safety risks or violations of policies. Protection against retaliation is paramount. Grievance redress refers to the formal process for handling complaints once raised. This involves acknowledging receipt, conducting fair and impartial investigations (often involving the Ethics Board), communicating findings and implementing appropriate remedies (e.g. system modification, compensation, policy changes, disciplinary action). This mechanism demonstrates commitment to accountability, provides a path to justice for affected parties and serves as an essential feedback loop for improving the overall governance system.

17.7. Metrics, reporting and continuous improvement

Moving beyond principles and frameworks, this section addresses the practical implementation and operationalization of ethical and social governance for AI-enabled supply chains. It focuses on how to measure performance, communicate it effectively and ensure the governance system evolves and improves over time. Without concrete metrics and feedback mechanisms, ethical governance remains aspirational rather than actionable.

17.7.1. *Defining key performance indicators (KPIs) for ethical and social performance of AI systems*

Defining key performance indicators (KPIs) for the ethical and social performance of AI systems is essential to translate abstract principles such as fairness, transparency and accountability into structured, trackable measures. This process involves aligning system behavior and impact with ethical challenges, enabling objective evaluation rather than subjective judgment. For instance, bias and fairness can be measured using demographic parity ratios, equal opportunity differences or complaint rates related to unfair AI decisions, while transparency and explainability may be assessed by tracking the use of explanation tools, user comprehension through surveys or model complexity. Accountability can be reinforced through documented ownership structures, incident resolution times and compliance with oversight protocols. Similarly, data privacy and security performance can be tracked via compliance with minimization principles, breach incidents and completion of AI-specific DPIAs. Labor impact indicators may include metrics on workforce augmentation versus automation, reskilling hours, mobility rates and employee sentiment. Environmental impact can be quantified by calculating the carbon footprint and monitoring efficiency improvements in AI operations (Sharma and Bhambri). Finally, stakeholder trust can be gauged through supplier satisfaction, customer trust in AI-driven claims and community sentiment towards deployments, thereby ensuring that ethical considerations are not only acknowledged but systematically measured and managed.

17.7.2. *Integrating ethical AI metrics into broader ESG reporting frameworks*

To avoid siloed reporting, ethical AI KPIs should be embedded within the broader Environmental, Social and Governance (ESG) framework, reinforcing that responsible AI governance is an integral part of organizational sustainability and credibility. Mapping these KPIs onto ESG pillars ensures coherence and addresses increasing investor and stakeholder demands for holistic disclosure. Under the social pillar, metrics such as labor impact, fairness in supplier relationships, worker well-being, data privacy, community effects and human rights due diligence directly contribute to diversity, equity and inclusion (DEI) goals, employee development and labor practices. The governance pillar encompasses KPIs tied to accountability structures, ethics boards, AI risk management, audit frequency, regulatory compliance and transparency mechanisms, highlighting oversight of emerging technology risks. Although less direct, the environmental pillar captures the carbon footprint and energy efficiency of AI operations, aligning technological growth with environmental responsibility. To ensure comparability and compliance, these AI-related KPIs should align with established standards such as GRI, SASB (now part of IFRS), TCFD and the EU's CSRD, with reporting that clearly demonstrates how AI is being ethically managed and its role in advancing or potentially challenging ESG objectives.

17.7.3. *Establishing feedback loops for continuous monitoring and improvement of AI governance practices*

Establishing feedback loops for continuous monitoring and improvement ensures that ethical AI governance evolves as technology, regulations and risks change, transforming governance from a static framework into a dynamic, learning system. This requires formal mechanisms for ongoing data collection from KPIs, incident reports, audits, feedback channels, grievance mechanisms, whistleblower reports, Ethics Board reviews and AI system performance logs. The collected information must then be regularly analyzed by the AI Ethics Board, governance committees and operational teams – typically on a quarterly or bi-annual basis – to identify trends, investigate root causes of issues such as spikes in bias, highlight successes and detect areas where governance controls or metrics fall short (Beta et al. 2025). Benchmarking against industry best practices and emerging standards further supports refinement, enabling organizations to adapt proactively and ensure that AI systems remain aligned with ethical principles and stakeholder expectations.

17.8. Case studies: navigating ethical dilemmas

This section presents anonymized or hypothetical real-world scenarios to demonstrate how organizations confront ethical challenges when deploying AI in supply chains. Each case focuses on a specific dilemma, analyzes the ethical tensions and outlines actionable governance strategies to resolve them.

17.8.1. *Illustrative examples (hypothetical or anonymized real-world) covering*

Global Retailer X implemented an AI tool to automate supplier vetting for efficiency and cost reduction, but audits revealed that the system disproportionately excluded SMEs from developing economies due to biased training data favoring large, established Western suppliers and proxies such as years in business or bank credit history. To address this, the company retrained the model with debiased datasets and fairness-aware algorithms, introduced human-in-the-loop checkpoints for SME applications and partnered with NGOs to identify high-potential marginalized suppliers. As a result, supplier diversity increased by 40%, strengthening supply chain resilience and aligning procurement practices with ESG objectives.

17.8.2. *Mitigating bias in AI-driven supplier selection*

Logistics Firm Y deployed an AI system to optimize delivery routes, achieving lower fuel costs and improved punctuality, but drivers soon raised concerns about unsafe routing through high-crime areas and unrealistic time pressures. The lack of transparency in the "black-box" algorithm left workers unable to challenge or understand the trade-offs being made, such as safety versus speed. To resolve this, the firm implemented Explainable AI (XAI) techniques such as SHAP values to clarify route-generation logic, introduced a driver feedback interface enabling real-time adjustments for safety and embedded ethical constraints in the model to avoid high-risk zones after dark. These changes improved both trust and safety, resulting in a 30% increase in driver satisfaction and a reduction in accident rates, effectively balancing efficiency with worker well-being.

17.8.3. *Implementing explainable AI for logistics routing affecting delivery workers*

E-Commerce Giant Z automated 60% of its warehouse picking and packing roles with AI-powered robots to enable round-the-clock operations, but this raised ethical concerns around worker displacement, lack of reskilling opportunities and disproportionate impacts on low-skilled labor. To address these challenges, the company adopted a "just transition" approach by launching a multi-year reskilling program in partnership with local technical colleges, offering redeployment guarantees such as transitioning displaced pickers into robot maintenance roles, and phasing automation rollouts gradually to reduce disruption (Sharma and Bhambri 2024). As a result, 85% of affected workers were successfully retained in new positions, helping the company maintain community trust and its social license to operate.

17.8.4. *Managing workforce transitions due to warehouse automation*

Pharma Company A leveraged IoT sensors to track temperature-sensitive shipments worldwide, but the collection of real-time location data raised risks of exposing sensitive delivery routes, such as vaccine shipments to conflict zones, and potential GDPR/CCPA violations through unintended employee tracking. To balance operational visibility with privacy, the company adopted federated learning to process data locally at the edge, reducing reliance on centralized pools, implemented role-based access controls that anonymized worker identities for non-security teams and introduced dynamic consent mechanisms enabling employees to disable location sharing during off-hours. These measures provided end-to-end supply chain visibility without privacy breaches, establishing a benchmark for ethical IoT deployment in the pharmaceutical sector.

17.9. Conclusion: toward responsible and trustworthy AI-powered supply chains

17.9.1. *Summarizing the critical role of ethical and social governance*

The deployment of AI within global supply chains is not merely a technological upgrade, it represents a profound transformation with far-reaching ethical and societal consequences. Throughout this chapter, we have established that ethical and social governance is not an optional add-on but a fundamental prerequisite for sustainable and resilient AI-powered operations. The core challenges – algorithmic bias leading to discriminatory sourcing or labor practices, the "black box" nature obscuring accountability, threats to data privacy, the potential for workforce displacement and the environmental costs of AI computation – pose significant risks to corporate reputation, legal compliance, operational stability and social license to operate (Rana and Bhambri 2024b). Robust governance acts as the essential safeguard against these risks. It ensures that AI-driven decisions align with human values, legal frameworks and societal expectations, thereby building trust – trust among workers whose jobs are impacted, suppliers competing in AI-driven marketplaces, consumers demanding ethical provenance and communities affected by supply chain activities. In a world increasingly focused on ESG performance, ethical AI governance is the linchpin connecting technological capability to long-term viability and positive social impact. It transforms AI from a potential source of disruption and harm into a force for efficiency and equity.

17.9.2. *Key takeaways for leaders: integrating ethics as a core strategic pillar*

For supply chain leaders and C-suite executives, the imperative is clear: ethics must be integrated as a core strategic pillar, not relegated to a compliance afterthought. This requires proactive and visible leadership commitment. Key actionable takeaways include (Moghadam et al. 2024):

– Ownership from the top: ethical AI governance requires explicit buy-in and accountability at the highest levels (CEO, Board). Leaders must champion ethical principles and allocate dedicated resources (budget, personnel).

– Embed ethics by design: ethical considerations must be woven into the entire AI lifecycle – from initial problem definition and data sourcing to model development, deployment and continuous monitoring. This demands a cross-functional collaboration between supply chain, IT, legal, HR and ethics/compliance teams.

– Prioritize transparency and explainability: invest in tools and processes (Explainable AI – XAI) that make AI decisions understandable to relevant stakeholders (e.g. why a supplier was deselected, how a delivery route was optimized). Develop clear communication strategies.

– Establish concrete governance structures: form dedicated AI Ethics Boards or Committees with diverse expertise (ethics, law, tech, SCM, social sciences) and clear mandates. Implement rigorous pre-deployment impact assessments and ongoing AI auditing protocols.

– Empower human oversight: define clear roles for "human-in-the-loop" or "human-in-command" oversight, ensuring that meaningful human judgment is applied to critical decisions, especially those impacting people or significant resources.

– Engage stakeholders proactively: actively involve workers, suppliers (especially SMEs), communities and civil society organizations in discussions about AI deployment impacts and governance frameworks. Foster co-creation where possible.

– Focus on workforce transition: develop and fund comprehensive strategies for reskilling and upskilling workers displaced or impacted by AI automation, ensuring a just transition.

– Measure and report: define specific KPIs for ethical AI performance (e.g. bias mitigation scores, audit completion rates, stakeholder satisfaction) and integrate these metrics into broader ESG reporting.

17.9.3. *The ongoing journey*

Achieving truly responsible and trustworthy AI-powered supply chains is not a destination, but a continuous journey of adaptation and improvement. The technological landscape is in constant flux, with new AI capabilities (such as generative AI) emerging rapidly, presenting novel ethical dilemmas. Regulatory frameworks are evolving globally (e.g. EU AI Act), demanding ongoing compliance vigilance. Societal expectations around fairness, privacy and corporate responsibility continue to rise. Therefore, governance frameworks cannot be static documents; they must be living systems capable of learning and evolving. Organizations must cultivate a culture of continuous ethical reflection, encouraging open dialogue about AI impacts and near-misses. Investment in ongoing education for all employees involved in AI development and deployment is crucial. Collaboration across industries, academia, policymakers and civil society is essential to share best practices, develop standards and address systemic challenges (Wang and Zhang 2025). Vigilance, adaptability and a long-term commitment to ethical principles are the hallmarks of organizations that will successfully navigate this complex terrain. By embracing this ongoing journey, businesses can ensure their AI-powered supply chains are not only efficient and resilient but also equitable, transparent and worthy of the trust of all stakeholders, thereby securing sustainable success in the disrupted world of tomorrow.

17.10. References

Beta, K., Nagaraj, S.S., Weerasinghe, T.D. (2025). The role of artificial intelligence on supply chain resilience. *J. Enterp. Inf. Manag.*, 38(3), 950–973.

Bhambri, P. (2025). Understanding AI and machine learning in security. In *Handbook of AI-Driven Threat Detection and Prevention: A Holistic Approach to Security*, Bhambri, P. and Anand, A.J. (eds). CRC Press, Boca Raton, 1–17. doi: 10.1201/9781003521020-1.

Bhambri, P. and Anand, A.J. (eds) (2025). *Handbook of AI-Driven Threat Detection and Prevention: A Holistic Approach to Security*. CRC Press. doi: 10.1201/9781003521020.

Bhambri, P. and Bajdor, P. (2024). Technological sustainability unveiled: A comprehensive examination of economic, social, and environmental dimensions. In *Handbook of Technological Sustainability: Innovation and Environmental Awareness*, Bhambri, P. and Bajdor, P. (eds). CRC Press, Boca Raton, 80–98. doi: 10.1201/9781003475989-8.

Bhambri, P. and Bajdor, P. (2025). AI-powered predictive analysis for proactive cyber defense. In *Handbook of AI-Driven Threat Detection and Prevention: A Holistic Approach to Security*, Bhambri, P. and Anand, A.J. (eds). CRC Press, Boca Raton, 308–321. doi: 10.1201/9781003521020-18.

Bhambri, P. and Hamad, A. (2025). Quantum computing and AI synergies: Strengthening cybersecurity resilience. In *Handbook of AI-Driven Threat Detection and Prevention: A Holistic Approach to Security*, Bhambri, P. and Anand, A.J. (eds). CRC Press, Boca Raton, 337–352. doi: 10.1201/9781003521020-20.

Bhambri, P. and Kant, S. (2025a). A taxonomy of bias in machine learning: Classification, sources, and implications for ethical AI. In *Proc. Lincoln-SPAST Global Sustainability Programme (SGS-24), 1st Int. Conf. L-GPR Program, SPAST Proc.*, 1(2).

Bhambri, P. and Kant, S. (2025b). Ethical AI systems: A comprehensive framework for bias mitigation and fairness in machine learning. In *Proc. Lincoln-SPAST Global Sustainability Programme (SGS-24), 2nd Int. Conf. L-GPR Program, SPAST Proc.*, 1(2).

Bhambri, P. and Khang, A. (2024). Machine learning advancements in E-health: Transforming digital healthcare. In *Medical Robotics and AI-Assisted Diagnostics for a High-Tech Healthcare Industry*, Khang, A. (ed.). IGI Global, Hershey, 174–194. doi: 10.4018/979-8-3693-2105-8.ch012.

Bhambri, P. and Kumar, S. (2024). Protecting sustainable supply chains from cyber threats. In *Digital Sustainability: Navigating Entrepreneurship in the Information Age*, Bhambri, P. and Paweloszek, I. (eds). CRC Press, Boca Raton, 125–141. doi: 10.1201/9781003484226-9.

Bhambri, P. and Pawełoszek, I. (2025). Deep learning techniques for intrusion detection in critical infrastructure. In *Handbook of AI-Driven Threat Detection and Prevention: A Holistic Approach to Security*, Bhambri, P. and Anand, A.J. (eds). CRC Press, Boca Raton, 322–336. doi: 10.1201/9781003521020-19.

Bhambri, P. and Rani, S. (2024a). Advancements and future challenges in business intelligence. In *Developing Managerial Skills for Global Business Success*, Barrena-Martinez, J., Foncubierta-Rodríguez, M., Medina-Garrido, J.A., Dobrowolski, Z. (eds). IGI Global, Hershey, 271–290. doi: 10.4018/979-8-3693-3057-9.ch017.

Bhambri, P. and Rani, S. (2024b). Ethical issues for climate change and mental health. In *Impact of Climate Change on Mental Health and Well-Being*, Samanta, D. and Garg, M. (eds). IGI Global, Hershey, 178–198. doi: 10.4018/979-8-3693-2177-5.ch012.

Bhambri, P. and Starostka-Patyk, M. (2025). Integrating AI with blockchain for decentralized security and threat prevention. In *Handbook of AI-Driven Threat Detection and Prevention: A Holistic Approach to Security*, Bhambri, P. and Anand, A.J. (eds). CRC Press, Boca Raton, 353–370. doi: 10.1201/9781003521020-21.

Bhambri, P., Rana, R., Kautish, S. (2025). Sustainable digital transformation: Reducing carbon footprint in the metaverse. In *Metaverse and Sustainability: Business Resilience Towards Sustainable Development Goals*, W.L. Filho, S. Kautish, V.P. Gupta (eds). Springer, Cham, 105–128. doi: 10.1007/978-3-031-89545-6_7.

Camilleri, M.A. (2024). Artificial intelligence governance: Ethical considerations and implications for social responsibility. *Expert Syst.*, 41(7), e13406.

Chithra, N. and Bhambri, P. (2024). Ethics in sustainable technology. In *Handbook of Technological Sustainability: Innovation and Environmental Awareness*, Bhambri, P. and Bajdor, P. (eds). CRC Press, Boca Raton, 245–256. doi: 10.1201/9781003475989-21.

Condé, L. and Münch, C. (2025). Resilient by design: Exploring the social abilities and actor-network roles of artificial intelligence in supply chain management. *J. Bus. Logist.*, 46(4), e70032.

Moghadam, M.R.S., Mansouri, T., Sahebi, I.G. (2024). Ethical dilemmas and solutions in the adoption of AI technologies in supply chain. *Commun. IIMA*, 22(1), 10.

Orenuga, A., Oyeyemi, B.B., Olufemi John, A. (2024). AI and sustainable supply chain practices: ESG goals in the US and Nigeria. *Int J Future Eng Innovations*, 1(1), 127–137.

Rana, R. and Bhambri, P. (2024a). Ethical considerations in artificial intelligence for environmental solutions: Striking a balance for sustainable innovation. In *Handbook of Technological Sustainability: Innovation and Environmental Awareness*, Bhambri, P. and Bajdor, P. (eds). CRC Press, Boca Raton, 389–396. doi: 10.1201/9781003475989-31.

Rana, R. and Bhambri, P. (2024b). Generative AI-driven security frameworks for web engineering: Innovations and challenges. In *Generative AI for Web Engineering Models*, Shah, I.A. and Jhanjhi, N.Z. (eds). IGI Global, Hershey, 285–296. doi: 10.4018/979-8-3693-3703-5.ch014.

Rane, N., Choudhary, S., Rane, J. (2024). Artificial intelligence driven approaches to strengthening Environmental, Social, and Governance (ESG) criteria in sustainable business practices: A review. *SSRN*. doi: 10.2139/ssrn.4843215.

Sah, B.P. and Shaikh, S. (2024). AI-driven IoT and blockchain integration in Industry 5.0: A systematic review of supply chain transformation. *Innovatech Eng. J.*, 1(01), 99–116.

Sharma, R. and Bhambri, P. (2024). Digital duplicity and the disintegration of trust: A quantitative inquiry into the impact of deep fakes on media sustainability and societal equilibrium. In *Handbook of Technological Sustainability: Innovation and Environmental Awareness*, Bhambri, P. and Bajdor, P. (eds). CRC Press, Boca Raton, 273–291. doi: 10.1201/9781003475989-24.

Suljic, V. (2025). Strategic leadership in AI-driven digital transformation: Ethical governance, innovation management, and sustainable practices for global enterprises and SMEs. *SBS J. Appl. Bus. Res.*, 13(1), 17–35.

Wang, S. and Zhang, H. (2025). Enhancing environmental, social, and governance performance through artificial intelligence supply chains in the energy industry: Roles of innovation, collaboration, and proactive sustainability strategy. *Renew. Energy*, 245, 122855.

Wu, H., Liu, J., Liang, B. (2025). AI-driven supply chain transformation in Industry 5.0: Enhancing resilience and sustainability. *Journal of the Knowledge Economy*, 16, 3826–3868. doi: 10.1007/s13132-024-01999-6.

18

Revolutionizing Supply Chains with Artificial Intelligence and Machine Learning: A Conceptual Model

Supply chains today move faster, involve more players and generate far larger data volumes than they did only a few years ago. Artificial intelligence (AI) and machine learning (ML) are now central to many firms' efforts to make these networks more agile, resilient and even self-learning. This chapter presents a phased framework for embedding AI and ML tools across each supply chain function, with the specific goals of boosting visibility, sharpening forecasts, improving choices and strengthening risk defences. Drawing on resource-based view and dynamic capabilities theory, the model maps the resources, routines and performance gains that accompany smart-technology adoption. In addition to advancing scholarly discourse, the chapter seeks to direct researchers and managers toward practical research directions by putting forth testable hypotheses and suggesting proof-of-concept locations in digitally mature supply chains.

18.1. Introduction

Volatility, complexity and uncertainty characterize the current global supply-chain environment, which is a result of the Covid-19 pandemic's aftereffects, increased geopolitical tensions and the quick development of digital technologies. Traditional supply-chain models, which frequently remain overly slow, rigid and essentially blind to demand projections in quickly changing markets, have fundamental flaws that have been brought to light by these forces (Younis et al. 2022; Singh 2023). AI and machine-learning applications are leading the current digital transformation in supply chains by processing enormous datasets, uncovering previously hidden patterns and enabling real-time, evidence-based decisions. The wide umbrella of AI

Chapter written by Sunitaa TANK, Manika GARG and Bharat Kumar TANK.

includes natural-language processing, robotics, computer vision and various machine-learning techniques, all of which attempt to replicate specific human-cognitive functions. Within this framework, ML sits as a narrower but powerful branch that teaches computers to learn from experience instead of strictly following pre-written rules. As supply networks often face rapid, unpredictable shifts, this adaptive trait makes ML particularly useful in that domain (Tirkolaee et al. 2021). Scholarly reviews of contemporary supply-chain management now regard ML and AI as foundational rather than adjunct technologies. Their disciplined application routinely underpins demand forecasting, inventory optimization, warehouse automation, transportation scheduling, and the identification and mitigation of systemic risk (Woschank et al. 2020). Unified AI dashboards permit risk officers to spot, assess and neutralize anomalies well ahead of traditional lagging signals, thereby safeguarding operational continuity and extending value beyond narrow efficiency gains (Baryannis et al. 2019). Recent analyses show that these systems function as strategic platforms that build durable value, spur innovation and strengthen resilience instead of mere stand-alone instruments (Belhadi et al. 2024). Current publications usually focus on discrete uses within particular industries or stages of the chain, leaving academics and practitioners without a shared reference that connects all findings through a single narrative strand (Younis et al. 2022). What the field needs now is an integrated blueprint that clearly illustrates how AI and ML features engage with each SCM function and aligns those encounters with larger strategic aims, such as operational agility, systemic resilience and overall firm performance.

To fill this noticeable gap in the literature, the present work introduces an early-stage conceptual framework that maps, in logical sequence, how AI and ML tools can be woven into routine supply-chain tasks. Built on resource-based-view (RBV) reasoning and bolstered by principles of dynamic-capability theory (DCT), the model identifies discrete AI and ML resources, traces their deployment through interrelated SCM activities and connects that flow to observable performance outcomes. By presenting these steps in a structured, visual manner, the framework hopes to steer future scholars toward system-wide questions while offering managers a straightforward guide for positioning AI and ML as deliberate levers of supply-chain improvement (Bhambri and Kumar 2024).

18.2. Literature review

Organizations have strengthened their supply chains through AI and ML, motivated by a quest for sharper data insights, leaner operations and networks capable of absorbing shocks. A systematic review by Younis et al. (2022) maps leading use cases, including demand forecasting, inventory optimization, supplier-risk assessment and logistics routing. Expanding on that theme, Tirkolaee et al. (2021) proposed a five-pillar framework for supply-chain management, grouping ML methods under demand forecasting, production planning, inventory control, logistics and risk management.

Demand-forecasting systems that combine long-historical-sales series with near-real-time indicators routinely outperform classical econometric benchmarks in out-of-sample examinations (Rai et al. 2021). On the factory floor, AI sorts production schedules, reallocates resources at speed and sustains either semiautonomous or fully autonomous decision nodes along the line (Cioffi et al. 2020). In transport and warehousing, ML engines power adaptive route optimization, enable live asset tracking, and direct robotic arms or automated stackers for unit handling (Woschank et al. 2020). Singh (2023) argues that these data-saturated workflows make supply chains both leaner and more reactive, perpetually balancing inventory and compressing lead times.

Risk management is emerging as the next proving ground for the discipline. Cloud-hosted risk-analytics dashboards can replay disruption scenarios, map supplier vulnerabilities and recommend tactical contingencies within minutes (Baryannis et al. 2019). As the platforms also ingest social media feeds, earnings releases and other unstructured streams, they translate qualitative signals into early warnings immediately actionable by logistics managers.

As global supply networks face more frequent and unpredictable shocks, many firms are turning to AI and ML to strengthen resilience and speed up response times. Belhadi et al. (2024) present empirical evidence showing that, when the business environment becomes highly volatile, AI-based innovations boost both overall supply-chain performance and resilience. Their study suggests that these digital tools help organizations sense, decide and adapt more quickly to a wide range of disruptions, whether triggered by geopolitical tensions or by health emergencies, such as the most recent pandemic. In a related line of enquiry, Soori et al. (2023) demonstrate that, when combined with AI, advanced robotics speeds up order processing and sharpens last-mile delivery, two core activities that underpin genuinely agile supply chains.

Adoption of AI and ML techniques is uneven across different industries. Sircar et al. (2021) examined the oil-and-gas supply chain and reported that predictive-maintenance models reduced equipment downtime, while ML forecasts streamlined inventory decisions. In agriculture, Liu (2020) demonstrated how AI-linked sensors track produce from the farm gate to supermarket shelves and how yield now estimates incorporate real-time weather data. Taking that research further, Belhadi et al. (2025) developed an ensemble-model framework that evaluates credit risk for small-and-medium agricultural firms, thereby connecting supply activities with finance and investment choices. Onukwulu et al. (2023) presented an end-to-end energy-logistics model guided by real-time demand forecasts, and Saurabh and Dey (2021) showed that pairing AI with blockchain improves transparency in sustainable agri-food networks. Together, these studies confirm that AI and ML tools are flexible enough to meet the distinct requirements of many different sectors.

Research on AI and ML in supply-chain management is expanding rapidly, but several fundamental gaps remain. First, many published accounts consist mainly of descriptive case studies or experimental prototypes, without a unifying theoretical framework that ties particular AI and ML techniques to strategic and operational objectives (Younis et al. 2022). Rigorous future investigations could close this gap by developing formal models that connect each tool with dynamic capabilities and measurable supply-chain outcomes, tested across different contexts. Second, factors such as a robust digital backbone, disciplined data governance and ongoing executive support are seldom examined, yet they often determine whether organizations can successfully deploy new technologies (Dhamija and Bag 2020). As a result, scholars have yet to offer clear, evidence-based pathways that managers can follow to prepare their firms for larger-scale, sustainable adoption.

Security threats arising from AI-generated insights such as adversarial inputs and latent backdoors have yet to receive sustained attention in supply-chain research, leaving central issues of trust and regulatory compliance inadequately addressed (Gu et al. 2017). Similarly, scholars recognize that AI now operates alongside IoT, blockchain and edge computing (Hassija et al. 2020; Mohanta et al. 2020), but systematic evidence on how this technology convergence alters supply-chain performance is still thin and urgently needed.

18.3. Methodology

This chapter takes a conceptual tack, a choice that proves valuable when researchers encounter thin or fast-moving empirical evidence and still need to weave a coherent theoretical story. AI and its narrower sibling, ML, are spreading through virtually every supply-chain function at break-neck speed; by focusing on the big ideas first, the authors can corral scattered reports into a single, step-by-step map of future possibilities. Rather than launching new surveys or experiments, they lean on deductive reasoning, strategic theory-mixing and close reading of published work to sketch out a model for how AI and ML might reshape supply chains at the strategic level. In building the model, the authors systematically sifted the literature for anchor concepts, key technologies and measurable business outcomes tied to AI and

ML in SCM. They searched Scopus, Web of Science and ScienceDirect with the targeted phrases AI, machine learning, supply-chain management, logistics, inventory optimization and demand forecasting, and narrowed the results to articles published between 2017 and early 2024.

The review strategically chose a publication window that captures the discipline's leading-edge software and present-day usage patterns. During the final search phase, the team restricted attention to peer-reviewed articles in English only, deliberately omitting conference abstracts, editorials and gray-unpublished papers as a safeguard for methodological soundness. Studies describing AI and ML initiatives with explicit bearing on supply-chain management were therefore preserved. As a result, investigations of predictive analytics, risk mitigation, delivery routing, warehouse automation and intelligence-augmented procurement cleared the initial screen. After applying those thematic filters alongside a demanding quality threshold, 30 records from respected regional and international journals emerged for systematic scrutiny (Bhambri et al. 2024). The investigators then performed inductive thematic coding to map recurring concepts, tools, competencies and performance indicators across diverse industries and jurisdictions. Illustrative entries on the resulting matrix include Baryannis et al. (2019), Cioffi et al. (2020), Younis et al. (2022) and Belhadi et al. (2024), each demonstrating how AI and ML interweave with particular supply-chain tasks. The ensuing analysis draws on RBV and DCT as its primary theoretical anchors.

18.4. Conceptual model

The increasing complexity of contemporary supply chains – from geopolitical shocks and market uncertainty to rapid digitization – requires management systems that are not only advanced but also continuously adaptive and intelligent. Drawing on existing research and anchored in the RBV and DCT, the following model articulates a strategic pathway for embedding AI and ML into supply-chain management, with the aim of lifting overall performance, resilience and agility.

Theoretical foundation

Resource-based view theory maintains that a firm's lasting edge arises from its ability to acquire and deploy resources that are valuable, rare, inimitable and non-substitutable. In today's digital economy, integrated AI and ML platforms achieve that VRIN mark only when paired with a sturdy data foundation, seasoned personnel and processes shaped for a specific context. Dynamic-capabilities theory adds that companies operating in rapidly changing markets must continuously sense, seize and reconfigure their resource mix. AI and ML undergird these actions by delivering near-real-time sensing instruments, such as anomaly detectors, demand-forecast algorithms that steer seizing moves and automated routing engines that smooth the path to ongoing reconfiguration.

Key constructs in the conceptual model: the model is organized in three distinct yet interconnected layers.

18.4.1. *AI/ML capabilities (input layer)*

– Predictive analytics.

– Reinforcement learning.

– Natural language processing (NLP).

– Computer vision.

– Deep learning and neural networks.

18.4.2. *SCM functional integration (process layer/mediators)*

– Demand forecasting: accuracy and responsiveness using real-time data (Rai et al. 2021).

– Inventory management: stocking levels through predictive consumption models (Tirkolaee et al. 2021).

– Procurement and supplier selection: risk assessment using historical and real-time information (Younis et al. 2022).

– Logistics and distribution: route optimization, delivery tracking and warehouse automation (Woschank et al. 2020).

– Risk and disruption management: early detection and corrective action through scenario simulation (Baryannis et al. 2019; Belhadi et al. 2024).

18.4.3. *Performance outcomes (output layer)*

– Supply-chain agility: speed of reaction to market changes and unforeseen events.

– Supply-chain resilience: ability to recover and remain stable during stress.

– Operational efficiency: optimization of costs, time and resources.

– Firm performance: sustained competitive advantage and enhanced value creation.

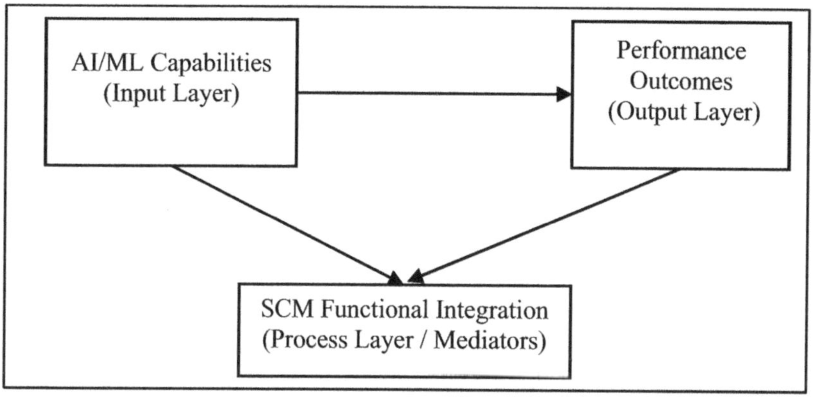

Figure 18.1. *Conceptual model*

18.5. Findings

An extensive literature review demonstrates that AI and ML tools are steadily becoming routine elements of supply-chain management (SCM). Guided by the RBV and DCT, this chapter draws together recent empirical studies and singles out five interlinked topics summarizing the strategic promise and the day-to-day practices reshaped by these technologies. The first topic documents firms embedding AI and ML into core SCM tasks such as demand forecasting, inventory tuning, logistics routing, procurement pricing and risk appraisal. By doing so, organizations are moving away from reactive, rule-of-thumb choices and toward proactive, data-informed operations steered by real-time evidence. Demand-forecasting platforms now enriched with AI combine streaming market signals with decades of historical data, boosting accuracy, cutting safety stock and relieving both stock-outs and excess inventory (Tirkolaee et al. 2021; Singh 2023). Likewise, machine-learning engines in logistics revise routes and schedule fleets continuously, speeding deliveries while reducing transport costs (Woschank et al. 2020). The review also isolates a second, closely related point: senior executives increasingly treat resilience and agility as prima-facie corporate assets in an environment shaken by geopolitical tensions and public-health crises.

Recent studies demonstrate that AI-driven insights now detect potential disruptions sooner, adapt supply chains on the fly and offer real-time recommendations at moments of peak uncertainty (Baryannis et al. 2019; Belhadi et al. 2024).

Correspondingly, organizational agility profits from predictive analytics and smart automation, enabling firms to alter their course almost instantaneously whenever market signals, or urgent customer requests, shift. Nevertheless, these advantages cannot simply emerge by chance; realizing them depends on a coherent data architecture, a digital-first attitude across the organization, competent staff capable of turning strategy into practice, and continuous backing from senior leaders (Rana and Bhambri 2024a). Companies that build solid data ecosystems and map precise digital trajectories consistently leave rivals behind, converting the potential of AI and ML into concrete performance improvements and lasting competitive edge. Due to this, context shapes value realization and should occupy a central position in any framework guiding technology deployment. The framework advanced here clarifies the causal pathways through which AI and ML produce superior firm performance, identifying enhancements in supply-chain-management functions as the key mediating conduit; consequently, gains arise not from a simple mathematical formula but from shorter lead times, higher service levels and improved cost efficiency.

The proposed pyramid explicitly translates digital indicators into tactical results and provides a graduated guideline for scholars intending to validate the construct in practice. Beyond the conceptual overview, the case studies itemize distinct, domain-driven uses and recent breakthroughs. In agriculture, for instance, machine-learning routines autonomously authenticate product origin, while in the energy sector, prognostic algorithms schedule turbine repairs ahead of imminent breakdown (Liu 2020; Onukwulu et al. 2023). These illustrations demonstrate that AI and its associated tools can be finely tuned to the unique limitations and prospects present in any given chain. Taken together, the empirical findings map out a coherent path for embedding such systems into day-to-day supply-chain operations. With that foundation, the assembled analysis positions AI and ML as catalysts for heightened agility, durability and performance in networks orientated toward a digital-first economy. By anchoring this assertion in established theoretical models, the framework begins to fill an important void in the academic debate about the large-scale evolution of supply systems.

18.6. Implications

Current applications of AI and ML in supply-chain management supply practical insights for both senior executives and front-line operations teams. The framework laid out in this chapter shows that these technologies do much more than lower personnel costs or perform routine tasks more quickly: they force organizations to reconsider strategic priorities, to redesign execution workflows and to create sustainable advantages in fast-moving markets. For supply-chain executives, the evidence confirms that digital technologies should be woven into the wider corporate strategy instead of managed as separate sets of gadgets or pilots. The roll-out of AI and ML thereby becomes a leadership responsibility, demanding a clear vision, ongoing executive backing and a workplace culture that elevates every decision with accurate, real-time data (Rana and Bhambri 2024b). Senior managers are therefore urged to sponsor only those AI and ML projects that strengthen priorities such as operational agility, customer-focused service and organizational resilience. Sustaining such initiatives calls for disciplined funding of the basic digital infrastructure clean, live datasets, scalable secure platforms and clear pathways for their expansion and for skilled personnel able to exploit them. Teams perform best when data scientists, supply-chain planners and IT specialists work side by side; managers should formalize this collaboration in cross-functional pods and commit budget, time and incentives to up-skilling existing staff in data literacy and change-management practices.

Performance-assessment frameworks must evolve on an ongoing basis; contemporary success is no longer defined solely by lower costs or higher output, but by sharper predictive accuracy, increased resilience to disruption and a faster response to shifting market conditions. In light of these broader objectives, the associated key performance indicators and escalation protocols embedded in each framework should be systematically recalibrated to record and analyze the new dimensions of performance. Equally important, sustained stakeholder engagement, coupled with structured change-management practices, remains essential for translating upgraded technical capabilities into enduring business value. When team members, suppliers, partners and end customers lack trust in the system and in one another, momentum toward automation and data-driven decision-making typically falters. To mitigate this risk, managers are encouraged to involve vendors alongside their own staff in continuous training, open, transparent communication, and a series of small joint pilot projects that demonstrate immediate benefits and gradually acclimate all participants to the use of AI.

18.7. Conclusion

Guided by a structured review and framed through the resource-based view alongside dynamic capabilities theory, this chapter puts forward a fresh model that shows that these technologies can boost agility, resilience and overall performance in digitally connected supply networks. Evidence drawn from the literature points to a wide range of applications that demand forecasting, inventory control, transport planning, procurement and risk assessment, where AI and ML deliver tangible gains in accuracy, speed and responsiveness. Beyond these operational wins, the tools strengthen firms' dynamic abilities by improving their capacity to sense shifts, seize new opportunities and rearrange processes on-the-fly. However, the promise of AI and ML will be realized only when advanced algorithms sit atop clean, timely data, when people and culture are ready to adapt, and when leaders steer the effort with a clear digital vision. In this way, the study adds a coherent blueprint to supply-chain scholarship, mapping how AI and ML resources link with specific functions and, ultimately, with superior organizational performance. The model not only clarifies existing theories but also offers a coherent platform on which later researchers can build the empirical tests needed to confirm or adjust the proposed links. As supply chains grow increasingly volatile, the deliberate embedding of AI and ML shifts from a forward-looking possibility to an immediate necessity. For managers, analysts and academic scholars alike, this work serves as both a guiding map and an urgent invitation: treat AI and ML not as stand-alone gadgets, but as integral, learning-driven elements of a resilient, responsive supply-chain architecture.

18.8. Future research directions

This chapter advances a conceptual model that connects AI and ML with both strategic and operational supply-chain outcomes, yet multiple noteworthy research paths remain untapped. As these technologies improve at an unprecedented pace and supply chains are becoming more digital and decentralized, scholars are called to test, fine-tune and widen the framework presented here. The first priority is to conduct large-sample empirical tests of the model in varied industries and geographic regions. Although the current version offers general pathways through which AI and ML shape supply-chain functions, sector-specific factors in manufacturing, agriculture, pharmaceuticals or e-commerce may strengthen or weaken those links. Surveys, combined with structural-equation modeling (SEM), are well suited to examine the model's predictive power and to reveal how context alters its structures. A second important avenue is the identification of organizational enablers and obstacles to AI and ML adoption in supply-chain management. Researchers should measure how leadership, data infrastructure, digital skills and corporate culture influence the success of these technologies. Longitudinal case studies will then illustrate the step-by-step transformation of firms moving from conventional systems to AI-enhanced supply chains. Third, investigations are needed into how AI and ML merge with other up-and-coming tech, including the Internet of Things, blockchain, edge computing and fifth-generation mobile networks. These tools increasingly work together to create smart operating environments, so their joint influence on supply-chain management processes and decision-making deserves a close study. Questions abound: for instance, in what ways does AI-IoT coupling deepen real-time visibility for cold-chain logistics? Also, how do shared ledgers and ML jointly boost supplier trust and item traceability? Fourth, as talk of algorithm bias, misuse and data breaches climbs, attention must turn to the risks and guardrails tied to AI within supply-chain ecosystems. Scholars might craft practical frameworks that promote responsible model use, uphold transparency and ensure fairness in choices such as vendor selection, staff scheduling or credit assignment. Fifth, the study of the human–AI partnership remains urgent. Much existing writing pictures AI as an independent decision engine, but real supply chains are social–technical blends where people and machines co-act. New research should map ways to align human judgment and artificial insight, spotlighting trust, interpretability and targeted training as vital links. Finally, scholars can build performance-score systems that look well beyond cost and output speed. Sustainable rankings might include measures of customer experience, ecological impact and social equity. A comprehensive evaluation of AI and ML in sustainable supply chains could include metrics such as predictive accuracy, flexibility to new conditions, carbon abatement and overall customer experience.

18.9. References

Baryannis, G., Validi, S., Dani, S., Antoniou, G. (2019). Supply chain risk management and AI: State of the art and future research directions. *International Journal of Production Research*, 57(7), 2179–2202.

Belhadi, A., Mani, V., Kamble, S.S., Khan, S.A.R., Verma, S. (2024). AI-driven innovation for enhancing supply chain resilience and performance under the effect of supply chain dynamism: An empirical investigation. *Annals of Operations Research*, 333(2), 627–652.

Belhadi, A., Kamble, S.S., Mani, V., Benkhati, I., Touriki, F.E. (2025). An ensemble MLapproach for forecasting credit risk of agricultural SMEs' investments in agriculture 4.0 through supply chain finance. *Annals of Operations Research*, 345(2), 779–807.

Bhambri, P. and Kumar, S. (2024). Protecting sustainable supply chains from cyber threats. In *Digital Sustainability: Navigating Entrepreneurship in the Information Age*, Bhambri, P. and Paweloszek, I. (eds). CRC Press, Boca Raton, 125–141. doi: 10.1201/9781003484226-9.

Bhambri, P., Rani, S., Khang, A. (2024). AI-driven digital twin and resource optimization in Industry 4.0 ecosystem. In *Intelligent Techniques for Predictive Data Analytics*, Singh, N., Birla, S., Ansari, M.D., Shukla, N.K. (eds). Wiley-IEEE Press, New York, 47–69. doi: 10.1002/9781394227990.ch3.

Cioffi, R., Travaglioni, M., Piscitelli, G., Petrillo, A., De Felice, F. (2020). AI and ML applications in smart production: Progress, trends, and directions. *Sustainability*, 12(2), 492.

Dhamija, P. and Bag, S. (2020). Role of AI in operations environment: A review and bibliometric analysis. *The TQM Journal*, 32(4), 869–896.

Gu, T., Dolan-Gavitt, B., Garg, S. (2017). Badnets: Identifying vulnerabilities in the MLmodel supply chain. *arXiv preprint*. doi: 10.48550/arXiv.1708.06733.

Hassija, V., Chamola, V., Gupta, V., Jain, S., Guizani, N. (2021). A survey on supply chain security: Application areas, security threats, and solution architectures. *IEEE Internet of Things Journal*, 8(8), 6222–6246. doi: 10.1109/JIOT.2020.3025775.

Liu, S.Y. (2020). AI in agriculture. *IT Professional*, 22(3), 14–15.

Mohanta, B.K., Jena, D., Satapathy, U., Patnaik, S. (2020). Survey on IoT security: Challenges and solution using machine learning, AI and blockchain technology. *Internet of Things*, 11, 100227.

Onukwulu, E.C., Agho, M.O., Eyo-Udo, N.L. (2023). Developing a framework for AI-driven optimization of supply chains in energy sector. *Global Journal of Advanced Research and Reviews*, 1(2), 82–101.

Pallathadka, H., Ramirez-Asis, E.H., Loli-Poma, T.P., Kaliyaperumal, K., Ventayen, R.J.M., Naved, M. (2023). Applications of AI in business management, e-commerce and finance. *Materials Today: Proceedings*, 80, 2610–2613.

Rai, R., Tiwari, M.K., Ivanov, D., Dolgui, A. (2021). ML in manufacturing and Industry 4.0 applications. *International Journal of Production Research*, 59(16), 4773–4778.

Rana, R. and Bhambri, P. (2024a). Hybrid MCDM (multi-criteria decision-making) approaches for sustainable energy management. In *Modern SuperHyperSoft Computing Trends in Science and Technology*, Smarandache, F. and Majumder, P. (eds). IGI Global, Hershey, 149–184. doi: 10.4018/979-8-3693-6875-6.ch006.

Rana, R. and Bhambri, P. (2024b). Environmental challenges and technological solutions. In *Handbook of Technological Sustainability: Innovation and Environmental Awareness*, Bhambri, P. and Bajdor, P. (eds). CRC Press, Boca Raton, 187–200. doi: 10.1201/9781003475989-17.

Saurabh, S. and Dey, K. (2021). Blockchain technology adoption, architecture, and sustainable agri-food supply chains. *Journal of Cleaner Production*, 284, 124731.

Singh, P.K. (2023). Digital transformation in supply chain management: AI and ML as catalysts for value creation. *International Journal of Supply Chain Management*, 12(6), 57–63.

Sircar, A., Yadav, K., Rayavarapu, K., Bist, N., Oza, H. (2021). Application of ML and AI in oil and gas industry. *Petroleum Research*, 6(4), 379–391.

Soori, M., Arezoo, B., Dastres, R. (2023). AI, ML and deep learning in advanced robotics: A review. *Cognitive Robotics*, 3, 54–70.

Syam, N. and Sharma, A. (2018). Waiting for a sales renaissance in the fourth industrial revolution: ML and AI in sales research and practice. *Industrial Marketing Management*, 69, 135–146.

Tirkolaee, E.B., Sadeghi, S., Mooseloo, F.M., Vandchali, H.R., Aeini, S. (2021). Application of ML in supply chain management: A comprehensive overview of the main areas. *Mathematical Problems in Engineering*, 2021(1), 1476043.

Woschank, M., Rauch, E., Zsifkovits, H. (2020). A review of further directions for AI, machine learning, and deep learning in smart logistics. *Sustainability*, 12(9), 3760.

Younis, H., Sundarakani, B., Alsharairi, M. (2022). Applications of AI and ML within supply chains: Systematic review and future research directions. *Journal of Modelling in Management*, 17(3), 916–940.

19

Enabling AI in Supply Chain Transformation: An MCDM-Based Analysis of Critical Success Factors

This chapter examines the transformative role of artificial intelligence (AI) in improving proficiency and transparency within supply chain management (SCM). Determined by the strains of Industry 4.0 and the rise of Logistics 4.0, AI offers significant potential for optimizing various aspects of the supply chain, including transportation, demand forecasting, inventory control and warehousing operations. Through a comprehensive literature review and the application of the Simple Multi-Attribute Rating Technique (SMART), this chapter identifies critical success factors for AI adoption in SCM and evaluates the effectiveness of different AI-powered strategies. A sensitivity analysis further examines the robustness of these strategies under varying conditions.

The findings highlight the dominance of a data-driven approach in maximizing the benefits of AI in SCM, emphasizing the need for strategic technology investments, workforce training and a supportive organizational culture. This research provides valuable insights for manufacturers seeking to leverage AI for enhanced efficiency, transparency and competitiveness in the evolving landscape of Industry 4.0.

19.1. Introduction

The rapidly evolving business landscape today necessitates the adoption of advanced technologies to augment the performance and transparency of supply chain management (SCM). One of the key facilitators in this evolution has been artificial intelligence (AI), which has become an intrinsic part of the transition from Logistics 4.0 to a new set of operational paradigms across various sectors, and one such sector has been agri-food.

Chapter written by Tripti SHARMA, Akash RAI, Indrajit GHOSAL and Md. Rahat KHAN.

The use of AI in SCM extends beyond traditional optimization methods and often holds transformative potential. This includes strategic decision-making facilities like selecting suppliers under operation efficiency, coupled with sustainability evaluation. This capability also becomes more pertinent with rising acceptance of a new management approach under the label of green supply chain management (GSCM), which is increasingly popular due to greater environmental awareness around the world.

AI in SCM applications is complex, with functionalities ranging from optimizing transportation routes to increasing the accuracy of demand forecasting and inventory management. AI automates these convoluted processes and allows companies to significantly cut down on operational costs, shorten the delivery window and improve customer satisfaction.

AI has been a similarly important catalyst in driving supply chain transparency. AI leads the new era of SCM by giving stakeholders visibility of the physical and digital movement of goods and services in real time, enabling all parties involved across the network to access timely, accurate information upon which they can rely for improved performance partnerships within an interdependent operational ecosystem.

This research looks into the different uses of AI for more efficient and transparent supply chains. This chapter also investigates the prospects of employing AI in SCM and some of the hurdles that come with it and provides a perspective on how organizations could configure these technologies to improve their competitiveness in today's industrial scenario.

19.1.1. *Background*

A move toward Industry 4.0 (and soon also Industry 5.0), with a range of different supply chain aspects in the process of being digitized, has provided fertile ground for Logistics 4.0 to take over. At the heart of this is AI centered around how products and services are created, delivered and consumed. AI is the enabler behind Logistics 4.0, as it has the potential to process massive datasets, automate intricate workflows and enable intelligent decision-making processes. AI is ripe with possibility in SCM, allowing myriad benefits that can lead to efficiency, transparency and sustainability.

Key uses of AI in SCM:

– Advanced demand prediction: AI delivers a new dimension to the domain of demand forecasting, where it can appear by leveraging historical sales data, market trends and several other factors. This allows them to keep inventory levels in check and prevents stockouts while reducing waste.

– Enhanced inventory management: real-time inventory follow-up and automatic replenishment make it much easier for AI-infused systems to control the inventory more efficiently. This method reduces inventory storage costs, prevents stockouts and increases order-fill rates.

– Automation of warehouses: AI automation enables robots to perform their needs in core warehouse activities such as picking, packing and shipping. This automation in turn leads to productivity gains, reduces labor costs and minimizes the possibility of operational errors.

– Real-time tracking and monitoring: real-time tracking of cargo via AI provides the concerned parties with continuous visibility throughout the life cycle of an order. This level of visibility builds trust, creates stronger partners and improves total supply chain awareness.

– Using these capacities concurrently, AI not only enhances operational effectiveness but also supports strategic goals of building an environmentally friendly and transparent supply chain aligned with the principles of the Fourth Industrial Revolution.

19.1.2. *Objective of study*

– Develop an evaluation of key AI technologies and apps that can improve efficiency and transparency in supply chains.

– Ensure programming/model functioning works closely with the tech development team.

– Build the multi-criteria decision-making (MCDM) model for assessing intelligent combination strategies from the supply chain perspective.

– Apply the MCDM model to a case study of real life and thus emphasize the importance of AI on supply chain efficiency and transparency.

19.2. Literature review

Chen et al. (2024) reviewed a wide range of AI techniques such as machine learning (ML), metaheuristics and reinforcement learning (RL) for routing, fleet planning and network design under carbon and energy constraints. Their research laid the groundwork for bridging techniques with problems such as VRP variants as well as insights into intermodal planning with AI-optimization hybrids. The authors emphasized quantifiable Key Performance Indicators (KPIs), including both fuel and

CO_2 emissions, as well as lead time, while also giving an account of how carbon pricing comes into play with the model objectives. Two potential bottlenecks for adoption are identified as data fragmentation and explainability, while a research agenda on greener, AI-supported logistics operations is suggested.

Qu and Kim (2024) provided a Preferred Reporting Items for Systematic Reviews and Meta-Analyses (PRISMA)-guided review of 170 Scopus articles related to AI, Big Data, IoT and decision support systems against Sustainable Supply Chain Management (SSCM) outcomes. They uncovered ten themes according to the nature of operation and deployment based on topic modeling Latent Dirichlet Allocation (LDA) proving from supplier selection, transport optimization to renewable energy integration. While environmental and economic dimensions seem well covered, their review suggests that social sustainability is still underexplored. The authors presented a mechanical framework of a dynamic SSCM, outlining 20 specific research propositions and offering practical guidance for aligning AI projects with the Supply Chain Operations Reference (SCOR) process to effectively achieve sustainability goals.

Moosavi et al. (2024) surveyed XAI techniques such as SHAP, LIME, saliency maps and counterfactual explanations in a broad context of quality control, predictive maintenance and process optimization within manufacturing/industrial CPS. They examined the trade-offs between fidelity and interpretability, followed by an exploration of run-time considerations in shop-floor settings. To this end, the authors suggested the use of model cards and traceability mechanisms in regulated sectors and aligns XAI principles with ISO/IEC AI governance guidance. They also recommended some design patterns, for instance, integration of digital twins and XAI dashboards.

A systematic review by Drissi Elbouzidi et al. (2023), which synthesizes 277 publications, identified 22 core studies on AI-driven Warehouse Digital Twins (WDTs). The research charted the progression of WDT maturity from digital models to digital shadows and finally to integrated digital twins. The analysis connected specific AI techniques to operational functions; for example, reinforcement learning optimizes flow control, while computer vision ensures safety and quality. The authors concluded that interoperability and a lack of standards are significant barriers and, in response, developed a maturity scale to evaluate WDT implementation in intralogistics.

Bhattacharya et al. (2023) investigated the human-in-the-loop (HIL) paradigm in production intensification, drawing a line from Industry 4.0 to Industry 5.0 and promoting an "Industry X.0" mixed strategy during transformational stages. The study reviewed the cases of cyber–physical systems in which human operators oversee and control AI for scheduling, visualization and cyber-security. The authors also highlighted the need to adopt metric and standards to field HIL performance evaluation while also drawing attention to the fact that, despite factories being highly automated, human intervention is critical for safety checks and ethical oversight. As a result, they determined shortcomings concerning benchmarking methods and coping with bias within human–machine interaction pipelines.

Teixeira et al. (2025) explored what it is that brings together AI use cases across the successive value-adding processes of SCM identified in plan, source, make, delivery, return and enable phases. Some of the applications featured in the review included ML for demand forecasting, natural language processing for risk detection, computer vision for quality control and RL for dynamic routing. Finally, the number of authors comparing datasets and evaluation metrics between studies is a few paragraphs longer, but fundamental considerations around governance, data quality, model drift management and ethical guidelines are presumably welcomed. They suggested a research agenda that focuses on interpretability and human–AI cooperation in the supply chain.

A critical review by Douaioui et al. (2024) explored classical ML techniques to deep learning (DL) architectures, such as Convolutional Neural Networks (CNNs), Recurrent Neural Networks (RNNs) and Transformers forecasting models of SCM. We investigated their behavior for various forecast horizons: how they can deal with seasonality (if at all), whether exogenous variables are supported, and which kind of cross-validation is available. Some of the most common include data leakage, using error metrics in a detrimental way and weak baselines. The authors suggested a combination of hybrid models and probabilistic forecasts as ways to address supply risks and share learnings for dataset design and deployment.

Samuels (2025) found state-of-the-art synthesis on the application of AI in SCM from Industry 4.0 to Industry 6.0, specifically around forecasting, inventory optimization and resilience. The main recommendation from the review was sustainability and cybersecurity. The two most important issues facing AI in the future will be favored by an insistence on human–AI co-working and skill development. The study documents the efforts of supply chain partners around AI, characterizes governance and interoperability as perpetual roadblocks in bridging them and highlights a series of recommended readings for policymakers and practitioners to effectively leverage AI.

Daios et al. (2025) provided a comprehensive overview and analysis of AI applications in key supply chain functions, including customer relationship management, procurement, inventory management, delivery forecasting, and risk management. This presents an algorithm-task-fit matrix and includes research in a supply network with graph neural networks, routing with RL and disruption news analysis by NLP. The authors then discussed the common practice of MLOps such as drift monitoring, retraining schedules and data lineage, along with the need for ethical and explainability considerations to create partner trust. The study provides a seminal source for companies establishing the path to AI adoption in supply chains.

Xu et al. (2021) offered a fresh take on multi-agent supply chain automation since the technology for integrative consumer-driven manufacturing is now more mature, thanks to capabilities in IoT, distributed ledgers and ML. The authors suggest it enables intelligent agents to go beyond basic automation and achieve full autonomy in perception, planning and action. In particular, a new framework is considered for supply chain using modern strategies by using agent technology and research issues are explained, such as interoperability problems while sharing the structure of legal responsibilities among various parties who contributed to the contract. The research establishes the relationship between agent-based systems and recent transparency and traceability cyber–physical structures suitable for the Logistics 4.0 landscape.

Tran (2021) gives an overview of the role of AI as the "brain" of smart manufacturing and covers emerging topics including predictive maintenance, RL in scheduling, explainable monitoring and digital twins. As in the current literature, this perspective serves as an introduction to a special issue in "sensors", bringing together 19 contributions on these related topics (specified below) and setting future research directions. It provides a top-level entry point for drivers and reacts to directed readings on applications of AI in manufacturing.

19.3. Methodology

Simple Multi-Attribute Rating Technique (SMART) is a decision support tool in the form of a structured methodology used to evaluate and rank different choices in smart manufacturing transformation initiatives. It starts by establishing a list of criteria that are context-dependent criteria (e.g. technological readiness, net benefit ratio, risk of business operation disruption and alignment with company goals). Alternatives are then judged against these criteria, while each criterion is given a weight based on its relative importance. These weighted evaluations are summed up to a number, which allows decision-makers to know what the best strategy for their transformation journey should be. Hence, this methodology enables a robust, transparent and continuous assessment process which achieves decision-making informed by the competitive and swift-shifting manufacturing industry.

19.3.1. *Framework of methodology*

– Step 1: critical success factor (CSF) weightage.

A total of 19 critical success factors (CSFs) were extracted, and then 19 weights were assigned to show the significance level out of these CSFs.

– Step 2: normalization of weights.

Then, weights assigned to each criterion were normalized so as they summed up to 1.0.

– Step 3: choice of data-driven vs. phase-based.

The effectiveness of the two strategies (data-driven, phased-based) was assessed in relation to five CSFs using a 1–3 performance scale (1 = poor, 3 = excellent).

– Step 4: calculate weighted scores.

These weighted scores were calculated by multiplying the assessment score of a CSF by its normalized weight. We present these results in two bar charts, which show performance distinctions across the strategies.

– Step 5: final score comparison.

All CSFs had an aggregated score, which were compared, and the data-driven way had a higher overall score on comparison. It was thus a better strategy here.

– Step 6: sensitivity analysis.

Through sensitivity analysis, the most impactful CSFs were isolated, and wiser knowledge was highlighted to drive risk mitigation and strategic scheduling of actions.

Through this systematic SMART-based evaluation, we can identify a data-driven pathway as the optimal strategy toward smart manufacturing transition over efficiency and adaptability with minimal risks.

Critical success factor (CSF)	Weight guideline	Normalized weight
Top management support	5	0.0793651
Resilient supply chain (SC)	5	0.0793651
Recycling factories	5	0.0793651
Metaheuristics	5	0.0793651

Critical success factor (CSF)	Weight guideline	Normalized weight
Operations research (OR)	–	0.047619
Gas consumption	3	0.047619
Carbon footprint	3	0.047619
Green supplier criteria	3	0.047619
Data-driven simulation	3	0.047619
Non-dominated sorting genetic algorithm	5	0.0793651
Predictable behavior	5	0.0793651
Digital SCM	3	0.047619

Table 19.1. *Assigning weights to critical success factors (CSFs)*

The identified weight guidelines of the identified CSFs for smart manufacturing technologies and practices are presented in Table 20.1 with their normalized weights.

– CSF: key elements or strategic factors that are critically important for the acceptance, adoption and effectiveness of smart manufacturing initiatives.

– Weight recommendation: this represents the weight with which each CSF has started. Hence, higher values imply high importance assigned to transformation objectives.

– Normalized weight: once initial weights were assigned, they were then normalized so the total sum of all weights averaged at 1.0. This standardization maintains the relative importance of each CSF while ensuring equal comparisons when it comes to evaluation.

Top management support, resilient supply chain, recycling factories, metaheuristics, operations research (OR), gas consumption, carbon footprint, green supplier criteria, data-driven simulation, non-dominated sorting genetic algorithm (NDSGA), predictable behavior and digital SCM are referred to as key CSFs for this study.

Top management support has the highest normalized weight in this group, giving 0.0793651, demonstrating its strategic importance, followed by resilient supply chain and recycling factories with balancing scores maintaining their strategic positioning. On the contrary, CSFs (gas consumption, carbon footprint, green supplier criteria, data-driven simulation, OR and digital supply chain context) were considered a normalized weight of 0.047619 due to their relative importance.

These normalized weights guarantee that the impact of each factor is represented in the overall evaluation to some extent and can be further analyzed according to a SMART methodology.

19.3.2. *Sensitivity analysis*

– CSF: the main focus areas, or measures of achievement, must be sufficiently realized to enable an innovative deployment of SM technologies and practices.

– Weight guideline: this is the initial importance of each CSF. So, the higher the value, the more important it is to a successful smart transformation from a manufacturing perspective.

– Normalized weight: the weight after adjustment in weighting where weights are assigned to each interpreting item, so that the sum of all of the weights equals 1.0. This method keeps the weight of individual CSFs constant with one another and, thus, allows for direct comparability between all factors.

The sensitivity analysis results are spread out through line charts, showing how overall scores only change from the data-driven and phased approaches when we increase (by 10%, 20% or 30%) the weight of each of the top five CSFs in comparison to the other sectors.

Critical success factor (CSF)	Data-driven score (0.1)	Data-driven score (0.2)	Data-driven score (0.3)	Phased score (0.1)	Phased score (0.2)	Phased score (0.3)
Top management support	64.625	64.250	63.875	40.250	40.500	40.750
Resilient supply chain (SC)	65.250	65.500	65.750	40.250	40.500	40.750
Recycling factories	65.250	65.500	65.750	39.625	39.250	38.875
Metaheuristics	65.250	65.500	65.750	40.250	40.500	40.750
Predictable behavior*	64.625	64.250	63.875	39.625	39.250	38.875

Table 19.2. *Sensitivity analysis of top critical success factors (CSFs)*

Key observations

In each of these scenarios, we increase the weights of individual CSFs by 10%, 20% and 30%. This shows that the data-driven approach is more favorable not solely due to their initial weight allocations.

The overall scores from the results are more sensitive to the increased weights of IoT and data fusion for both approaches. However, their impact is more beneficial when data-driven (compared to the phased approach).

3D printing had the lowest sensitivity, which means that it plays a separate type of role in smart manufacturing, one that does not distinguish the strategy performance relative to each other for other key top CSFs.

19.4. Findings and discussion

SMART analysis on the overall score points to the data-driven approach as the best choice for smart manufacturing transformation, compared to a phased approach. As we can see in both the weighted (150 vs. 102) and normalized (2.38 vs. 1.62) scores, the data-driven approach will more effectively match up with the CSFs identified.

Critical success factor (CSF)	Weight guideline	Normalized weight
Top management support	5	0.0793651
Resilient supply chain (SC)	5	0.0793651
Recycling factories	5	0.0793651
Metaheuristics	5	0.0793651

Table 19.3. *Top five critical success factors (CSFs)*

The focus on data, communication and the use of advanced tech in promoting smart manufacturing is already reflected through these top CSFs. Strategic flexibility and business model transformation both point to the fact that top management support and business resiliency/sustainable supply chain sustenance are of paramount importance for maintaining the sea change. The mention of recycling factories reflects the increased priority of sustainable manufacturing, and metaheuristics, as an advanced optimization algorithm, further elaborates on increasing decision-making efficiency. Together, these illustrate new accelerators of manufacturing transition success: technology innovation integrated with strategic and sustainable priorities.

19.4.1. *Implications of study*

Several lessons for future smart manufacturing decisions emerge from the results of the SMART analysis; most notably, the data-driven approach is shown as clearly dominant. This comprehensive diagnostic can be used to identify major CSFs that will help manufacturers devise a strategic framework to govern their initiatives, ensuring the effective prioritization and allocation of resources in order to gain maximum benefits from transformations.

The following are the main takeaways:

– Strategic technology investments: this process of the data-driven approach is only possible when we have a good degree of technical capabilities, which will enable the organization to leverage collecting, storing, analyzing and applying the insights generated by the application of data. This includes investments in sensors, IoT hardware, data storage and advanced analytics. Top management support and a resilient supply chain remain the top CSFs, so an approach by which new technologies/technological upgrades are aligned with these will help maximize the effectiveness of a data-driven strategy.

– Workforce training and data literacy process: a data-driven process becomes sustainable only if there is a workforce to provide competencies in data literacy, analysis and interpretation. Manufacturers need to invest in specialized upskilling programs that give employees the competencies they need to turn data insights into decisions. This helps in operational improvement, which is key to sustaining a competitive edge.

– Fostering a data-driven organizational culture: this adoption of a data-driven approach needs a cultural shift in the organization. They must facilitate an atmosphere where data is promoted, distributed and leveraged for decision-making across the operational layers. This includes encouraging innovation and experimentation and enforcing clean data, as well as facilitating increased teamwork between marketing and technology peers.

By focusing on the highest CSFs, such as top management support and the embedding of explainable AI for transparency, manufacturers will be more able to set a clear path for their smart manufacturing transformation journey. Addressing these priority areas will not only help deliver better returns on investment but also speed up the digital transformation process in line with Industry 4.0 plans.

Aligning strategies with these CSFs can yield numerous benefits for manufacturers:

– *Improved efficiency:* data-driven insights can identify bottlenecks, optimize processes and reduce waste, leading to significant efficiency gains.

– *Increased productivity:* by leveraging data to monitor and control production in real time, manufacturers can enhance productivity and throughput.

– *Enhanced innovation:* data-driven approaches can uncover new opportunities for product and process innovation, enabling manufacturers to stay ahead of the competition.

– *Greater competitiveness:* by adopting smart manufacturing technologies and practices, manufacturers can improve their cost-effectiveness, quality and responsiveness to customer demands, thereby strengthening their competitive position in the market.

The insights from this analysis can be used to develop a comprehensive roadmap for smart manufacturing transformation. This roadmap should outline the following steps:

1. *Assess current state:* evaluate the organization's existing data infrastructure, technology capabilities and workforce skills to identify gaps and areas for improvement.

2. *Define objectives:* clearly articulate the goals and objectives of the smart manufacturing transformation, such as improving efficiency, reducing costs or increasing innovation.

3. *Develop a strategy:* formulate a data-driven strategy that outlines the specific technologies, processes and cultural changes required to achieve the defined objectives.

4. *Implement and monitor:* execute the strategy in a phased manner, starting with pilot projects and gradually scaling up. Continuously monitor progress and adjust the approach as needed, based on data-driven insights.

5. *Sustain and evolve:* establish mechanisms for ongoing data collection, analysis and utilization to ensure that the smart manufacturing transformation is sustained and continuously improved over time.

Linking smart manufacturing strategies to predefined CSFs has great potential payoff in improving operational efficiency and competitive stay. However, by using data-driven insights, manufacturers can root out bottlenecks, optimize processes for efficiency and effectively eliminate waste. Optimized real-time monitoring and control can maximize productivity and throughput, while advanced analytics find the solutions to both new product opportunities and capabilities hotspots, ensuring companies stay at least on par with competitors. In addition, the advancement of smart manufacturing increases company market within the Industry 4.0 landscape by allowing process optimization to reduce cost, improve quality and enhance customer responsiveness.

This detailed roadmap backstopping the SMART analysis would be the basis of any transformation initiatives. The roadmap to building an AI- and data-capable environment should start with an assessment of the current state, by evaluating data infrastructure, technology capabilities and human resources skills to pinpoint the company's strengths and weaknesses. This is then followed by clear objectives and a data-driven strategy that defines the technologies, processes and cultural changes needed to deliver against those objectives. The execution should be gradual, where it should start with pilot projects and progresses based on quantifiable results and ongoing evaluations to adjust via analytical feedback. Finally, an infrastructure to support long-term data collection, analysis and utilization needs to be established that is sustainable so both quality assurance and continuous improvement are institutionalized. Adopting a systematic method enables the manufacturers to expedite their transformational journey, ensuring that they can optimize returns on investments and guarantee sustainable success in the transforming industrial scenario.

19.5. Conclusion and future work

The final methodology was based on a combination of expert opinion, but during the initial assessment role-out, each factor in the SMART analysis had been assigned a subjective weight (now normalized to ensure comparability across all criteria). Priorities emerging out of these normalized weights are strong leadership support, creation of a robust supply chain, recycling practices in sourcing and use to the largest extent possible and advanced optimization techniques such as metaheuristics and genetic algorithms. These characteristics further reinforce an even attention to reasonableness and sustainability. Each of these areas is critical, but the strength that top management support holds confirms our own findings, indicating how important leadership is to the success of smart manufacturing initiatives. While the study explicitly mentions operations research and data-driven simulation — implying a focus on systematic trend analysis and data pipeline optimization — it lacks the necessary methodological detail to support deeper interpretation of its findings. To gain a richer interpretation of the implications, we really must read the whole paper and also examine how other studies in this field stack up against it (Bhambri and Kumar 2024; Rana and Bhambri 2024).

In this chapter, a SMART analysis was performed as an evaluation framework of strategic smart approaches for smart manufacturing. However, SMART is not devoid of shortcomings. This means that the weightings for the CSFs are, at the base level, always highly subjective and likely to differ in their specification by manufacturer as a result of contextual priorities and operational constraints. Furthermore, the metric space for comparison of data-driven to phased approaches is narrow and may not therefore reflect that the complexities of smart manufacturing are well substantiated. More evaluation factors should be considered in future research, and the study should be extended to other industrial contexts. Moreover, in further developments, we will seek to validate our results with empirical performance data from case studies on a more extensive range of companies.

19.6. References

Bhambri, P. and Kumar, S. (2024). Protecting sustainable supply chains from cyber threats. In *Digital Sustainability: Navigating Entrepreneurship in the Information Age*, Bhambri, P. and Paweloszek, I. (eds). CRC Press, Boca Raton, 125–141. doi: 10.1201/9781003484226-9.

Bhattacharya, M., Penica, M., O'Connell, E., Southern, M., Hayes, M. (2023). Human-in-Loop: A review of smart manufacturing deployments. *Systems*, 11(1), 35. doi: 10.3390/systems11010035.

Chen, W., Ouyang, H., Chen, X., Li, Z. (2024). Artificial intelligence in logistics optimization with sustainable criteria. *Sustainability*, 16(21), 9145 [Online]. Available at: https://www.mdpi.com/2071-1050/16/21/9145.

Daios, A., Kladovasilakis, N., Kelemis, A., Kostavelis, I. (2025). AI applications in supply chain management: A survey. *Applied Sciences*, 15(5), 2775. doi: 10.3390/app15052775.

Douaioui, K., Oucheikh, R., Benmoussa, O., Mabrouki, C. (2024). Machine learning and deep learning models for demand forecasting in supply chain management: A critical review. *Applied System Innovation*, 7(5), 93 [Online]. Available at: https://www.mdpi.com/2571-5577/7/5/93.

Drissi Elbouzidi, A., Ait El Cadi, A., Pellerin, R., Lamouri, S., Tobon Valencia, E., Bélanger, M.-J. (2023). The role of AI in warehouse digital twins: Literature review. *Applied Sciences*, 13(11), 6746 [Online]. Available at: https://www.mdpi.com/2076-3417/13/11/6746.

Moosavi, S., Leitão, P., Indri, M. (2024). Explainable AI in manufacturing and industrial cyber–physical systems: A survey. *Electronics*, 13(17), 3497 [Online]. Available at: https://www.mdpi.com/2079-9292/13/17/3497.

Qu, C. and Kim, E. (2024). Reviewing the roles of AI-integrated technologies in sustainable supply chain management: Research propositions and a framework for future directions. *Sustainability*, 16(14), 6186 [Online]. Available at: https://www.mdpi.com/2071-1050/16/14/6186.

Rana, R. and Bhambri, P. (2024). Hybrid MCDM (multi-criteria decision-making) approaches for sustainable energy management. In *Modern SuperHyperSoft Computing Trends in Science and Technology*, Smarandache, F. and Majumder, P. (eds). IGI Global, Hershey, 149–184. doi: 10.4018/979-8-3693-6875-6.ch006.

Samuels, A. (2025). Examining the integration of artificial intelligence in supply chain management from Industry 4.0 to Industry 6.0. *Frontiers in AI*, 7 [Online]. Available at: https://www.frontiersin.org/articles/10.3389/frai.2024.1477044/full.

Teixeira, A.R., Ferreira, J.V., Ramos, A.L. (2025). Intelligent supply chain management: A systematic literature review on artificial intelligence contributions. *Information*, 16(5), 399. doi: 10.3390/info16050399.

Tran, K.P. (2021). Artificial intelligence for smart manufacturing: Methods and applications. *Sensors*, 21(16), 5584 [Online]. Available at: https://pmc.ncbi.nlm.nih.gov/articles/PMC8402272/.

Xu, L., Mak, S., Brintrup, A. (2021). Will bots take over the supply chain? Revisiting agent-based supply chain automation. *arXiv preprint*. doi: 10.48550/arXiv.2109.01703.

20

Sustainable Intelligence: Aligning Ethical AI in Global Supply Chain Systems

This chapter aims to explore the ethical considerations in artificial intelligence (AI)-powered supply chain management practices. It outlines various ethical and sustainable technological issues in contemporary supply chain practices. The current supply chain practices incorporate AI procedures to enable process streamlining, predict future needs and optimize logistics operations. Automation and predictive analytics are constantly applied to streamline the supply chain procedures. This results in the creation of issues concerning bias, establishing accountability and data protection. Ethical AI practices should be duly investigated to prevent negative AI outcomes, maintain trust and guarantee fairness across global supply networks. The study employs a qualitative research design and conducts a meta-analysis of existing literature, case studies and regulatory guidelines on AI ethics, and introduces guidelines for responsible AI development and deployment adapted to supply chain contexts, assimilating the dimensions of fairness, explainability and sustainability metrics. The proposed framework detects critical and ethical AI dangers in AI applications. Such dangers are connected with supplier assessment methodologies, predictive analytics tools and demand planning systems. It presents workable approaches for a proactive and systematic approach to incorporating ethical considerations throughout the entire AI lifecycle within the supply chain. This research work provides a structured approach to constructing future-ready and sustainable supply chains, which promotes responsible innovation and builds trustworthy AI systems.

20.1. Introduction

The surge in the use of sophisticated technologies and their integration in global supply chain mechanisms has presented a transformative shift in the way supply chain operations are handled with respect to efficiency, accuracy and real-time decision-making (Brau et al. 2024; Beta et al. 2025). The entire process pertaining to inventory optimization and forecasting of demand, and the assessment of supplier

Chapter written by Gagandeep SINGH, Jasdeep Singh WALIA and Priya MANDIRATTA.

risks, is done through artificial intelligence (AI)-driven technologies (Abdullahi et al. 2022). The use of intelligent and sustainable technologies is presented in innovative ways in which goods and services are delivered across different countries (Hamdan 2021). The integration of intelligent technologies into the supply chain mechanisms presents multiple opportunities to the way the supply chain is managed and governed, yet it is facing complex challenges, which are exposing the supply chain networks to multiple risks (Musa et al. 2014; Barman 2025). The AI-embedded supply chains are enabling businesses to take multiple advantages of cost-effectiveness, augmented speed and responsiveness of the supply chains (Oluwafunmilayo Esan et al. 2024). At the same time, it is facing multiple challenges concerning the absence of a structured approach and a framework that could mitigate the AI-driven risks and cause multiple inequalities (Suljic 2025). Such a scenario raises a critical question concerning the application of artificial intelligence and its alignment with sustainability practices (Danach et al. 2024).

Contemporary businesses have enabled AI-driven mechanisms to streamline their supply chain operations, yet they are facing multiple issues concerning accountability, ethics and the rise of AI in equality (Boyer 2024; Hasan and Ojala 2024). The lack of upgraded and standardized governance mechanisms and equitable access to digital technologies is increasing further. These risks thereby create a scenario where technological upgrades are outpacing the ethics and accountability on the part of businesses (Teixeira et al. 2025).

20.2. Review of the literature

The present study considers three realms of literature concerning: (1) the integration of AI mechanisms and sustainable supply chain practices, (2) ethical dimensions of AI usage in global supply chain networks, and (3) governance, transparency and accountability in the AI-enabled supply chain management systems. These are described in the following sections.

20.2.1. *The integration of AI mechanisms and sustainable supply chain practices*

The convergence of AI mechanisms into global supply chain systems is emerging as a new horizon in the way modern businesses are governed and operated (Vann Yaroson et al. 2025). Such technological changes are not witnessed as small incremental changes, but present a transformative development in the way products and services are produced, sourced, transported and delivered across various nations (Balthrop et al. 2023). The implementation of AI mechanisms ensures that the data is processed on a real-time basis, permits predictive analytics and ensures autonomous decision-making (AL-Khatib and Shuhaiber 2022; Lin 2025). All these processes allow the businesses to respond quickly to the various challenges arising on account of logistics and efficiency management (Varun Sridharan 2025).

The past literature explores the aspects of sustainable practices and outlines that these capabilities have been shown or strive to achieve the objectives connected with environmental degradation, the improvement of energy efficiency and the achievement of responsible sourcing goals (Aggarwal et al. 2024; Attri et al. 2024). Several works highlighted the importance of implementing machine learning models to accurately forecast demand and achieve the objectives of cutting down on overproduction and wastage (Di Vaio et al. 2024). The collective outcomes of the studies focusing on the application of intelligent systems in sustainable supply chain practices highlighted that intelligent routing systems should enable lower fuel consumption by recognizing the various optimal delivery paths (Akhtar et al. 2023; Shawon et al. 2025). Several studies explored the significance of using AI monitoring tools and linked them with the compliance management systems of environmental standards (Khan et al. 2024; Rashid et al. 2025). It was outlined in their research work that changing climatic conditions and resource scarcity mean that AI will be a critical factor in ensuring sustainable supply chain practices for businesses (Hao and Demir 2024).

Certain studies pointed out the various challenges of applying AI mechanisms in supply chain practices. Their outcomes revealed that issues such as cost reduction and operational speed may overpower the critical challenges of maintaining ecological balance and social welfare (Richey et al. 2023; Yadav et al. 2024). It was suggested in their research studies that the environmental footprint of training large AI models raises various issues concerning excessive energy utilization in the AI data centers and achieving net sustainability outputs (Zhao and Gómez Fariñas 2023; Coniglio et al. 2024). It was furthermore highlighted that optimizing AI system processes for ensuring delivery speed causes a surge in carbon emissions by favoring the use of air transportation rather than following slower and greener alternatives of transportation (Hamdan 2021; Brau et al. 2024).

A consensus among scholars was witnessed in their research work regarding AI mechanisms in supply chain practices and their uneven distribution. It was suggested in their research studies that businesses operating in developed economies are more likely to employ sophisticated AI tools, while businesses operating in developing and underdeveloped countries are facing significant issues concerning digital infrastructure, financial resources and the technical expertise to manage their supply chain systems (Musa et al. 2014; Boyer 2024; Danach et al. 2024). It was put forward that the digital divide in the supply chain mechanisms creates challenges such as the dictation of terms and reinforcement of existing imbalances (Di Vaio et al. 2024). A recurring theme across past literature relates to the opacity of AI algorithms, which are creating difficulties for the regulatory authorities in ensuring that the AI-driven decisions of businesses align with sustainable practices (Attri et al. 2024; Akhter et al. 2025; Shawon et al. 2025). A prominent issue was raised in the past literature concerning the limited standardization of sustainability indicators, and the way they are defined, measured and weighted within the algorithm mechanisms of AI (Teixeira et al. 2025; Vann Yaroson et al. 2025). The absence of universally accepted sustainability benchmarks creates challenges for making comparisons and ensuring accountability across different businesses. In view of the above, a research gap is witnessed, and there is a need to develop a framework in which AI mechanisms can be effectively used as a tool for efficiency enhancement and for ensuring systematic sustainability transformation.

20.2.2. *Ethical dimensions of AI usage in global supply chain networks*

The use of artificial intelligence mechanisms and maintaining ethics in global supply chain systems calls for managing the issues concerning justice, transparency and human dignity (Richey et al. 2023; Cannas et al. 2024). The past literature outlines that the use of AI mechanisms calls for ensuring greater responsibility while making significant decisions concerning supplier selection, workforce allocation and risk assessments (Chauhan et al. 2020; Segun-Ajao 2025). Several studies underscore the significance of reshaping the economic conditions of the workforce, specifically in the low-income economy, which includes a noteworthy amount of manufacturing and raw materials extraction facilities (Meena et al. 2025; Moghaddam and Karimzadeh 2025). The application of automated performance monitoring systems and predictive algorithms should be applied to assess the credit scoring of the suppliers and to identify the need for training on the underrepresented information (Balthrop et al. 2023; Štreimikienė et al. 2025). A case study approach was used in a few prominent studies, and an AI model was evaluated in terms of factory compliance. This compliance was assessed based on past audit outcomes to identify weak regulatory enforcement and requirements for current improvement (Tsolakis et al. 2023; Gadi et al. 2024).

Moreover, certain studies acknowledged the importance of applying demand forecasting algorithms to cut labor costs and ensure cost efficiency in supply chain management. It was stressed that ethical considerations should be given due importance in the system design of businesses to prevent inequity under the elements of innovative practices (Kulkov et al. 2024). The collective outcomes of a few studies focused on developing an ethical AI framework, which considers the aspects of balancing innovation with accountability, equity and automation with the human workforce.

The issues of AI governance were outlined in a few studies, and it was established that an ethical AI system cannot be achieved merely on the lines of technical fixation. It was suggested that stakeholder inclusion and accountability are required for achieving the desired governance of the AI mechanisms (Shawon et al. 2025; Suljic 2025). The concept of value-sensitive design and integration of ethical principles was given due importance in the prior research work. It was underscored that principles such as transparency, fairness and human ethics must be implemented in the development of AI processes (Richey et al. 2023; Coniglio et al. 2024). A prominent example was highlighted where the AI platform was effectively used for order allocation among the suppliers, and it was programmed to cut down the cost and delivery times by giving due consideration to carbon emission practices (Hamdan 2021; Beta et al. 2025). It was established that standardization should be ensured in making AI standards, for ensuring industry collaboration and for exercising various verification mechanisms (Oluwafunmilayo Esan et al. 2024). A prominent concern was raised in the past literature concerning algorithmic explainability. The AI system must be designed to extract a reasonable number of explanations for all the affected parties in the supply chain (Alhaili and Mir 2024; Hasan and Ojala 2024). The past scholar works also raised concerns relating to AI risk and safeguarding those risks in the supply chain management practices. It was put forward that there is a need to develop a participatory governance framework, involving local communities, the workforce and producers, that should affect the way AI systems run in businesses. This should ensure the maintenance of trust and compliance with the required standards.

20.2.3. *Governance, transparency and accountability in AI-enabled supply chain management systems*

Effective governance mechanisms are essential for ensuring that the AI processes contribute in a meaningful manner to ensuring sustainability and adherence to ethics in global supply chain systems (Boyer 2024; Danach et al. 2024). The established literature raised concerns related to the absence of mechanisms that consider the aspects of compliance, oversight and technological management (Hao and Demir 2024; Vann Yaroson et al. 2025). It was outlined that advanced technologies and their usage are not properly applied by collective entities such as businesses, logistics providers and technological vendors.

The intensification of AI mechanisms and their complexity is creating difficulties in the way they are audited, traced and managed (Gadi et al. 2024; Yadav et al. 2024). A prominent example of the downgrading of suppliers' rating was discussed, which results in the re-routing of shipments based on predictive risk analysis (AL-Khatib and Shuhaiber 2022; Attri et al. 2024). The issues of lack of transparency undermine accountability and management and result in manipulation and AI bias (Alhaili and Mir 2024; Varun Sridharan 2025). It was underscored that governance structures should suitably match the scale of technological advancements and ensure the efficiency and well-being of the human and ecological systems (Kulkov et al. 2024; Moghaddam and Karimzadeh 2025).

The collective outcomes of past literature fostered the development of new forms of collaboration among various participatory concerns for establishing proper monitoring mechanisms and redressing the issues arising in AI-governed supply chain systems (Orenuga et al. 2024). Several studies recognized that governance mechanisms cannot properly address the issues of the transnational and dynamic nature of AI-driven supply chain systems (Cannas et al. 2024; Segun-Ajao 2025). It was recommended in the past literature that codes of conduct and certification programs must be established to ensure their proper governance (Zhao and Gómez Fariñas 2023; Moghaddam and Karimzadeh 2025). Some studies proposed the development of regulatory interventions, such as AI disclosure requirements and compulsory algorithmic impact assessments, to be applied in supply chain management systems.

The issues concerning jurisdictional challenges were highlighted in a few studies, where concerns relating to enforcement capacities were addressed. A prominent example of the European Union's AI legislation was showcased, outlining significant enforcement for ensuring the regulation of high-risk AI tools (Chen et al. 2024; Shawon et al. 2025). It is important to address concerns relating to labor management and critical infrastructure for ensuring governance in global supply networks (Attri et al. 2024; Gadi et al. 2024). It was fostered that regulatory authorities cannot solely resolve the issues and shall be suitably complemented by organizational change within the businesses (Orenuga et al. 2024; Coniglio et al. 2024). There is a need to develop an internal ethics committee and invest heavily in AI literacy programs to report various algorithmic harms (Hamdan 2021; Barman 2025). The application of blockchain and distributed ledger technologies is offered as a solution for ensuring immutable records of transactions and meeting the sustainability challenges (Zhao and Gómez Fariñas 2023; Segun-Ajao 2025). This sophisticated technology can properly verify the origin of raw materials, track carbon emissions and authenticate labor practices in the supply chain systems (Balthrop et al. 2023; Vann Yaroson et al. 2025). It was underscored in the established literature that independent oversight bodies shall be constituted to conduct auditing of AI systems within businesses (Chauhan et al. 2020; Tsolakis et al. 2023). Such bodies can properly assess the fairness of the AI supply chain model and evaluate the environmental impacts. There is a need to focus on the important aspects of technical expertise, inclusivity and financial independence for advancing sustainable intelligence in the global supply chain systems.

20.3. Research gap

The growing literature on the integration of AI mechanisms in supply chain systems has presented several critical gaps in comprehending. The ethical considerations in the way the systems are managed and controlled (Lin 2025; Shawon et al. 2025). The AI-driven decision-making in supply chain management calls for the development of a comprehensive framework that caters to the various sustainability issues. The established literature has extensively focused on the technical capabilities of AI concerning demand, forecasting, logistics, optimization and predictive analytics, and there remains a gap in how these AI mechanisms are governed at the core level in businesses (Musa et al. 2014; Di Vaio et al. 2024). The focus of past studies is on the application of AI as a tool for ensuring efficiency in the supply chains. However, this technological aspect does not consider the environmental and ethical consequences of using AI mechanisms in global supply chains (Chen et al. 2024; Varun Sridharan 2025). Various issues are witnessed related to labor vulnerabilities, AI asymmetry and environmental degradation, which need to be suitably met (Richey et al. 2023; Segun-Ajao 2025). The prior research work lacks a comprehensive framework that aligns AI mechanisms with the ethical principles of fairness, accountability and inclusivity in managing supply chains. The absence of a holistic framework has created a disconnect between the use of sophisticated technologies and the achievement of sustainable development goals.

Few studies acknowledge the risk of AIL algorithmic bias and data exclusion, but these concerns are highlighted in isolation rather than as connected components of broader governance issues (Aggarwal et al. 2024; Barman 2025; Lin 2025). It is witnessed that there does not exist a consensus in the way ethical performance of AI tools in the supply chain is measured (Balthrop et al. 2023; Teixeira et al. 2025). Furthermore, there is an absence of standardized mechanisms meant for auditing and reporting of AI algorithmic biases. Moreover, it is witnessed that significant lies in stakeholder participation in the AI government supply chain (Alhaili and Mir 2024; Brau et al. 2024). The overall design of AI mechanisms is controlled by tech, data, scientists and businesses, while the primary participants in the supply chain systems are affected by algorithmic decisions, and they are excluded from the overall process (Hao and Demir 2024; Kulkov et al. 2024). Their concerns are not properly incorporated in the development of protocols, guidelines and in making impact assessments. This undermines the trust, legislation of AI governance and increases the risk of AI bias (Musa et al. 2014; Oluwafunmilayo Esan et al. 2024; Orenuga et al. 2024). It is also witnessed that the issues concerning energy consumption are not properly accounted for while making sustainability assessments, ultimately leading towards high carbon emissions (Tsolakis et al. 2023; Coniglio et al. 2024). It is concluded that the established literature does not provide a holistic and practical actionable model for sustainable intelligence in supply chain practices. It calls for the need for the development of aspects related to governance, ethics and environmental responsibility into the core framework of AI-enabled supply chain systems. The concerns of all the stakeholders should be accounted for, empowering the stakeholders at all levels to achieve the required goals of contemporary sustainable supply chain practices.

20.4. Theoretical framework

The theoretical framework of the study lays its foundation by integrating the perspectives from interdisciplinary domains. These perspectives are taken from social development theory, technology, ethics, institutional theory and systems thinking theory to construct a well-inclusive framework related to AI-powered global chain systems (Tsolakis et al. 2023; Chen et al. 2024; Shawon et al. 2025). The framework proposed in the present chapter intervenes in AI mechanisms as a socio-technological system that is integrated with broader objectives of economic and environmental structures. The overall aim is to extend beyond instrumental views of AI and position it as an efficiency-enhancing mechanism for ensuring long-term sustainability and accountability in supply chain systems (Hamdan 2021; Boyer 2024; Vann Yaroson et al. 2025).

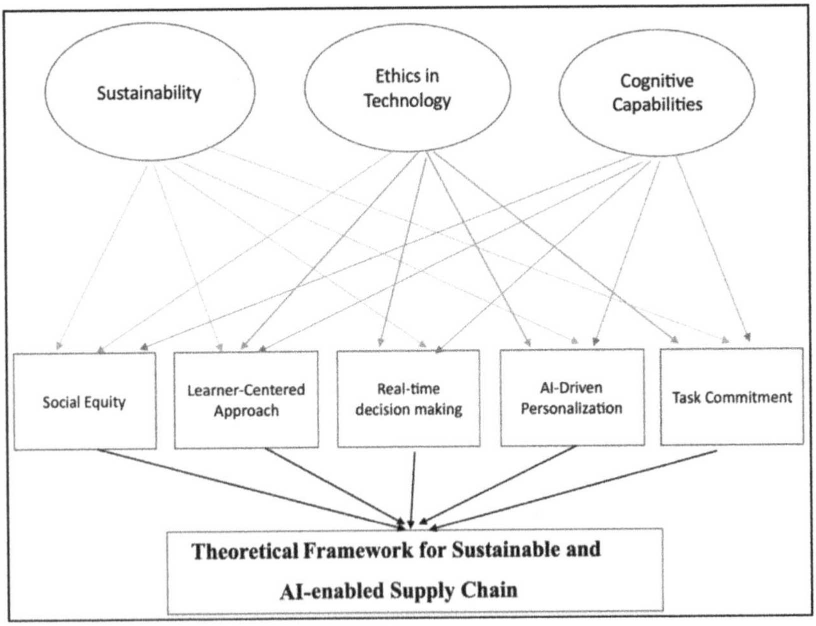

Figure 20.1. *Theoretical framework concerning sustainable and AI-enabled supply chain (source: author's creation). For a color version of this figure, see www.iste.co.uk/bhambri/nextgensupply.zip*

The study summarizes significant theoretical constructs to establish a strong framework that aids in guiding the AI alignment with a sustainability perspective across international supply chain networks. The sustainable development theory is the foundational pillar of the framework proposed in the study (Akhter et al. 2025; Cannas et al. 2024; Suljic 2025). It emphasizes the integration of aspects concerning environmental protection and social equity. In the context of current research work, sustainability is not only considering waste reduction, but also empowering the workforce rights in the system of supply chain (Orenuga et al. 2024; Segun-Ajao 2025). The aspects of speed, cost and inventory turnover are the core aspects of this theory, which is meant to create proper delivery schedules and cut down on automated workforce reduction. The outcomes of sustainable development theory demand developing sustainable AI models by balancing the concerns of economic and social variables (Danach et al. 2024; Vann Yaroson et al. 2025).

Institutional theory is the second critical aspect that outlines the formation of regulations, cognitive abilities in shaping the organizational behavior within the businesses. The core aspect of this theory is to consider that businesses should be properly embedded by considering legitimate and acceptable supply chain practices (Musa et al. 2014; Brau et al. 2024; Cannas et al. 2024). The integration of AI in suppliers should be properly adopted to ensure innovative business practices and compliance with the standards. This theory focuses on making a coordinated action across governing bodies to ensure a normative ecosystem is followed, meeting all the stakeholder interests (Tsolakis et al. 2023; Chen et al. 2024). The third significant theory relates to the ethics of technology, which focuses on creating a value-sensitive design and responsible innovation. The significant aspect of this theory involves giving due value and priority to the needs of the stakeholders (Darman 2025). It must consider the voices of suppliers, workers and local communities to efficiently manage the global supply chain.

The use of AI should be ethical and should be designed by taking into account the interests of the various stakeholders. This theory guided the design of a framework that embeds ethical values of transparency and fairness at its outset. The concerns relating to explainability also form an integral part of the AI-enabled supply chain, which involves comprehending the automated decisions and challenging them whenever required (Attri et al. 2024; Lin 2025). The fourth important theory taken into consideration relates to systems thinking, which views a supply chain system as a dynamic and interconnected network. It outlines that AI systems do not operate in isolation but involve required interaction with the market forces and workforce. The feedback mechanisms are an integral part of the overall system of the global supply chain (Meena et al. 2025; Moghaddam and Karimzadeh 2025). In this regard, the present research work has considered the aspect of agent-based modeling and resilience mapping as an integral part while designing the framework settings (Brau et al. 2024). The collective outcomes of all the theories have set the guidance for the construction of a comprehensive framework that gives due consideration to the aspects connected with meeting stakeholder demands, ensuring ethical guidelines and adhering to sustainable practices.

Theoretical pillar	**Core principle**	**Key components**	**Role in AI-powered supply chain framework**
Sustainable Development Theory	Integration of economic, environmental and social equity goals	Environmental protection, social justice, long-term resource stewardship and workforce rights	Positions AI not just for efficiency but to advance sustainability by balancing cost, speed, and social impact
Institutional Theory	Organizational behavior shaped by regulations, norms and legitimacy	Regulatory compliance, industry standards, normative pressures and cross-border governance	Ensures AI adoption aligns with legitimate and accepted practices and promotes coordinated action among governments, firms and international bodies to build a trustworthy, standardized ecosystem
Ethics of Technology (Value-Sensitive Design & Responsible Innovation)	Technology must reflect human values and ethical principles	Fairness, transparency, stakeholder inclusion, explainability and accountability	Guides ethical AI design by embedding stakeholder voices (workers, suppliers, communities) and ensures decisions are understandable, contestable and aligned with human rights
Systems Thinking Theory	Supply chains as dynamic, interconnected systems with feedback loops	Interdependence, adaptability, resilience, agent-based modeling, scenario analysis	Treats AI as part of a complex system interacting with markets, labor and environment and supports adaptive decision-making, shock responsiveness and holistic impact assessment

Table 20.1. *Aspects of the theoretical framework and its governing principles (source: author's creation)*

20.5. Proposed framework concerning sustainable intelligence in AI-enabled supply chains

This chapter proposes a comprehensive and inclusive framework that promotes sustainable intelligence in AI-enabled supply chain systems. This framework aims to bridge the gaps between the aspects of amalgamating AI mechanisms with ethical and environmental practices. The dimensions of this framework treat AI mechanisms as transformative, which, when integrated with ethical and systematic structures, result in the delivery of meaningful and reasonable outcomes. The entire framework is based upon five important aspects connected with ethical design, sustainability, strong governance, accountability of stakeholders and adaptive systems. Each of the components aims to meet the complexities arising in supply chain management (Bhambri and Bajdor 2025). This framework enables businesses to scrutinize their contemporary AI mechanisms, recognize various misfits with the sustainability objectives and implement required strategies for enabling long-term viability in the supply chain system.

The initial aspect of the framework relates to ethically designing the AI processes. It sets the guide for the adequate development of AI mechanisms in the supply chain systems. This aspect takes into consideration various ethical dimensions that are integrated within the architecture of the system. The framework is built upon the concerns raised in the established literature concerning responsible innovation and sensitive AI design. In this regard, this dimension focuses on training the AI models that are ethically sound and diverse in operations. Another important aspect of this dimension relates to ensuring algorithmic transparency and redefining the confidentiality of the entire AI ecosystem (Bhambri and Kant 2025). The application of explainable AI is an integral part of the framework which suitably permits the regulatory authorities and auditing firms to comprehend the main logic behind making automated decisions. The evaluation of AI mechanics should be made by a proper review board, which should consider ethics and environmental safeguards. The algorithms governed by ethical standards should be used to prohibit the selection of suppliers with a history of violating the regulations and the use of carbon-intensive practices.

The second main aspect of the framework relates to ensuring a sustainable matrix aligned with the AI mechanisms. The established literature highlighted that traditional supply chains focused on cost reduction and efficiency management at the cost of sustainability. Therefore, in this regard, the framework proposed in the study aims to build a holistic indicator reflecting equity and environmental practices (Bhambri and Kumar 2024). The AI system used in supply chain management should balance environmental and social issues. It should aim to cut down the carbon intensity of various energy sources applied in logistics management. The demand forecasting models should aim to reuse and re-manufacture products to meet the sustainable guidelines. This aspect of the framework highlights setting various standards connected with labor equity, water usage, carbon emissions and diversity of suppliers.

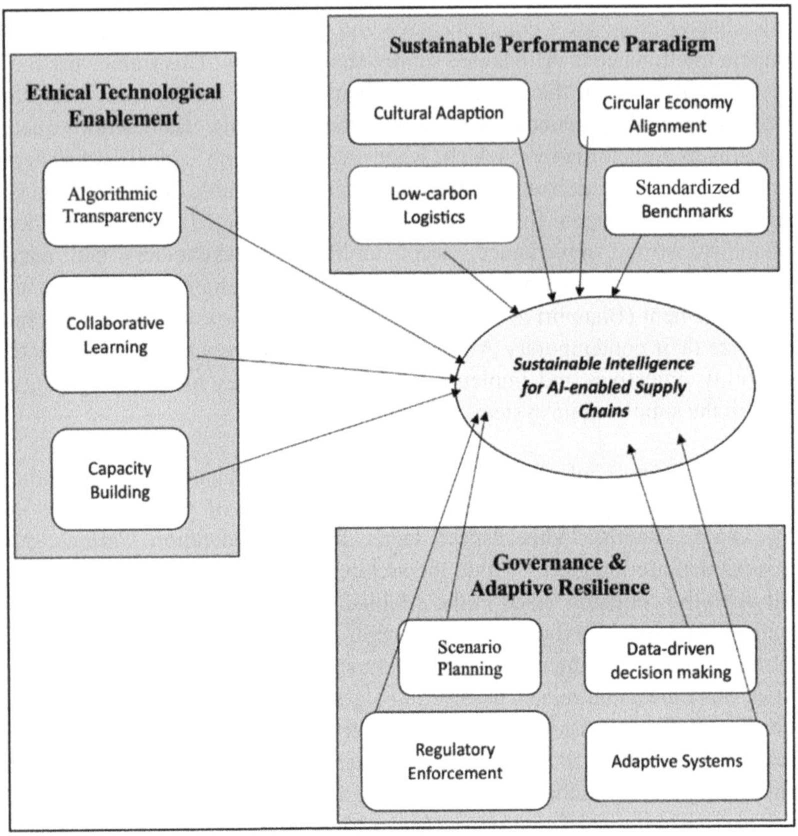

Figure 20.2. *Framework for sustainable intelligence for AI-enabled supply chain (source: author's creation)*

The third aspect of the framework relates to ensuring governance that meets the challenges of regulating the AI mechanisms across supply chain networks. The framework outlines the deployment of ethical AI mechanisms and ensures its governance within the firms, within the industry and at the national and global levels. It is underscored that within the businesses, a proper AI governance unit should be formulated that considers risk assessment at all levels (Bhambri and Starostka-Patyk 2025). The industry level should develop different guidelines and standards for ensuring ethical AI practices. At the national level, the regulatory authorities should enforce mandatory audit procedures and various certification schemes to meet required AI ethical standards. The concerns relating to algorithmic bias should be met by exercising whistleblower protection policies. At the global level, international organizations should coordinate among themselves to bring harmonization in the regulations. The ultimate objective of this layer is to ensure that accountability and ethical oversight are reinforced properly in the entire management of the supply chains.

Another significant aspect of the framework relates to ensuring accountability on the part of all the stakeholders to derive AI-based decisions at all levels within the organization. This phase requires the deployment of AI systems by ensuring participatory mechanisms and including all the required stakeholders, such as suppliers, the workforce and community officers, in the design and development of AI mechanisms.

The study proposes the development of advisory councils meant for the stakeholders to ensure that the proper testing and feedback mechanisms are always enforced (Bhambri et al. 2025). The businesses should strive for the development of grievance redressal mechanisms to provide relief to the affected parties for raising their issues concerning algorithmic bias and inadequate AI use. It is put forward that the digital mechanisms applied in the organizations should be used to collect real-time feedback and should focus on making continuous improvements. There is a need to develop capacity-building activities and knowledge-sharing platforms to empower all the stakeholders involved in the global AI-connected supply chain networks. The last phase of the framework relates to ensuring the resilience of AI-embedded supply chains. The stakeholders involved in the overall conduct of supply chain management should aid in developing an ethical supply chain system, which continuously evolves and responds properly to any uncertainties. This aspect of the proposed framework aims to counter any kind of disruption that is raised in the business of the supply chain. The design process of AI-enabled supply chains should be adaptive and continuously update its data models in response to the changing business scenarios (Rana and Bhambri 2024a). In this regard, it is imperative that businesses make use of various AI simulation tools and aid in the development of scenarios. Planning practices should continuously check the working mechanisms of their supply chain systems. The development of such practices will prevent them from the sudden shocks raised by continuous trade wars and any uncertain economic events.

It is concluded that all five important aspects proposed in the comprehensive framework aim at achieving actionable and cohesive guidelines concerned with the operation of the intelligent supply chain systems. It aims to build, assess, refine and improve sustainable AI mechanisms in the uncertain business world. The outcomes of this framework provide sites to the policymakers, regulatory authorities and tech developers to develop a global supply chain system that is smart, resilient and regenerative.

Aspects	Core principle	Key components	Implementation mechanisms
Ethical AI Design	Embed ethics in AI from the start	Value-sensitive design, bias mitigation, explainability, ethical constraints	Ethics review boards, XAI tools, bias audits, human rights integration
Sustainable Performance Integration	Optimize AI for ESG, not just efficiency	Multi-objective goals, ESG data, sustainability KPIs	Redefine AI objectives, real-time ESG dashboards
Multi-level Governance	Ensure oversight across levels	Internal units, industry standards, national regulation, global coordination	AI governance teams, industry consortia, regulatory compliance, international frameworks
Stakeholder-centric Accountability	Include affected voices in AI processes	Participatory design, redressal, feedback, capacity building	Advisory councils, digital feedback platforms, appeal mechanisms, training programs
Adaptive Resilience	Enable AI to learn and respond to shocks	Dynamic learning, scenario planning, diversification, continuous updates	Adaptive models, AI simulations, shock-responsive routing, feedback loops

Table 20.2. *Integral components of the sustainable and AI-enabled supply chain (source: author's creation)*

20.6. Implications of the study

The outcomes of the current study present significant implications for the policymakers, regulatory authorities and tech innovators involved in the intelligent supply chains system. These implications guide them in their proper design, deployment and adequate governance. The integration of AI mechanisms in logistics, procurement and supplier management calls for developing an ecosystem that is built upon the principles of equity and sustainability (Rana and Bhambri 2024b).

The embedding of AI mechanisms calls for suitable oversight and proper direction to curb inefficiencies and various inequalities in the management of the supply chain. The study outlines five major implications that aim to provide suitable insights to the authorities for enabling ethical and sustainable transformative activities in supply chain practices.

20.6.1. *Development of binding standards for ethical AI in the supply chain*

The outcomes of the current study outline that the existing regulations concerning ethical AI operations in supply chain management are fragmented, which often leads to concerns related to data privacy and its compliance. The framework proposed in the study outlines such a significant aspect and calls for developing adequate guidelines that should require businesses to run proper algorithmic impact assessments. Such assessments should be deployed in the AI systems before they affect the various stakeholders connected in the supply chain. These assessments should have the ability to investigate various biases in the automated systems. It is imperative for the regulatory authorities to mandate the application of explainable AI in systems requiring credit, scoring, supplier assessment and workforce scheduling.

20.6.2. *Establishment of sustainability metrics in AI mechanisms*

The proposed framework calls out for the development of a proper sustainability matrix and for it to be integrated into the digital transformation guidelines. The outcomes of the study necessitate the policymakers bringing a re-orientation in the AI framework, and they should include bringing aspects of sustainability into the supply chain systems. Policymakers must develop proper incentives for those AI systems that tend to bring down carbon emissions and adhere to the principles of the circular economy (Rana and Bhambri 2024c). The establishment of AI systems must be based upon predefined sustainability criteria, and standardized data platforms should be developed to bring transparency to the supply chain systems. The government should launch various tax incentives for businesses showing significant improvements in their sustainability performance and exhibiting responsible AI use.

20.6.3. *Adoption of value-sensitive design as a core principle of the intelligent supply chain system*

The framework highlighted in the study calls for considering the ethical and social aspects of AI applications. It reflects that the principles of value creation should be embedded in the AI mechanisms to ensure fairness and transparency in the architecture of the supply chain. The tech developers should focus on designing a suitable algorithm that avoids discriminatory results and ensures proper stakeholder feedback. The outcomes of the study encourage the technologies to prioritize the inter-operator ability of the sustainable supply chain framework. The application and use of open-source tools and ethical AI tool kits should be promoted. This should enable suppliers operating at a small scale to participate properly in the digital transformation process of supply chain management without having any dependency on the AI proprietary systems.

20.6.4. *Development of governance structures considering AI oversight*

The present study calls for addressing any ethical lapses and misalignments in sustainability practices. In this regard, businesses must aim to establish a dedicated board that should frame and exercise AI governance; the board would be responsible for assessing the algorithmic risks and ensuring compliance with the ethical standards. A proper review and monitoring of the long-term impact of AI usage on the stakeholders should be conducted. The board should include requisite members who are experts in ensuring ethical conduct, adherence to sustainability standards and ensuring the AI-related performance is properly conducted. The audit management procedures should be in line with superior and ethical AI practices and should involve the conduct of algorithmic auditing at proper intervals.

20.6.5. *Ensuring inclusive and equitable AI deployment*

The outcomes of the study call on the policymakers to establish requisite stakeholder advisory councils, which should properly meet the expectations and interests of the workforce, suppliers and small-scale businesses. This should enable them to coexist in the AI-enabled supply chain system and also to review their performance using digital feedback platforms. This scenario should allow them to conduct real-time reporting of any algorithmic issues (Rana and Bhambri 2025). The government authorities should aim to promote and develop capacity-building programs to equip the members with the requisite supply chain management practices. This should allow them to conduct businesses under the purview of ethical and sustainable oversight. The regulatory authorities should aim to develop laws concerning data rights, algorithmic literacy and digital compliance.

It is therefore concluded that the five implications presented in the current research work formulate a roadmap for making an effective transformation towards sustainable supply chain assistance by embedding AI mechanisms. The study stresses the application of a holistic viewpoint and presents a value-driven approach for guarding innovative practices in the supply chain systems. The regulatory authorities and the policymakers should create such an ecosystem, where these stakeholders are empowered to take ethical decisions for exercising suitable conduct of the overall supply chain. The implications call for a coordinated and multilevel action that can build contemporary supply chain systems into smart, resilient and intelligent AI-based integrated mechanisms.

20.7. Conclusion and scope for future research work

The amalgamation of AI mechanisms into supply chain systems has presented a transformative change in the way the management of logistics, procurement and sustainable supply chain practices are carried out throughout the world. The integration of AI into supply chain management is exhibiting a pivotal shift intended to cut down waste, improve responsiveness and augment the efficiency of the system from the perspective of sustainability dimensions. The current research work underscores that AI mechanisms cannot be treated merely as a technical tool, but rather should be embedded properly, considering their technical dimensions. The study calls for alignment with the sustainability principle to reduce the inequities and imbalances arising from the use of AI systems. The proposed framework of sustainable intelligence in the AI-integrated supply chain outlines a comprehensive and adaptive ability to integrate ethics, stakeholder participation and ensure governance at all levels. The proposed model underscores the necessity of embracing a holistic view of intelligence, exercising efficiency-centric ability and prioritizing accountability and social equity. The outcomes of the study indicate that the overall task of sustainable intelligence in the supply chain should not merely lie in technological advancement; rather, it requires careful and skilled design of the AI-embedded supply chain intelligence. The study calls for integrating the sustainability metrics for removing any algorithmic bias, ensuring transparency and establishing a proper governance mechanism in supply chain systems. The outcomes of the study provide insights to policymakers, regulatory authorities and tech innovators for creating suitable standards that ensure data sovereignty and protect the interests of vulnerable stakeholders. It is imperative that the AI system prevents inefficiency, digital colonialism and ensures an equitable sharing of the benefits at all levels. Ensuring and creating adaptive resilience is the core area on which the entire framework of the study is built, which further emphasizes that AI mechanisms should be proactive to learn from various economic and social distractions and should adopt simulating capabilities to assess future risks.

The current study has proposed innovative solutions for enabling sustainable intelligence in AI-integrated supply chains. However, it also proposes several avenues for carrying out future research work in this dimension. Further research should be carried out to validate the sustainable AI-enabled supply chain framework across various businesses and geographic areas. The practical application of this framework must be suitably tested across different sectors as well as businesses in light of sustainability challenges. Moreover, future research work can focus on making a comparative analysis between different businesses. In this way, they adopt ethical AI practices and ensure the aspects of resilience and stakeholder trust are maintained in the holistic process of the supply chain. In addition, future research can also aim to explore the construction of standardized aspects and various auditing tools to scrutinize the sustainability performance of AI mechanisms. There is a lack of accepted methodology, and the established literature has not presented any framework that adequately measures the algorithmic fairness, environmental impact and its accountability in supply chain mechanisms. A suitable development of such benchmarks should enable stakeholders to properly evaluate AI mechanisms objectively to ensure responsible innovation at all stages of the supply chain.

The study also calls for exploring the role of emerging technologies based on blockchain systems and federated learning to oversee and inspect the interaction of variables, such as transparency and data privacy, within the AI-enabled supply chain. The verification of sustainability claims can be carried out by scrutinizing the aspect of decentralized data sharing and technical aspects within the businesses. The pertinent issues related to technical literacy and incentive structures, which can hinder the adoption of sustainable intelligence practices, can be explored. The aspects of change management, capacity, building programs and various leadership strategies can be explored to enable practical guidance for businesses and their supply chain systems. Longitudinal research should be carried out to comprehend the response management systems of the businesses considering changing economic situations. It is therefore concluded that sustainable intelligence in the supply chain mechanisms calls for technical innovation, establishment of ethics, adequate governance and institutional reforms. The current study lays a suitable foundation for directing such transformative practices by offering a comprehensive framework that is resilient and regenerated in building scalable supply chain mechanisms.

20.8. References

Abdullahi, M., Baashar, Y., Alhussian, H., Alwadain, A., Aziz, N., Capretz, L.F., Abdulkadir, S.J. (2022). Detecting cybersecurity attacks in Internet of Things using artificial intelligence methods: A systematic literature review. *Electronics*, 11(2), 198. doi: 10.3390/electronics11020198.

Aggarwal, M., Yadav, A., Garg, R.K. (2024). Enabling a green supply chain with machine learning and Industry 4.0: Certain investigations for research and applications. In *Optimization of Production and Industrial Systems*, Bhardwaj, A., Pandey, P.M., Misra, A. (eds). Springer, Singapore, 51–65. doi: 10.1007/978-981-99-8343-8_5.

Akhtar, P., Ghouri, A.M., Khan, H.U.R., Amin Ul Haq, M., Awan, U., Zahoor, N., Khan, Z., Ashraf, A. (2023). Detecting fake news and disinformation using artificial intelligence and machine learning to avoid supply chain disruptions. *Annals of Operations Research*, 327(2), 633–657. doi: 10.1007/s10479-022-05015-5.

Akhter, S., Arefin, J., Hossen, M.S., Bhuyan, M.H., Taslim, S. Md. B., Zishan, Md. S.R., Amanul Islam, M. (2025). Neuro-symbolic AI for IoT-driven smart cities: A next-generation framework for urban intelligence. *Journal of Computer Science and Technology Studies*, 7(2), 36–55. doi: 10.32996/jcsts.2025.7.2.4.

AL-Khatib, A.W. and Shuhaiber, A. (2022). Green intellectual capital and green supply chain performance: Does Big Data analytics capabilities matter? *Sustainability*, 14(16), 10054. doi: 10.3390/su141610054.

Alhaili, S. and Mir, F. (2024). The role of artificial ethics principles in managing knowledge and enabling data-driven decision making in supply chain management. In *Information Systems*, Papadaki, M., Themistocleous, M., Al Marri, K., Al Zarouni, M. (eds), vol. 501, Springer, Cham, 263–277. doi: 10.1007/978-3-031-56478-9_19.

Attri, A., Yadav, A., Garg, R.K. (2024). Enhancing supply chain sustainability through Industry 4.0 and additive manufacturing technologies: A bibliometric-based review. In *Optimization of Production and Industrial Systems*, Bhardwaj, A., Pandey, P.M., Misra, A. (eds). Springer, Singapore, 67–77. doi: 10.1007/978-981-99-8343-8_6.

Balthrop, A., Scott, A., Miller, J. (2023). How do trucking companies respond to announced versus unannounced safety crackdowns? The case of government inspection blitzes. *Journal of Business Logistics*, 44(4), 641–665. doi: 10.1111/jbl.12353.

Barman, A. (2025). Sustainability, supply chain management, and machine intelligence: Overcoming challenges and shaping the future. *Procedia Computer Science*, 258, 993–1002. doi: 10.1016/j.procs.2025.04.336.

Beta, K., Nagaraj, S.S., Weerasinghe, T.D.B. (2025). The role of artificial intelligence on supply chain resilience. *Journal of Enterprise Information Management*, 38(3), 950–973. doi: 10.1108/JEIM-12-2023-0674.

Bhambri, P. and Bajdor, P. (2025). AI-powered predictive analysis for proactive cyber defense. In *Handbook of AI-Driven Threat Detection and Prevention: A Holistic Approach to Security*, Bhambri, P. and Anand, A.J. (eds). CRC Press, Boca Raton, 308–321. doi: 10.1201/9781003521020-18.

Bhambri, P. and Kant, S. (2025). A taxonomy of bias in machine learning: Classification, sources, and implications for ethical AI. In *Lincoln-SPAST Global Sustainability Programme (SGS-24), 1st International Conference of L-GPR Program, SPAST Proceedings*, 1(2) [Online]. Available at: https://spast.org/techrep/article/view/5387/724.

Bhambri, P. and Kumar, S. (2024). Protecting sustainable supply chains from cyber threats. In *Digital Sustainability: Navigating Entrepreneurship in the Information Age*, Bhambri, P. and Paweloszek, I. (eds). CRC Press, Boca Raton, 125–141. doi: 10.1201/9781003484226-9.

Bhambri, P. and Starostka-Patyk, M. (2025). Integrating AI with blockchain for decentralized security and threat prevention. In *Handbook of AI-driven Threat Detection and Prevention: A Holistic Approach to Security*, Bhambri, P. and Anand, A.J. (eds). CRC Press, Boca Raton, 353–370. doi: 10.1201/9781003521020-21.

Bhambri, P., Rana, R., Kautish, S. (2025). Sustainable digital transformation: Reducing carbon footprint in the metaverse. In *Metaverse and Sustainability: Business Resilience towards Sustainable Development Goals*, Leal Filho, W., Kautish, S., Gupta, V.P. (eds). Springer, Cham, 105–128. doi: 10.1007/978-3-031-89545-6_7.

Boyer, A. (2024). Navigating complexity: Interdisciplinary approaches to sustainable supply chain management. *Management Research Quarterly*, 1(3). doi: 10.63029/78v84162.

Brau, R.I., Sanders, N.R., Aloysius, J., Williams, D. (2024). Utilizing people, analytics, and AI for decision making in the digitalized retail supply chain. *Journal of Business Logistics*, 45(1), e12355. doi: 10.1111/jbl.12355.

Cannas, V.G., Ciano, M.P., Saltalamacchia, M., Secchi, R. (2024). Artificial intelligence in supply chain and operations management: A multiple case study research. *International Journal of Production Research*, 62(9), 3333–3360. doi: 10.1080/00207543.2023.2232050.

Chauhan, A., Kaur, H., Yadav, S., Jakhar, S.K. (2020). A hybrid model for investigating and selecting a sustainable supply chain for agri-produce in India. *Annals of Operations Research*, 290(1–2), 621–642. doi: 10.1007/s10479-019-03190-6.

Chen, W., Men, Y., Fuster, N., Osorio, C., Juan, A.A. (2024). Artificial intelligence in logistics optimization with sustainable criteria: A review. *Sustainability*, 16(21), 9145. doi: 10.3390/su16219145.

Coniglio, I.M., Cimino, A., Corvello, V. (2024). Artificial Intelligence and the future of supply chain management. In *Research and Innovation Forum 2024*, Visvizi, A., Troisi, O., Corvello, V., Grimaldi, M. (eds). Springer, Cham, 43–52. doi: 10.1007/978-3-031-78623-5_4.

Danach, K., Dirani, A.E., Rkein, H. (2024). Revolutionizing supply chain management with AI: A path to efficiency and sustainability. *IEEE Access*, 12, 188245–188255. doi: 10.1109/ACCESS.2024.3474531.

Di Vaio, A., Latif, B., Gunarathne, N., Gupta, M., D'Adamo, I. (2024). Digitalization and artificial knowledge for accountability in SCM: A systematic literature review. *Journal of Enterprise Information Management*, 37(2), 606–672. doi: 10.1108/JEIM-08-2022-0275.

Esan, O., Ajayi, F.A., Olawale, O. (2024). Supply chain integrating sustainability and ethics: Strategies for modern supply chain management. *World Journal of Advanced Research and Reviews*, 22(1), 1930–1953. doi: 10.30574/wjarr.2024.22.1.1259.

Gadi, V., Govani, P., Grover, V., Balusamy, B. (2024). AI-enabled supply chain planning and execution: A pathway to sustainability. In *Blockchain, IoT, and AI Technologies for Supply Chain Management*, Grover, V., Balusamy, B.B., Milanova, M., Felix, A.Y. (eds). Apress, Berkeley, CA, 123–145. doi: 10.1007/979-8-8688-0315-4_5.

Hamdan, A.M.M., Hassanien, A.E., Razzaque, A., Alareeni, B. (2021). *The Fourth Industrial Revolution*. Springer, Cham.

Hao, X. and Demir, E. (2024). Artificial intelligence in supply chain decision-making: An environmental, social, and governance triggering and technological inhibiting protocol. *Journal of Modelling in Management*, 19(2), 605–629. doi: 10.1108/JM2-01-2023-0009.

Hasan, R. and Ojala, A. (2024). Managing artificial intelligence in international business: Toward a research agenda on sustainable production and consumption. *Thunderbird International Business Review*, 66(2), 151–170. doi: 10.1002/tie.22369.

Khan, S.I., Rahman, M.S., Ashik, A.A.M., Islam, S., Rahman, M.M., Hossain, E. (2024). Big Data and business intelligence for supply chain sustainability: Risk mitigation and green optimization in the digital era. *European Journal of Management, Economics and Business*, 1(3), 262–276. doi: 10.59324/ejmeb.2024.1(3).23.

Kulkov, I., Kulkova, J., Rohrbeck, R., Menvielle, L., Kaartemo, V., Makkonen, H. (2024). Artificial intelligence – driven sustainable development: Examining organizational, technical, and processing approaches to achieving global goals. *Sustainable Development*, 32(3), 2253–2267. doi: 10.1002/sd.2773.

Lin, K.-Y. (2025). Generative artificial intelligence - driven sustainable supply chain management: A UNISONE framework for smart logistics and predictive analytics under Industry 5.0. *International Journal of Logistics Research and Applications*, 1–32. doi: 10.1080/13675567.2025.2540855.

Meena, R., Sahoo, S., Malik, A., Kumar, S., Nguyen, M. (2025). Artificial intelligence and circular supply chains: Framework for applications and deployment from the triple bottom line model perspective. *Annals of Operations Research*. doi: 10.1007/s10479-025-06510-1.

Moghaddam, G.K. and Karimzadeh, M. (2025). AI-driven digital transformation and sustainable logistics: Innovations in global supply chain management. Preprint. doi: 10.21203/rs.3.rs-6086101/v1.

Musa, A., Gunasekaran, A., Yusuf, Y. (2014). Supply chain product visibility: Methods, systems and impacts. *Expert Systems with Applications*, 41(1), 176–194. doi: 10.1016/j.eswa.2013.07.020.

Orenuga, A., Oyeyemi, B.B., John, A.O. (2024). AI and sustainable supply chain practices: ESG goals in the U.S. and Nigeria. *International Journal of Future Engineering Innovations*, 1(1), 127–137. doi: 10.54660/IJFEI.2024.1.1.127-137.

Rana, R. and Bhambri, P. (2024a). Environmental challenges and technological solutions. In *Handbook of Technological Sustainability: Innovation and Environmental Awareness*, Bhambri, P. and Bajdor, P. (eds). CRC Press, Boca Raton, 187–200. doi: 10.1201/9781003475989-17.

Rana, R. and Bhambri, P. (2024b). Ethical considerations in artificial intelligence for environmental solutions: Striking a balance for sustainable innovation. In *Handbook of Technological Sustainability: Innovation and Environmental Awareness*, Bhambri, P. and Bajdor, P. (eds). CRC Press, Boca Raton, 389–396. doi: 10.1201/9781003475989-31.

Rana, R. and Bhambri, P. (2024c). Hybrid MCDM (multi-criteria decision-making) approaches for sustainable energy management. In *Modern SuperHyperSoft Computing Trends in Science and Technology*, Smarandache, F. and Majumder, P. (eds). IGI Global, Hershey, 149–184. doi: 10.4018/979-8-3693-6875-6.ch006.

Rana, R. and Bhambri, P. (2025). Reliability analysis of energy networks. In *Neural Networks and Graph Models for Traffic and Energy Systems*, Bhambri, P. and Anand, J. (eds). IGI Global, Hershey, 259–292. doi: 10.4018/979-8-3373-0290-4.ch010.

Rashid, A., Baloch, N., Rasheed, R., Ngah, A.H. (2025). Big data analytics-artificial intelligence and sustainable performance through green supply chain practices in manufacturing firms of a developing country. *Journal of Science and Technology Policy Management*, 16(1), 42–67. doi: 10.1108/JSTPM-04-2023-0050.

Richey, R.G., Chowdhury, S., Davis-Sramek, B., Giannakis, M., Dwivedi, Y.K. (2023). Artificial intelligence in logistics and supply chain management: A primer and roadmap for research. *Journal of Business Logistics*, 44(4), 532–549. doi: 10.1111/jbl.12364.

Segun-Ajao, E. (2025). AI and sustainable procurement: A path to green supply chains. Preprint. doi: 10.20944/preprints202501.1516.v1.

Shawon, R.E.R., Hasan, M.R., Rahman, M.A., Ghandri, M., Lamari, I.A., Kawsar, M. and Akter, R. (2025). Designing and deploying AI models for sustainable logistics optimization: A case study on eco-efficient supply chains in the USA. *arXiv*. doi: 10.48550/arXiv.2503.14556.

Sridharan, V. (2025). Ethical AI integration in enterprise resource planning systems: A framework for balancing innovation and responsibility in B2B environments. *Journal of Computer Science and Technology Studies*, 7(5), 489–504. doi: 10.32996/jcsts.2025.7.5.56.

Štreimikienė, D., Bathaei, A., Streimikis, J. (2025). Enhancing sustainable global supply chain performance: A multi-criteria decision-making-based approach to Industry 4.0 and AI integration. *Sustainability*, 17(10), 4453. doi: 10.3390/su17104453.

Suljic, V. (2025). Strategic leadership in AI-driven digital transformation: Ethical governance, innovation management, and sustainable practices for global enterprises and SMEs. *SBS Journal of Applied Business Research*, 13(1), 17. doi: 10.70301/JOUR/SBS-JABR/2025/13/1/2.

Teixeira, A.R., Ferreira, J.V., Ramos, A.L. (2025). Intelligent supply chain management: A systematic literature review on artificial intelligence contributions. *Information*, 16(5), 399. doi: 10.3390/info16050399.

Tsolakis, N., Schumacher, R., Dora, M., Kumar, M. (2023). Artificial intelligence and blockchain implementation in supply chains: A pathway to sustainability and data monetisation? *Annals of Operations Research*, 327(1), 157–210. doi: 10.1007/s10479-022-04785-2.

Vann Yaroson, E., Abadie, A., Roux, M. (2025). Human-artificial intelligence collaboration in supply chain outcomes: The mediating role of responsible artificial intelligence. *Annals of Operations Research*. doi: 10.1007/s10479-025-06534-7.

Yadav, A., Garg, R.K., Sachdeva, A. (2024). Artificial intelligence applications for information management in sustainable supply chain management: A systematic review and future research agenda. *International Journal of Information Management Data Insights*, 4(2), 100292. doi: 10.1016/j.jjimei.2024.100292.

Zhao, J. and Gómez Fariñas, B. (2023). Artificial Intelligence and sustainable decisions. *European Business Organization Law Review*, 24(1), 1–39. doi: 10.1007/s40804-022-00262-2.

List of Authors

P. Ashok
Symbiosis Institute of Digital and Telecom Management
Symbiosis International (Deemed) University
Pune
Maharashtra
India

Paula Bajdor
Warsaw University of Technology
Poland

Pankaj Bhambri
Department of Information Technology
Guru Nanak Dev Engineering College
Ludhiana
Punjab
India

Rik Das
Department of Data and Analytics
PwC India
Kolkata
India

Debjit Dhar
Department of Data and Analytics
PwC India
Kolkata
India

Mingyue Fan
School of Management
Jiangsu University
Zhenjiang
China

Manika Garg
Senior Research Analyst
New Delhi
India

Indrajit Ghosal
Department of Management
Brainware University
Kolkata
West Bengal
India

Milind GODASE
Department of Computer Applications
Sinhgad Institute of Management
Pune
Maharashtra
India

Jeffy JOHNSON
Department of Law
Bengaluru School of Law and Justice
Karnataka
India

Bhagwat KAULWAR
Department of Computer Applications
Sinhgad Institute of Management
Pune
Maharashtra
India

S. KAVITHAMBIKA
School of Agribusiness & Rural Management
Dr. Rajendra Prasad Central Agricultural University
Samastipur
Bihar
India

Md. Rahat KHAN
Department of Management
Army Institute of Business Administration
Savar
Bangladesh

Mudassir KHAN
Department of Computer Science
King Khalid University
Abha
Asir
Saudi Arabia

Muhammad Asif KHAN
Department of Business Management
College of Business and Economics
University of Johannesburg
Gauteng
South Africa

R. KIRAN
School of Agribusiness & Rural Management
Dr. Rajendra Prasad Central Agricultural University
Samastipur
Bihar
India

Helena KOŚCIELNIAK
Faculty of Social Sciences
University of Kalisz
Poland

K. Murali KRISHNA
Department of Electronics and Communication Engineering
Rajalakshmi Engineering College
Chennai
Tamil Nadu
India

Pushan KUMAR DUTTA
Department of Electronics and Communication Engineering
Amity University
Kolkata
India

Saranik MAHAPATRA
Department of Data and Analytics
PwC India
Kolkata
India

Priya MANDIRATTA
Beta College of Business & Technology
Nelson Street West
Brampton
Canada

Balajee MARAM
School of Computer Science and Artificial Intelligence
SR University
Warangal
Telangana
India

Rafał NIEDBAL
Faculty of Management
Czestochowa University of Technology
Silesian
Poland

Agnieszka PACUD
Faculty of Social Sciences
University of Kalisz
Poland

Paula PYPŁACZ
Faculty of Management
Czestochowa University of Technology
Silesian
Poland

Akash RAI
Department of Business Administration
Ahmedabad Institute of Technology
Gujarat
India

Venkatesh RAMAMURTHY
NETS-International
Dubai
United Arab Emirates

Sita RANI
Department of Computer Science and Engineering
Guru Nanak Dev Engineering College
Ludhiana
Punjab
India

Ranjeeta SADHWANI
Department of Economics and Management
University of Brescia
Lombardy
Italy

Krishi Pallab SAIKIA
Department of Data and Analytics
PwC India
Kolkata
India

K.M. SANTHOSHA
School of Agribusiness &
Rural Management
Dr. Rajendra Prasad Central
Agricultural University
Samastipur
Bihar
India

Himani SHARMA
Department of Information
Technology
Guru Nanak Dev
Engineering College
Ludhiana
Punjab
India

Tripti SHARMA
Department of Business
Administration
Ganpat University
Ahmedabad
Gujarat
India

Chandrani SINGH
Department of Computer
Applications
Sinhgad Institute of Management
Pune
Maharashtra
India

Gagandeep SINGH
Mittal School of Business
Lovely Professional University
Phagwara
Punjab
India

Vijay Kumar SINHA
Chitkara University School of
Engineering & Technology
Solan
Himachal Pradesh
and
School of Computer Science and
Artificial Intelligence
SR University
Warangal
Telangana
India

Safia SOOMRO
Department of Education
Begum Nusrat Bhutto
Women University
Sukkur
Sindh
Pakistan

Sanam SOOMRO
School of Management
Jiangsu University
Zhenjiang
China

S. Lakshmi SRIDEVI
Department of Computer Science
and Engineering
Chennai Institute of Technology
Tamil Nadu
India

Marta STAROSTKA-PATYK
Faculty of Management
Warsaw University of Technology
Poland

Bharat Kumar TANK
RICS School of Built Environment
Amity University
Noida
Uttar Pradesh
India

Sunitaa TANK
ATL
Niti Aayog
Leader in Making
New Delhi
India

Jasdeep Singh WALIA
Mittal School of Business
Lovely Professional University
Phagwara
Punjab
India

Karina ZACHARSKA
CNC Construct
Żarki
Czestochowska
Poland

Index

S, T, U

Other titles from

iSTE

in

Computer Engineering

2026

DARCHE Philippe
Computer Memories 1: Core Concepts

MAHOUT Vincent, ROCACHER Thierry, AURIOL Guillaume
Programming of Embedded Systems: Applications to SM32F10x μControllers

2025

CHIKH Azeddine
Systemic Approach to Categorizing and Modeling Requirements

KUMAR Abhishek, BATTA Priya, AHUJA Sachin, RATHORE Pramod Singh
AI-driven Innovations in Physiotherapy and Oncology 1
AI-driven Innovations in Physiotherapy and Oncology 2

TANEJA Ashu, KUMAR Abhishek, LIMKAR Suresh Vishnudas, OUAISSA Mariya, OUAISSA Mariyam
Driving Innovation through AI and Digital Twin for 6G Powered Sustainable Ultra Smart Cities

TANEJA Ashu, KUMAR Abhishek, LIMKAR Suresh Vishnudas,
OUAISSA Mariya, OUAISSA Mariyam
6G Urban Innovation: AI and Digital Twin for Next-Gen Sustainable Cities

2024

CHAKRABORTY Rajdeep, GHOSH Anupam, KUMAR MANDAL Jyotsna,
CHOUDHURY Tanupriya, CHATTERJEE Prasenjit
Smart Edge Computing: An Operation Research Perspective
(International Perspectives in Decision Analytics and Operations Research Set – Volume 2)

HOMÈS Bernard
Fundamentals of Software Testing (2nd edition, revised and updated)

JERBI Abdessalem
Discrete-Event Simulation: Concepts and Production in Arena

PRADHAN Devasis, KUMAR SAHU Prasanna, MYO TUN Hla,
CHATTERJEE Prasenjit
Artificial and Cognitive Computing for Sustainable Healthcare Systems in Smart Cities
(International Perspectives in Decision Analytics and Operations Research Set – Volume 3)

2023

CHOUDHURY Tanupriya, KHANNA Abhirup, CHATTERJEE Prasenjit,
UM Jung-Sup, BHATTACHARYA Abhishek
Blockchain Applications in Healthcare: Innovations and Practices
(International Perspectives in Decision Analytics and Operations Research Set – Volume 1)

PAI G A Vijayalakshmi
A Textbook of Data Structures and Algorithms 1: Mastering Linear Data Structures
A Textbook of Data Structures and Algorithms 2: Mastering Nonlinear Data Structures
A Textbook of Data Structures and Algorithms 3: Mastering Advanced Data Structures and Algorithm Design Strategies

2022

HOMÈS Bernard
Advanced Testing of Systems-of-Systems 1: Theoretical Aspects
Advanced Testing of Systems-of-Systems 2: Practical Aspects

MEHTA Shikha, TIWARI Sanju, SIARRY Patrick, JABBAR M.A.
Tools, Languages, Methodologies for Representing Semantics on the Web of Things

SIDHOM Sahbi, KADDOUR Amira
Systems and Uses of Digital Sciences for Knowledge Organization (Digital Tools and Uses Set – Volume 9)

ZAIDOUN Ameur Salem
Computer Science Security: Concepts and Tools

2021

DARCHE Philippe
Microprocessor 4: Core Concepts – Software Aspects
Microprocessor 5: Software and Hardware Aspects of Development, Debugging and Testing – The Microcomputer

DELHAYE Jean-Loïc
Inside the World of Computing: Technologies, Uses, Challenges

HARDIN Thérèse, JAUME Mathieu, PESSAUX François, VIGUIÉ DONZEAU-GOUGE Véronique
Concepts and Semantics of Programming Languages 1: A Semantical Approach with OCaml and Python
Concepts and Semantics of Programming Languages 2: Modular and Object-oriented Constructs with OCaml, Python, C++, Ada and Java

MKADMI Abderrazak
Archives in The Digital Age: Preservation and the Right to be Forgotten
(Digital Tools and Uses Set – Volume 8)

TOKLU Yusuf Cengiz, BEKDAŞ Gebrail, NIGDELI Sinan Melih
Metaheuristics for Structural Design and Analysis
(Optimization Heuristics Set – Volume 3)

2020

DARCHE Philippe
Microprocessor 1: Prolegomenes – Calculation and Storage Functions – Models of Computation and Computer Architecture
Microprocessor 2: Core Concepts – Communication in a Digital System
Microprocessor 3: Core Concepts – Hardware Aspects

DUVAUT Patrick, DALLOZ Xavier, MENGA David, KOEHL François, CHRIQUI Vidal, BRILL Joerg
Internet of Augmented Me, I.AM: Empowering Innovation for a New Sustainable Future

LAFFLY Dominique
TORUS 1 – Toward an Open Resource Using Services: Cloud Computing for Environmental Data
TORUS 2 – Toward an Open Resource Using Services: Cloud Computing for Environmental Data
TORUS 3 – Toward an Open Resource Using Services: Cloud Computing for Environmental Data

LAURENT Anne, LAURENT Dominique, MADERA Cédrine
Data Lakes
(Databases and Big Data Set – Volume 2)

OULHADJ Hamouche, DAACHI Boubaker, MENASRI Riad
Metaheuristics for Robotics
(Optimization Heuristics Set – Volume 2)

SADIQUI Ali
Computer Network Security

VENTRE Daniel
Artificial Intelligence, Cybersecurity and Cyber Defense

2019

BESBES Walid, DHOUIB Diala, WASSAN Niaz, MARREKCHI Emna
Solving Transport Problems: Towards Green Logistics

CLERC Maurice
Iterative Optimizers: Difficulty Measures and Benchmarks

GHLALA Riadh
Analytic SQL in SQL Server 2014/2016

TOUNSI Wiem
Cyber-Vigilance and Digital Trust: Cyber Security in the Era of Cloud Computing and IoT

2018

ANDRO Mathieu
Digital Libraries and Crowdsourcing
(Digital Tools and Uses Set – Volume 5)

ARNALDI Bruno, GUITTON Pascal, MOREAU Guillaume
Virtual Reality and Augmented Reality: Myths and Realities

CARDON Alain
Beyond Artificial Intelligence: From Human Consciousness to Artificial Consciousness

HOMAYOUNI S. Mahdi, FONTES Dalila B.M.M.
Metaheuristics for Maritime Operations
(Optimization Heuristics Set – Volume 1)

JEANSOULIN Robert
JavaScript and Open Data

PIVERT Olivier
NoSQL Data Models: Trends and Challenges
(Databases and Big Data Set – Volume 1)

SEDKAOUI Soraya
Data Analytics and Big Data

SALEH Imad, AMMI Mehdi, SZONIECKY Samuel
Challenges of the Internet of Things: Technology, Use, Ethics
(Digital Tools and Uses Set – Volume 7)

SZONIECKY Samuel
Ecosystems Knowledge: Modeling and Analysis Method for Information and Communication
(Digital Tools and Uses Set – Volume 6)

2017

BENMAMMAR Badr
Concurrent, Real-Time and Distributed Programming in Java: Threads, RTSJ and RMI

BOUHAÏ Nasreddine, SALEH Imad
Internet of Things: Evolutions and Innovations
(Digital Tools and Uses Set – Volume 4)

HÉLIODORE Frédéric, NAKIB Amir, ISMAIL Boussaad, OUCHRAA Salma, SCHMITT Laurent
Metaheuristics for Intelligent Electrical Networks
(Metaheuristics Set – Volume 10)

MA Haiping, SIMON Dan
Evolutionary Computation with Biogeography-based Optimization
(Metaheuristics Set – Volume 8)

PÉTROWSKI Alain, BEN-HAMIDA Sana
Evolutionary Algorithms
(Metaheuristics Set – Volume 9)

PAI G A Vijayalakshmi
Metaheuristics for Portfolio Optimization: An Introduction using MATLAB®
(Metaheuristics Set – Volume 11)

REYES-GARCIA Everardo
The Image-Interface: Graphical Supports for Visual Information
(Digital Tools and Uses Set – Volume 3)

REYES-GARCIA Everardo, BOUHAÏ Nasreddine
Designing Interactive Hypermedia Systems
(Digital Tools and Uses Set – Volume 2)

SZONIECKY Samuel, BOUHAÏ Nasreddine
Collective Intelligence and Digital Archives: Towards Knowledge Ecosystems
(Digital Tools and Uses Set – Volume 1)

2016

BLUM Christian, FESTA Paola
Metaheuristics for String Problems in Bio-informatics
(Metaheuristics Set – Volume 6)

DEROUSSI Laurent
Metaheuristics for Logistics
(Metaheuristics Set – Volume 4)

DHAENENS Clarisse, JOURDAN Laetitia
Metaheuristics for Big Data
(Metaheuristics Set – Volume 5)

LABADIE Nacima, PRINS Christian, PRODHON Caroline
Metaheuristics for Vehicle Routing Problems
(Metaheuristics Set – Volume 3)

LEROY Laure
Eyestrain Reduction in Stereoscopy

LUTTON Evelyne, PERROT Nathalie, TONDA Alberto
Evolutionary Algorithms for Food Science and Technology
(Metaheuristics Set – Volume 7)

MAGOULÈS Frédéric, ZHAO Hai-Xiang
Data Mining and Machine Learning in Building Energy Analysis

RIGO Michel
Advanced Graph Theory and Combinatorics

ZELM Martin, DOUMEINGTS Guy, MENDONÇA Joao Pedro
Enterprise Interoperability: in the Digitized and Networked Factory of the Future

2015

BARBIER Franck, RECOUSSINE Jean-Luc
COBOL Software Modernization: From Principles to Implementation with the BLU AGE® Method

CHEN Ken
Performance Evaluation by Simulation and Analysis with Applications to Computer Networks

CLERC Maurice
Guided Randomness in Optimization
(Metaheuristics Set – Volume 1)

DURAND Nicolas, GIANAZZA David, GOTTELAND Jean-Baptiste, ALLIOT Jean-Marc
Metaheuristics for Air Traffic Management
(Metaheuristics Set – Volume 2)

MAGOULÈS Frédéric, ROUX François-Xavier, HOUZEAUX Guillaume
Parallel Scientific Computing

MUNEESAWANG Paisarn, YAMMEN Suchart
Visual Inspection Technology in the Hard Disk Drive Industry

2014

BOULANGER Jean-Louis
Formal Methods Applied to Industrial Complex Systems
Formal Methods Applied to Complex Systems: Implementation of the B Method

EXPOSITO Ernesto, DIOP Codé
Smart SOA Platforms in Cloud Computing Architectures

GARDI Frédéric, BENOIST Thierry, DARLAY Julien, ESTELLON Bertrand, MEGEL Romain
Mathematical Programming Solver based on Local Search

KRICHEN Saoussen, CHAOUACHI Jouhaina
Graph-related Optimization and Decision Support Systems

LARRIEU Nicolas, VARET Antoine
Rapid Prototyping of Software for Avionics Systems: Model-oriented Approaches for Complex Systems Certification

LAURAS Matthieu, ZELM Martin, ARCHIMÈDE Bernard, BÉNABEN Frédérick, DOUMEINGTS Guy
Enterprise Interoperability: Interoperability for Agility, Resilience and Plasticity of Collaborations

OUSSALAH Mourad Chabane
Software Architecture 1
Software Architecture 2

QUESNEL Flavien
Scheduling of Large-scale Virtualized Infrastructures: Toward Cooperative Management

RIGO Michel
Formal Languages, Automata and Numeration Systems 1: Introduction to Combinatorics on Words
Formal Languages, Automata and Numeration Systems 2: Applications to Recognizability and Decidability

SAINT-DIZIER Patrick
Musical Rhetoric: Foundations and Annotation Schemes

TOUATI Sid, DUPONT DE DINECHIN Benoit
Advanced Backend Code Optimization

2013

ANDRÉ Étienne, SOULAT Romain
The Inverse Method: Parametric Verification of Real-time Embedded Systems

BOULANGER Jean-Louis
Safety Management for Software-based Equipment

DELAHAYE Daniel, PUECHMOREL Stéphane
Modeling and Optimization of Air Traffic

FRANCOPOULO Gil
LMF — Lexical Markup Framework

GHEDIRA Khaled
Constraint Satisfaction Problems: CSP Formalisms and Techniques

GOVAERT Gérard, NADIF Mohamed
Co-Clustering: Models, Algorithms and Applications

LANDRAGIN Frédérick
Man–Machine Dialogue: Design and Challenges

LUCAS Laurent, LOSCOS Céline, REMION Yannick
3D Video: Models, From Capture to Diffusion

ROCHANGE Christine, UHRIG Sascha, SAINRAT Pascal
Time-Predictable Architectures

WAHBI Mohamed
Algorithms and Ordering Heuristics for Distributed Constraint Satisfaction Problems

ZELM Martin, VAN SINDEREN Marten, FERRAIRA PIRES Luis, DOUMEINGTS Guy
Enterprise Interoperability: Research and Applications in the Service-oriented Ecosystem

2012

ARBOLEDA Hugo, ROYER Jean-Claude
Model-Driven and Software Product Line Engineering

BLANCHET Gérard, DUPOUY Bertrand
Computer Architecture

BOULANGER Jean-Louis
Industrial Use of Formal Methods: Formal Verification
Formal Methods: Industrial Use from Model to the Code

CALVARY Gaëlle, DELOT Thierry, SÈDES Florence, TIGLI Jean-Yves
Computer Science and Ambient Intelligence

MAHOUT Vincent
Assembly Language Programming: ARM Cortex-M3 2.0: Organization, Innovation and Territory

MARLET Renaud
Program Specialization

SOTO Maria, SEVAUX Marc, ROSSI André, LAURENT Johann
Memory Allocation Problems in Embedded Systems: Optimization Methods

2011

BICHOT Charles-Edmond, SIARRY Patrick
Graph Partitioning

BOULANGER Jean-Louis
Static Analysis of Software: The Abstract Interpretation

CAFERRA Ricardo
Logic for Computer Science and Artificial Intelligence

KORDON Fabrice, HADDAD Serge, PAUTET Laurent, PETRUCCI Laure
Distributed Systems: Design and Algorithms
Models and Analysis in Distributed Systems

LORCA Xavier
Tree-based Graph Partitioning Constraint

RIDHA MAHJOUB A.
Progress in Combinatorial Optimization: ISCO2010

TRUCHET Charlotte, ASSAYAG Gerard
Constraint Programming in Music

VICAT-BLANC Pascale, GOGLIN Brice, GUILLIER Romaric,
SOUDAN Sébastien
Computing Networks: From Cluster to Cloud Computing

2010

AUBRUN Christophe, SIMON Daniel, SONG Ye-Qiong
Co-design Approaches for Dependable Networked Control Systems

AUDIBERT Pierre
Mathematics for Informatics and Computer Science

BABAU Jean-Philippe, BLAY-FORNARINO Mireille, CHAMPEAU Joël,
ROBERT Sylvain, SABETTA Antonino
Model Driven Engineering for Distributed Real-Time Systems: MARTE Modeling, Model Transformations and their Usages

BOULANGER Jean-Louis
Safety of Computer Architectures

SIGAUD Olivier, BUFFET Olivier
Markov Decision Processes in Artificial Intelligence

MONMARCHÉ Nicolas, GUINAND Frédérick, SIARRY Patrick
Artificial Ants

SOLNON Christine
Ant Colony Optimization and Constraint Programming

2009

FOURNIER Jean-Claude
Graph Theory and Applications: with exercises and problems

GUÉDON Jeanpierre
The Mojette Transform: theory and applications

JARD Claude, ROUX Olivier H.
Communicating Embedded Systems: Software and Design

LECOUTRE Christophe
Constraint Networks: Techniques and Algorithms

2008

BANÂTRE Michel, MARRON Pedro Jose, OLLERO Anibal, WOLITZ Adam
Cooperating Embedded Systems and Wireless Sensor Networks

MERZ Stephan, NAVET Nicolas
Modeling and Verification of Real-time Systems: Formalisms and Software Tools

PASCHOS Vangelis Th.
Combinatorial Optimization and Theoretical Computer Science: Interfaces and Perspectives

WALDNER Jean-Baptiste
Nanocomputers and Swarm Intelligence

2007

BENHAMOU Frédéric, JUSSIEN Narendra, O'SULLIVAN Barry
Trends in Constraint Programming

JUSSIEN Narendra
A to Z of Sudoku

2006

BABAU Jean-Philippe, CHAMPEAU Joël, GÉRARD Sébastien
From MDD Concepts to Experiments and Illustrations – DRES 2006

HABRIAS Henri, FRAPPIER Marc
Software Specification Methods: An Overview Using a Case Study

MURAT Cécile, PASCHOS Vangelis Th.
Probabilistic Combinatorial Optimization on Graphs

PANETTO Hervé, BOUDJLIDA Nacer
Interoperability for Enterprise Software and Applications: Proceedings of the Workshops and the Doctorial Symposium of the Second IFAC/IFIP I-ESA International Conference: EI2N, WSI, IS-TSPQ 2006

2005

GÉRARD Sébastien, BABAU Jean-Philippe, CHAMPEAU Joël
Model Driven Engineering for Distributed Real Time Embedded Systems

PANETTO Hervé
Interoperability of Enterprise Software and Applications: Workshops of the INTEROP-ESA 2005 International Conference (EI2N, WSI, ISIDI and IEHENA 2005)

Printed and bound by CPI Group (UK) Ltd, Croydon, CR0 4YY

24/08/2026

14947835-0007